The History of French Literature on Film

HISTORY OF WORLD LITERATURES ON FILM

Series Editors
Greg M. Colon Semenza
Bob Hasenfratz

Also Published in the Series

The History of British Literature on Film, 1895–2015
Greg M. Colon Semenza and Bob Hasenfratz
The History of American Literature on Film
Thomas Leitch

Forthcoming Volumes in the Series

The History of German Literature on Film
Christiane Schonfeld
The History of Russian Literature on Film
David Gillespie
The History of Sub-Saharan African Literatures on Film
Sara Hanaburgh

The History of French Literature on Film

KATE GRIFFITHS AND ANDREW WATTS

BLOOMSBURY ACADEMIC
LONDON • NEW YORK • OXFORD • NEW DELHI • SYDNEY

BLOOMSBURY ACADEMIC
Bloomsbury Publishing Inc.
1385 Broadway, New York, NY 10018, USA
29 Earlsfort Terrace, Dublin 2, Ireland

BLOOMSBURY, BLOOMSBURY ACADEMIC and the Diana logo are trademarks of
Bloomsbury Publishing Plc

First published in the United States of America 2021
This paperback edition published in 2022

Copyright © Kate Griffiths and Andrew Watts, 2021

For legal purposes the Acknowledgements on p. xi constitute an extension
of this copyright page.

Cover images: Still from *A Trip To The Moon*, 1902, *dir*. Georges Méliès © Collection Christophel / ArenaPAL; Cécile de France, in *Mademoiselle de Jonquières*, 2018, *dir*. Emmanuel Mouret © Moby Dick Films / Collection Christophel / ArenaPAL

All rights reserved. No part of this publication may be reproduced or transmitted in any form or by any means, electronic or mechanical, including photocopying, recording, or any information storage or retrieval system, without prior permission in writing from the publishers.

Bloomsbury Publishing Inc does not have any control over, or responsibility for, any third-party websites referred to or in this book. All internet addresses given in this book were correct at the time of going to press. The authors and publisher regret any inconvenience caused if addresses have changed or sites have ceased to exist, but can accept no responsibility for any such changes.

Library of Congress Cataloging-in-Publication Data

ISBN: HB: 978-1-5013-1184-0
PB: 978-1-5013-7240-7
ePDF: 978-1-5013-1181-9
eBook: 978-1-5013-1182-6

Series: History of World Literatures on Film

Typeset by Newgen KnowledgeWorks Pvt. Ltd., Chennai, India

To find out more about our authors and books visit www.bloomsbury.com
and sign up for our newsletters.

Contents

List of Figures vii
Acknowledgements xi

    Introduction Deceptive binaries: Adaptations and their literary sources 1
    Kate Griffiths

1 The currency of adaptation: Art and money in silent cinema (1899–1929) 19
    Andrew Watts

2 Who is adaptation? Interpersonal transactions in film (1927–39) 63
    Kate Griffiths

3 Politics, propaganda and the censored screen: Adapting French literature during the German Occupation (1940–44) 105
    Andrew Watts

4 The formative function of the dominant film poetics: The impact of film movement, moment and genre (1945–70) 147
    Kate Griffiths

5 The history of adaptation/adaptation and history (1970–2004) 189
    Kate Griffiths

6 Textual migration and adaptive diaspora: French literature adaptations beyond France (1996–2016) 225
    Andrew Watts

Conclusion 267
Andrew Watts

Bibliography 283
Index 297

Figures

0.1 *Carmen, la de Triana* (*Carmen the Girl from Triana*) (1938, dir. Rey) 12

0.2 *Carry On Emmanuelle* (1978, dir. Thomas) 14

0.3 *The Tender Tale of Cinderella Penguin* (1981, dir. Perlman) 15

1.1 *Cendrillon* (*Cinderella*) (1899, dir. Méliès) 24

1.2 *L'Enfant de la barricade* (*The Child of the Barricade*) (1907, dir. Guy) 29

1.3 *Carmen* (1915, dir. DeMille) 34

1.4 *L'Atlantide* (*Atlantida*) (1921, dir. Feyder) 44

1.5 *Crainquebille* (*Old Bill of Paris*) (1922, dir. Feyder) 46

1.6 *L'Auberge rouge* (*The Red Inn*) (1923, dir. Epstein) 50

1.7 *L'Argent* (*Money*) (1929, dir. L'Herbier) 56

2.1 *La Bête humaine* (*Judas Was a Woman*) (1938, dir. Renoir) 71

2.2 *Unholy Love* (1932, dir. Ray) 73

2.3 *The Count of Monte-Cristo* (1934, dir. Lee) 75

2.4 *Camille* (1936, dir. Cukor) 86

2.5 *Mad Love* (1935, dir. Freund) 89

2.6 *La Chienne* (*The Bitch*) (1931, dir. Renoir) 90

3.1 *Pontcarral, colonel d'empire* (*Pontcarral, Colonel of the Empire*) (1942, dir. Delannoy) 113

3.2 *La Main du diable* (*Carnival of Sinners*) (1943, dir. Tourneur) 118

3.3 *Goupi Mains Rouges* (*It Happened at the Inn*) (1943, dir. Becker) 127

FIGURES

3.4 *Goupi Mains Rouges* (*It Happened at the Inn*) (1943, dir. Becker) 128

3.5 *Le Dernier des six* (*The Last of the Six*) (1941, dir. Lacombe) 132

3.6 *Le Dernier des six* (*The Last of the Six*) (1941, dir. Lacombe) 133

3.7 *L'Assassin habite au 21* (*The Murderer Lives at Number 21*) (1942, dir. Clouzot) 134

3.8 *L'Assassinat du Père Noël* (*The Killing of Santa Claus*) (1941, dir. Christian-Jaque) 140

4.1 *Le Rouge et le Noir* (*The Red and the Black*) (1954, dir. Autant-Lara) 152

4.2 *Jules et Jim* (*Jules and Jim*) (1962, dir. Truffaut) 156

4.3 *Carmen Jones* (1954, dir. Preminger) 161

4.4 *L'uomo, l'orgoglio, la vendetta* (*Man, Pride, and Vengeance*) (1967, dir. Bazzoni) 167

4.5 *Anuradha* (1960, dir. Mukherjee) 170

4.6 *Ryan's Daughter* (1970, dir. Lean) 176

5.1 *Emmanuelle* (1974, dir. Jaeckin) 192

5.2 *Carry On Emmanuelle* (1978, dir. Thomas) 200

5.3 *The Tender Tale of Cinderella Penguin* (1981, dir. Perlman) 201

5.4 *Germinal* (1993, dir. Berri) 207

5.5 *Moulin Rouge!* (2001, dir. Luhrmann) 209

5.6 *Un long dimanche de fiançailles* (*A Very Long Engagement*) (2004, dir. Jeunet) 215

6.1 *Planet of the Apes* (2001, dir. Burton) 233

6.2 *Diabolique* (1996, dir. Chechik) 235

6.3 *Untold Scandal* (2003, dir. E. J-yong) 240

6.4 *Thirst* (2009, dir. Park) 244

6.5 *Atomised* (2006, dir. Roehler) 250

6.6 *Bel Ami* (2012, dir. Donnellan/Ormerod) 253

6.7 *Suite française* (2015, dir. Dibb) 255

6.8 *The Skin I Live In* (2011, dir. Almodóvar) 260

C.1 *Au revoir là-haut* (*See You Up There*) (2017, dir. Dupontel) 273

C.2 *Laissez bronzer les cadavres* (*Let the Corpses Tan*) (2017, dir. Cattet and Forzani) 277

C.3 *Mademoiselle de Joncquières* (2018, dir. Mouret) 278

Acknowledgements

Some of my analysis in this book is about the interpersonal and the people who shape works. And the people behind this book are important. It is dedicated to my daughters, Evie and Mari, with all the love in the world. Caru chi'n fwy na'r byd i gyd yn grwn. Rwyf mor falch ohonch chi'ch dwy. And to Richard Sheppard who helped make the space for me to write and weather life's twists in and around its making. It is dedicated to John and Maggie Griffiths for years of love and laughter. Dwi'n dy garu Dad. Dwi'n dy golli di. It is also dedicated to a circle of friends who never cease to bring sunshine: Cerian Arianrhod, Kathryn Collins, Samantha Deeks, Siân Keepin and Nicole Kennedy.

I am grateful to be able to record in print my thanks to the team of people who have made Cardiff a happy place to work. Thanks are more than due to Rachael Langford and Helen Walker for their back-up and leadership, to Claire Gorrara for her helpful nudges, to Hanna Diamond for her support, to Liz Wren-Owens for more than fits into a phrase, to Cathy Molinaro for always being there, to Carlos Sanz-Mingo for laughter and to Sue Birch for covering and, with Mrs Wenzwig, Mrs Anderson, Mrs P. George and the teachers at Caerleon Comprehensive, being part of my coming to study French in the first place. I am thankful for the extra miles you put in. I am grateful too to my translation colleagues – Loredana Polezzi, Cristina Marinetti, Dorota Goluch and Abdel-Wahab Khalifa – for their willingness to let me pick their brains as I wrangled in both this book and another with how translation and adaptation studies intersect.

Of the team of people beyond Cardiff who have been invaluable to the book's creation, my co-author Andrew Watts is first in line. I am grateful for his endless patience, for his willingness to run with my new ideas and directions even when well into the progress of the book and for the flexibility of our writing partnership. I am thankful to the series editors Bob and Greg for giving us the chance to reprise our book writing collaboration and bearing with me while I completed the manuscript. I am grateful to be able to thank Graham Nelson and the team at Legenda for allowing me the time and space to juggle my book for them and this one for Bloomsbury. Sincere thanks are also due to Bradley Stephens for his willingness to read and cut to the heart of things adaptive, to Kathryn Jones for advice and to Susan Harrow for support at the various twists and turns of my career.

Kate Griffiths

When I first started working on this book in 2015, I could not have imagined that it would become so closely entwined with significant changes in my personal life. At that time, Kate and I were delighted to have been asked to write a history of French literature on film, especially since this gave us an opportunity to co-author a second book together. However, before I had even put pen to paper on the first of my chapters, this exciting challenge took on a very different complexion with the news that my mother, Janet, was seriously ill. Mum passed away in July 2016, and as my family and I tried to make some sense of her loss, I wondered where I might find the time and mental energy for a major research project. While moving forward with this book was undoubtedly difficult, I am grateful that writing it gave me a clear sense of purpose in those weeks and months after my mother's death. This volume was the last of my research projects that she knew about during her lifetime, and with its completion another link to the life that I shared with her begins to fade into memory. However, I take comfort in knowing that she would have been delighted to see this book in print. In so many ways, my contributions to this volume are for her.

Life, my mother used to say, isn't meant to stay the same, and in May 2018, it took a much happier turn when my wife, Claire, and I celebrated the arrival of our son, James. Finishing a book with a new baby in the house was never going to be easy, but James brought fun, laughter and a radiant warmth back into our lives at a time when we needed them the most. For me, this book will forever be associated with the little boy who bashed my keyboard gleefully and made off with the mouse every time my back was turned. I hope one day he will find in these pages not just a history of film adaptations of French literature but a reflection of the joy and excitement that he brought us during his first year.

In completing this project, I have been overwhelmed by the support of my family, friends and colleagues. At home, Claire listened, encouraged and offered advice whenever it was needed. Most importantly, she has always been there, and without her love and support, this book simply would not have come to fruition. I am equally grateful to my father, John, who in the wake of his own loss found the greatest of inner strength to support me and my work. Dad and I stood together in our determination to see this project completed and to honour the example my mother set for us. This achievement is as much his as it is mine.

ACKNOWLEDGEMENTS

Among my friends in academia, many have taken the time to discuss this book with me and to comment on draft chapters. I am particularly indebted to Masha Belenky, Michelle Cheyne, Martyn Cornick, Lisa Downing, Nigel Harris, Sara Jones and Rob Stone for their insightful readings and constructive criticism and to Kay Chadwick for her kindness in checking a key reference for me during the very final stages of the project. Special thanks are due to Tim Unwin, who showed endless patience in helping me to develop and refine some of my very first drafts. Most of all, Kate Griffiths has proved once again to be a wonderful co-author and an inspiring source of ideas and knowledge on all things adaptation. I am enormously thankful both for her support and for her intellectual generosity.

I would also like to place on record my thanks to the various academic institutions that have provided essential support for this project. I am especially grateful to the University of Birmingham for granting me an extended period of research leave in 2016–17 to complete two of my three chapters and to our institutional library for securing copies of films and other key research materials. In Paris, the Bibliothèque Nationale de France and the Cinémathèque Française granted invaluable access to newspapers, cinema journals and film reviews, particularly from the Occupation period.

Finally, to our series editors, Greg Semenza and Bob Hasenfratz, I extend my warmest thanks for inviting me to co-author this book and for following the progress of my chapters with such rigour and enthusiasm. I hope this volume will make a worthy addition to your series and that it will, like many of the films discussed within its pages, stand the test of history.

Andrew Watts

Introduction
Deceptive binaries: Adaptations and their literary sources

Kate Griffiths

Claude Autant-Lara's 1954 film adaptation of Stendhal's *Le Rouge et le Noir* (*The Red and the Black*) fetishizes the book from which it derives. Its opening images do not lead with the iconic good looks, marketability and draw of its star, Gérard Philipe – then at the apogee of his short but glorious career. Rather, Autant-Lara's first images revel in the beauty, marketability and canonical draw of the French literary source from which they are derived. The camera lingers lovingly on the worn red leather of a clearly well-thumbed copy of Stendhal's novel, contrasting it with the watermarked silk blackness of the subsequent inner page before offering us an imprint page identifying the novel as the Editions Sauret version. The camera leafs page by page into the flow of the film in point-of-view shots which simultaneously and impossibly situate us as readers of a cinematic adaptation. Imprinting himself and his film literally on the pages of Stendhal's work, Autant-Lara turns from the title page of the novel – which hails Stendhal (Henri Beyle) as its creator – to a fabricated page which reads thus: 'A film by Claude Autant-Lara.' The film's opening credits are printed as pages in this novel before segueing into a dramatic fade to red, which echoes the red of the courtroom velvet as Julien Sorel (Philipe) stands trial for murder. Cinema thus springs from Stendhal's novel in an adaptation which proudly proclaims itself as filmed literature.

Autant-Lara's obsession with the novel behind his cinematic adaptation has, as Chapter 3 will argue, much to do with the cinematic movement with which he associated himself: the Tradition of Quality. It privileged craft over innovation, established directors over novices and, above all, great literary works of the canonical tradition. Autant-Lara's foregrounding of the materiality of the source novel behind his adapted images, though particularly obsessive, is not unique. It foregrounds a commercial and creative veneration of literary sources within the adaptation industry which is unsurprising. Hosts of film adaptations flick, in their opening images, through the pages of a book before dissolving into their own creative action, tacitly seeking to claim for themselves a measure of the commercial success or canonical status of their literary forebear. Autant-Lara's obsession with the literary source behind his images, though, reaches beyond his movement and the generic conventions of the art form in which he works. It gestures to a comparable obsession in key strands of adaptation studies more broadly, which have historically struggled to read and account for the shape, form and artistry of a film adaptation beyond the vector of its source text.

The first volume in the series to which *The History of French Literature on Film* belongs, *The History of British Literature on Film*, was persuasive in its identification of adaptation studies' historic obsession with the source text. Greg Semenza and Bob Hasenfratz write:

> In spite of major recent advances in adaptation studies, the literary text too often continues to dominate the conception and structure of most book-length studies of British literature on film, which usually focus on cinematic adaptations of a particular canonical literary author …, a particular literary period …, or a particular literary genre (e.g., the novel, drama). Such approaches cannot avoid privileging literature over film. In contrast, our book – and its forthcoming companions in the 'History of World Literatures on Film' series – explores how adaptations evolved within movie history itself.[1]

The title of our book, *The History of French Literature on Film*, implies we might lead with literature, replicating the constraints of the restrictive critical framework Semenza and Hasenfratz, among others, work to undo. The current volume, though, speaks to Semenza and Hasenfratz's critical intent, to their belief that adaptations cannot fully be understood without reference to the formative function of the intersections of history they inhabit. Our book uses the complex, compelling creative outputs crafted from French works from the dawn of the medium to the modern day to pluralize and examine the very different histories that shape the adaptive process. Our aim is not exhaustive coverage of every piece of French literature on film. Rather, through global clusters of adaptations that speak to common themes, this book works to assess the formative function of different types of history on the adaptation of French sources in different times, nations, genres and languages. The adaptations of French sources at the heart of this book are not merely shaped by their literary precursor; they are fashioned, in intriguing ways, by the economic, personal, political, cultural and national moments of their making. They are complex historical documents shaped by an intricate range of factors above and beyond the literary sources they rework. Moreover, far from being passive recipients of the aforementioned economic, personal, political, cultural and national moments of their making, the adaptations at the core of this study impact upon those histories. They shape the context from which they derive. This book thus does not seek to catalogue all French sources made into film. Instead, it seeks to underline why key strands and clusters of adaptations from French sources both speak to the historical turn in adaptation studies and develop it.

Adaptations are more than the sum of their source: Furthering the historical turn in adaptation studies

'Under most literary lenses', writes Kamilla Elliott, adaptations are considered 'an inferior reproduction of a superior original'.[2] Adaptation studies has not only struggled to shake off these so-called literary lenses; it has also, to an extent, seen itself through them in key debates and moments of its evolution. This book builds on Semenza and Hasenfratz's persuasively enunciated belief in the first of this World Literatures on Film series that adaptation studies has over-privileged the source text in its assessments of both the genesis and value of adaptations as art works. Books do matter in the adaptation of French sources into film – and this current volume will evaluate them. But to seek only the source text in a cinematic reworking of a French source is to misunderstand what adaptation is and does, and indeed to ascribe a fixity and singularity to the concept of the source text which often it does not have. D. W. Griffith's *The Drunkard's Reformation* (1909) offers a powerful case in point. Griffith's film, a version of Zola's famous work *L'Assommoir*, stems not from the author's novel but from the British/North American theatrical version of Octave Gastineau and William Busnach's French theatrical adaptation of Zola's text. Writing on early cinema's links with the world of theatre, Rick Altman argues:

> Take any list of silent films apparently derived from novels, submit it to a few hours' research in a serious library and you will have little trouble discovering that a very high proportion of the novels were turned into extremely popular stage shows in the years preceding the film. Yet, systematically, it is the novel that gets the attention, the novel that is mentioned in the end, the novel that draws the screen credit. For by the turn of the century novels were clearly a drawing card, cinema's tenuous connection with culture.[3]

Source texts are often mobile things in the adaptations of French literature made in the silent era as filmmakers adapt at times source texts, at times subsequent adaptations made of them for different media. Such mobility is, Julie Sanders argues, a key feature of the adaptive process long after the silent era as adaptations work and rework both the source text and the adaptations, canonical or otherwise, which have accreted, palimpsest-like, on the surface of said text in different eras and cultures.[4] Adaptations of French literature often spring from such a palimpsest of sources. Griffith's *The Drunkard's Reformation* clearly adapts history as much, if not more so, than its putative literary source. It is clearly shaped by the temperance debates of its era as well as contemporary cinematic debates about the moral value and rectitude of cinema. But, far from being passively shaped by either of those histories – social or cinematic – it seeks to impact upon and enter into a dialogue with them. History is key to what Griffith's adaptation of a French source is and does. To ignore it is to engage with Griffith's work in half measure.

Semenza and Hasenfratz articulate in their *History of British Literature on Film* a move towards a historical turn in adaptation studies, offering a clear mission statement

> that *history matters*. It matters not merely in the sense that cultural, economic, artistic, and political contexts (to mention a few) will influence and even determine the ways in which adaptations are produced, consumed, and theorized, but also in the sense that a greater understanding of how adaptations have changed over time will directly influence the ways we define them and how they are to be evaluated.[5]

They draw on what they situate as the newest phase of scholarship in adaptation studies, the 'sociological approach to adaptation' enunciated by Simone Murray, and its commitment to 'foregrounding those issues usually pushed to the margins of adaptation studies work: the industrial structures, interdependent networks of agents, commercial contexts, and legal and policy regimes in which adaptations come to be'.[6] This *History of French Literature on Film* speaks to the historical turn at the heart of the work of these adaptation scholars, evaluating the formative function of the economics, people, politics, genres, historic moments and nations in which its case study adaptations are created. But it also seeks to bring additional voices to these debates. These voices come perhaps most notably from translation theory, a discipline whose cultural turn resonates in intriguing ways with the historical turn in adaptation studies. The translation theory of thinkers such as André Lefevere, and his belief that translations and their critical receptions are both fashioned by and act upon the cultural and historical moments in which they are produced, is instrumental to the structure of our *History of French Literature on Film*. Lefevere explores the shaping impact of the financial systems, people, politics, genre conventions, times and spaces of a translation's creation on its shape and artistry. Though Lefevere features directly only in one chapter, this *History of French Literature on Film* crafts its overarching structure from the cultural formative forces he enunciates, affording each a chapter as it seeks to do justice to the complex interplay of histories from which the art of adaptation springs.

History, this book works to show, is no simple, single, linear thing. The temporal structure of this book perhaps suggests at first glance that it is. The work is divided into significant eras which encompass key movements, films, world events or phenomena in film adaptation: 1899–1929, 1927–39, 1940–4, 1945–70, 1970–2004, 1996–2016. The chapters showcase that different eras adapt differently as a result of technological limitations or innovations, social and cultural conventions as well as production values. The chronology of our chapter structure, though, is deliberately not smooth. There are overlaps and jumps as chapters turn and re-turn to enter into dialogue with works from different eras. For the chronology of adaptation as a process is not smooth. Source novels often change nation in adaptation. So too do they frequently change historical era. And if, as this book argues, the space of adaptation is intriguing, so too is its time. Heritage adaptations of French literary sources are big business, and examples feature in all of the eras showcased in our chapters. But their temporality is intriguing. They purport to take us back to an earlier novel and its far-flung historical era, yet the history they offer is very much of our present. It is shaped and conditioned by the cultural values of our present and by the production values of contemporary film. Films like *Germinal* (1993, dir. Berri) thus stand, Janus-like, impossibly adapting their contemporary context and the past to which they simultaneously seek to return. Berri's film moves between historical eras, posing intriguing questions about what and where history might be.

Defining French literature: Spaces in transit

Film's love affair with French literature is an abiding one. Drawing on novels, poems, operas, plays and short stories written in French, filmmakers from around the world have, since the birth of the medium, made and remade French literature for the big screen. Cinema, in its early developmental years, had strong roots in France thanks to pioneering figures such as the Lumière brothers. The Lumière brothers may have seen film as a new form of science, but for those working in the magic lantern tradition, it offered the possibility of cheap, mass, sensational entertainment. French filmmakers, as soon as films were technologically advanced and long enough to offer narrative development, immediately turned to French literary sources. They did so for myriad reasons. Successful novels generated audiences. They provided a degree of cultural legitimacy for the nascent medium as it tried to define itself. And literature provided ready-made material from which filmmakers could craft their own vision and creative identity. The cinematic output of 1902 is a case in point. Georges Méliès's *Le Voyage dans la lune* (*A Trip to the Moon*) used Jules Verne's adventure writing as a means to indulge the director's interest in trick photography. In the same year, Ferdinand Zecca's *Les Victimes de l'alcoolisme* (*Alcohol and Its Victims*) offered viewers a five-minute adaptation of Émile Zola's Naturalist novel *L'Assommoir* (1877) in five tableaux. The same novel would be adapted a further three times in France before the outbreak of the First World War. And while adaptations of French sources were frequent in French film, the international trade in silent film – a trade sometimes undertaken legally, often not – meant that said films were trafficked around the world, their lack of sound rendering nearly non-existent the language constraints which might otherwise have confined them to France. This transnational movement of texts continues to the current day. French source texts move around the globe, inhabiting new cultures, nations and languages in diasporic existences which make clear adaptations' status as spatially intriguing art works; works that simultaneously inhabit the nation and space of their source and, impossibly, those of their target audience. In spatial terms, adaptations are works endlessly in motion as they travel to new contexts, neither fully willing nor entirely able to shake off the contexts of their source.

The wealth of adaptations of French sources remade for cinema compels their presence in a series that sets out to chart the history of world literatures on film. But the case studies in the current volume merit attention as a collective corpus not merely as a result of their number. In the global reach of their forms and audiences as well as their frequent self-reflexivity in relation to their own adaptive acts, our case study adaptations ask intriguing questions about their own identities. Space is key to this current volume. This book is firmly anchored in the literary output of Francophone nations, output which has proved so attractive to filmmakers around the world. But if key adaptations studied in this book play with the teleology of time/history, others play with the borders and boundaries of nations. The cinematic afterlives crafted from the novels of Émile Zola are key to our line of argument here. Zola's novels are obsessed by space. As a Naturalist novelist he tries to pin it down, capturing both its panoramas and its close detail in the print of his pages. As a disciple of the work of Hippolyte Taine, space is still more resonant for Zola. He conceives of it as one of the determining forces shaping human behaviour, along with era and genetic inheritance. The geographical spaces which Zola seeks so intently to pin down shift and slip into different national spaces as his novels are adapted and readapted around the world. His 1894 novel *Lourdes* was adapted in Sweden in 1913 under the title *Miraklet* (*The Miracle*, dir. Sjöström). In 1920 Zola's novel *Madeleine Férat* (1868) was adapted in Italy by directors Febo Mari and Roberto Roberti. His writing has been reworked for film in Argentina,[7] Germany,[8] the United States,[9] Mexico[10] and South Korea in the adaptation of *Thérèse Raquin* under the title *Thirst* (2009, dir. Park). The adaptations of Zola around the world, when read in conjunction, pose probing questions of adaptation studies in relation to space. Adaptation studies, as this introduction has already suggested, has traditionally privileged the space of the source text as the principal shaping force in the adaptive process. But the national spaces for which adaptations are made are comparably important. They shape adaptations in complex ways. The BBC's 1980 adaptation of Zola's *Thérèse Raquin* (1868) is a notable case in point.[11] The adaptation is performed in geographically recognizable BBC English, by recognizably British BBC stars in an adaptive vehicle whose performances and production values are entirely consonant with the mores and standards of the national corporation making the piece. However, the BBC adaptation retains elements of its French source culture and space. The characters' names are French. They reference French locations, cultural habits and words. As a case study it points to the spatial complexity of the adaptive artefact, which is worthy of examination. The BBC *Thérèse Raquin* underscores that works cross the boundary not only between literature and film but also nations. It makes clear that adaptations adapt national spaces/moments as well as their source text. They offer complex spatial composites which are neither fully French nor fully of the nation to which they have been transplanted. Finally, the BBC's 1980 *Thérèse Raquin* warns us not to essentialize film, the medium placed in the foreground of this book's title, as a space. Created as a television series, it was subsequently released by the Masterpiece Theater on DVD to be consumed as a film. This book may promise to be a history of French literature on film, but just as it explores the borders and boundaries of texts as they traverse nations, it is alive to the shifting borders and boundaries of film as a medium. Film is as mobile a medium as the source texts it adapts. Evolving beyond recognition from its birth images, film has moved from silence to sound, from cinematic projection to personal home viewing devices, from set projection times to on-demand, controllable viewing platforms which enable the viewer to select the time, space and means of consumption.

Defining French literature: Who is French literature?

This book works from lynchpin adaptations in key eras to emphasize both the importance of specific French sources and authors to adaptation studies and their ability, in adapted form, to ask paradigm-shifting questions of the history of the discipline they inhabit. It works from authors both canonical and not. It aims to probe the complex relationship between adaptation and canonicity. It is far from insignificant that the two French source authors discussed in detail thus far in this introduction – Stendhal and Zola – are canonical for our era. Adaptation often draws on canonical authors who provide well-known plot lines, a ready-made audience of fans, commercial promise and creative credibility. But the relationships between adaptation and canonicity are far more complex than that. A consideration of the adaptive afterlives of Jules Verne powerfully makes this point. Verne, one of the most adapted authors in the French language, is something of a constant on cinema screens. Claude Faber notes that around forty adaptations of the novelist's works were made in the silent era.[12] If anything, sound film's passion for Verne is even stronger. As early as 1929 Maurice Tournier, Benjamin Christensen and Lucien Hibbard created a silent adaptation revolving around Verne's Nemo character that featured specific sound sequences. More than 148 adaptations of a variety of Verne's texts have appeared on the big and small screen in works whose flow shows no signs of abating. Verne clearly makes cinematic sense.[13] Verne, though, was not canonical in his lifetime and, arguably, still has not fully attained canonical status, whatever that might be, in literary form. He might easily, however, on the basis of the film adaptations of his works which are explored in this book, be argued to be canonical in film. Canonicity works in intriguingly different ways in literature and in film adaptation.

The adaptations of Verne's source texts for film speak further to our subtitle for this section, 'Who is French Literature?', for they alert us to the fact that adaptations often adapt the star identity of their source author above and beyond his/her literary work. Cinema's attraction to Verne stems as much from the thrills and spills of his adventure narratives as from the powerful persona which has cumulatively been crafted from his work, making him a worldwide brand. Many of the adaptations of his works are adaptations of this mythical persona. The 1958 Czechoslovak *Vynález zkázy* (*The Fabulous World of Jules Verne*, dir. Zeman) is, as its English title makes clear, a case in point. Adapting and moving between several Verne source texts, it unites them in its adaptation of Verne the man. We have, according to Timothy Unwin, fallen for the seductive and misleading image of Verne as 'the great Jules Verne, honorary world citizen and dreamer of scientific tomorrows, the writer translated into dozens of languages and adapted into every existing medium, still astonishing us with his "uncanny" insights into the future'.[14] We adapt Verne's image and brand as much, if not more so, than his sprawling oeuvre. We do so in works which demonstrate that any dogged focus on the source text as the only means to assess adaptive quality obfuscates key and compelling elements of the play of influences from which the adaptive artefact is formed.

If this book looks at authors who are clearly canonical and those who attain a measure of canonicity via adaptation, so too does it consider those who clearly sit on the margins of the canon or decisively beyond it. It does so in order to explore whether the primacy of the source text and source author still pertains in discussions of adaptations made from works not of the canon. In each of the era-based chapters, canonical writers feature alongside non-canonical writers to assess the different means and modes of their adaptation and critical reception. Thus, in its study of the *théâtre filmé* (filmed theatre) of the years 1927 to 1939 this book evaluates adaptations of the plays of André Picard, Paul Armont, Louis Verneuil and Félix Gandéra as well as a novel by André Reuze. It assesses little-known writers as well as those who were hugely popular and acclaimed in their era but whose works have not, for whatever reason, stood the test of time and the canon. The canon, it would appear, is itself a concept that adapts and shifts in its sources. This book evaluates Henri-Pierre Roché's novel *Jules et Jim* (*Jules and Jim*, 1953). Practically unknown before New Wave filmmaker François Truffaut adapted it in 1962, Roché's novel still lies largely hidden behind the canonicity of Truffaut's film, a film many do not know as an adaptation.[15] The vast majority of reviews of Truffaut's film do not seek Roché's novel in Truffaut's film or use it as a vector for quality assessment, for Roché's novel, in its comparative obscurity, is eclipsed by its cinematically canonical adaptation. Few people know Henri Murger's 1851 work, *Scènes de la vie de Bohème*, the novel on which Giacomo Puccini's *La Bohème* (1896) is based. Adaptations such as *Mimi* (1935, dir. Stein) and *Moulin Rouge!* (2001, dir. Luhrmann) work from Puccini as much if not far more so than Murger. Filmmakers adapt the canonical adaptive precursor rather than the lesser-known literary source. Our study also explores literature decisively beyond the canon, such as Emmanuelle Arsan's pornographic novel *Emmanuelle* (1967). Far from being hindered by their source's non-canonical status, adaptations of the novel form their own canon, elevating Arsan's novel, and Just Jaeckin's infamous soft-porn adaptation of it, to canonical status within the porn genre, relentlessly returning to references of these landmark works in the history of sex.[16] There are, our case study adaptations of French sources reveal, alternative canons, multiple canons, canons with which this volume seeks to engage.

Organization and contents

This book's chapters have been designed to underscore the creative complexity and power of the adaptive artefact and the multiple historical forces shaping its form. Its aim is not to assess the merits of adaptations, or lack thereof, solely on the basis of the extent to which they replicate their literary source. Such a limited critical framework, as this book argues, has two major shortcomings. First, adaptations do not occur in a vacuum, and to work in a binary fashion, seeking only a source in the adapted images, is to ignore the creative, compelling multiplicity of forces shaping adaptations above and beyond their stated or presumed source. The binary between source text and adaptation reads only part of the adaptive process. It ignores the powerful formative impact of money, the creative personnel involved, the politics of the era for which the adaptation is made, the movement with which it is associated, the history of its source text and of its recreation as well as the national context for which a given adaptation is made.

This *History of French Literature on Film* is designed to study the range of forces shaping adaptations from a number of different angles. Chapter 1, 'The currency of adaptation: Art and money in silent cinema (1899–1929)', focuses on currency, both real and metaphorical. It asks, why adapt French sources? All too often adaptations are written off as money-spinners, as derivative secondary works whose artistry is somehow lessened by their need to recoup and profit from their costs. Chapter 1 traces the financial imperatives driving filmmakers to adapt French sources in the silent era as they quickly recognized the potential for attracting paying audiences by recreating well-known works for the screen. Money was needed for the creation of Georges Méliès's adaptation of fairy tales such as *Cinderella* and the novels of Jules Verne in his composite adaptation *Le Voyage dans la lune*. But money was also generated by the same adaptation. Driven by a need to meet the increasing audience thirst for new films and sensations in the new medium of film, commercially savvy cinematographers turned to well-known novels and long-running stage plays. Such works offered cheap, marketable material. But, as Chapter 1 argues, they also offered valuable creative currency. As film in its early years grappled with its place in the creative world, literary adaptation of French sources offered directors both cultural validity in their pre-validated sources and, crucially, a blank canvas on which to cultivate their own artistry in a medium rapidly developing new techniques and capacities. Marcel L'Herbier's version of Zola's *L'Argent* (1929) brings together all of these imperatives. Its plot revolves around the relentless movement of financial capital in a cinematic vehicle which both depends on the accepted artistry of its source novel and forges a space for its own experimental artistry in its complex cinematography. The adaptation of French literature in the silent era is driven by multiple currencies, by the need to recoup and profit from the costs of production, by the need to wrest a sense of cultural currency for film as a medium via the reworking of a culturally valuable source, by the need to experiment with the possibilities of what film could do as art. Adaptations of French sources in film drew on the currency of their source in order to generate critical and literal currency for themselves and their medium.

If Chapter 1 considers the economic histories of adaptation, Chapter 2 – 'Who is adaptation? Interpersonal transactions in film (1927–39)' – works to uncover the personal histories behind the process. It argues that one cannot just seek texts in adaptations; one must consider the people shaping them. And by 'people' the chapter does not mean just directors. Drawing on Christiane Nord's theory of the interpersonal in the context of translation, it argues that adaptations are complex creative artefacts shaped by shifting networks of people whose influence is key to the form they ultimately take.[17] Source authors are key to this interpersonal reading of adaptation, their texts and personalities wielding a formative force on the adaptations made of them in this era. Thus, this chapter explores adaptations of the now-canonical Victor Hugo, Zola and Gustave Flaubert in France (*Les Misérables*, 1934, dir. Bernard, and *La Bête humaine*, 1938, dir. Renoir) and the United States (*The Hunchback of Notre Dame*, 1939, dir. Dieterle, and *Unholy Love*, 1932, dir. Ray). It contrasts them with the multiple transformations of the popular Alexandre Dumas *père* (*The Iron Mask*, 1929, dir. Dwan, and *The Three Musketeers*, 1935, dir. Lee) as well as the wealth of so-called *théâtre filmé* from well-known authors (such as Marcel Pagnol) and others now forgotten. The interpersonal transactions of the adaptations of this era are not, though, the chapter argues, confined to source authors. Stars and their formative influence on the films in which they act must also be considered, as the examples of Douglas Fairbanks, Jean Gabin, Greta Garbo and Peter Lorre make clear. Directors too are part of this interpersonal reading of adaptations. Focusing on Jean Renoir, this chapter makes visible his attempt in his films to wrest a distinct directorial presence and originality from the wealth of creative personalities and influences around him. The figures in the interpersonal adaptive transactions of this era, though, are not always visible, Chapter 2 suggests. Focusing on the political figures and situations authoring the Spanish-German *Carmen, la de Triana* (*Carmen, the Girl from Triana*) (1938, dir. Rey) on the eve of war, the chapter explores the power of political patrons (to use André Lefevere's term) such as the Reich Minister of Propaganda Joseph Goebbels to shape the adaptive output of this epoch in Germany and, in this instance, Spain (see Figure 0.1).[18] The people at the heart of the numerous adaptive transactions between 1927 and 1939 are numerous. Their interpersonal exchanges are complex and intriguing. They underscore that to seek only a source text in a work of adaptation from a French source in this era is to misunderstand what adaptation is and the range and depth of people who shape it.

Chapter 3, 'Politics, propaganda and the censored screen: Adapting French literature during the German Occupation (1940–44)', underlines that sometimes the source text is not the determining force in shaping an adaptation; politics is. During the German occupation of France between 1940 and 1944 politics shaped which French texts were adapted into film, how they were adapted and how they were received. Moreover, adaptations in this era were not just shaped by politics but often sought to have a political

FIGURE 0.1 Carmen, la de Triana (Carmen, the Girl from Triana) *(1938, dir. Rey)*.

impact in their own right, offering political comment explicitly or implicitly on the context in which they were produced. As this chapter suggests, directors used adaptation to respond to the political circumstances of the time, whether this meant paying homage to the spirit of resistance in *Pontcarral, colonel d'empire* (1942, dir. Delannoy) or adopting a collaborationist stance in *La Main du diable* (*Carnival of Sinners*) (1943, dir. Tourneur). And politics shaped the critical reception of these films in their contemporary era, just as it continues to shape our approach to them now. The political ambiguity and escapism of so many of the adaptations of French sources made in this era is, far from being an escape from politics, political comment in and of its own right. It shows the constraints on adaptations and their makers, and the political forces attempting to prevent them from speaking freely. Like the shifting camera work in *Goupi Mains Rouges* (*It Happened at the Inn*) (1943, dir. Becker), the French literature adaptations of this period rarely settle fully on any one political position. Filmmakers used French texts to vent their deep anxieties over what France had become under German rule.

Adaptations are shaped not only by the politics and history of their time but also, importantly, by those of their medium. Chapter 4, 'The formative function of the dominant film poetics: The impact of film movement, moment and genre (1945–70)', assesses the influence of film movement on adaptations. It seeks to analyse the ways in which adaptations are clearly products of their cinematic heritage, moment and film affiliations as well as being reworkings in film of an earlier source. Focusing on the years 1945 to 1970, the chapter analyses how Claude Autant-Lara's aforementioned version of Stendhal's novel *Le Rouge et le Noir* is shaped by his affiliations with the French Tradition of Quality and its monumentalization of literature and cultural value. It contrasts this with François Truffaut's *Jules et Jim*, a work both shaped by the French New Wave movement in France and designed to further said movement. To seek only Henri-Pierre Roché's source novel in this adaptation is to ignore the monumental import of the film movement within which Truffaut was working: the movement at least as visible in the adaptation's images as its source text. The import of film movement on the adaptation of French source texts is tangible in a host of international movements of this era. And the chapter moves between them, looking at the shaping impact of the musical film genre on Otto Preminger's 1954 *Carmen Jones*, the fundamental import of the Italian Spaghetti Western genre on Luigi Bazzoni's adaptation of the same Carmen plot line in *L'uomo, l'orgoglio, la vendetta* (*Man, Pride and Vengeance*, 1967), the moulding influence of the Golden Age of Indian film on Hrishikesh Mukherjee's *Anuradha* (1960) in its reworking of Gustave Flaubert's 1856 novel *Madame Bovary* and the import of the conventions of epic film to David Lean's *Ryan's Daughter* (1970). Lean's film reworks the same novel as

Mukherjee, yet the national context, era and particularly the film movements or moments within which both directors worked mean that the adaptations produced are starkly different.

Chapter 5 – 'The history of adaptation/adaptation and history (1970–2004)' – argues that history is key to understanding any piece of adaptive art. Adaptations of French sources in this chapter's case study years document the history of their time, alongside that of their chosen source text. Just Jaeckin's soft-porn film *Emmanuelle* adapts the sexual revolution of the 1960s and 1970s in society, literature and film, pushing up against the limits of what it can show. The *Black Emmanuelle* unauthorized spin-offs of this film undertaken by a variety of directors, but most often associated with Joe d'Amato, adapt Italy's complex relationship with its colonial pasts and peoples, using their exotic spaces to challenge the borders of porn history in their topics and style. The British *Carry On* spin-off of the Emmanuelle franchise, the disastrous *Carry On Emmanuelle* (1978, dir. Thomas), adapts British social and class history of the era. It also adapts the history of the *Carry On* franchise for which it was one of the death knells, reflecting on the British film phenomenon which it was bringing to an end (see Figure 0.2).

But history, this chapter argues, is a complex source to adapt. Claude Berri's *Germinal* (1993) powerfully makes this point as it highlights the multiplicity of voices and versions of the past it could adapt, approaching history as a subjective, shifting thing. And the adaptations of this era do not just document

FIGURE 0.2 Carry On Emmanuelle *(1978, dir. Thomas)*.

history; they ask and evaluate what it is as source. Baz Luhrmann's *Moulin Rouge!* (2001) deconstructs the historical genre it ostensibly inhabits, re-energizing it in so doing. Luhrmann's film exuberantly proffers and simultaneously refuses both its source history and a range of French literary sources, whetting the viewer's appetite for a return in history and literature to a source but refusing to allow history to exist as distinct from the present. It circles dizzyingly between past and present, underscoring the fictitious nature of the history we construct for our world. If Luhrmann's film traps itself in the impossible cycles of a return to an earlier time and source, *The Tender Tale of Cinderella Penguin* (1981, dir. Perlman), an animation based on the fairy tales of Charles Perrault (1697), does likewise (see Figure 0.3). It adapts the history of Perrault in adaptation, trapping the viewer in the circles and cycles of the text's retellings in history and different media. If Perlman's adaptation probes history gently, Jean-Pierre Jeunet's *Un long dimanche de fiançailles* (*A Very Long Engagement*, 2004) deconstructs it as a stable source. An adaptation of a historical era, the First World War and Sébastien Japrisot's novel based on it (1991), Jeunet's adaptation takes history as its source while showing the very impossibility of history as source. Jeunet adapts in his film a history which – he makes clear – he cannot grasp in any tangible way. History, Jeunet's film

FIGURE 0.3 The Tender Tale of Cinderella Penguin *(1981, dir. Perlman)*.

suggests, is personal, subjective, multiple and at times false. It functions as a source text but is itself something of an adaptation.

Chapter 6 – 'Textual migration and adaptive diaspora: French literature adaptations beyond France (1996–2016)' – moves to contemplate the space of adaptations in reworkings of French literature produced outside France between 1996 and 2016. As France's population has, over the centuries, migrated to the four corners of the globe, forming diasporic communities, this chapter contemplates adaptations in different nations in a similarly diasporic light. While the migration of films transnationally was a prevalent feature of the silent era, the intense globalizing impulses of the late twentieth and early twenty-first centuries have brought them to a new intensity. Chapter 6 explores what happens to French sources as they are uprooted from their home language and integrated into new nations, cultures and contexts. It does so using Tim Burton's 2001 version of *Planet of the Apes*, a work which both takes us back to author Pierre Boulle's text (1963) and transfigures it for a different nation. The chapter also considers *Thirst* (2009), a combination of Zola's Naturalist novel *Thérèse Raquin* with elements of vampire horror in a Korean contemporary setting. *Thirst* underscores the cultural hybridity innate to the diasporic movement of both peoples and texts around the globe. Intriguingly, diasporic adaptations do not only embrace their transnational status in this era; at times they also evaluate it in their images. Diasporic adaptations, this chapter argues, often expose a self-conscious awareness of their own status as cross-cultural artefacts. In Declan Donnellan and Nick Ormerod's 2012 adaptation of Maupassant's 1885 novella *Bel-Ami* their reference to the *Twilight* saga is far from insignificant.[19] By casting Robert Pattinson as the predatory social climber Georges Duroy, the film invites spectators to compare the character to Pattinson's vampiric incarnation of a hero in the *Twilight* series, gesturing to the ingestion of different cultures, films and nations which is central to the adaptive enterprise. Like Pattinson's vampiric hero, adaptations shift depending on the different geographical contexts in which they find themselves.

Adaptations of French literature in film matter. They matter because of their prevalence – they have wielded a formative influence on the shape and form of adaptation history and enable us to trace that history. They matter because of their range and diversity, which cumulatively affords us the power to ask critical questions about what adaptation is, how it is formed and, crucially, how we should evaluate it. They matter because they force us to question whether we can actually seek just a source text in an adaptive work of art or whether this is to misunderstand the adaptive process, to ignore the creative forces shaping film recreations of these French literary sources. The adaptations showcased in this book do rework their French source texts. But they also sit at the interstices of multiple creative currents. They are shaped by the money funding them, by their medium's technological possibilities, by film's quest for artistic validity, by the networks of people behind them, by the politics of their time and by the movement within which they were made or those against which they are reacting. They interact with the history of their time and that of their source, pushing us to contemplate the multiplicity of sources from which they work, sources literary, historical and personal. They ask us probing questions about the time of adaptation and its space as texts move and mutate the world over. They remind us that adaptations, in their creative complexity, matter. Far from being commercial derivatives, designed to make a fast buck, adaptations, this book argues, shed light on the complex, contested and creative pathways via which art is created.

Notes

1 Greg Semenza and Bob Hasenfratz, *The History of British Literature on Film (1895–2015)* (New York: Bloomsbury, 2015), 5.
2 Kamilla Elliott, *Rethinking the Novel/Film Debate* (Cambridge: Cambridge University Press, 2003), 128. Also cited in David Baguley, '*Riduttore, Traditore*? On Screening Zola', *Excavatio* 21 (2006): 198–212 (206).
3 Rick Altman, 'Dickens, Griffith, and Film Theory Today', in *Silent Film*, ed. Richard Abel (London: Athlone Press, 1996), 148.
4 'Adaptation and appropriation … provide their own intertexts such that they often perform in cultural dialogue with one another, so perhaps it will increasingly serve us better to think in terms of complex filtration, and in terms of networks, webs and signifying fields, rather than simplistic one-way lines of movement from source to adaptation.' Julie Sanders, *Adaptation and Appropriation* (London: Routledge, 2006), 33.
5 Semenza and Hasenfratz, *The History of British Literature on Film*, 8.
6 Simone Murray, *The Adaptation Industry: The Cultural Economy of Contemporary Literary Adaptation* (New York: Routledge, 2012), 6.
7 *La Bestia humana* (1957, dir. Tinayre).
8 *Zum Paradies der Damen* (*The Ladies' Paradise*, 1922, dir. Pick).
9 *Human Desire* (1954, dir. Lang).
10 *Nana* (1944, dir. Gorostiza and Gavaldón) and *Nana* (1985, dir. Baledón).
11 *Thérèse Raquin* (1980, dir. Langton).
12 Claude Faber, *Jules Verne: Le roman de la terre* (Milan: Éditions Milan, 2005), 50.
13 Verne is far from the only French-speaking writer who is adapted and readapted in different decades, languages and film moments. Prosper

Mérimée's *Carmen* (1845), Alexandre Dumas *père*'s Musketeer novels (1844–50), Alexandre Dumas *fils*'s *La Dame aux Camélias* (*The Lady with the Camellias*, 1848) and Henri Murger's *Scènes de la vie de Bohème* (1851), a text made famous in adaptive form in Giacomo Puccini's *La Bohème* (1896), turn and re-turn in the history of cinema based on French source works. And, to underline this, each of these texts turns and re-turns in successive chapters and eras of this book, which seeks to bring them into dialogue with each other.

14 Timothy Unwin, *Jules Verne: Journeys in Writing* (Liverpool: Liverpool University Press, 2005), 1.
15 *Jules et Jim* (*Jules and Jim*, 1962, dir. Truffaut).
16 *Emmanuelle* (1974, dir. Jaeckin).
17 Christiane Nord, *Translating as a Purposeful Activity: Functionalist Approaches Explained* (Manchester: St Jerome, 1997).
18 André Lefevere, *Translation, Rewriting and the Manipulation of Literary Fame* (London: Routledge, 2016).
19 *Twilight* (2008, dir. Hardwicke), *The Twilight Saga: New Moon* (2009, dir. Weitz), *The Twilight Saga: Eclipse* (2010, dir. Slade), *The Twilight Saga: Breaking Dawn – Part 1* (2011, dir. Condon), *The Twilight Saga: Breaking Dawn – Part 2* (2012, dir. Condon).

1

The currency of adaptation: Art and money in silent cinema (1899–1929)

Andrew Watts

The enthusiasm of filmmakers for adapting French literature is as old as the medium of cinema itself. After brothers Louis and Auguste Lumière had exhibited their cinematograph for the first time in 1895, others were quick to recognize the potential for using this new technology to create fiction as well as documentary films. The period between 1899 and 1929 – the year in which the first sound film, *The Jazz Singer* (dir. Crosland), was released in France – subsequently witnessed the emergence of a vibrant interest in recreating French literary texts for the screen. As the nascent medium hungered for new material, adaptations represented a quick and inexpensive way of making money and promoting cinema as a form of entertainment. Moreover, adapting the works of canonical writers such as Balzac, Hugo and Zola served as a reliable means of attracting spectators, who were often curious to see how re-imaginings of classic texts appeared on film. The present chapter explores these early drivers of cinematic adaptation by drawing on key French literature films produced in France, Germany and the United States. More specifically, it uses the concept of currency – in both a literal and figurative sense – to ask why French literature exerted such a powerful fascination for silent cinematographers and how they, in turn, reflected on the questions of art and money which shaped the early film industry.

In analysing the key reasons for which silent filmmakers adapted French literature, this chapter employs the idea of currency on a variety of interrelated levels. Most obviously, it defines currency as money and shows that the desire to amass profits was one of the strongest motives behind the reinvention of French literary texts for the silent screen. At the same time, however, my discussion argues that money was merely one of a number of currencies that early cinematographers used and actively pursued. First, as cinema strove to establish its credibility as a new medium, it aspired to garner currency in the Bourdieusian sense of cultural value and legitimacy, particularly in comparison with the more prestigious medium of the theatre. Second, cinema sought to acquire its own creative currency and to develop artistic techniques and innovations that were genuinely cinematic as opposed to being derived from the well-worn conventions of the stage. Third, this chapter interprets some of the early stars of silent cinema as human currencies, commercial assets who were used both to promote the films in which they appeared and to generate large box office revenues. Finally, currency can be viewed as a key subject of silent adaptations of French literature. Together with its associated themes of circulation, rotation and exchange, the subject of currency captivated many early cinematographers, who identified it as a conduit through which to reflect on the development of their medium.

By exploring this array of literal and figurative currencies, this chapter rethinks the long-standing critical assumption that silent filmmakers embraced adaptation merely for financial gain. Making money was of course a key objective of the early film industry, and studios were often prepared to break the law in their pursuit of profits. As Jane M. Gaines has argued, plagiarism and financial profiteering were especially rampant during this period:

> In the years before copyright in the moving picture was tested, the major players in both the US and Europe all were involved in a variety of copying practices in an effort to profit quickly. They all attempted to undercut their competitors either by striking duplicate prints or by remaking short films which they then sold as their own.[1]

Within the context of silent adaptations of French literature, this characterization of early cinema as an unscrupulous, money-orientated industry is by no means inaccurate. In 1910, for example, Alice Guy's *Esmeralda* (1905), the earliest known cinematic version of Hugo's *Notre-Dame de Paris* (1831), was pirated by two companies in the United States, Vitagraph and Selig, which reissued it under the titles *Hunchback* and *Hugo the Hunchback*, respectively.[2] By representing early filmmakers as plagiarists and profiteers, scholars have nevertheless tended to ignore the much wider range of artistic, cultural and financial imperatives that drove the practice of adaptation during this period. In so doing, they have also perpetuated old critical stereotypes of adaptation as a parasitic activity that exploits the prestige of canonical literature for commercial ends.[3]

The first part of this chapter focuses on French cinema between 1899 and the end of the First World War, since analysing the notion of currency during this period deepens our understanding of the adaptive impulses that underpinned the silent era. This opening section considers the work of early filmmakers Georges Méliès and Alice Guy. In particular, it shows how they used adaptation not only to generate commercial revenues but also to give cultural currency to a medium that had its origins in fairgrounds and popular theatre.[4] The second part of this chapter explores the adaptation of French literature in the United States between 1913 and 1921. Through its discussion of this key period in which North America established itself as the pre-eminent commercial power in world cinema, this section examines how silent filmmakers in the United States used adaptation to bring artistic, cultural and monetary currency to the cinema. It reflects more specifically on the role of stardom in films such as *The Count of Monte Cristo* (1913, dir. Porter), which sought to garner substantial profits by casting well-known stage actor James O'Neill in the title role. Finally, this chapter returns to European cinema and to the tension between art and money that can be observed in both French and German adaptations during the 1920s. In *L'Argent* (*Money*) (1929), especially, Marcel L'Herbier reflects self-consciously on the creative and commercial drivers behind the production of his film, not least through his emphasis on images of rotation and monetary exchange.

In studying the importance of art and money during the silent era, this analysis draws on the work of key film scholars including Richard Abel, Tino Balio and Susan Hayward, whose research enables us to situate the practice of cinematic adaptation within the broader historical context of the period. However, in contrast to the critical approach favoured by these earlier scholars, who have tended to focus on the diachronic history of silent film, this chapter explores the fundamental role that adaptation played in the early development of cinema as a medium. In my discussion of films spanning the advent of the cinematograph to the arrival of sound film, I argue that the desire of early filmmakers for currency – whether artistic or financial, literal or metaphorical – was integral to establishing the new medium. This desire for currency is of course not unique to the silent era. Throughout the subsequent history of cinema, filmmakers have continued to be motivated by the pursuit of money and artistic innovation. As this chapter shows, however, the interaction between different forms of currency takes on a specific resonance in the context of silent cinema. In the early film industry, currencies were the source of a productive tension that drove the technical development of cinema and fuelled the medium's eventual awareness of itself as an art form.

Adaptive commerce and the pursuit of cultural currency in early French cinema (1899–1917)

For the earliest filmmakers in France, money appeared as a key driver of cinema's enthusiasm for adapting French literature and its attempts to establish itself as a narrative medium. Financial imperatives helped to shape the early development of cinema. This is particularly clear in the case of Georges Méliès, who was born in 1861 to a prosperous family of Parisian shoe manufacturers. Prior to embarking on his career as a cinematographer, Méliès had been employed in his parents' business. In 1884, he travelled to London with a view to extending his family's commercial contacts in the city. During his year-long stay in Britain, he developed an interest in theatrical illusions, in particular those of the popular magician David Devant. Such was his fascination for stage magic that following his return to Paris, Méliès sold his share in the family business and combined these funds with his wife's dowry to purchase the Théâtre Robert-Houdin in 1888. Over the next seven years, the theatre staged numerous magic shows and *féeries*, fantastical plays which combined elements of music, dance, acrobatics and pantomime whose aesthetic would greatly influence both Méliès's own subsequent film production and the development of cinema as a medium more generally.

In providing Méliès with a financial platform to establish himself in the entertainment industry, money also proved crucial to his subsequent turn to filmmaking, adaptation in particular. In the hope of increasing revenues at the Théâtre Robert-Houdin by incorporating film screenings into his shows, Méliès attempted to buy a cinematograph from the Lumière brothers in December 1895. Eager to retain the commercial benefits of this new technology for themselves, the Lumières refused his offer of 10,000 francs, prompting him to acquire a more rudimentary projector known as an Animatograph from British inventor Robert William Paul. The Animatograph enabled him to show films at the Théâtre Robert-Houdin and, as he modified and improved the equipment, to build a new camera with the capacity to record images. In the early summer of 1896, Méliès made his first film, *Une partie de cartes* (*Playing Cards*), in which he, his brother Gaston and two of their friends are shown playing cards in what was a direct adaptation of the Lumière brothers' earlier film *Partie d'écarté* (*Card Game*) (1895). By the end of the year, he had also begun construction on his own studio in the garden of his home in Montreuil, a structure he built to the same specifications as the stage at the Théâtre Robert-Houdin. With its large glass panels designed to provide sufficient light for filming, it resembled an oversized greenhouse. Money had enabled Méliès to launch his career in the theatre, and the commercial acumen that he continued to show thereafter was integral to his ambition to extend his work into film.

Literary adaptations formed a key part of Méliès's plans to use film screenings to boost revenues at his theatre and ultimately sell his films to an international market. Not surprisingly, given his artistic passion for *féeries*, he drew extensively on the seventeenth-century fairy tales of Charles Perrault and recreated at least four of these stories for the screen during his career. The earliest of these adaptations was *Cendrillon* (*Cinderella*) (1899), based on Perrault's 1697 tale of the same title. Totalling 120 metres in length, the six-minute film is described in the catalogue of Méliès's Star Film Company as a 'grand and extraordinary *féerie* in 20 tableaux', a claim which rather overstates the number of sequences in the film by counting each plot element as a scene in its own right. Despite this exaggeration of the film's complexity, *Cendrillon* was clearly an ambitious adaptation, it being the first of Méliès's films to use multiple *tableaux*, with the narrative unfolding across six different sets and incorporating five scene transitions. The film also featured a large cast of dancers and extras which Georges Sadoul speculates might have been drawn – along with some of the costumes and décors – from a production of *Cendrillon* staged at the Théâtre Robert-Houdin in December 1897.[5]

If Méliès appropriated artistic materials from the stage in his adaptation of Perrault's fairy tale, he also sought to highlight the technical dexterity of cinema as a new medium. Key to the cinematic quality of *Cendrillon* in this respect is its playful use of the substitution splice, in which two pieces of film are joined together in order to create the effect of people or objects appearing, disappearing or changing in some way. The first such splice occurs when the fairy godmother (Bleuette Bernon) materializes suddenly in the fireplace of Cinderella's kitchen, where she proceeds to turn a mouse into a carriage driver and two larger mice into footmen. After Cinderella has carried a pumpkin into frame and placed it on a stool, a rapid series of splices sees the pumpkin double in size and become a carriage and Cinderella's rags replaced with an elegant ballgown (see Figure 1.1). Finally, this opening scene blends subtly into the ball sequence by means of a dissolve. In using a well-known fairy tale to attract spectators, Méliès demonstrated through the visual effects of *Cendrillon* that cinema was capable of developing its own artistic techniques and that these were not simply borrowed in their entirety from the stage.

FIGURE 1.1 Cendrillon (Cinderella) *(1899, dir. Méliès).*

The commercial success of *Cendrillon* – and the monies it generated from screenings throughout Europe and the United States – would have a significant impact on the kind of films that Méliès produced subsequently and on his approach to adapting literary material. Together with his eleven-episode reconstruction of the Dreyfus Affair, *Cendrillon* provided him with the financial stability to start making longer films. 'It's thanks to them [*Cendrillon* and *L'Affaire Dreyfus* (The Dreyfus Affair)],' writes Sadoul, 'that he is able to abandon the standard film length of 20 metres and contemplate making two or three films per year, each of which can reach up to 300 metres in length and run beyond a quarter-of-an-hour.'[6] Among these longer, more complex films was *Le Voyage dans la lune*, in which Méliès can be seen to adapt numerous motifs drawn widely from literature, popular culture and the stage. Produced in 1902, *Le Voyage dans la lune* was first screened at the Théâtre Robert-Houdin between September and December of that year. The film, in which a group of astronomers travels to the moon in a capsule fired from a giant cannon, captivated audiences and quickly became an international sensation. In the United States, where it was released in October 1902, *Le Voyage dans la lune* drew enthusiastic crowds in New York, Washington and a host of major cities. In Italy, it was still being screened in 1904, two years after its initial release.[7] The extent of the film's international distribution resulted in substantial profits, though as Matthew Solomon points out, the widespread pirating of the film during this period of scant copyright protection for filmmakers meant that Méliès received only a small portion of the receipts it generated.[8] Whereas *Cendrillon* had equipped him with the funds he needed to make more ambitious films, the unauthorized circulation of copies of *Le Voyage dans la lune* deprived Méliès of much of the financial benefit of his work.

In addition to its status as one of the most widely distributed – and pirated – films of the silent era, *Le Voyage dans la lune* is particularly important as an artistic amalgam in which Méliès recreates several different sources and sends them back into artistic circulation. The first and most obvious of these sources for *Le Voyage dans la lune* were Jules Verne's novels *De la terre à la lune* (*From the Earth to the Moon*) (1865) and *Autour de la lune* (*Around the Moon*) (1869). In an interview in 1930, Méliès himself drew a direct parallel between his film and Verne's novels when he explained that in *Autour de la lune*,

> the men were unable to land on the moon, orbited around it, and returned to Earth after, in fact, failing in their mission. By using the method proposed by Verne (cannon and shell), I thus imagined getting to the moon in such a way that would allow me to compose a certain number of magical and amusing views of its interior and exterior.[9]

However, while it is tempting to take Méliès at his word, Thierry Lefebvre has shown that the film actually has very little in common with either *De la terre à la lune* or *Autour de la lune*, other than a passing similarity between the 'Astronomic Club' depicted in the opening sequence of the film and the Baltimore Gun Club represented by Verne. Even the cannon that launches Méliès's astronomers into space differs from the one described in *De la terre à la lune*, where its barrel stretches beneath a mountain, in contrast to the much more visible apparatus that points skywards in the film. 'In truth,' writes Lefebvre, '*A Trip to the Moon* is a heterogeneous film, taken from a patchwork of sources, which are probably more complex and varied than Méliès made out to be the case.'[10]

Rather than a reinvention of any one particular source, *Le Voyage dans la lune* can be viewed as the product of a series of adaptive exchanges through which Méliès obtained the artistic material that he needed for his film. As Lefebvre has argued, the filmmaker's potential sources included the 'Trip to the Moon' attraction at the Pan-American Exhibition held at Buffalo, New York, in 1901, which thrilled visitors with its simulated flight to the moon and tour of the caverns beneath the lunar surface.[11] More obviously, Méliès appears to have been inspired by aspects of Jacques Offenbach's fairy-opera *Le Voyage dans la lune* (1875), which was itself an unauthorized parody of Verne's *De la terre à la lune*. The film reveals several similarities with Offenbach's earlier work, not least the names of the six astronomers – Cosinus, A-plus-B, Omega, Coefficient, Rectangle and Phichipsi – whose counterparts in the film are identified by the similarly playful names of Nostradamus, Alcofribas, Micromegas, Parafaragaramus, Omega and Barbenfouillis (the latter played by Méliès himself). In a further, telling parallel, the astronomers in the film, like those in the operetta, travel to the moon with umbrellas.[12] By appearing to adapt a range of sources beyond the purely literary, *Le Voyage dans la lune* can be situated within a network of artistic exchanges from which Méliès gathered material before recasting it as a distinct work of cinema.

Whereas Méliès first identified adaptation as a means of generating commercial revenues, his contemporary Alice Guy was eager to appropriate the cultural currency of nineteenth-century French literature. Guy began her career working as a secretary for Léon Gaumont, with whom she attended a demonstration of the Lumières' cinematograph in March 1895. Having viewed the short documentary film *La Sortie de l'Usine Lumière à Lyon* (*Workers Leaving the Lumière Factory in Lyon*), she recognized the potential for using the new medium to create fiction films. 'As the daughter of a publisher,' she recalled later, 'I had read a lot, and retained quite a bit of it. I had done a little amateur theatre and thought that one could do better [than *Workers Leaving the Factory*].'[13] Convinced that she could add an artistic dimension to the emerging film industry, Guy made her first film, a fantasy tale entitled *La Fée aux choux* (*The Cabbage Fairy*), in 1896. The following year, she was promoted to head of production at Gaumont, where over the next decade she directed and produced more than a thousand films before emigrating to the United States in 1907.

While Guy worked across a diverse range of genres including comedies, Westerns and biblical epics, adaptation played a key role in her attempts to enhance the cultural respectability of her medium. The works of Victor Hugo, in particular, were an important source of inspiration for Guy, starting with her 1905 adaptation of *Notre-Dame de Paris* under the title *Esmeralda*. As Delphine Gleizes has argued, silent filmmakers quickly identified the writings of Hugo as 'an instrument of legitimation'[14] whose cultural prestige they hoped would rub off on their own medium and help to elevate it above the status of fairground attraction. Little is known about why Guy chose to adapt *Notre-Dame de Paris* specifically, though the status of the novel as an acknowledged classic of French literature would certainly have made it an attractive choice for adaptation. The film itself is now lost. However, Guy's memoirs give a valuable insight into her ambitions for the project. *Esmeralda* was the first film produced at the Cité Elgé, the studios at Buttes-Chaumont which Gaumont had constructed in 1905. Mindful of her employer's financial investment in both this new facility and her film, Guy was determined that her version of *Notre-Dame de Paris* would reflect the artistic richness of Hugo's text. However, the production threatened to descend into farce when she arrived on set to discover that her scene decorator had painted a backdrop of medieval Paris with houses that looked askew and were crumpled into incongruously futuristic spiral shapes. To exacerbate this unintentionally comic effect, Guy found herself unable to shake off the attention of Esmeralda's goat, which followed her persistently around the set. Finally, the balls of cotton with which actor Henry Vorins had stuffed his hunchback costume kept falling out just as the crew was preparing to shoot the scene in which Quasimodo is tortured. Exasperated by the practical challenges involved in adapting *Notre-Dame de Paris*, Guy found that *Esmeralda* risked undermining both Gaumont's monetary investment in its new studio and the cultural credibility that she hoped to bring to her medium through this production.

Analysis of still photographs of *Esmeralda* nevertheless gives a more positive indication of the artistic value and complexity of the film, as evidenced in particular by the manner in which Guy adapts the creative resources of the theatre. Notably, one of these photographs, which Sadoul published in his 1947 volume *Les Pionniers du cinéma*, shows Quasimodo in the towers of Notre-Dame opposite his rival Claude Frollo. The image makes obvious the theatrical staging of the production, which like most films from the first decade of cinema was shot from a single static camera position in the centre of the frame. Moreover, behind the Gothic arches of the cathedral there appears a view of the city below, with its buildings painted in miniature in order to give the impression that we are looking down on them from a great height. Sadoul observed that this particular aspect of the film's mise en scène set a precedent for subsequent adaptations of *Notre-Dame de Paris*, including the 1939 Hollywood version starring Charles Laughton, which used the same shot of the streets and houses of Paris viewed from the elevated vantage point of the cathedral towers. More problematically, however, Sadoul argued that this distancing effect would not have been possible in the theatre.[15] His claim appears as a fundamental misrepresentation of Guy's adaptive technique in *Esmeralda*, not least because it was scenery obtained from a theatre that made this effect possible. As Guy recalled of her preparations for the film, 'we had bought some outdated curtains from the theatre in Belleville or Porte Saint-Martin. Using one of the sections of portico scenery, I had hung behind it one of the curtains representing a city in the distance.'[16] As her use of this painted backdrop shows, Guy sought to enhance the artistic capabilities of early cinema not by discarding the creative materials of the theatre but by incorporating them into her filmmaking practices.

If Guy attempted to bring cultural legitimacy to her medium by adapting *Notre-Dame de Paris*, her 1907 film *L'Enfant de la barricade* (*The Child of the Barricade*) reflects the way in which she used Hugo's poetry to give artistic depth and sophistication to her own work. Inspired by the poem 'Sur une barricade' ('On a barricade'), a depiction of the Paris Commune which appeared in Hugo's 1872 collection *L'Année terrible* (*The Terrible Year*), the film is, in the assessment of Alison McMahan, one of Guy's weaker scripts.[17] As a re-imagining of its poetic source, *L'Enfant de la barricade* nevertheless illustrates the director's willingness to experiment with Hugo's work and bring a new artistic resonance to it in adaptation. Her cinematic version of the poem begins with an interior scene in which an adolescent boy is shown sitting at the dinner table with his mother. Seeing a group of soldiers run past outside, the boy grabs a milk pail, inventing the pretext of an errand in order to find out what is happening in the street. After becoming embroiled in a popular uprising, he is captured by government troops and sentenced to death by firing squad. Still carrying his milk pail, the boy pleads to be allowed to deliver it to his mother, which he does before bravely returning to face his sentence. *L'Enfant de la barricade* stands out especially for the way in which it reconfigures Hugo's poem, taking only the basic plotline and moulding it into a reflection on the mother–son relationship.

The changes that Guy makes to the source text are significant in this respect. In contrast to the poem, in which the boy asks to be allowed to return home with a watch, Guy prefers the maternal symbol of milk as a signifier of the bond that exists between mother and child. In a further creative departure from the poem, it is the mother's intervention that saves the boy from execution, rather than the sight of his courage and the shame that this causes the commanding officer (see Figure 1.2). In recreating 'Sur une barricade' as a powerful expression of maternal love, Guy does not treat Hugo's work as a priceless cultural artefact but as source material that can be reinvested with new layers of depth and meaning in adaptation.

Guy's attempts at investing her medium with greater cultural respectability were echoed in more formal terms by the establishment of a new production company, Film d'Art, in 1908. Founded by the writer and journalist Paul Lafitte, Film d'Art aimed to dismantle negative perceptions of cinema as merely cheap fairground entertainment by making high-quality narrative films. Working in collaboration with his brother Léon, Lafitte sought in particular to attract middle-class spectators to the cinema by producing films starring some of the leading theatrical actors of the day. He turned in the first instance to the Comédie-Française, recruiting one of its most eminent members, Charles Le Bargy, both to feature in Film d'Art productions and to serve as the company's artistic director. Le Bargy would star in the studio's first release, *L'Assassinat du Duc de Guise* (*The Assassination of the Duke of Guise*) (dir. Le Bargy/Calmettes), in 1908.

FIGURE 1.2 L'Enfant de la barricade (The Child of the Barricade) *(1907, dir. Guy)*.

Although based on an original screenplay by Henri Lavedan, the film stands as an important landmark in the development of French 'art films' and literary adaptations, not least because it sought to adapt both the cultural prestige and artistic techniques of highbrow theatre for the new cinematic medium. On-screen, the film – which relates the plot hatched by King Henri III to murder his rival the Duc de Guise in 1588 – borrows extensively from the conventions of the stage.[18] The action is filmed from a camera planted in the centre of the frame and at waist height to the actors, thus mimicking the position of a spectator in the theatre stalls. Moreover, the gestures and movements of the actors appear exaggerated in a manner reminiscent of theatrical performance. 'Forgetting that one could not hear them,' wrote director Henri Fescourt of seeing the film for the first time, 'they articulated their words by emphasizing each of them with a change of facial expression, a movement of their hands, arms, or body. They behaved as if they were on the boards.'[19] In seeking to appropriate the cultural legitimacy of the theatre, *L'Assassinat du Duc de Guise* adapted the artistic techniques of the stage in a manner that now seemed incongruous with the demands of the new medium.

L'Assassinat du Duc de Guise nevertheless had a significant impact on the practice of literary adaptation in France, especially since its commercial success enabled Film d'Art to launch production on a series of films based on the work of canonical writers. In 1908–9, the company was responsible for no fewer than twenty-eight films, including versions of Mérimée's *Carmen* and Balzac's *La Grande Bretèche*. After the studio changed ownership in 1909, adaptations, particularly of nineteenth-century fiction, remained a staple of its output. Notably, these films encompassed recreations of Dumas *fils*'s *La Dame aux camélias* (*The Lady with the Camellias*) (1912, dir. Pouctal/Calmettes) and *Les Trois Mousquetaires* (*The Three Musketeers*) (1912, dir. Pouctal/Calmettes) and Zola's *Travail* (*Work*) (1920, dir. Pouctal). The advent of Film d'Art also sparked the emergence of rival organizations which used literary adaptations to garner large profits by playing on the curiosity of French audiences to see works from their national canon presented on-screen. In 1908, Pathé established the Société cinématographique des auteurs et gens de lettres (SCAGL) under the leadership of Pierre Decourcelle. Like Film d'Art, SCAGL's mission was to produce highbrow art films, with former actor and theatre director Albert Capellani employed to direct adaptations of Zola's *L'Assommoir* (*The Drinking Den*) (1909) and Hugo's *Les Misérables* (1911) and *Quatre-vingt-treize* (*Ninety-Three*) (1914; released 1921). Having set out to exploit the cultural prestige of the theatre, Film d'Art proved the catalyst for a period of vibrant interest in adapting French literature, resulting in a series of films that often achieved widespread circulation and substantial box office receipts.

While it is clear that Film d'Art brought both commercial revenues and cultural currency to the cinema, the artistic merit of the adaptations it produced is more difficult to assess given that most of these films are now lost. One of the few Film d'Art productions that has survived, however, is the 1917 adaptation of Dumas *père*'s *Le Comte de Monte Cristo* (dir. Pouctal). Originally screened as an eight-part serial, the film was later re-released in a three-hour version, a copy of which has been conserved by the Cinémathèque Royale in Belgium. This reinvention of the story of the fictional Edmond Dantès, a sailor who is wrongfully imprisoned after becoming embroiled in a Bonapartist conspiracy, appears as an intriguing example of Film d'Art's approach to adapting popular classics of French literature. In particular, it reflects the way in which the company strove to maximize the artistic value of its films by presenting them as highly faithful recreations of their source material. Despite working with only a small budget of 3,500 francs per day, Pouctal was determined to shoot his film at some of the actual locations described in the novel. Accordingly, he made extensive use of the port at Marseilles and the Château d'If, the island fortress that in 1917 was still a detention facility for foreign prisoners. These locations would play a key role in the cinematography of the film, as evidenced in particular by the sequence in which Dantès arrives at the prison. Struggling with his guards, the former sailor (Léon Mathot) is shown being escorted up the steps of the island before passing through an archway into the main courtyard. The sequence is notable especially for the way in which it uses these different locations to call attention to changes in the natural light, as each step of Dantès's journey shows the sunlight diminishing in size behind him. Starting with the bright sun that beats down as his protagonist disembarks on the island, Pouctal employs the prison archway and then the cell door as frames for a light that becomes progressively smaller, thereby reflecting the gradual extinction of Dantès's liberty. Finally, this sunlight becomes only a sliver that illuminates the character's eyes as he contemplates the outside world through the narrow opening in the door. As this early sequence in the film illustrates, fidelity was not for Pouctal an end in itself but rather a starting point from which he sought to develop his own cinematic techniques.

Pouctal's recreation of *Le Comte de Monte Cristo* stands as a significant achievement during a period in which French film production had ground to a near-complete halt. By 1917, the First World War had stripped the country's film industry of its artistic and economic assets. Numerous actors, directors and technical staff had left their profession either to join the armed forces or to continue their careers abroad. Many studios had also closed or were being used to accommodate military equipment and supplies.[20] When viewed through the lens of this historical context, *Le Comte de Monte Cristo* appears particularly impressive as a film that defied budgetary constraints to articulate its own, richly cinematic vision of the source text. Adaptations of such complexity would prove the exception rather than the norm in France at this time. As the First World War neared its end, French cinema would be faced with attempting to repair the damage it had suffered as a result of the conflict and regaining some of the artistic and commercial influence that the United States had by now appropriated.

Commercialism, creativity and stardom: Adaptive currencies in American silent film (1913–21)

By the time the First World War broke out in Europe in 1914, American cinematographers had already produced numerous screen versions of French literary texts. The extent of their enthusiasm for adapting such works can be gauged from an index of films based on literary sources published by *Motion Picture World* in July 1915. The record indicated that since 1910, no fewer than eleven adaptations of the work of Dumas *père* had been produced in the United States, in addition to five films inspired by the novels of Verne and a further four adaptations of works by Hugo.[21] As Eileen Bowser observes, literary adaptations far outnumbered original screenplays during the early years of American cinema, as the new medium struggled to satisfy the public's appetite for fiction films.[22] For silent filmmakers in the United States, French literature provided a cheap and accessible source of material that for the most part was unencumbered by copyright restrictions. Like their counterparts in France, they were also quick to identify popular classics of French fiction as a reliable means of attracting spectators to the cinema and maximizing profits.

In seeking to bring French literature films to the largest paying audiences possible, early American cinematographers had often recreated successful theatrical versions of canonical texts. In his 1913 adaptation of *Le Comte de Monte Cristo*, for example, Edwin S. Porter aimed to capitalize on the popularity of a long-running stage adaptation of Dumas *père*'s novel starring James O'Neill. O'Neill had played the role of Edmond Dantès more than six thousand times in theatres across the United States, a run that stretched back to 1883. However, in attempting to transpose O'Neill's celebrated stage performance to the screen, Porter revealed that he had little interest in developing the artistic techniques of cinema as a new medium. Instead, the film borrowed heavily from theatrical conventions and contained only one shot – a close-up of a locket – that could be considered authentically cinematic. 'Seen only in long, medium, and full-figure form,' writes William K. Everson, 'his [O'Neill's] performance is reduced to an arm-waving, stiffly posing pantomime, with never a good look at his face, let alone the opportunity for that face to register nuances of emotion.'[23] Moreover, the film readily destroys the illusion that spectators are watching a work of cinema by addressing them directly. As Bowser explains, this willingness to break the fourth wall is reflected most obviously in the scene in which O'Neill's Dantès escapes from the Château d'If, but not before indicating to the audience the hole in his cell wall that he intends to use as his route out of the prison.[24] Far from striving to develop the artistic potential of film as a medium, Porter's version of *Le Comte de Monte Cristo* was concerned primarily with making money by appropriating the narrative conventions of the theatre and the star persona of O'Neill.

As the American film industry evolved both technically and commercially during the First World War, silent cinematographers began to discard the 'canned theatre' format that had previously typified French literature adaptations in the United States. At the same time, however, they continued to draw on the artistic resources of the stage, and in particular its stars, as a means of generating revenues and promoting film as a legitimate art form.

This tendency is illustrated strikingly by Cecil B. DeMille's 1915 version of Prosper Mérimée's novella *Carmen* (1845). With a running time of 65 minutes, the film was produced by the Lasky Company, which, in an attempt to draw an upper-class audience to the cinema, recruited opera star Geraldine Farrar to play the eponymous heroine. Farrar's status as one of the leading figures of grand opera invested the production with a strong element of cultural authority. 'An American-born singer and Hohenzollern protégée,' explains Sumiko Higashi, '[Farrar] had made her debut in Berlin and was an accomplished diva who could sing in German, Italian, and French. She brought to the film the aura of high culture patronized by European royalty.'[25] In order to emphasize that his company's version of *Carmen* was intended for consumption by the social elite, producer Jesse Lasky held the premiere at Boston's Symphony Hall, where a full orchestra accompanied the screening with a live performance of Hugo Riesenfeld's score, which the composer had based on Bizet's opera *Carmen* (1875). Following its general release on 1 November 1915, DeMille's film proved a stunning success with audiences. Some contemporary estimates claimed that a million spectators flocked to see the film in a single month, with box office receipts totalling $147,599 against production costs of $23,429. Reviews of the film were also effusive in their praise, particularly of Farrar's performance. As one critic wrote in the *New York Dramatic Mirror*:

> Geraldine Farrar has put her heart and soul into this picture, and without the aid of the magic of her voice, has proved herself one of the greatest actresses of all times. ... Her acting in this production is one of the marvels of the stage and screen, so natural, so realistic that it is hard to believe it is acting.[26]

As well as bringing cultural cachet to this adaptation, the casting of Farrar proved key to the commercial success of the film and to the positive reaction from critics who were captivated by her ability to perform beyond the confines of the opera stage.

DeMille's version of *Carmen* is notable for the way in which it mobilizes the cultural currency both of Farrar as an opera star and of grand opera as a medium. The first shot in which Farrar appears on-screen gestures towards her star persona at the outset. Following an intertitle that announces her as Carmen, the film cuts to a medium close-up of the actress as she peers through bushes and then steps forward smiling, in a manner reminiscent of a singer stepping through the curtains and onto the stage. A further sequence later in the film reinforces this evocation of Farrar's career in grand opera, as the bullfighter Escamillo enquires impatiently after the whereabouts of Carmen at Pastia's tavern. In reply, the innkeeper points to a door at the back of the frame, which then opens suddenly to reveal Carmen, who waves regally to the customers on the floor below, as if they were spectators in the theatre stalls.

As Phil Powrie has argued, however, DeMille does not simply punctuate his film with repeated allusions to Farrar's status as an opera diva. On the contrary, his version of *Carmen* can be seen to blend the artistic resources of opera with the nascent language of cinema in a highly innovative way. DeMille's integration of the two media is reflected in his use of the film's operatic score to produce specific stylistic effects. Powrie points out that it is impossible to know the precise extent to which the visual narrative of the film aligned with Riesenfeld's score. However, his analysis of the 2006 DVD release of *Carmen*, which set the film against a performance of this original score by the London Philharmonic Orchestra, suggests that DeMille sought to achieve some synchronicity between sound and image.[27] In the sequence entitled 'The Game Begins', for example, in which Carmen initiates her seduction of Don José, a series of three shots corresponds to three separate occurrences of the word 'amour' sung in the 'Habanera', the most famous aria of Bizet's opera, which Riesenfeld adapted in his own score. In the first of these shots, a close-up of Carmen shows her taking a rose from her mouth before flicking her head haughtily on the final consonant of the word 'amour' (see Figure 1.3). A further close-up focuses on Don José, who on the second

FIGURE 1.3 Carmen *(1915, dir. DeMille)*.

occurrence of the word 'amour' looks towards Carmen with an expression of boyish embarrassment. Finally, we see the couple in shot together as Carmen steps away and the third vocalization of 'amour' emphasizes the love that has now sparked between them. As this sequence shows, DeMille was able to work both through and outside the reputation of Farrar as an opera star and to integrate the artistic materials of her medium into his cinematic retelling of the story.

While DeMille engaged closely with opera, he was also determined to highlight the artistic currency of film by exploring its potential as a new medium of creative expression. His version of *Carmen* invites us in particular to contemplate the range and quality of its cinematic techniques. The film uses colour tints, for example, to add visual resonance to specific sequences, such as the blue tint that accompanies the opening shots of the sea or the deep red tint that covers the screen when tarot cards predict Carmen's death. One of the sequences that best illustrates DeMille's drive towards pushing the artistic boundaries of his medium, however, is the climax of the film set in the Plaza de Toros in Seville. Foreshadowing the epic scale and spectacle of his later sound films *The Ten Commandments* (1956) and *Ben-Hur* (1959), the director shows Carmen watching her lover Escamillo as he faces a bull in the ring below. Lasky's promotional campaign for the film boasted that twenty thousand extras had participated in this sequence, creating a sense of grand spectacle to which the film's cinematography clearly draws attention.

In one notable high-angle shot filmed from within the crowd, we see Carmen from behind as she watches the bullfight, a shot that gestures towards the position of spectators in the cinema as they view the spectacle unfolding before them on-screen. However, despite the lavish scale of the bullfight, a closer reading of this sequence reveals that DeMille's creative contributions to the film were often subtle, as can be seen from his careful use of lighting techniques. Working in tandem with his regular cameraman Alvin Wyckoff, the filmmaker proved adept at representing contrasts of light and shade in what would subsequently become known as 'Lasky lighting' or, as DeMille preferred to describe it, 'Rembrandt lighting'. Such contrasts are evident in the final scene of the film, in which Don José murders Carmen beneath the terraces of the Plaza de Toros. This violent scene takes place behind a large wooden door, above and below which light penetrates from outside. As Don José struggles with Carmen, DeMille shows the heroine attempting to claw her way back into the arena, only for Don José to pull her back into the shadows towards her death. By the time Escamillo returns and opens the door to the enclosure, allowing the light to flood in, Don José has already stabbed both Carmen and himself. The final shot of the film underscores this interplay of light and shade, as José cradles the dying Carmen, her shadow at first visible beneath her before it is gradually extinguished by her head falling lifeless to the ground. Through its use of lighting and cinematography, DeMille's version of *Carmen* deploys its own visual language and storytelling techniques and, in so doing, presents itself as an inherently cinematic work.

In contrast to the highbrow ambitions of *Carmen*, *20,000 Leagues under the Sea* (1916, dir. Paton) traded on the popularity and commercial appeal of Jules Verne. Verne's work proved particularly attractive to silent cinematographers, many of whom were tempted by the prospect of being able to sell adaptations of it to a worldwide market. Brian Taves writes:

> To early filmmakers, Jules Verne was not only a legend but also a contemporary author of international repute, and his global reputation was still at its peak. ... Verne's tales were already regarded as classics that appealed to every audience and geographical locale.[28]

The Frenchman's works were certainly well known in the United States, where they had been widely translated and adapted for the stage on numerous occasions. The advent of cinema further increased the circulation of Verne's fiction in North America. In 1914, for example, a French version of his 1868 novel *Les Enfants du Capitaine Grant* (*The Children of Captain Grant*), directed by Victorin Jasset, was reissued for American audiences under the title *In Search of the Castaways*. The period between 1895 and 1915 also yielded at least three film versions of *Michael Strogoff* (1876) in the United States, including the first feature-length adaptation of the novel directed by Lloyd B. Carleton and released by Popular Plays and Players in 1914. With a plot that combined adventure and science fiction, Verne's 1870 novel *Vingt mille lieues sous les mers (20,000 Leagues under the Sea)* appeared as a natural choice for cinematic adaptation, despite the technical challenges involved in recreating its extensive underwater sequences. Moreover, given that the story was one of the author's best-known works, adapting it for the screen represented a potentially lucrative opportunity to draw large audiences to the North American box office.

If Paton's version of *Vingt mille lieues sous les mers* adapted Verne's work for commercial gain, the film also sought to promote film as a new art form. In order to recreate the tale of the fictional Captain Nemo and his submarine the Nautilus, Paton enlisted the help of brothers Ernest and George Williamson, who had pioneered a method of filming underwater. The Williamsons' invention, which they called the 'photosphere', consisted of a small steel capsule that was attached to a barge by means of a watertight tube. This capsule could be lowered to a depth of 25 metres and was large enough to accommodate a cameraman, who captured footage through a porthole. Determined to exploit the commercial potential of this equipment,

Universal's marketing campaign trumpeted *20,000 Leagues under the Sea* as 'the only production of its kind in the world – the only photo-drama actually photographed at the bottom of the ocean'. In a further attempt to highlight the invention that had made its underwater sequences possible, the film itself also included a short prologue featuring the Williamson brothers, in which they remove their hats, smile and nod warmly to the audience. As well as seeking to profit financially from the international popularity of Verne's fiction, Paton's reworking of *Vingt mille lieues sous les mers* showcased the technical innovation of which the new medium of film was capable.

Despite Universal's obvious attempt to capitalize on the novelty value of this adaptation as 'the first submarine photoplay ever filmed', *20,000 Leagues under the Sea* engaged seriously with the figure of Verne as a writer. As Kate Griffiths points out in the introduction to this book, adaptations of Verne's work have often focused on his image as a scientific visionary and boundless adventurer. Paton's film clearly illustrates this tendency. In particular, it foregrounds the Verne who sought to transport readers to new worlds through the series of fictions to which he gave the collective title *Voyages extraordinares (Extraordinary Journeys)* (1863–1905). The underwater sequences in the film are key to adapting this aspect of Verne's authorial personality, as evidenced by a notable scene in which Nemo invites Professor Aronnax, the harpooner Ned Land and Aronnax's daughter (a character not featured in the novel) to join him in contemplating the seabed through a large porthole in his cabin. There follows a long sequence in which the camera pans over the seaweed and coral reefs, occasionally cutting back to the inside of the Nautilus, where Nemo explains each of the sights as they pass before them. The intertitles which articulate the Captain's dialogue emphasize the wondrous nature of this experience, as he encourages his guests to 'behold the beautiful marine gardens' and 'notice how brilliant is the reflection of the sun's rays on these coral reefs'. Finally, a shark swims into view, prompting Nemo to observe that 'only the crystal plates of our window protect us from these man-eaters'. Clearly, such statements were also directed at the film's first spectators, inviting them to share with the fictional Aronnax and his companions the thrill of seeing the bottom of the ocean and its marine life on-screen. More importantly, the sequence illustrates how Paton used his medium to recast Verne's exploration of the natural world in a visually striking way.

The captivating underwater sequences of *20,000 Leagues under the Sea* helped to ensure that the film was a major critical and commercial success when it was released in the United States on 24 December 1916. Writing in *The Moving Picture World*, Edward Weitzel praised its combination of adventure and underwater photography, in particular the scene in which

Nemo rescues a pearl diver from the clutches of an octopus by hacking at the creature's tentacles with an axe:

> The picture is full of mystery to the uninitiated, the fight with the octopus being a case in point. The illusion here is perfect. The views of the coral beds are things of beauty and won hearty applause from the audience which witnessed the first showing of the picture at the Broadway theater, New York.[29]

As Weitzel's review suggests, *20,000 Leagues under the Sea* also performed well at the North American box office, with some four hundred thousand people viewing it in New York alone. Subsequent scholarly appraisals of the film have nevertheless been decidedly mixed. While identifying Paton's version as one of the few adaptations of *Vingt mille lieues sous les mers* to represent Nemo's ethnicity, Brian Taves, for example, criticizes the film for making radical changes to Verne's portrayal of the fictional submariner. 'From the outset of the adaptation,' observes Taves, 'Nemo weakens in the resolve to remain isolated from his fellow men, and no explanation is provided for why or how the Nautilus came to be built or its scientific achievement.'[30] In contrast to Verne's representation of Nemo as a political revolutionary, Paton reinvents the character as a man on a personal mission to avenge the attempted rape of his wife and the abduction of his daughter. Moreover, Taves complains, the film makes spurious claims about Verne himself, not least that, according to an intertitle at the start of the film, the author 'died a disappointed man because the world did not take him seriously'.[31] In a charge so often levelled at adaptations, such negative criticisms accuse Paton of being too liberal in his approach to recreating *Vingt mille lieues sous les mers* and of failing to respect either the artistic value of the novel or the cultural importance of Verne himself.

To judge Paton's version of *Vingt mille lieues sous les mers* principally on the basis of its fidelity to the source text and the author's biography is nevertheless to underestimate how the film generates its own narrative from the raw material of Verne's fiction. One of the most intriguing features of the film in this respect is the way in which it combines plot elements from both *Vingt mille lieues sous les mers* and another Verne novel, *L'Île mystérieuse* (*The Mysterious Island*) (1874). In the opening section of the film, the USS *Abraham Lincoln* is dispatched to investigate sightings of a mysterious sea monster that is revealed subsequently as the Nautilus. When the two vessels collide, Nemo plucks Aronnax, Ned Land and Aronnax's daughter from the sea and takes them captive on board his submarine. The action then switches to a different plotline – corresponding broadly to that of *L'Île mystérieuse* – in which five Union soldiers escape from a Confederate prison in a balloon and land on an island in the Pacific, where, in a departure from the plot of the source text, they discover a primitive girl dressed in animal skins. Paton continues to alternate between the Nautilus and the island, and it is only in the final part of the film that the connection between the two stories becomes clear. Following an intertitle which announces this narrative resolution as 'the story that Verne never told', Nemo reveals himself as an Indian prince who left his homeland in despair after an American merchant, Charles Denver, had assaulted his wife and kidnapped his daughter, whom he later abandoned on the remote island. After being reunited with the girl, Nemo dies and is buried in a grave at the bottom of the ocean.

Taken at face value, Paton's description of these closing scenes as original material is misleading. In *L'Île mystérieuse*, Verne had identified Nemo as the Indian prince Dakkar, whose family was killed during the Sepoy Rebellion of 1857. Moreover, the conclusion to the film can be viewed as conventional for its time, not least because it recycles melodramatic tropes in a manner that was highly characteristic of silent cinema. In particular, it punishes the villain Denver, who dies when the Nautilus torpedoes his yacht and restores the happiness of Nemo by repairing some of the damage wrought to his family years before. More importantly, however, this ending illustrates Paton's ability to adapt material from across the *Voyages extraordinaires*. Instead of restricting himself to a single source text, the director borrows elements from *Vingt mille lieues sous les mers* and *L'Île mystérieuse* and uses them to create a story of his own design. In so doing, his film appears not as a travesty of these two novels, as Taves claims,[32] but as an adaptation that skilfully recasts and reinterprets its Vernian sources.

In addition to harnessing the contemporary popularity of writers such as Verne, North American cinema proved adept during this period at exploiting the commercial value of well-known actors and performers. By the early 1910s, many American producers recognized the importance of recruiting star names for their films and, as we saw earlier in this chapter, often turned to the stage in search of established performers capable of attracting large audiences. However, as the new medium evolved beyond its early dependence on the artistic resources of the theatre, so, too, did it begin to develop its own stars. Although many of these performers – such as Charlie Chaplin, Douglas Fairbanks and Mary Pickford – had launched their careers on stage, it was their subsequent appearances on-screen that brought them to the attention of a much wider audience and won them a devoted following both in the United States and abroad. As Tino Balio explains, the emergence of this star system had significant commercial benefits for the major American studios. 'A star's popularity', writes Balio, 'created a ready-made market for his or her pictures, which reduced the risks of production financing – an insurance policy of sorts, but also a production value and a trademark enhancing the prestige of the producer.'[33] Several of the leading performers in this star system were also quick to understand their own value as commercial assets. In an attempt to secure greater control over the distribution of their films and a larger share of the profits arising from them, Chaplin, Fairbanks and Pickford allied themselves with director D. W. Griffith to establish their own studio, United Artists, in 1919. Despite producing an average of only five films per year until 1924, the venture clearly reflected the importance of stardom as one of the key commercial drivers of the early American film industry.

The star system had a significant impact on the adaptation of French literature in the United States, as increasingly studios used leading actors as human currencies, commercial assets that could be exploited in order to maximize revenues. One of the adaptations that best exemplifies this tendency is *The Three Musketeers* (1921, dir. Niblo), based on Dumas *père*'s 1844 novel *Les Trois Mousquetaires* and starring Douglas Fairbanks. Having begun his Hollywood career at Triangle Pictures in 1915 under the guidance of D. W. Griffith, Fairbanks quickly became known for the physical athleticism he displayed in his screen performances. However, it was his thirtieth film, *The Mark of Zorro* (1920, dir. Niblo), that launched him into a succession of swashbuckling roles that would become integral to his screen persona. As the masked vigilante Zorro, who protects the people of Spanish California from mistreatment at the hands of the fictional Governor Alvarado, the actor combined energetic swordsmanship with comic bravado in a film that proved so popular with American audiences that it recouped more than three times its production cost of $169,187.[34] With the commercial success of *The Mark of Zorro*, Fairbanks established his image as a daring romantic hero that filmmakers would continue to adapt and recirculate throughout his career.

Made by Fairbanks's own production company, *The Three Musketeers* aimed to attract spectators and maximize profits by redeploying his swashbuckling screen persona. Fairbanks had long aspired to play the character of D'Artagnan on-screen and initially considered starring in a French serial version of Dumas's novel directed by Henri Diamant-Berger.[35] Ultimately, the actor expressed his preference for working in Hollywood feature films and recruited Fred Niblo, his director in *The Mark of Zorro*, to work with him in producing their own adaptation of the novel. Their subsequent version of *Les Trois Mousquetaires* emphasizes those aspects of Fairbanks's screen image that had delighted audiences in his earlier performance as Zorro, most notably the actor's athleticism. This attribute is particularly evident in a thrilling sequence early in the film in which D'Artagnan joins the eponymous musketeers in a swordfight against Cardinal Richelieu's guards. One of sixteen duels represented in the film, the sequence begins with D'Artagnan arriving behind the Palais du Luxembourg in the expectation of crossing swords with Porthos, Athos and Aramis, only for the four men to be interrupted by Richelieu's guards. Deciding to join forces, D'Artagnan and the musketeers confront their common enemy, with Fairbanks advancing immediately to the front of the frame in a manner that underscores his status as the star of the film. Niblo proceeds to highlight the actor's physical prowess in this scene, as we see D'Artagnan leap over the crossed blades of Aramis and one of the guards, whom he swiftly dispatches with a blow to the chest. The camera switches then to show D'Artagnan coming to the aid of Porthos, who, believing that he has won his own duel, turns his back on his injured assailant, thus allowing the man to take aim at him with a pistol. The moment gives rise to the most difficult stunt in the film, as Fairbanks performs a left-handed handspring, plunging a dagger into the guard's chest and forward-rolling over him while still balancing on the handle of the blade. In its emphasis on Fairbanks's athleticism and acrobatic skills, Niblo's adaptation of *Les Trois Mousquetaires* plays overtly on the physicality that underpinned both the actor's screen persona and his reputation as an international star.

Fairbanks's determination to protect the commercial value of his screen image would also shape the way in which *The Three Musketeers* adapted its source material. Working in tandem with scriptwriter Lotta Woods, Niblo and Fairbanks configured their version of the story in order to align the character of D'Artagnan with the actor's star persona and his own expectations of the role. On reading Dumas's work, Fairbanks had been surprised to discover that D'Artagnan was by no means the idealized hero he had envisaged, as the actor told *Motion Picture Magazine* in November 1922:

> You know if you get right down to cases, that fellow [D'Artagnan] was a brute and a bully. He went around picking quarrels with everybody and killing folks who hadn't done anything to get killed for. ... It sounded all right in the book, but when you showed it in the picture you had to show men being run thru with swords and dying ... that could have been a horrible thing.[36]

As a result, the violence that Fairbanks perpetrates in the role of D'Artagnan often resembles innocent slapstick in which those involved rarely suffer serious injury. Following their duel with the musketeers behind the Luxembourg Palace, for example, Richelieu's guards stagger to their feet and live to report the incident to the cardinal. As Jeffrey Vance explains, the film elides the darker aspects of D'Artagnan's behaviour portrayed by Dumas and replaces them with 'the familiar "Doug" characteristics that audiences had come to expect'.[37]

Most notably, Fairbanks's D'Artagnan displays a kind of comic exuberance that the actor had developed earlier in his career, not least as Zorro. The sequence in which the aspiring musketeer rushes back to Paris with the Queen's diamonds reflects this comic tone. As D'Artagnan arrives at the city gates, an intertitle informs us that he 'scents danger', before the camera cuts to a shot of him sniffing the air. In a further moment of comic ebullience, he then leaps onto an empty cart and launches himself into the river, paddling furiously across the water in an attempt to evade Richelieu's guards. This strategy of exploiting the familiar elements of Fairbanks's star persona proved highly popular with audiences, resulting in domestic box office receipts of $1.4 million, almost double the film's production cost. By capitalizing on the popularity of Fairbanks's screen image, *The Three Musketeers* illustrates both the economic value of stars in American silent cinema and the fundamental role of stardom in determining how French literature was adapted in the United States during this period.

Fluctuating currencies: French literature films between art and commerce (1921–9)

By the early 1920s, the French film industry had recovered sufficiently from the paralysing effects of the First World War to begin to confront the commercial dominance of North American cinema. Literary adaptations once again would prove key to this development, as illustrated by the emphasis on producing large-scale adaptations, or 'superproductions', that gripped French filmmaking briefly during the first part of the decade. Characterized by high production values and underwritten by enormous financial budgets, these superproductions aimed to re-establish French-made films in both the national and international market and, in so doing, open major new revenue streams for their parent studios. One of the earliest examples of this superproduction strategy was *L'Atlantide* (*Atlantida*) (1921) directed by Jacques Feyder.[38] Inspired by Pierre Benoit's best-selling novel *L'Atlantide* (1919), the film relates the story of a Saharan queen, Antinéa, who lures European men to her desert palace and takes them as lovers before turning them into metallic statues. Enthralled by the possibility of bringing this popular work to the screen, Feyder paid 10,000 francs to acquire the rights to adapt the novel, in the process fending off competition from a number of Hollywood studios.

With production costs that eventually soared to 1.8 million francs, *L'Atlantide* was a highly ambitious project, especially since Feyder insisted on shooting the film entirely on location in Algeria. In choosing to make his film in the desert, where temperatures regularly reached forty-five degrees, Feyder was determined to show that this major project was both possible and financially viable. 'With *L'Atlantide*,' he recalled later in *Le Cinéma, notre métier*, 'I attempted a work of considerable proportions whose scope and cost terrified the producers; I showed myself that such an undertaking is possible, the distributors that it can be profitable, and that henceforth cinema can take on large-scale subjects.'[39] The commercial success of *L'Atlantide* would certainly repay Feyder's faith in the production. Following its premiere on 4 June 1921, the film ran for fifty-two consecutive weeks in Paris and was widely distributed to overseas territories. Sadoul estimates that between ten and fifteen million spectators saw the film in France alone, making it one of the most notable and enduring box office attractions of the silent era.[40]

From the very outset, the epic scale of *L'Atlantide* assails the viewer through an opening sequence in which Feyder introduces the mystery surrounding the repeated disappearances of French soldiers in the Sahara. Following a brief iris shot of Antinéa reclining on her throne, the director cuts to a further shot showing a wide, empty expanse of desert. Emphasizing the inhospitality of this environment, an intertitle warns that camels which stray from their route are likely to meet with death, before Feyder cuts to shots of the skeletal remains of a camel and lizards crawling on the sand. The sequence proceeds to foreground the vastness of the desert as a caravan of horses and camels carrying French soldiers advances from the left of frame across the distant horizon. In a further reflection of the scale and openness of the space, two riders on horseback turn to approach the camera, seemingly taking an age to reach the front of the frame, despite riding over the dunes at full gallop. Finally, we see the body of a man – later revealed as the missing soldier Saint-Avit – lying on the sand in a state of exhaustion, the length of his arduous journey illustrated by the line of footsteps extending from the point at which he has fallen and continuing beyond the top of the frame. These opening shots of the desert captivated many of the film's first critics, most notably Louis Delluc, who claimed – albeit with a hint of sarcasm – that 'there is a great actor in *L'Atlantide*, and that is the sand'.[41] In his representation of the desert, Feyder highlighted both the vast scale of his project and the striking cinematography that could be achieved with large-scale investment.

While it clearly belonged to the vogue for superproductions that swept through French cinema in the early 1920s, *L'Atlantide* was by no means merely a vacuous commercial product. On the contrary, analysis of the film reveals that it is both artistically and ideologically sophisticated, particularly in its engagement with questions of French imperialism. As one of the earliest French colonial films, Feyder's adaptation is notable for the way in which it glorifies France's civilizing mission in North Africa, not least by depicting the officers Morhange and Saint-Avit as courageous explorers who are prepared to risk their lives to cross the desert in search of their missing comrades. Moreover, the film can be seen to reflect a desire to escape from the painful realities of the war and its aftermath that Susan Hayward identifies as a key feature of the French national mindset during this period.[42]

This escapist impulse is illustrated by a sequence early in the film, in which Saint-Avit returns to Paris on medical leave but remains preoccupied by memories of the Sahara. As we see the character at various locations around the city – sitting on a bench near the Eiffel Tower and walking in the Place de l'Opéra – Feyder incorporates a series of images of the desert accompanied by intertitles which describe Saint-Avit as experiencing 'nostalgia for those magical horizons' and the 'mysterious attraction towards those great lonely expanses' (see Figure 1.4). However, the film's representation of this pull

FIGURE 1.4 L'Atlantide (Atlantida) *(1921, dir. Feyder).*

towards the colonies is by no means uniformly positive. While associating the desert with escapist fantasy, Feyder also dramatizes the mortal dangers posed by French involvement in North Africa. The figure of Antinéa, in particular, appears as a temptress who lures French soldiers to her palace only to kill them and display their bodies as golden statues. In his novel, Benoit had made clear that his female protagonist repeats this process of seduction and murder out of revenge for the centuries of abuse and betrayal that women have endured at the hands of colonial adventurers. 'It is an old quarrel, a very old quarrel,' explains Professor Le Mesge, the resident scholar of Antinéa's palace, to Morhange. 'Have you really forgotten to what extent the beautiful queens of antiquity had just cause to complain of the strangers whom fortune brought to their borders?'[43] Feyder's version of L'Atlantide struggles to recreate this image of Antinéa as a murderous seductress, a shortcoming of the film that critics have often attributed to the fact that actress Stacia Napierkowska gained thirty pounds in weight before the start of production. Images of death nevertheless feature strongly in this adaptation, reflecting what we might interpret as a sense of anxiety that France will continue to lose its young men to North Africa as it had done to the war. The closing shots of L'Atlantide appear as an implicit expression of this concern, as Saint-Avit, accompanied by another French soldier who takes the place of his dead comrade Morhange, declares himself unable to resist the temptation of rediscovering Antinéa's kingdom, knowing that he will meet an inevitable end by returning there. In associating the colonies with death as well as escapism, Feyder invested these familiar exotic tropes with new meaning by resituating them within a post-war context of loss and national uncertainty.

Whereas *Les Trois Mousquetaires* and *L'Atlantide* aimed to generate vast commercial revenues, the early 1920s in France also spawned a number of smaller – and in some cases experimental – adaptations which rejected the money-driven ethos of the superproduction strategy. Feyder himself was a key figure in developing a cinematic alternative to the big-budget spectaculars that proved so popular with audiences during this period. Having completed work on *L'Atlantide*, the director sought to produce not another superproduction, but rather a film that would enable him to explore the artistic possibilities of his medium on a smaller scale. As Charles Ford explains, '*L'Atlantide* was above all a daring commercial venture, and Feyder aspired to something else. Calm, reflective, and honest with himself, he now had a firm desire to sample an experience that would be more fulfilling from an artistic point of view.'[44]

The work that Feyder chose as the basis for this new project was *L'Affaire Crainquebille* (*The Crainquebille Affair*), a novella by Anatole France first published in 1901. Adapted under the title *Crainquebille* (1922), the film revolves around an elderly fruit and vegetable seller (Maurice de Féraudy) who goes to

FIGURE 1.5 Crainquebille (Old Bill of Paris) *(1922, dir. Feyder).*

prison after being accused of insulting a police officer (see Figure 1.5). Despite accepting his punishment without bitterness, upon his release Crainquebille finds himself shunned by his former customers, sending him into a downward spiral of alcoholism and homelessness. Reworking this story for the screen presented Feyder with significant challenges. 'Everyone had advised him against it,' writes Ford of the director's intention to adapt the novella. 'It was generally thought that the purely psychological tale of the misadventures of Crainquebille was entirely anticinematic and that, moreover, the character of a modest fruit and vegetable seller from the Rue Lepic ... would hardly be of interest to cinema audiences.'[45]

Feyder was nevertheless determined to confront the technical challenges involved in recreating this supposedly unadaptable text and, in so doing, to highlight the artistic – as opposed to the merely commercial – possibilities of his medium. In adapting *L'Affaire Crainquebille*, the director focused first on producing a realist film in which images of Parisian trade and commerce feature prominently. Urban realist films emerged as a key strand of French literature adaptations during this period, a vogue that Abel attributes to the popularity of Henri Pouctal's depiction of factory life in his 1920 version of Zola's *Travail*. 'On the strength of *Travail*'s success,' claims Abel, 'several producers tried to turn other works of nineteenth-century urban fiction into profitable realist films',[46] a tendency exemplified in particular by Jacques de Baroncelli's adaptation of Balzac's *Le Père Goriot* (*Old Goriot*) (1835) in 1921. Although based on an early-twentieth- rather than a nineteenth-century text, *Crainquebille* can be viewed as an extension of this vogue for urban realism. The opening sequence of the film appears particularly striking in this respect, as Feyder shows a convoy of horse-drawn carts making their way through the streets of Paris towards the market at Les Halles. Beginning with a shot of the Eiffel Tower in darkness, this initial sequence follows the traders as they pass through the various districts of the city at night. Pausing to introduce us to characters who will feature in the film's plot, Feyder shows first the doctor, Mathieu, being awoken by the noise of the carts outside his apartment, followed by the lawyer Maître Lemerle returning home accompanied by two women and finally the prostitute Madame Laure, one of Crainquebille's long-standing customers. The realist centrepiece of this sequence, however, is its depiction of Les Halles. Tilting down from a high-angle shot of the buildings and crowded streets of this bustling commercial district, Feyder presents a series of shots of the traders and throngs of customers, piles of vegetables and crates loaded with other goods. Allusions to different forms of trade continue to accumulate in the second part of this prologue, which intersperses shots of handcarts being prepared to be wheeled outwards across the city with images of prostitutes being loaded into a police wagon and the young newspaper seller 'La Souris' ('Mouse') (Jean Forest) clamouring to collect his batch of papers for the day. Only at the end of this series of realist vignettes does Feyder introduce the title character, as we see him pushing his own cart through the crowds. As this opening sequence illustrates, *Crainquebille* uses images of trade and commerce to establish its own credentials as an urban realist film.

To view *Crainquebille* purely as a realist production would nevertheless be to neglect both the artistic complexity of the film and the acuteness of its social commentary. Feyder's representation of Crainquebille's treatment at the hands of the French judicial system is replete with social irony, as evidenced most obviously by the courtroom sequence that follows the old man's arrest. Using a combination of visual effects and trick shots, Feyder shows the indifference of the court to Crainquebille's situation and the character's own awareness of the intrinsic bias of the proceedings. The sequence begins with the defendant shuffling nervously in the dock waiting for his case to be heard. A series of point-of-view shots reflect the old man's confusion, starting with a blurred image of a policeman's uniform, followed by jerky camera movements as Crainquebille looks towards the public gallery. The court nevertheless ignores his agitated state and, worse still, shows little interest in his case. In a state of obvious boredom, the public prosecutor makes paper shapes at his bench and stares out of the window towards the towers of Notre-Dame. Meanwhile, the defence lawyer Lemerle studiously marks off his bets in a copy of the horseracing newspaper *Le Jockey*. Most notably, Feyder represents Crainquebille's perception of the biased manner in which the court treats the evidence of the different witnesses. For example, during the testimony of Agent 64, the policeman whom Crainquebille stands accused of having insulted, the director uses a visual effect to show the officer assuming gigantic proportions and towering over the courtroom. By contrast, Doctor Mathieu appears to diminish in size, reflecting the court's apparent lack of faith in his evidence. At the close of this sequence, Feyder confirms Crainquebille's perspective that the court has taken a very partial view of his case and that it cares little for what happens to him thereafter. Once sentence is passed, Maître Lemerle rushes from the room without stopping to explain the verdict to his client, leaving a bewildered Crainquebille to enquire of a policeman, 'I'm a criminal, then?' Far from restricting himself to producing a work of documentary realism, Feyder uses his adaptation of the courtroom sequence to deploy visually striking effects while simultaneously underscoring his ability to engage in social commentary.

Following its release in France in November 1922, *Crainquebille* was greeted enthusiastically by audiences and garnered praise from Anatole France, who was impressed by the film's technical dexterity. Of the visual effects used in the courtroom sequence, in particular, the author observed that 'these are captivating techniques [that would be] unworkable in the theatre'.[47] In the United States, where *Crainquebille* was released in 1923 under the title *Bill*, D. W. Griffith, for his part, lauded the film's urban realism. According to Sadoul, Griffith emerged from a screening of *Crainquebille* in New York and proclaimed 'I have seen a film which, for me, precisely symbolizes Paris.'[48] Within the sphere of literary adaptation, the success of *Crainquebille* also coincided with the decline of the French superproduction strategy, which, as Abel points out, had failed to establish a stronger foothold for French films abroad or to break the commercial dominance of American films in France.[49]

Faced with this reality, many French studios focused once again on maximizing profits by producing low-budget adaptations of popular nineteenth-century novels. Balzac's work in particular inspired several adaptations during the first half of the 1920s in France, including versions of *Ferragus* (1924, dir. Ravel) and *Le Cousin Pons* (1924, dir. Robert). Despite being made without significant financial investment, some of these films proved highly sophisticated artistic works. This was clearly true in the case of Jean Epstein's

1923 adaptation of Balzac's short story *L'Auberge rouge* (*The Red Inn*) (1831), in which a young army surgeon, Prosper Magnan (played in Epstein's version by Léon Mathot), stands accused of having murdered a wealthy diamond merchant at a roadside inn in Alsace. With a plot that revolved around murder, mystery and the moral dilemma of inheriting money acquired through crime, *L'Auberge rouge* fitted neatly with the director's vision of cinema as a medium for all. 'It is wrong to talk about cinema for the elite,' Epstein claimed, 'because then it is no longer cinema, it's literature. Cinema needs its hundred million spectators, its two hundred million eyes … in order to live and to progress.'[50]

Adapting Balzac's text afforded Epstein an opportunity to showcase the kind of artistic developments that he sought to bring before a mass cinema audience. His version of *L'Auberge rouge* abounds in examples of innovative shot-making, such as the circular tracking shot that the director uses to introduce the participants in the drama, which reviewer Jean Eyre described at the time of the film's release as 'most strange'.[51] However, while Epstein was determined to highlight the artistic capabilities of his medium, he was also profoundly aware of the wider commercial context in which he was operating. This awareness is reflected clearly in the thunderstorm sequence that serves as the film's most spectacular visual set-piece. Filmed using thousands of gallons of water supplied by the Paris fire brigade, this sequence was conceived by Epstein in part as a means of rivalling the big-budget special effects beloved of his counterparts in American cinema. Describing the scene when he visited the set of *L'Auberge rouge*, Jean Eyre recalled in an article for *Mon Ciné* that 'an enormous aeroplane propeller blew bursts of fake rain across the set and stirred the leaves of the trees with a storm wind. It was very … American'. Later in the night, Eyre spoke to Epstein himself, who boasted, tongue in cheek, that the scene had cost him 500,000 francs.[52] However, creating a stunning visual effect of the kind popularized by Hollywood cinema was only part of Epstein's ambition in this sequence. This cinematic thunderstorm also functions as a conduit through which he explores how to represent the silent workings of Magnan's mind as the character contemplates killing the diamond broker with whom he and Taillefer are sharing a room. Through a series of closely related shots, Epstein conveys visually the shifts in his protagonist's mental state.[53] From an initial shot of Magnan sitting awake in the corner of the room, the director proceeds to alternate between images of the storm outside and dream-like shots of diamonds falling like drops of rain. As Magnan removes his scalpel from his pouch and prepares to strike, he stops himself, as if realizing the gravity of his murderous plan (see Figure 1.6). Epstein continues to link the storm outside to Magnan's thought process, as quick fades cut repeatedly across the screen,

FIGURE 1.6 L'Auberge rouge (The Red Inn) *(1923, dir. Epstein).*

not only simulating the effect of lightning but also foreshadowing the slashing of the diamond broker's throat.

As Abel has noted in his own discussion of *L'Auberge rouge*,[54] this sequence contains the earliest example of a theoretical principle that Epstein had developed two years earlier in his 1921 volume *Bonjour cinéma*. In this work of film criticism, the director had stated his ambition to merge objective and subjective viewpoints in his films, so that the audience not only sees the performers on-screen but also experiences the action from their perspective:

> When a character goes to meet another, I want to go with him, not behind or in front, or even beside him, but in him, so that I see through his eyes and see his hand stretch outwards from underneath me as if it were my own.[55]

With a combination of shots that evokes Magnan's lust for the diamonds and his thoughts of obtaining them through murder, the thunderstorm of *L'Auberge rouge* encapsulates Epstein's determination to take us inside the subjective experience of his protagonist. Taking as his starting point a spectacular, American-style visual effect, he uses this sequence to represent the psychological dimensions of the story and, in so doing, put into practice his own cinematic theory.

The tension between art and commerce that so often underpinned literature adaptations in France during the 1920s was similarly reflected in German cinema during the 1920s. The economic context in which French and German cinematographers operated was nevertheless very different. While the French film industry had been virtually crippled by the First World War, German cinema emerged in the 1920s as the main competitor to Hollywood. For major American producers, the German market appeared rich territory for exhibiting their films, particularly as German currency began to stabilize towards the end of 1923. The influx of over a hundred American feature films per year brought moments of financial crisis for German cinema during this period, culminating in the near-bankruptcy of the prestigious national film company UFA in 1927. However, as Stephen Brockmann observes, the 1920s saw German films continue to generate larger revenues than their American counterparts in the domestic market. Between 1926 and 1928, for example, German films retained a 42.5 per cent market share compared to 39.5 per cent for Hollywood productions.[56] The 1920s also witnessed substantial investment in the exhibition infrastructure in Germany, as the number of cinemas increased from 3,731 in 1920 to over 5,000 a decade later.[57]

As the German film industry lurched between financial crisis and relative prosperity during this period, literature adaptations provided studios with a reliable means of maximizing profits. Not surprisingly, given that the two countries had so recently been at war, German cinematographers showed relatively little interest in adapting French literature during the 1920s. More often, the works they chose to recreate for the screen were based on traditional German sources that were likely to appeal to audiences whose sense of national pride had been severely damaged by defeat in the First World War. In 1924, for example, Fritz Lang reworked the medieval epic poem *Nibelungenlied* (c.1200) as a two-part film, *Die Nibelungen* (*The Song of the Nibelungs*). Similarly, in 1926, F. W. Murnau directed *Faust*, based on the German folktale in which the eponymous protagonist sells his soul to the Devil. Such films provided studios with inexpensive subject matter and therefore represented low risks at a time when the German industry was often under severe commercial pressure.

Although only a small number of French literature adaptations appeared in Germany during the 1920s, *Manon Lescaut* (1926) stands out as a film that reflects self-consciously on its status as both an artistic artefact and a commercial product. Directed by Arthur Robison for UFA, the film was inspired by Abbé Prévost's 1731 novel *L'Histoire du Chevalier des Grieux et de Manon Lescaut* (*The Story of the Chevalier des Grieux and Manon*

Lescaut), in which a young nobleman falls in love with a beautiful courtesan just as he is about to take holy orders and enter a monastery. Robison's version of the story was produced by Erich Pommer, a leading figure in Weimar cinema who was well attuned to the demands of literary adaptation, having overseen work on both Lang's *Die Nibelungen* and Murnau's *Herr Tartüff* (1925), based on Molière's 1664 play *Tartuffe*. As Hans-Michael Bock has explained, Pommer strove during his career at UFA to synthesize the sometimes conflicting demands of art and business in cinema. In so doing, writes Bock, he allowed his 'production teams great creative freedom to perform their artistic and technical experiments [which] led to over-extended budgets and contributed to UFA's growing financial crisis'.[58] The considerable artistic and financial latitude that Pommer granted cinematographers at UFA is illustrated clearly by *Manon Lescaut*, which presents itself at the outset as a film based on high production values. In a manner which highlights that this is not merely a studio-based film, the opening shot of this adaptation shows a carriage speeding through the countryside and transporting Manon to a convent. Accompanied by her two aunts, the eponymous heroine shares the carriage with an aristocratic gentlemen and two peasants. Each of the characters wears authentic period costume, including the gentleman's finely embroidered coat, which can be seen to gesture towards the extravagance of the production as a whole. Following a further shot in which the carriage races past the camera towards its destination, an intertitle announces its arrival at an inn in Amiens. The large, open set was designed by art director Paul Leni, who had already established his reputation as a renowned set designer in Berlin theatre and an accomplished filmmaker in his own right. Combining exterior shooting with a rich variety of period costumes and ambitious set design, this opening sequence reflects the high production values that Pommer was determined to achieve in order to maximize the film's success at the box office.

In emphasizing its own status as a lavish period adaptation, *Manon Lescaut* echoes the artistic dimension of Pommer's cinematic vision through its intricate camera technique. The sequence set in the inn at Amiens early in the film illustrates in particular a series of cuts, juxtapositions and visual exchanges which carefully establish the key strands of the plot. The opening shot of this sequence introduces us to the Marquis de Bli as he gnaws on a chicken bone. After identifying the Marquis as an official tax collector, Robison cuts between shots of the character eating and a peasant family struggling to settle their taxes at the next table. The Marquis's gluttony as he continues to strip the meat greedily from the bones on his plate anticipates his subsequent lust for the flesh of Manon, who will in turn strip him of money to satisfy her own taste for wealth and luxury. However, these initial shots are particularly notable for the way in which they trigger a series of exchanges between the characters in the plot. Following the Marquis's angry instruction that the peasants should be thrown out, Robison cuts to a shot of Des Grieux and his friend Tiberge, who have witnessed the scene from their own table. An intertitle explains Des Grieux's dismay at the callousness he has just witnessed: 'At the sight of such barbarity, Tiberge, it is easy to renounce the pleasures of the world and enter Holy Orders.' His reaction prompts a cut to another vignette, as a prostitute, having overheard Des Grieux from the next table, strolls over to predict that entering a monastery would please the young man's father. Robison's dexterity in linking these exchanges between four different tables extends to the presentation of Manon herself, whose arrival causes the immediately captivated Marquis to rise from his table to greet her. This moment initiates another sequence of visual exchanges within the scene, as the director first switches back and forth between Manon and the Marquis and then between Manon and Des Grieux, whom she notices by accident after tripping at the bottom of the stairs. A series of rapid cuts captures the first sparks of attraction between her and the young nobleman before we see them in shot together. Finally, cutting back to a shot of a worried-looking Tiberge, Robison underscores that this particular exchange of glances will have significant implications for the rest of the plot, it being the starting point of the tempestuous relationship that follows. Through the intercutting of shots that knits together the various exchanges in this sequence, the director both lays out the parameters of the plot and announces his film as a carefully crafted artistic project.

While Robison clearly foregrounds his own cinematic techniques in *Manon Lescaut*, much of his cinematography also seeks to exploit the star persona of Lya de Putti in the title role. As Brockmann observes, the 1920s were a decade in which 'the German star system blossomed, with major male and female actors becoming celebrities throughout the country'.[59] Hungarian actress de Putti achieved her own celebrity within this system by playing sultry, seductive characters. Most notably, in the 1925 film *Varieté*, she appeared as a sideshow dancer and trapeze artist, Berta-Marie, who, following her arrival in Berlin from San Francisco, stirs the violent passion of two of her male co-performers.

Robison's adaptation of *Manon Lescaut* plays explicitly on de Putti's vampish screen persona. The film abounds particularly in lingering close-ups of her face and eyes as Manon bewitches a succession of men from the Marquis de Bli to Des Grieux and Bli's son. Moreover, Robison presents de Putti explicitly as possessing a body that excites male desire. In the scene in which Manon smashes some of the Marquis's porcelain ornaments, for example, one of Bli's friends briefly spies the young woman's bare shoulder through a pair of glasses, an action which invites the film's spectators to participate in the illicit pleasure of gazing at her body. Similar invitations to contemplate de Putti's physical beauty recur throughout the film, such as when Manon visits an area described in an intertitle as the 'Parisian Fashion Centre'. Having acknowledged that she cannot afford any of the fine clothes on display, Manon unexpectedly encounters the Marquis de Bli's son, who offers to buy her a new dress. The elegant garment instantly transforms her once again into an object of envy and curiosity. Interspersed with shots of Des Grieux gambling at cards, in which his opponent fails to notice that he is cheating, Manon attracts a growing crowd of onlookers. Outside the shop in which she models the dress, people press themselves against the bars to see her. Later in the sequence, as she descends the stairs on the arm of Bli's son, another woman pauses to look over her shoulder at her. Finally, when she returns to her apartment, she looks down at herself in a manner that invites Des Grieux to cast his own admiring gaze over her appearance. In maximizing the effect of de Putti's seductive screen persona, Robison's adaptation of *Manon Lescaut* encourages us to contemplate the physical beauty of its star and to share in the feelings of desire and sometimes envy that her character inspires.

The capacity of silent filmmakers to reflect on the artistic and commercial impulses behind their productions reached a clear apogee with *L'Argent* (dir. L'Herbier) in 1929. Inspired by Zola's 1891 novel of the same title, *L'Argent* was a co-production between L'Herbier's own studio and the Cinéromans film company in France and UFA in Germany. Under the terms of this partnership, the film featured cast members from both countries, including French actors Pierre Alcover (Saccard) and Marie Glory (Line) and their German counterparts Alfred Abel (Gunderman) and Brigitte Helm (Baronne Sandorf). In an attempt to rival the kind of large-scale studio spectaculars produced by Hollywood during the 1920s, *L'Argent* also benefited from a considerable budget of 3 million francs, a sum that eventually soared to almost 5 million as a result of the costs involved in building some of the film's vast sets and of shooting in locations such as the Paris Stock Exchange.[60] However, despite the significant funds at his disposal, it was L'Herbier's contempt for money – a hatred born of long-term struggles to finance the production of his films – that was the key imperative behind his desire to adapt Zola's novel. 'After ten years of cinematic headaches,' the director recalled in his memoirs, 'riddled with bleeding financial wounds, I was obsessed with just one idea: filming at whatever cost, even (what a paradox) at great cost, a fierce indictment of money.'[61] In order to maximize the resonance of this scornful representation of money, L'Herbier resituated Zola's story in a contemporary context, transposing the action from the Second Empire to the early twentieth century. Accordingly, the plot of the film revolves around the fictional Saccard's attempt to rescue his Banque

Universelle from financial disaster by sponsoring the aviator Jacques Hamelin's pioneering flight across the Atlantic. Updating the narrative in this way enabled L'Herbier to depict money in what he described as its 'enduring power and modern virulence'.[62] At the level of plot, the film abounds in examples of the destructiveness of money. Having been forced to collaborate with Saccard in order to fund his transatlantic flight, Jacques loses his eyesight – albeit only temporarily – and faces a trial over his involvement in Saccard's financial malpractice. While her husband is away, Line Hamelin falls prey to Saccard's unwanted advances and suffers the profound emotional distress of believing that Jacques has been killed. Finally, Saccard, who at the start of the film had witnessed the virtual collapse of the Banque Universelle, finds himself imprisoned – though by no means remorseful – for having manipulated share prices by withholding the news of Jacques's successful landing. As L'Herbier stated of the film, 'all in all, it was a cry of detestation against money, amplified by a cry of love for its victims'.[63]

In tandem with the film's emphasis on the subject of currency, L'Herbier clearly used the financial investment behind his version of *L'Argent* to produce one of the most ambitious and artistically complex adaptations of the silent era. The film is particularly striking for its location filming, not least the sequences shot in the Paris Stock Exchange, which L'Herbier rented for three days and packed with some 1,500 extras. As Ginette Vincendeau observes, however, *L'Argent* is equally notable for the way in which it was shot. 'The film', she writes, 'is a riot of mobile camerawork, with truly dizzying shots, for example with the camera dangling from the high ceiling in wide sweeping movements, giving a sense of the stock exchange as a mad zoo.'[64] Key to the artistic intricacy of the film is the way in which L'Herbier uses editing and camera movement to represent the circulation of money itself. In recreating Zola's novel, not once does the director actually show money on-screen. Instead, he evokes the movement of capital metaphorically, most notably through images of rotation as shares are bought and sold. Such images feature prominently in the sequence in which Jacques prepares to depart on his pioneering flight. As the aviator bids farewell to Line in the airfield control tower, L'Herbier cuts in shots of the engineers outside starting the propeller of his plane. Once the aircraft is running, the sequence alternates between shots of the airfield and the Stock Exchange, where a broker announces excitedly that the 'engine is turning over marvellously'. The director strengthens this link between the rotation of the engine and the movement of capital by cutting from a close-up of the propeller to a swirling overhead shot of the circular trading table of the Bourse (see Figure 1.7).[65] As the sequence builds towards its climax, we then see the aircraft accelerating over the grass before the camera swoops over the floor of the Stock Exchange, a movement which emphasizes that the

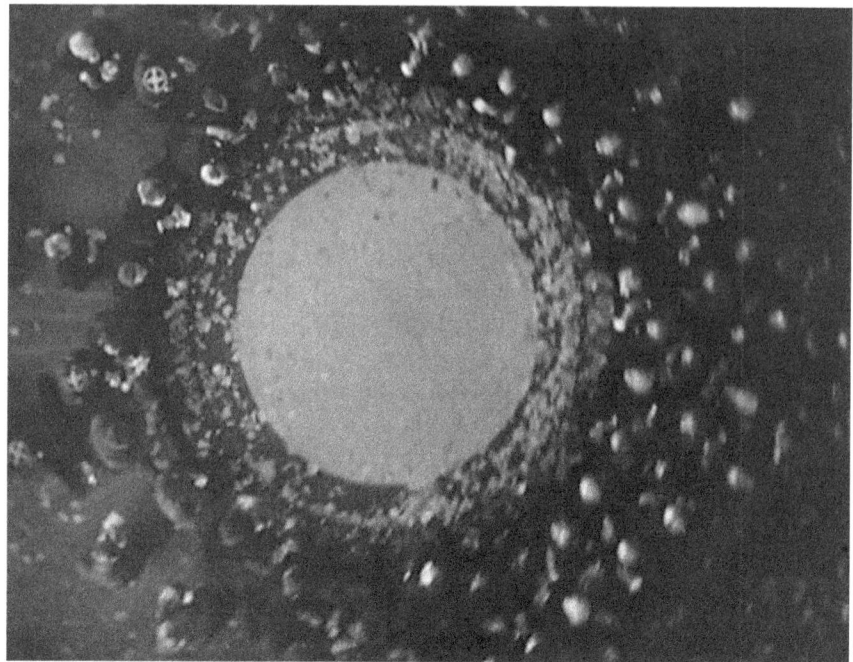

FIGURE 1.7 L'Argent (Money) *(1929, dir. L'Herbier)*.

financial world as much as the aircraft itself has launched Hamelin into flight. During the premiere of *L'Argent* at the Aubert-Palace in Paris in January 1929, this sequence was accompanied by a recording of sound effects consisting of aircraft noise and the tumult of the Stock Exchange. However, rather than match these effects to the corresponding images on-screen, the recording blended them together in what Abel terms 'one continuous simultaneous flux'.[66] While the practical difficulty of synchronizing sound and images meant that this effect was not repeated in future screenings, its use at the premiere highlights the dexterity with which L'Herbier amalgamated his cinematic techniques with the film's monetary theme. Through its emphasis on images of rotation, *L'Argent* exposes the way in which it deploys mobile camerawork and shot sequencing to represent money as a force in perpetual circulation.

If *L'Argent* represents clearly the importance of financial circulation to its plot, the film can also be viewed as a self-conscious reflection of its own production process and of the sometimes divisive role of money within it. L'Herbier's adaptation often appears deeply self-reflexive, especially in its portrayal of Jacques Hamelin's attempt to secure funding for his transatlantic flight. 'Jacques's uneasy, compromised relation to the world of finance', writes Abel, 'parallels that of the narrative avant-garde filmmaker in the French film industry. Like Daedulus or, more precisely, Icarus, neither can escape the labyrinth of capitalist speculation that supports their efforts.'[67] Such self-reflexivity extends to other aspects of the film, in particular its association of money with instances of failed and sometimes violent exchange. As L'Herbier revealed in his memoirs, *L'Argent* was a difficult shoot that was beset by problems. The director's relationship with producer Jean Sapène proved especially troubled, culminating in a physical confrontation between the pair after the sequence in which Saccard holds a lavish celebration party had to be reshot. 'He [Sapène] burst out of his office,' L'Herbier remembered, 'took hold of me by the shoulders and we rolled around on the rug after I fell and dragged him down with me. Immediately I felt the heavy hand of this colossal man grab me by the throat much like Saccard's had gripped Sandorf.'[68] As L'Herbier's recollection of this incident suggests, the sequence in which Saccard confronts Sandorf over her involvement with rival banker Gunderman can be interpreted as a reflection of the director's own relationship with his producer. In particular, the scene features several moments of failed or frustrated exchange before erupting into violence. While hosting a group of gamblers in her home, Sandorf learns that Saccard is waiting for her in a sunken room screened off from the gaming area. In the first of a series of failed interactions, a point-of-view shot shows the baroness catching sight of Saccard, who continues to look in the opposite direction. After the two initiate their conversation, the banker proceeds to ask Sandorf where she got her glittering bracelet, a question to which she does not at first respond. Stung by the accusation that he is heaping money on his new lover, Saccard then demands to know what else the gossips are saying about him, prompting Sandorf to pull away as she again refuses to answer. In a final example of blocked exchange, a rapid alternation of shots captures Saccard placing his hands around the throat of his former mistress, who resolutely avoids his gaze until he makes the telling admission that his Banque Universelle will soon be worth 200 million francs. In a manner reminiscent of L'Herbier's difficult professional relationship with Sapène, this meeting between Saccard and Sandorf is hampered by failed and frustrated exchanges that erupt in violence. As analysis of this sequence illustrates, *L'Argent* can be seen to reflect self-consciously on the role that money played in its own production process, a role that was both destructive and essential to the artistic achievement of the film.

Analysis of French literature adaptations of the silent era proves invaluable for understanding the importance of currency as a driver of the adaptive process. For many early filmmakers such as Georges Méliès, recreating popular literary classics appeared as a quick way of making money and bringing cinema to a mass audience. As this chapter has shown, however, the first cinematographers were not simply financial profiteers. Money was only one of an array of currencies that drove the practice of adaptation during this period. In turning to the works of canonical writers such as Victor Hugo, Alice Guy sought to invest cinema with cultural value and legitimacy and to show that it deserved to be taken seriously as a form of artistic expression. Such ambitions were clearly shared by key silent filmmakers in the United States, who used the virtual collapse of the French film industry during the First World War to cement their international dominance of film production and distribution. Many of these American silent adaptations borrowed extensively from the artistic resources and prevailing currencies of the stage, including its star performers. However, with the improvement of production techniques and the abandonment of old formats such as short one- and two-reel films, they also revealed a striking creative artistry of their own. Films such as Stuart Paton's 1916 version of *20,000 Leagues under the Sea* were largely unconcerned with fidelity to their source material, preferring instead to explore and extend the technical possibilities of their medium. Finally, this chapter has unpicked some of the tensions between the currencies of art and money that can be observed in French and German adaptations between 1921 and 1929. From heavily commercialized superproductions such as *L'Atlantide* to low-budget films such as *L'Auberge rouge*, the last decade of silent cinema saw some filmmakers reflect openly on the combination of artistic and financial imperatives behind their adaptive undertakings. Fittingly, given the theme of this chapter, these reflections reach a self-conscious peak in *L'Argent*, in which L'Herbier aligns the film's core theme of monetary circulation with the innovativeness of his own cinematic techniques. In so doing, his film exposes the ultimately productive relationship between commerce and creativity that emerged during the silent era. Far from merely exploiting their source texts for financial benefit, adaptations of French literature show art and money as the dual currencies with which cinema gained its own sense of identity as a narrative art.

Notes

1 Jane M. Gaines, 'Early Cinema's Heyday of Copying: The Too Many Copies of *L'Arroseur arrosé* (*The Waterer Watered*)', *Cultural Studies* 20.2–3 (2006): 227–44 (227).

2 For a brief discussion of these pirated films within the broader context of film adaptations of Hugo's novel, see Michael F. Blake, *The Films of Lon Chaney* (Lanham, MD: Vestal, 1998), 136.

3 On the history of these claims of parasitism in relation to adaptation, see, for example, Imelda Whelehan, 'Adaptations: The Contemporary Dilemmas', in *Adaptations: From Text to Screen, Screen to Text*, ed. Deborah Cartmell and Imelda Whelehan (London: Routledge, 1999), 3–19; and Robert Stam,

'The Theory and Practice of Adaptation', in *Literature and Film: A Guide to the Theory and Practice of Film Adaptation*, ed. Robert Stam and Alessandra Raengo (Oxford: Blackwell, 2005), 3–8.

4   For further background on the popular origins of silent cinema, see Tom Gunning, 'Cinema of Attractions: Early Film, Its Spectator and the Avant-Garde', in *Early Cinema: Space Frame Narrative*, ed. Thomas Elsaesser and Adam Barker (London: BFI, 1990).

5   Georges Sadoul, *Les Pionniers du cinéma (de Méliès à Pathé), 1897–1909* (Paris: Denoël, 1947), 122. Unless otherwise stated, all translations in my contributions to this volume are my own.

6   Sadoul, *Les Pionniers du cinéma*, 122.

7   For additional background on the international reception of *Le Voyage dans la lune*, see Matthew Solomon, ed., *Fantastic Voyages of the Cinematic Imagination: Georges Méliès's 'Trip to the Moon'* (Albany: State University of New York Press, 2011), 2–3.

8   Solomon, *Fantastic Voyages of the Cinematic Imagination*, 2.

9   Cited by Philippe d'Hugues and Michel Marmin, *Le Cinéma français: Le Muet* (Paris: Atlas, 1986), 42.

10 Thierry Lefebvre, '*A Trip to the Moon*: A Composite Film', in *Fantastic Voyages of the Cinematic Imagination*, ed. Solomon (Albany: State University of New York Press, 2011), 53.

11 Lefebvre, '*A Trip to the Moon*: A Composite Film', 51–3.

12 Lefebvre, '*A Trip to the Moon*: A Composite Film', 54, 57.

13 Alice Guy, *Mémoires: autobiographie de la première femme cinéaste*, ed. Catherine Laboubée (Paris: Autists Artists Associats, 2018), 51.

14 Delphine Gleizes, ed., *L'Œuvre de Victor Hugo à l'écran: des rayons et des ombres* (Paris: L'Harmattan; Quebec: Presses de l'Université Laval, 2005), 21.

15 Sadoul, *Les Pionniers du cinéma*, 382.

16 Guy, *Mémoires*, 63.

17 Alison McMahan, *Alice Guy Blaché: Lost Visionary of the Cinema* (New York: Continuum, 2002), 106.

18 On the relationship between theatrical and cinematic modes of representation in this film, see Richard Abel, *The Ciné Goes to Town: French Cinema 1896–1914* (Berkeley: University of California Press, 1998), 249–53.

19 Henri Fescourt, *La Foi et les montagnes ou la septième art au passé* (Paris: Photo-Cinéma/Paul Montel, 1959), 41.

20 For additional detail on the paralysing effect of the First World War on the French film industry, see Richard Abel, *French Cinema: The First Wave, 1915–1929* (Princeton, NJ: Princeton University Press, 1984), 9.

21 Eileen Bowser, *The Transformation of Cinema: 1907–1915* (Berkeley: University of California Press, 1994), 256.

22 Bowser, *The Transformation of Cinema*, 256.

23 William K. Everson, *American Silent Film* (New York: Da Capo Press, 1998), 59.
24 Bowser, *The Transformation of Cinema*, 91.
25 Sumiko Higashi, *Cecil B. DeMille and American Culture: The Silent Era* (Berkeley: University of California Press, 1994), 21.
26 Cited by Robert S. Birchard, *Cecil B. DeMille's Hollywood* (Lexington: University Press of Kentucky, 2004), 60.
27 Phil Powrie, '1915: The Year of the Two *Carmens* (DeMille, Walsh)', in *Carmen on Film: A Cultural History*, ed. Phil Powrie, Bruce Babington, Anne Davies and Chris Perriam (Bloomington: Indiana University Press, 2007), 49.
28 Brian Taves, *Hollywood Presents Jules Verne: The Father of Science Fiction on Screen* (Lexington: University of Kentucky Press, 2015), 13.
29 Edward Weitzel, 'Twenty Thousand Leagues under the Sea', *The Moving Picture World* (13 January 1917): 240.
30 Taves, *Hollywood Presents Jules Verne*, 25.
31 Taves, *Hollywood Presents Jules Verne*, 26.
32 Taves, *Hollywood Presents Jules Verne*, 25.
33 Tino Balio, ed., *The American Film Industry* (Madison: University of Wisconsin Press, 2006), 115.
34 Jeffrey Vance, *Douglas Fairbanks* (Berkeley: University of California Press, 2008), 99.
35 Henri Diamant-Berger, *Il était une fois le cinéma* (Paris: Jean-Claude Simoën, 1977), 82.
36 Douglas Fairbanks, 'Kind of Crazy', *Motion Picture Magazine* (November 1922): 43, 94.
37 Vance, *Douglas Fairbanks*, 111.
38 Another notable example of this superproduction strategy was Henri Diamant-Berger's version of *Les Trois Mousquetaires* (1921–2). The film was made on a vast budget of 2.5 million francs and released by Pathé as a twelve-part serial. It subsequently generated seventeen million francs in box office receipts. For further background on this film, see Richard Abel, *French Cinema: The First Wave*, 21.
39 Jacques Feyder and Françoise Rosay, *Le Cinéma, notre métier* (Geneva: Albert Skira, 1944), 21.
40 Georges Sadoul, *L'Art muet, 1919–1929 (I. L'Après-guerre en Europe)* (Paris: Denoël, 1975), 178.
41 Louis Delluc, 'Notes', *Cinéa* (10 June 1921): 9.
42 Susan Hayward, *French National Cinema* (London: Routledge, 1993), 113.
43 Pierre Benoit, *Atlantida*, trans. Mary C. Tongue and Mary Ross (New York: Ace, 1920), 101.
44 Charles Ford, *Jacques Feyder* (Paris: Seghers, 1973), 19.

45 Ford, *Jacques Feyder*, 20.
46 Abel, *French Cinema: The First Wave*, 123.
47 Louis Guilloux, 'Une heure chez le maître Anatole France: à propos de *Crainquebille*', *Le Petit Journal* (16 March 1923): 4.
48 Cited by Sadoul, *L'Art muet*, 182.
49 Abel, *French Cinema: The First Wave*, 27.
50 Cited by Marcel Lapierre, *Les Cent Visages du cinéma* (Paris: Grasset, 1948), 159.
51 Jean Eyre, '*L'Auberge rouge*', *Mon Ciné* (4 October 1923): 19. On the cinematic artistry of *L'Auberge rouge*, see also Andrew Watts, 'Diamond Thieves and Gold Diggers: Balzac, Silent Cinema and the Spoils of Adaptation', in Kate Griffiths and Andrew Watts, *Adapting Nineteenth-Century France: Literature in Film, Theatre, Television, Radio and Print* (Cardiff: University of Wales Press, 2013), 59–61: '"Rien ne crie plus fort que le silence": *L'Auberge rouge* de Jean Epstein', in *Balzac à l'écran*, ed. Anne-Marie Baron, *CinémAction* (Athis-de-l'Orne: Éditions Charles Corlet, 2019), 173, 42–51.
52 Jean Eyre, 'Comment on tourne un orage la nuit', *Mon Ciné* (21 June 1923): 7.
53 For further detail on the shots used in this sequence, see Abel, *French Cinema: The First Wave*, 354–5.
54 Abel, *French Cinema: The First Wave*, 355.
55 Jean Epstein, *Écrits sur le cinéma*, 2 vols (Paris: Seghers, 1974–5), v. 1: 95.
56 Stephen Brockmann, *A Critical History of German Film* (Rochester, NY: Camden House, 2010), 53.
57 Brockmann, *A Critical History of German Film*, 51.
58 Hans-Michael Bock, 'Erich Pommer', in *The Oxford History of World Cinema*, ed. Geoffrey Nowell-Smith (Oxford: Oxford University Press, 1996), 145.
59 Brockmann, *A Critical History of German Film*, 51.
60 By the 1920s, Hollywood had firmly established its reputation for producing large-scale studio spectaculars. Adaptations in this mould included two films starring Lon Chaney: *The Hunchback of Notre Dame* (1923, dir. Worsley) and *Phantom of the Opera* (1925, dir. Julian). For further discussion of these films, see, for example, Blake, *The Films of Lon Chaney*, 132–7 and 147–51, respectively.
61 Marcel L'Herbier, *La Tête qui tourne* (Paris: Belfond, 1979), 149.
62 L'Herbier, *La Tête qui tourne*, 150.
63 L'Herbier, *La Tête qui tourne*, 150.
64 Ginette Vincendeau, 'Show Me the Money', *Sight and Sound*, 19 (January 2009): 92.
65 For further discussion of this image of rotation within the wider context of the film's cinematography, see Prosper Hillairet, 'Les Pieds dans le

tapis: *L'Argent* de Marcel L'Herbier', *Jeune Cinéma* 322–3 (Spring 2009): 102–5 (102–3).
66 Abel, *French Cinema: The First Wave*, 525.
67 Abel, *French Cinema: The First Wave*, 516.
68 L'Herbier, *La Tête qui tourne*, 159–60.

2

Who is adaptation? Interpersonal transactions in film (1927–39)

Kate Griffiths

In the seismic economic, political, social and technological changes of the years between 1927 and 1939, film's love affair with French source texts continued undimmed. The Great Depression struck, dictators rose, swathes of the globe inched towards war and sound transformed the essence of film. Global cinema both reacted to these changes and reflected on them in its adaptations of French sources, whether canonical, popular or comparatively unknown. While France was, perhaps not unexpectedly, the most prolific adaptor of French source texts in this era, the nation's literary outputs travelled far and wide, reaching Japan, China and Soviet Russia, among other nations, in filmic form.[1] Adaptation studies has frequently evaluated the adaptations of this era within an intertextual framework, seeking only the source in the subsequent film. But this chapter proposes a new way of reading adaptations. It argues that to seek only a text in an adaptation is to ignore the complex and compelling networks of people via which adaptations are produced and shaped. Adaptation, it suggests, needs to be read in interpersonal terms rather than intertextual ones. It is done by people for people, and we ignore those people at our peril. Drawing on the theories of André Lefevere and Christiane Nord as a critical framework, this chapter analyses the ways in which source authors, directors, actors, stars, studio personnel, politicians and censors shape the adaptations on which they work in visible and less visible ways. The chapter's case study years provide an ideal backdrop for this interpersonal analysis of adaptation as directors in an increasingly confident medium negotiate their creative identity alongside that of their source author in film, while the star system developed in intriguingly different ways in different nations and in relation to different genders, and networks of censors and politicians tried to shape adaptations to convey starkly different messages. Analysing adaptations of French sources from Britain, France, the United States, Germany and Spain, this chapter assesses the influence and impact of the networks of personalities which interpret, shape and define the art of adaptation between 1927 and 1939.

In a discussion of the networks of people behind adaptations, the people and voices from whom this chapter fashions its critical frame need to be visible. This interpersonal reading of adaptation studies constructs itself from the thought of Christiane Nord and André Lefevere. In different ways and from starkly different schools of thought, Nord and Lefevere argue that people lie at the heart of the recreative process as works are remade in different linguistic and national contexts. For Nord, recreative works are born of the interactions between the source author, the target audience, the recreative artist and the people funding that artist to reproduce an earlier work. Designating her vision of the recreative artist's need to meet the needs of all of these people under the term 'loyalty', Nord is clear that her interpersonal vision poses a direct challenge to the intertextual vision of fidelity frameworks. She writes:

> As an inter*personal* category referring to a social relationship between individuals who expect not to be betrayed in the process, loyalty may replace the traditional inter*textual* relationship of 'fidelity', a concept that usually refers to a linguistic or stylistic similarity between the source and the target *texts*, regardless of the communicative intentions and/or expectations involved.[2]

Lefevere, in contrast, explores the power of patrons as well as that of the critics, writers and censors who uphold the dominant poetics according to which reproductive works of art are judged. Patronage, an elastic category for Lefevere, may be economic, ideological or related to status, but its influence, the theorist argues, is pronounced:

> Patronage can be exerted by persons, such as the Medici, Maecenas or Louis XIV, and also by groups of persons, a religious body, a political party, a social class, a royal court, publishers, and, last but not least, the media, both newspapers and magazines and larger television corporations.

Patrons try to regulate the relationship between the literary system and the other systems which, together, make up a society, a culture. As a rule they operate by means of institutions set up to regulate, if not the writing of literature, at least its distribution.[3]

This chapter's case studies showcase the fertility of applying the interpersonal visions of Nord and Lefevere to the adaptive output of 1927–39. They not only respond to the work of these theorists but also evaluate and extend it, pushing, for example, Lefevere's concept of patronage into new contexts and capacities. They underscore that in the 1920s and 1930s, actors in the nascent star system could be patrons, commissioning and shaping the outputs in which they ostensibly only performed. So too could studios and film production companies function in that capacity, along with directors with a pet project, and political figures in the dictatorship of Nazi Germany. In a less generative capacity, the curtailing actions of the censors in Britain and the United States might even be seen to fall into the patronage category. The case studies at the heart of this chapter compel us to engage with the interpersonal nature of their genesis.

Collectively the case study films of this chapter enable us to focus on different identities in the interpersonal transaction that is adaptation. The first identity analysed in the interpersonal construction of adaptations is that of the source author. The chapter focuses on authors already canonical by the time of their adaptation into film, or authors who achieved a canonicity in film precisely as a result of their cinematic afterlives. It explores Victor Hugo, Émile Zola and Gustave Flaubert in France – *Les Misérables* (1934, dir. Bernard) and *La Bête humaine* (*Judas Was a Woman*) (1938, dir. Renoir) – and the United States – *The Hunchback of Notre Dame* (1939, dir. Dieterle) and *Unholy Love* (1932, dir. Ray). It contrasts them with the multiple transformations of the popular Alexandre Dumas *père* in different cultural blocs (*The Iron Mask*, 1929, dir. Dwan, and *The Three Musketeers*, 1935, dir. Lee). It contrasts them with less canonical authors assessing the wealth of so-called *théâtre filmé* (filmed theatre) from well-known authors (Marcel Pagnol), less acclaimed artists and those whom cinematic history has largely forgotten. The source author, this chapter argues, is a far from unproblematic concept. The source authors behind adaptations can be multiple, visibly and complexly composite, as *Mimi* (1935, dir. Stein) makes clear. It is simultaneously an adaptation of Henri Murger's little-studied *Scènes de la vie de bohème* (1851) and the operas, principally Puccini's canonical version, based upon it. Similarly, *Camille* (1936, dir. Cukor) adapts both Alexandre Dumas *fils*'s non-canonical *La Dame aux camélias* (*The Lady with the Camellias*, 1848) and its canonical adaptive successor in the form of Verdi's *La Traviata* (1853). The adaptations of this era reflect the composite authorial identities behind adaptations. They enable us to ask probing questions about the construction, fixity and integrity of the concept of the source author as well as the shifting canons with which they may be associated.

The interpersonal transactions of the adaptations of this era are not, though, confined to their source authors. The era is notable for the way in which actors (with the help of their studios) constructed themselves into stars, building their personalities to cult status and using them to shape the selection, production, reception and longevity of the adaptations made. The chapter will analyse Douglas Fairbanks senior, perhaps the first and brightest of the stars in the Hollywood firmament, in the aforementioned version of *The Iron Mask*. It parallels Fairbanks with the impact of rising star Jean Gabin in French film of the 1930s and the acting persona of Robert Donat in Britain to consider stardom in different national contexts. Stardom, this chapter's case studies underline, has a starkly gendered divide, as the marketing and formative influence of Greta Garbo in *Camille* shows. Male and female stars are both marketed differently and perceived to have a different impact in the adaptations in which they headline. Stardom too works differently, shapes adaptations differently, when it moves beyond the heroic mode. Serial bad guy Peter Lorre in *Mad Love* (1935, dir. Freund) – an adaptation of Maurice Renard's fantasy horror novel *Les Mains d'Orlac* (*The Hands of Orlac, 1920*) – is key to this chapter's intent to examine and nuance the impact of stars on the adaptations they make.

Directors are no less key to the interpersonal networks via which adaptations are formed. This chapter looks at the creative identities they seek to shape for themselves in works that are crowded with the creative signatures of others. It analyses the influence they exert on the adaptations they release as well as the inter-directorial exchanges that shape adaptations as directors make and remake earlier adaptations in new timeframes, countries, languages and directorial contexts. The films of Jean Renoir will be key to this chapter's line of argument here, for they make visible the complexities of Renoir's attempt to wrest a distinct directorial presence and originality from the wealth of creative personalities and influences around him. So strong is the creative signature which Renoir crafts for himself that directors such as Fritz Lang engage with and adapt it as a source text in different national contexts. Lang remade two of Renoir's films from this era for Hollywood. Renoir's *La Chienne* (*The Bitch*, 1931) became Lang's *Scarlet Street* (1945) and Renoir's *La Bête humaine* (*Judas Was a Woman*, 1938) became Lang's *Human Desire* (1954). Lang reworks Renoir as source rather than his source authors, posing intriguing questions of what and where the source text/author is.

The figures in the interpersonal adaptive transactions of this era, though, are not always visible, as the case study films of this chapter will make clear. Focusing on the complex political figures and situations authoring the Spanish-German *Carmen, la de Triana* (*Carmen, the Girl from Triana*) (1938, dir. Rey), a film with a German-language mirror version produced at the same time – *Andalusische Nächte* (*Nights in Andalusia*) (1938, dir. Maisch) – the chapter explores the power of political patrons (to use Lefevere's term), such as the Reich Minister of Propaganda Joseph Goebbels, to shape the adaptive output of this epoch in Germany and, in this instance, Spain. The people at the heart of the numerous adaptive transactions between 1927 and 1939 are thus countless. Their interpersonal exchanges are deeply intriguing. They remind us that to seek only a source text in a work of adaptation in this era is to misunderstand what adaptation is and the range and depth of people via whom it is refracted.

Who is adapted? The adaptive canon (1927–39)

Authors now labelled as canonical have a clear presence in the adaptive output of 1927–39. Both they and their canonicity shape the adaptations made from their work. Yet, taking three authors now associated with that epithet – Victor Hugo, Émile Zola and Gustave Flaubert – as a case study, it becomes clear that the reworking of these writers in film forces us to ask difficult questions about what we mean by the term 'canonicity': its formation, its fixity and its transferability across media.

Victor Hugo's presence in film in the years 1927–39 is strong. The novelist's *Les Misérables* (1862) is, Keith Reader argues, 'the most often-filmed of canonical French novels' and this chapter's case study years support his findings.[4] The novel was adapted in the United States in 1935 (*Les Misérables*, dir. Boleslawski), in France in 1934 (*Les Misérables*, dir. Bernard) and in Japan in 1938 (*Kyojin-den*, *The Giant*, dir. Itami).[5] Bernard's version of the film clearly seeks to harness the canonicity of its source text to its adaptive fictions. As Delphine Gleizes points out, 'the tagline for Bernard's adaptation, "the immortal masterpiece of the French *screen*" … assimilates the novel and the film within one common glory'.[6] What is interesting, though, about debates on canonicity is that they canonize the author as person, rather than or perhaps by means of the works produced. Harold Bloom's *The Western Canon* is a case in point. It may discuss specific works or collections of them, but it structures itself around the towering identities who attain the status of canonicity from their works (Shakespeare, Montaigne, Cervantes and Dante).[7] This personality- and individual-based conceptualization of canonicity is potent and clearly inflects Bernard's adaptation. Bernard adapts Hugo as well as his novel. The film begins with a section of Hugo's novel. The text is in Hugo's hand and marks the adaptation with Hugo's personality, as does the portrait of the author himself. The paratextual material of the adaptation reinforces Hugo's personal canonicity. It reminds us that the author is adapted in this film alongside his source text.

That the film monumentalizes Hugo as authorial personality is perhaps unsurprising. It mirrors the well-documented and concerted campaign of self-monumentalization that Hugo orchestrated to fashion himself into a self-styled *grand homme* (great man). In his eulogy to Balzac, Hugo spoke of great men, a category he sought to apply to himself, precisely in monumental terms: 'Great men make their own pedestal; the future takes care of the statue.'[8] Grossman argues that 'Hugo's metamorphosis into a media star clearly began with Hugo himself. The poet's sense of self and destiny was evident from the outset.'[9] Hugo's self-monumentalization finds intriguing echoes in Bernard's adaptation, in which the camera relentlessly aggrandizes both Jean Valjean and the fictional identity or alter ego that he fabricates for himself. In the film's opening sequence, Valjean – played by Harry Baur – is filmed in a low-angle shot at the base of some scaffolding. The function of the shot is threefold. First, it allows Valjean to tower over and dominate a shot in a scene in which the rest of the prisoners are filmed with a focus on their chained feet, symbolizing their faceless, powerless fate in captivity. Second, it links him to the statuary on the building he protects with his monumental muscle power – he supports part of the building's structure and the statues above serve a comparable function. Third, it sets a precedent for the camera angles the character will occupy throughout the film, which ennoble and aggrandize him, even in the most abject of situations. The adaptation does encode Valjean's power when he plays the part of M. Madeleine in different shots. He watches Cosette's brush with the law in the street below in a high-angle shot from his first-floor office, the elevation of the shot speaking to both his mastery of the situation on which he will shortly rule and Cosette's entrapment beneath the overbearing height of the camera. But the monumentalizing low-angle shot from Valjean/M. Madeleine's feet is prevalent – it appears even in the moments of greatest threat to the character. M. Madeleine denounces himself as Valjean the convict in court to save a falsely accused man. The scene is shot at an extremely low angle from his feet, as the camera signals both the towering majesty of his altruism and the magnitude of what he has achieved in the new life he has forged. The monumentality of the adaptation's hero resonates with that of his literary creator in the nineteenth century.

Bernard's adaptation may adapt Hugo as canonical identity, but it has not achieved canonical status for itself, largely as a result of the lack of canonicity of its director and leading man. Bernard's film remained, as Keith Reader points out, unavailable to the public until its DVD release in 2008, and has triggered comparatively little critical attention since that release.[10] Indeed, Reader's article explicitly sets itself the task of rectifying the critical neglect into which the adaptation has fallen. Canonicity, it appears, is not directly transferable. And, more intriguingly, there are competing canonicities at play in adaptive film. Bernard's adaptation is not canonical in part because its director has not achieved that status. Reader writes of Bernard:

> Not (as even his most ardent admirers would concede) on a par with Renoir, Carné or even Jean Grémillon – by comparison with whom he is too easily dismissed as an old-fashioned journeyman – Bernard clearly occupies a subaltern position in French film history.[11]

In an omission which speaks volumes, Rémi Fournier Lanzoni's *French Cinema from the Beginnings to the Present* – as Reader points out – makes no reference to Bernard in its survey chapter on French film in the 1920s and 1930s.[12] Bernard's adaptation is not canonical in part because its genre has not achieved that status. Reader claims of the adaptation's non-canonicity that the film's 'exclusion' results from the fact that '*Les Misérables* is a precursor of what Truffaut *famously* reviled as the *cinéma de papa* or *cinéma de qualité* with its stress on literary adaptation and scripting along with (by the standards of its time) lavish production values.'[13] Finally, Bernard's adaptation is not canonical in part because its actor, Harry Baur, no longer inhabits or perhaps never succeeded in inhabiting the canon of actors as others from his era did. Despite the fact that Baur was one of the big names in the 1930s – he was the most successful actor at the French box office in 1936 – he has fallen off the critical radar. Baur's fall from grace, Reader suggests, is in part the result of his 'heavy-duty' acting style, too reminiscent of pre-film stage acting to stand the test of time.[14] However, it is also, Reader argues, the result of Baur's actions as a person. During the Occupation, Baur made much of his Aryan status, even getting a certificate of Aryanness from the Propaganda Staffel – the German censorship authority – in addition to attending numerous collaborationist receptions.[15] He starred in Christian-Jaque's *L'Assassinat du Père Noël* (*The Killing of Santa Claus*) (1941, dir. Jaque), the first French film to be financed by the German-funded and -run production company Continental, set up by Goebbels in September 1940 as a means to counter the French film industry and its messages. He left for Berlin in 1942 to star in *Symphonie eines Lebens* (*Symphony of Life*) (1942, dir. Bertram), a decision that was to prove costly, for he was ultimately arrested by the Gestapo, is believed to have been tortured and died six months later. For directorial, genre- and actor-related reasons, Bernard's film is not canonical. But it emphasizes key things about canonicity. Canonicity is not transferable from literature to film; it needs to be approached as a multiple thing, for in film adaptations there are numerous canons at play: those of the literary source and its author, those that relate to the film's genre and director and finally that which is constructed around its stars or actors. The canonicities of the people involved in films have multiple impacts on the adaptations they shape.

Zola's presence in the adaptive canon of this chapter's case study years is as strong as that of Hugo. But the processes of canonicity work differently in relation to him as source author. Hugo was canonical in the timeframe of this chapter. Zola was not. But Jean Renoir's 1938 adaptation of Zola's *La Bête humaine* is canonical in adaptive terms and arguably fed into the novelist's gradual move towards canonization. Renoir's adaptation of Zola owes its canonicity to three factors: its director, its movement and its star. It is the work of a reputed director, Jean Renoir, whose films are both award-winning and extensively studied in critical works and educational syllabi. It is an output from a now-canonical genre – the poetic realism that dominated French cinema in the 1930s. Poetic realism clearly meets Harold Bloom's requirement that works be aesthetically strange and innovative in order to meet the terms of canonicity.[16] Remi Fournier Lanzoni, affording a considerable critical space to poetic realism in his overarching history of French film, depicts it precisely in terms of aesthetic difference:

> Poetic Realism, also labelled *social fantastique* (or *cinéma du désenchantement*), brought a new aesthetic to films. The aim was to show real life and represent a reality detached from the mundane trepidations and clichés of bourgeois drama. With its heavy atmosphere of *banlieue* (suburban) landscape, new film subjects of everyday popular culture were revealed and defined: naturalistic reflections on wet cobblestones, suburban commuter trains in the early morning, factories' smoke mixing with fog, small cafes in popular districts – in short, realism.[17]

La Bête humaine is equally arguably canonical in its lead actor – Jean Gabin. That Gabin has attained a monumental status in French cinema is clear. Ginette Vincendeau persuasively critiques the mythical presence of the actor, situating its foundations in the 'type' Gabin played in the series of now-classic films that includes *La Bête humaine*, a working-class hero with a good heart, harmed by destiny, forces beyond his control or a treacherous woman.[18] The monumentality of the mythical identity of Gabin triggered comment as early as 1939, the year with which this chapter ends. René Barjavel wrote of his visibility and grandeur: 'You recognize him when he comes on screen. You already know him.'[19] The actor plays in La Bête humaine the type, discussed above, for which he became so well known (see Figure 2.1). Such, though, is Gabin's canonicity as an actor that he, as star, overrides the very part he plays. The protagonist in Zola's novel is a murderer with tainted blood who damages the society in which he lives. However, so strong was Gabin's image as a working-class hero that he was asked in 1989 on the bicentenary of the French Revolution to parade down the Champs Elysées in a wooden locomotive as Jacques Lantier in La Bête humaine. The parade organizers ostensibly offered the presence of Gabin in that part but in reality adapted and overrode it with the canonical presence of Gabin the star. The canonicity of the 1938 adaptation of Zola's novel stems from the canonicity of its movement and of its leading man, not from its source author.

This adaptation of La Bête humaine does draw on its source author but it contributes to his canonization rather than, as was the case with the Hugo adaptation discussed above, sustaining itself from it. Renoir's film, like Bernard's adaptation of Hugo, leads with a section of text from his source author. The adaptation accompanies the fragment of Zola's text with both a photograph of the author himself and his signature. But the signature is not

FIGURE 2.1 La Bête humaine (Judas Was a Woman) *(1938, dir. Renoir).*

offered in static form, rather it is signed by Zola's invisible hand on the screen. The adaptation claims for itself the endorsement of its source author. But Renoir, as the adaptation's director, is able, as a result of Zola's not-quite-canonical status, to negotiate a clear, confident and authoritative status for himself. He appears in a cameo role which marks the piece as his own. Such cameo appearances are not unusual in Renoir's oeuvre and might be seen to serve as a signature of the director. But Renoir's cameo in *La Bête humaine* is particularly intriguing, for he plays the part of a poacher. In so doing, he saucily references his appropriation of the goods of another, Zola, in his source text. Michel de Certeau famously writes: 'Readers are travellers; they move across lands belonging to someone else, like nomads poaching their way across fields they did not write.'[20] Renoir imprints his own now-canonical image on his adaptation and, in the chosen part he plays, also points out through his poaching metaphor that he has made his own what once was Zola's. Renoir's film, like Bernard's discussed above, offers revealing insights into the canonicity of the source authors adapted in this chapter's case study years. Renoir's film feeds into the canonization of his source author. It is the site of complex negotiations of different canonicities as the author, director and star intersect, fashioning complex creative presences for themselves in the interpersonal chain of adaptation.

If Bernard and Renoir lead with their source authors, engaging with their canonicity in complex ways, Albert Ray's 1932 *Unholy Love* disregards its source author, Gustave Flaubert, entirely. The film is, the credits proclaim, 'suggested by Gustave Flaubert's Famous Novel *Madame Bovary*'. Yet Ray uses Flaubert's novel as little more than a literary shield to harness a modicum of cultural capital and respectability to a salacious tale. Ray renames all the characters, relocates the action to New York and focuses on his contemporary era. Jerry, a spoiled and squeamish doctor, marries a hustling girl from the wrong side of the tracks, Sheila, much to the disappointment of his father and his long-suffering would-be love Jane (see Figure 2.2). Sheila has one implied affair and another more explicitly which her father-in-law halts, while simultaneously paying her debts. Consumed by love, Sheila drives at speed off a high bridge. Jane, pursuing her to save her, destroys the suicide note, protecting Jerry to the end. Not only does *Unholy Love* underscore the disparate approaches to the canon of French literature in the years 1927–39, it also begins to reveal the external, historical factors shaping the delivery of canonicity. *Unholy Love* is a pre-Hays Code production, and it shows. The Hays Code was the informal name for the Motion Picture Code adopted in 1930 but not enforced until 1934. The Code required that morality be upheld, that the 'correct' standards of life be depicted, that laws not be broken on screen and that nudity and references to the sexual act not appear on screen. Ray's film,

FIGURE 2.2 Unholy Love *(1932, dir. Ray)*.

hiding behind the sheltering protection of the canonicity of his source text and sneaking in before the Code was enforced, shows extramarital kissing, waking bed scenes, debt and a scheming female protagonist with no regard for moral or social structures. Intriguingly, contemporary reviews, while making clear the production's betrayal of Flaubert's novel as source, show that Ray's film still adapts canonicity largely by means of the acting style it showcases. The reviewer begins thus:

> Here, if you please, is Gustave Flaubert's immortal classic *Madame Bovary*. At first blush, it causes resentment that the title should have been changed to read 'Unholy Love'. After viewing the picture, however, anyone having anyone having any respect for the book is grateful the title has been disguised. The great Flaubert must be doing some heavy grave turning over this story version. Not only have the producers rewritten and restaged the entire story beyond recognition, but in an attempt to be literary and high hat they've allowed everybody on the lot to overact.[21]

Aping the production and acting styles of heavyweight adaptations of canonical source texts, Ray's film seeks protection for its scandalous themes and images. It has never acceded to the canon of Flaubert adaptations on film. If it features at all in critical discussion of adaptations, it is usually flagged for interest either as an early sound film adaptation of Flaubert's novel or as an example of pre-Code work to highlight the huge change in style, content and morality the Code would bring. The importance of Ray's film is twofold. It underlines the protective potential of canonical forebears in adaptations that seek to infringe and infract. It also underlines that canonicity is not catching. One may adapt a canonical source in film but not necessarily attain canonicity, or even seek to, in said film.

Film, though, between 1927 and 1939 adapts not just what might now be deemed the canon. It also turns to a range of writers perhaps not of the canon, writers with cultural capital that was valuable in the medium of film for a host of different reasons. Alexandre Dumas *père* is a key figure in this respect. He is one of the most adapted authors in film history and the case study years of this chapter are no exception.[22] There were at least eleven adaptations of his work in these years across the globe.[23] Yet Dumas *père* was not canonical in his era and has arguably never become so in literature. Dumas was, in the mid-nineteenth century, wildly popular in serial form, the medium whose development his fiction in many ways shaped. A comment by Théophile Gautier underscores both the ubiquity of Dumas's texts in serial form and the public thirst for them:

> These days, everyone is reading Alexandre Dumas's novels in serial form. Their lengthy plots, their cliffhangers, the cliffhangers to their cliffhangers have managed to etch themselves into the public consciousness as if they were contemporary reality. So present are the adventures of the numerous characters in Dumas's tales ... that these characters end up feeling like people in our lives.[24]

Ubiquity, though, critics were clear, did not equate to canonicity, and indeed Dumas *père*'s chosen form, the serial novel, was seen to be innately anti-canonical. As Edmund Birch points out, 'The *roman-feuilleton* was deemed, in certain quarters, both to corrupt the purities of literary form, and by extension to undermine the tastes of the reading public at large.'[25] He argues that 'the triumph of serial fiction came to mark new lows in the perception of literary standards', illustrating his claim with the string of debates recorded in Lise Dumasy's *La Querelle du roman-feuilleton* (1999).[26] Not only was Dumas's chosen publication form against him in the canonicity stakes, so too was his means of production. Canonicity, as Harold Bloom's *The Western Canon* makes clear, is conferred upon individuals whose work is aesthetically distinct, original and integral enough to mark them out in the play of influence that is literary creation.[27] Dumas's writing style, in stark contrast, was innately, visibly and controversially collaborative, working as he did with ghost writers.

Dumas set up a production studio of writers. He worked with assistants and collaborators, most notably Auguste Maquet.[28] Dumas, for a range of reasons, is not quite fully canonical.

Dumas, though, as an author makes clear adaptive sense. The popularity and ubiquity of his writing is clearly mirrored in the range of adaptations made of his texts and the capital they grossed in this era. The 1934 adaptation *The Count of Monte Cristo* (1934, dir. Lee) is a case in point. The second adaptation of the novel in five years, it provided, according to Philip Dunne, 'Eddie Small with a fortune almost as great as The Treasure of Spada.'[29] The film's aesthetic distinctness and value was recognized by contemporary critics (it was named one of the top ten films of 1934 by the National Board of Review of Motion Pictures). Intriguingly, moreover, it came to stand as something of an original source text in its own right as it triggered two sequels: *The Son of Monte Cristo* (1940, dir. Lee) and *The Return of Monte Cristo* (1946, dir. Levin).

The value of Lee's film is not just financial. In critical terms it demonstrates the way in which people, in the form of actors, were used to market the Dumas brand in film. But they were used in different ways in different nations of this film's release. The film's leading man, Robert Donat, is key to my line of argument here (see Figure 2.3). In the United States, the star system

FIGURE 2.3 The Count of Monte-Cristo *(1934, dir. Lee)*.

was core to the success of the nation's big studios. Studios and production companies marketed the personalities of the stars in the adaptations. These personalities were developed and sold in the media of the time with such intent that they remain intentionally visible and identifiable, sitting sometimes harmoniously, sometimes problematically, alongside the identities of the parts the stars take in these adaptations. In Britain, leading actors, wary of the star discourse, instead sought to show that true skill and craft lay in subsuming themselves entirely in the parts they played in these adaptations, making the audience forget their media personas, which nevertheless helped sell the films in which they appeared.[30] *The Count of Monte Cristo* made Donat a well-known name in the United States and in Britain. Film critic Caroline Lejeune writes on the North American context: 'The public rushed to see Monte Cristo. What they went to see was the story. What they came away remembering was the star.'[31] Intriguingly, for Lejeune, the stardom the adaptation conferred upon Donat competed with Dumas and his source text in its visibility. Victoria Lowe concurs that '*Monte Cristo* established Donat's star image initially as the classic swashbuckling adventure hero, in the mold of former star types such as Douglas Fairbanks.'[32] Donat's stardom adapted that of his Hollywood predecessors more than that of its source author. That the studio publicity machine for the film in the United States pushed Donat as overnight star is clear. Lowe writes:

> The checkered process of the film's production was replaced by a tried and tested star mythology, involving a transatlantic search by the film's producer for an actor to play Edmond Dantès. The press material gushes that 'almost every major star was considered' until they ran a print of *The Private Life of Henry VIII*, after which producer Edward Small 'knew that he had his man, [resulting in] the most sensational male film discovery since Ronald Colman.' The press books demonstrate how Hollywood studio era discourses suggested that stars created performance by playing themselves, and thus the category of star determined that a performance should be read as not involving acting skill.[33]

In the United States Donat as star was used to market Dumas's personal brand in film.

In stark contrast, British reviews of the film praised Donat's craft as an actor, his ability to erase himself as identity in his delivery of Dumas's hero. Donat himself was, as Lowe points out, keen to give credence to such readings of him as an actor rather than a star. Citing a newspaper article he gave a month after the film's release, she notes: 'Donat talked about his role in a way that emphasized that he was giving a performance, rather than lending his personality to a role.'³⁴ Intriguingly, the film plays out these tensions between Donat as star and Donat as skilled actor, casting him as both. Donat's status as star is played up in the early romantic scene between Dantès and his love Mercedes (Elissa Landi) as they tryst. Lowe writes:

> Donat is seen first kneeling over her in a romantic, pictorial, and static posture, as if indeed posing in the best position to seem handsome. In fact, he does not move much throughout the whole scene. ... Mercedes/Landi then asks for a proposal teasingly: at this point, Donat is framed in profile, with Landi facing and looking out and beyond the camera. ... They climb a tree, and the camera tracks back to show them in mid-shot, looking off-camera with cheeks side by side, again with Donat barely moving his body for the last part of the scene. Here he consciously appears to be posing rather than acting, giving up his body and face to be adored by the audience.³⁵

But if Donat the star dominates such scenes, Donat the skilled actor becomes visible as he works to erase his identity while playing a man doing the same in the film's plot line. Donat plays the part of the fictitious Count of Monte Cristo, play-acting a new life for himself in a role which, if it is done with enough craft, will ensure that his previous identity as Edmond Dantès can no longer be detected. Donat plays parts within his part, skilfully allowing Dantès to be visible even while Donat as Dantès plays the part of Monte Cristo:

> Donat does seem to be consciously signaling a different character inside as well: his gestures are now closed, economical, and precise; his voice is controlled and abrupt – he doesn't hold onto the sound of the sentences in a lyrical way as before but speaks in clipped, short bursts. This then justifies the older Mercedes's declaration that the Count is different from Dantès, so that 'even the soul is not the same.' The only time he varies this characterization is in his hesitation when Mondego's son challenges Dantès to a duel. ... Donat reveals the Count's vulnerability by letting his voice trail off at the end of his sentences and looking out beyond the camera into the distance to show that his words (which accept the duel) do not quite reflect what is going on in his mind. Thus, we are also reminded that Donat as the Count is playing a character who is similarly playing a role. For the narrative to work, it has to be clear that behind the Count is the innocent Dantès, who has by necessity adopted the persona of the ruthless avenger. Therefore, we are witness to the spectacle of [Donat] hidden behind not one role but two, the effect being to foreground the acting ability of the performer within the performance itself.³⁶

If, as this chapter is arguing, the years 1927–39 force us to contemplate adaptations of French sources as interpersonal transactions rather than intertextual ones, the 1934 adaptation *The Count of Monte Cristo* offers a powerful case study. It positions Dumas as a prominent personality among the authors adapted and readapted in this era. But it also unpicks the play of personalities in the star and actor discourses so key, even in their difference, to delivering Dumas in film in this era.

Which genres were adapted? Authors visible, forgotten and multiple

This chapter's focus on the canonical and popular novelists adapted in this era into film is misleading. For a roaring trade also took place in the adaptation of French playwrights into film between 1927 and 1939. Some, like adaptations of Marcel Pagnol, are highly visible in the history of film, their output having attained measures of canonicity. Pagnol, a famous playwright in France, began working with film in 1930 after being contacted by Robert Kane, an American executive for Paramount Studios in France who wished to make use of Pagnol's national reputation and readymade subject matter. Pagnol, as Rémi Fournier Lanzoni makes clear, welcomed the association between media, considering 'the cinematic medium a great tool with which to promote his theatrical oeuvre'.[37] The emphasis on the primacy of theatre here is important. Within three years, each of Pagnol's successful plays had been adapted for film: *Marius* (1931, dir. Korda), *Fanny* (1932, dir. Allégret) and *Topaze* (1933, dir. Gasnier). The films of Pagnol's plays were successful in geographically diverse nations.[38] Yet they were critically challenged precisely for their theatricality and for their failure to adapt the structures and styles of the stage into modern film. 'The devotees of "pure" motion pictures,' writes Fournier Lanzoni, 'reproached him [Pagnol] as merely a "lost" playwright whose personality and talent were incapable of adapting to the laws of the screen.'[39] Unmoved, Pagnol argued that the advent of sound in film meant that cinema was the art of printing and distributing theatre. Theatre was a powerful source text for the filmmakers of this era, yet in the case of Pagnol, it struggled to shake off the medium of its source when recreated in film.

If Pagnol remains a visible, partially canonical identity in this trend of *théâtre filmé* which makes up so much of the French literature remade for film in this era, there are myriad French playwrights who contributed to this phenomenon but whose identities have faded in the annals of film history. Their works, whatever their success between 1927 and 1939, are currently far less available physically or in film criticism than those of Pagnol. Intriguingly, many of the now nearly invisible French playwrights adapted for film around the world were taken up by the German film industry. Such films are a feature of the late silent years of this chapter's case study era: Georges Berr and Louis Verneuil's play *Ma soeur et moi* (*My Sister and I*) sits almost unacknowledged behind Manfred Noa's 1929 film *Meine Schwester und ich* (*My Sister and I*). Adaptations of comparatively lesser-known playwrights continued into the sound era in productions often made simultaneously in French and German, which are discussed at the end of this chapter in relation to German patrons who sought to capitalize on their international dominance in the industry and markets for political reasons. But they exceed this phenomenon, as the German film industry, thirsty for material, adapted – solely in German – plays by Jacques Natanson, Alfred Capus, Victorien Sardou, Henri Bataille, René Sorel, Henri Kistemaekers, Jacques Bousquet and Henri Falk, André Birabeau and Georges Dolley, as well as Félix Gandéra. While Germany did in this era sparingly adapt authors whom we might label canonical (Flaubert, Balzac, Molière),[40] intriguingly the vast majority of its adaptations of French literary sources stemmed, in the run-up to the Second World War, from playwrights whose personal visibility was far less pronounced in textual and canonical terms. Questions of the personal visibility of source authors, though, are always temporally conditioned. The work of Maurice Dekobra is a case in point. The novelist was one of the best-known French writers between the two world wars. His works were translated into at least thirty-two languages and they form the basis of countless adaptations in our case study years in different national contexts. Yet Dekobra has, as a novelist, fallen totally out of favour, becoming as Alfred Eibel suggests 'a forgotten best-selling author'.[41] Visible in his era as source author both in France and Germany, Dekobra, as a creative identity, has faded in the modern era. Playwrights provide filmmakers between 1927 and 1939 with vast amounts of adaptive material. They provoke thorny questions about the boundary between film and theatre as media in this era. They also show the wide range of now nearly invisible creative identities and source authors from whom film in this era is gleaned.

The influence of opera stemming from French source works is as important in this era as that of French original theatre. Works such as adaptations derived from Mérimée's *Carmen* and the operatic workings made of it, most famously that of Georges Bizet in 1875, illustrate the multiple, plural nature of the source authors behind specific adaptations. Film in this era at times adapts opera texts by authors who were themselves reworking earlier French literary artefacts. *Gypsy Blood* (1932, dir. Lewis) forms a key case study in this respect. *Carmen* is something of a constant in the adaptive film industry: at least five versions of the piece were made in this chapter's case study years, three of which were musical.[42] While silent stars such as Douglas Fairbanks senior bemoaned the control that sound technicians came to assume over the creative process with the onset of sound in film, such invisible figures changed the shape of film, making this paragraph's case study film, Lewis's *Gypsy Blood*, possible.[43] Lewis's film, moreover, alerts us to the difficulties of defining the source author in the singular in specific adaptations, testifying, to use Julie Sanders's term, to the 'complex filtration' via which adaptations are formed.[44] The film's opening credits proclaim it to be an adaptation of the novella by Prosper Mérimée. Yet the music that accompanies it is that of Bizet, arranged by Dr Malcolm Sargeant with the New Symphony Orchestra. Lewis's *Carmen* is at once an adaptation of both Mérimée and Bizet, or rather of Mérimée in Bizet. The palimpsestuous nature of creative identities, moreover, is not limited to the film's source authors. The piece was marketed as filmed opera, with audiences drawn to it by the established opera stars who took the lead roles, in which they remained visible as themselves even while pretending to be the characters of Mérimée and Bizet. Contemporary reviews are distinctly personality-based in their critical approach to Lewis's film. Leonard Wallace's column writes thus of the adaptation: 'Grand opera makes its bow to filmgoers, featuring no less famous personalities than Tom Burke and Marguerite Namara.'[45] Such stars bring an aura of prestige to the film, elevating it and perhaps, via their operatic backgrounds, providing a protective layer of canonicity which enables Lewis to maintain the sexual promiscuity and flightiness of his heroine in ways that were not characteristic in film of the time. Lewis's adaptation makes no bones about its heroine's sexual escapades and her availability for purchase, allowing her to proclaim from the outset 'When I'm in love, I'm in love with one man. For as long as it lasts.' Her sexual freedom is ultimately curtailed and punished in Lewis's adaptation: she dies in a tussle with her discarded lover outside a bullring in a scene shot in an extreme high angle which encodes both the forces of morality bearing down on this expression of rebellious female disobedience and the necessity of said lover acting thus. The tussle runs parallel with the bullfight inside. Carmen falls with the bull in a doubling that portrays her animality. Carmen's sexual freedom, though, is allowed for the duration of the film; a freedom protected by the canonicity of Bizet's opera as intermediate source. If Bizet's opera protects, so too does it prove the undoing of Lewis's film in critical terms, as contemporary reviews demonstrate. Leonard Wallace's column concludes that Lewis's work sticks too closely to the medium of opera: 'It would take, however, a director more sympathetic to the needs of the screen than Cecil Lewis to make *Carmen* into a real motion picture.'[46] For the reviewer, the clash of mocked-up theatrical sets in a clear opera vein and the more filmic action scenes shot on location is too great. The 'Pick of the Performances' column concurs: 'Considered cinematically *Gypsy Blood* is a gallant but not too successful attempt to film grand opera. Considered as a novelty – with the vocal attraction of Tom Burke and Marguerite Namara taken into account – it is an acceptable innovation.'[47] Lewis's *Carmen* is multiply interpersonal. It alerts us to the trend in this era to adapt authors from opera; authors who rework a range of earlier authors in their identities with varying degrees of visibility.

The complex interpersonal transactions of adaptation (1927–35): Actors, directors, politicians and censors

Readings of adaptations in this era as interpersonal rather than intertextual transactions should not restrict themselves to the person of the source author. Source authors are, as the above paragraph on the cumulative authors behind Lewis's *Gypsy Blood* makes clear, far from an unproblematic category. A collective of identities shape and mediate the adaptations in this era and merit critical attention. Prominent among them are key actors of the time, who either shaped or fed into the development of the star system in this era. While this chapter has already considered the differing impact of Robert Donat in the adaptations in which he starred, it is necessary to consider the formative function of stardom more deeply. Critical works have persuasively focused on the power of actors to shape the films in which they star, but they have done so in relation to individual actors. This chapter pluralizes the nature and gender of the stars studied, exploring the impact of male heroes (Douglas Fairbanks), female leads (Greta Garbo), character actors (Nigel de Brulier) and villains (Peter Lorre) on the films they released between 1927 and 1939. Stardom works differently and has a different impact in different role types and along different gender lines.

The body of work on the actor as auteur in this era is extensive. Patrick McGilligan argues persuasively that actors are not passive icons shaped by the director or, I would argue, the source text in which they star. Rather, key male actors have such star standing that they author, in intriguing ways, elements of the films in which they star. Writing of James Cagney, McGilligan maintains:

> If an actor is responsible for only acting, but is not involved in any of the artistic decisions of filmmaking, then it is accurate surely to refer to the actor as a semi-passive icon, a symbol that is manipulated by writers and directors. But actors who not only influence artistic decisions (casting,

writing, directing etc.) but demand certain limitations on the basis of their screen personas, may justly be regarded as 'auteurs'.[48]

McGilligan's reading encapsulates the impact Douglas Fairbanks senior had on the films in which he starred between 1927 and 1935. Fairbanks and his second wife Mary Pickford, along with Charlie Chaplin, were, Jeffrey Vance argues,

> Hollywood's first cinema superstars. They achieved truly global fame and adulation, with fans referring to them on an intimate, first-name basis as Mary, Charlie and Doug. It is difficult to appreciate, in this age of devalued celebrity, the impact they had on world cinema and world culture.[49]

Fairbanks not only cultivated his own star persona in skilled ways but also went out of his way to ensure it gave him creative control over the films, often adaptations of French texts, in which he starred. In February 1917 he formed the Douglas Fairbanks Pictures Corporation, which would distribute its own productions and enabled him to function as an actor-producer when, in 1919, he, Pickford, Chaplin and Griffith formed their own distribution company, United Artists. The company's name underlined its intent for stars to shape the films they made.[50] Most prominent in the adaptations in which Fairbanks senior starred in this time were the Musketeer series, in particular *The Iron Mask* (1929, dir. Dwan), on which this chapter will shortly focus. The attribution of the film to Dwan as director is intriguingly problematic for, as was his wont, Fairbanks senior oversaw all aspects of the film.[51] Douglas Fairbanks junior explains that his father's directors 'were basically "super assistants". They were day-to-day, hour-to-hour coordinators and executives on the set ... while he encouraged their honest expression of views and welcomed their reactions, he always reserved the right to overrule them.'[52] That Fairbanks senior wielded an auteur-like influence in the adaptations in which he starred is clear.[53] However, what is still more intriguing is the interpersonal composite of the parts he played in them. As one of the first and perhaps therefore the most stellar of stars in the Hollywood firmament, Fairbanks senior's heavily marketed personality was always visible in and alongside the roles he performed in adaptations. *Picture-Play* reviewed Fairbanks as D'Artagnan, a role he was to play in several films, thus: '[When Fairbanks] broke loose with his incredible adventures there was a wink beneath his plumes and curls which said plainer than words "Under all this fuss and feathers ... it's me!"'[54] That Fairbanks senior felt an affinity with D'Artagnan is clear in his reprisals of the part across successive films. Vance suggests: 'D'Artagnan was his touchstone, he looked to the exuberant Gascon youth as his ideal screen self.'[55] But the D'Artagnan he played is a composite of his own star persona and Dumas's character. Vance emphasizes that

> D'Artagnan was made to fit the personality and idealized characteristics of Douglas Fairbanks rather than the other way around. Instead of delving into the more unpleasant characteristics of D'Artagnan, the fourth musketeer, Fairbanks eliminated these qualities and replaced them with the familiar 'Doug' characteristics that audiences had come to expect.[56]

Fairbanks senior's roles were interpersonal in their adaptation both of their adaptive source text and that of the star persona the actor had so carefully crafted for himself.

Nowhere is this interpersonal transaction more visible than in the last of the Musketeer films Fairbanks senior was to make, *The Iron Mask*. The film is a complex adaptation of different Dumas novels. But it is also an adaptation of Fairbanks senior's life in film. Sound was breaking through in film, washing away the stars, acting methods and production processes of the silent screen on which Fairbanks senior had been so dominant. Fairbanks junior writes of his father:

> [He] did not care for sound films. He liked to tell a story visually. He thought of his films – silent films – as essentially pantomime and ballet – rather than as an actor, he saw himself as an athletic dancer leaping with graceful and visually effective movement across the adventures of history. Sound for his purposes was too literal, too realistic and too restricting.[57]

The Iron Mask functions as a eulogy both for the silent film Fairbanks senior so loved and for the athletic, youthful presence the now-ageing star had enjoyed in it. Writing of the production, its nominal director Dwan claimed: 'Doug seemed to be under some sort of compulsion to make this picture one of his best productions.'[58] He added, 'He had always meticulously supervised every detail of his pictures, but in this one I think he eclipsed himself. It was as if he knew this was his swan song.'[59] The film is darker in tone than Fairbanks senior's previous film and is the first in which the actor permits himself to die. Dumas's novel is a eulogy for a historic and lost past. Fairbanks senior's *The Iron Mask* is a eulogy for a silent film history now past and a star fading. Nowhere is this more visible than in the film's prologue. Fairbanks, in the role of D'Artagnan, appears in a *tableau vivant*, the three musketeers at his side, a *tableau* he breaks in order to swashbuckle with his sword and deliver the following prologue:

> Out of the shadows of the past
> As from a faded tapestry
> Of time's procession slow and vast
> I step to bid you bear with me
> The while your fancy I engage
> To look upon another age
> An age when on the human tide
> The plumed wave of chivalry
> Rose to its summit
> Sweeping wide across a nation's mighty sea
> France never shone a brighter power
> Than in this high romantic hour
> So come with me to France of old
> To fiery days when hearts beat high
> When blood was young and hate was bold
> And sword crossed sword to do or die
> For love and honor gloried them
> And friendship reached its peak with men
> Friends were friends in those brave days –
> Athos, Porthos, Aramis, I
> Graved our hearts with a mystic phrase
> Bound our lives with a mystic tie
> Come, stir yourself with our ringing call
> Of 'all for one and one for all.'

The prologue promises the audience a nostalgic return to the past of Dumas as both text and time. But what it actually returns us to is a nostalgia for the past of Fairbanks senior. It is the spoken commissioned prologue in verse which was written by Edward Knoblock for the extravagant world premiere of Fairbanks senior's *The Three Musketeers* on 28 August 1921 at the Lyric Theatre Broadway, a film from the actor at his zenith.[60] Vance suggests: 'It is as if Fairbanks is bidding farewell not only to the art form he had pioneered and perfected but also to the best part of himself and his work.'[61] Fairbanks senior had always insisted that his acrobatics appear effortless and that his physical tales of derring-do carry the film. However, *The Iron Mask* is more of an ensemble piece in which Fairbanks takes the decision to have almost no close shots, choosing instead to be shown at full or three-quarter length; perhaps, Vance suggests, to soften the effect of his advancing years.[62] *The Iron Mask* adapts the history of the star persona of its leading man.

While the authorial influence of the male hero in films has been evaluated in compelling ways, that of supporting and character actors is less visible yet no less informative in relation to the performative palimpsests that are adaptations in this era. Nigel de Brulier, the British-born character actor who subsequently moved to ply his trade in North America, is key to my line of argument here. While there was a significant and intentional crossover of acting personnel between Fairbanks senior's 1921 *The Three Musketeers* and his 1929 *The Iron Mask*, De Brulier played the part of Cardinal Richelieu in no fewer than four Musketeer films: *The Three Musketeers* (1921, dir. Niblo), *The Iron Mask* (1929, dir. Dwan), *The Three Musketeers* (1935, dir. Lee) and *The Man in the Iron Mask* (1939, dir. Whale).[63] The significance of De Brulier's repeat casting in the role is multiple. It underscores the palimpsest-like nature of these adaptations as they adapt both Dumas and their cinematic predecessors' reworkings of him in their overlapping casts. Each of the Musketeer adaptations was a huge success, and the move for these films to situate themselves in relation to their predecessors might be read as a quest for comparable box office takings or critical acclaim. De Brulier clearly made creative and financial sense to the directors and filmmakers who repeatedly cast him in this role. But De Brulier, the actor who habitually played authority figures, clearly made sense to the audience too in the Richelieu role with which he came to be synonymous, despite portraying very different Richelieus. De Brulier's identity transacts with itself across the Musketeer films in its very different incarnations. But the very different interpretations De Brulier gives under different directors do not undermine him in the part; rather, in their cumulative genealogy, they serve as a marker of authenticity. It is, in these films as a whole, unclear where De Brulier stops and Cardinal Richelieu begins. The opening credits of the 1935 *The Three Musketeers* are revealing in this respect. They list the part thus: 'Nigel De Brulier as the Cardinal Richelieu (as Nigel De Brulier).' The actor points to the part, which points ineluctably back to the actor. Impossibly, De Brulier is visibly both himself and Richelieu in an inextricable interpersonal relationship which highlights a different formative function for the actor in films of this era. In reprising his at times villainous turn, De Brulier came to mark Musketeer adaptations as authentic simply by his very presence.

If the visibility of supporting characters in this era exerts a different formative influence over the adaptations in which they feature than that of the male lead, so too does that of female actors. Stardom works along starkly gendered lines. The shaping impact of Greta Garbo in *Camille* (1936, dir. Cukor), her critically acclaimed adaptation of Alexandre Dumas *fils*'s 1848 novel and 1852 play, *La Dame aux camélias*, a play that was also the basis for Verdi's *La Traviata* (1853), powerfully makes this point. Garbo, perhaps at the apogee of her career, has the film constructed around her as star (see Figure 2.4). She sits in the theatre box at the film's opening. She is statue-like, offering

FIGURE 2.4 Camille *(1936, dir. Cukor).*

herself to the system of adoring gazes in the theatre, a system in which we partake from the darkness of the cinema as we consume her star body. Both Marguerite and Garbo, as E. Ann Kaplan puts it, use their body as spectacle, as object to be looked at.[64] Numerous point-of-view shots through theatre glasses look up with adoration or desire at Marguerite's carefully positioned body with its no less carefully constructed media image. Within the film Marguerite, a lowly farm girl, has fabricated a mythical, desirable persona for herself, a persona she sells as much as her body, a persona which resonates with that carefully crafted for Garbo by herself and the studio professionals around her in her career. Garbo, though, was no passive icon around which film narratives were spun. Her status as a potential auteur is clear, for she wielded influence both on the films in which she starred and on the quality of the scripts used for them. Yet her stardom works very differently from that, for example, of her male protagonist counterparts in Hollywood. If Douglas Fairbanks senior's adaptations market him as a unique personality, Garbo in *Camille* was marketed as the latest in a long line of illustrious Camilles, subsumed into a chain of actresses. As part of a continuum, her identity was merely the most recent incarnation of that collectivity. The complex nature of Garbo's stardom in relation to the film is enacted within the film itself. It profiles Garbo as star in a role as a heroine who constructs herself carefully as a star. Yet the trajectory of the film annihilates Marguerite as star in telling ways. E. Ann Kaplan persuasively points to the ways in which *Camille* was marketed, promising precisely this female annihilation or abdication of star power in images that intertwine Garbo and her character Camille:

> Posters for the film build up the love between Marguerite and Armand in terms of a romance between Garbo and Taylor; for example one poster text reads 'Greta Garbo loves Robert Taylor' while another has underneath an image of Garbo and Taylor in a deep embrace 'crush me in your arms until the breath is gone from my body' (words which do not, of course, occur in the play or the film); Garbo is, in another poster, 'the eternal woman ready to suffer and die for the man to whom she has given her affection.'[65]

Marguerite opens the film as the undisputed star among the demi-monde of the courtesans, inspiring envy and admiration in the colleagues who recognize her status. Yet, in keeping with many of Garbo's roles, Marguerite must give up her prominence, economic power and ultimately her life for the man she comes to love. Marguerite falls in love with a young man, Armand, climbing his way up the middle-class professional ladder, a man far removed from her wealthy protectors. However, as E. Ann Kaplan notes, she must renounce her desire in order for the bourgeois patriarchal system to remain intact. Marguerite does so and the film explores her consequent annihilation. It points, in their brief escape to the country, to the impossibility of their relationship. It can only exist in a place apart, in an idyllic nowhere outside of time and society. 'The fake sets and the artificial scenery,' Kaplan argues, 'here add to the film's meaning in that these cinematic elements underscore the "unreality" of the space the lovers are attempting to find.'[66] While Marguerite is shot in extreme long shots, with Armand revelling in the wide open space of the country, that space proves to be a lie, for it is symbolically bordered by the château of her former protector, a man who will take her back to society and a more suitable role within it. The self-annihilation to which Marguerite condemns herself is enacted as she lies to Duval to protect him and his place in society in a scene which points towards her death at the close of the film. Kaplan writes:

> In a magnificent scene, Garbo convinces Duval that she no longer loves him, and then, again gorgeously decked out in white, she sweeps through the open doors that look out on the Baron's castle far away on the skyline; the camera holds her as her frail, translucent form moves further and further into the distance, signifying her loss of herself, her surrender to the abyss.[67]

Female stardom, if the case of Garbo is indicative, might be seen to work in very different ways in this era than that of its male counterparts.[68]

The formative influence of the stardom of villains needs also to be considered, and Peter Lorre's appearance in *Mad Love* (1935, dir. Freund), an adaptation of Maurice Renard's 1920 novel *Les Mains d'Orlac* (*The Hands of Orlac*), both structures itself around the power of stardom and, ultimately, dissects it. The film is a star vehicle for Peter Lorre, the Hungarian actor who fled Germany for Hollywood following Hitler's rise to power. Lorre's previous villainous performances, most notably his powerful performance as the child killer in *M* (1931, dir. Lang), inform and are implicitly referenced in his role as Dr Gogol in *Mad Love*. The same inner madness drives both parts. Lorre as the villain in *M* describes the voices driving him to kill. *Mad Love* enacts the voices driving its incarnation of Lorre to do likewise, dramatizing them in voiceover as Gogol stands in front of a mirror. Multiple differently dressed visions of Gogol appear, each urging him to spill blood in order to gain his true but married love. The film was carried by Lorre's performance as star, a performance which stood out in the lacklustre reviews of the piece. The adaptation is more about Lorre as film personality and star than it is about Renard's novel, a notion supported by a powerful shot in the opening credits, many of which are written by an invisible finger on a misted window. They announce the film to be derived 'From the novel *Les Mains d'Orlac* written by Maurice Renard' and 'Translated and adapted by Florence Crewe Jones'. Dramatically the hands that Lorre, as Gogol, has brought back to life suddenly smash through the window which has the credits superimposed on it, breaking the text that binds the film to its source novel. If the previously discussed stars of the adaptations in this era display their bodies to be admired by the camera and the audience metaphorically behind it, Lorre, the villain, displays his body and identity not for admiration but to trigger horror. Gogol dresses up in a hideous get-up with a neck brace and mechanical accompaniments, pretending to be Rollo, the guillotined criminal whose hands he grafted onto Orlac (see Figure 2.5). He does so in order to convince Orlac that he has murdered his own father and must hand himself over to the police. But what is particularly striking about the star body Lorre presents to inspire horror both within and beyond the film is that it deconstructs stardom and its mechanisms. Gogol's horrific body when dressed as Rollo is not real and the camera lingers on its constructedness, underscoring that constructedness as Gogol casts off his disguise. But the identities beneath disguises in this film are always themselves constructed. The film's heroine, Yvonne – the object of Gogol's unrequited love – is a case in point. Gogol, like the audience of the film in which he stars, is thirsty for a star. He falls in love with her performance on stage and the plot line into which he inserts himself in fantasy. He watches her body displayed for his adoration

FIGURE 2.5 Mad Love *(1935, dir. Freund)*.

on stage from a private shadowed box which we share with him, a point-of-view shot of his programme aligning us with his thirst to both find and adore a star on stage. But what he falls in love with is a constructed illusion, his projection of an ideal identity. Yvonne is not the part she plays at the theatre of horrors. Nor is she actually Yvonne, but rather an actress playing a part in a film in which her identity is refracted multiply: in stage roles, statues, posters and the like. After buying a wax statue of Yvonne, used to advertise her role, Gogol adores it as Galatea (he tells the statue, and a drunk nearby, of the myth of Galatea). He adores the projection of his own desire. Rather than make an actual statue of the actress playing Yvonne, Frances Drake, Freund's film has her play the statue as well as herself, underscoring stardom as the malleable material from which we, like Gogol, fashion our fantasies. *Mad Love* not only pushes us to consider the different ways in which villainous stardom impacts on the films in which it occurs, it also deconstructs stardom as a concept.

If the influence of stars is potent in the adaptations in which they feature, the role of the director in the interpersonal transactions of adaptations of French sources in this era is no less so. The celebrated director Jean Renoir, as his appearance in this chapter already suggests, forms something of a lodestone in my argument in this respect. Much of his output between 1927 and 1939 was adapted from a French literary source.[69] Renoir's films may acknowledge the person of the source author with credit attributions, portraits, fragments of text from the source author and the use of their physical signature. Yet Renoir marks them as his own. He does so via the previously discussed cameos which he creates for himself in them, but also as a result of the tropes, acting cast and personal vision which mark him as an auteur in his films. So strong is Renoir as identity in his adaptation of Zola's *La Bête humaine* that subsequent filmmakers adapt Renoir and his vision of the text, rather than Zola as source. Fritz Lang is a case in point. That Lang was intrigued by Renoir's creatively and commercially successful oeuvre is clear. He remade both Renoir's 1938 *La Bête humaine* into the Hollywood film noir *Human Desire* in 1954 and Renoir's 1931 *La Chienne* into *Scarlet Street* in 1945. Lang mirrored Renoir's intent to imprint his own identity on his films. Lang claimed to have imprinted traces of his own hands, symbols of his creative signature, across his body of work.⁷⁰ Lang's film clearly works from Renoir even as it seeks to make space for itself, as Lang's teasing inversion of tiny details shows. In *La Chienne*, Renoir has Lulu (the female protagonist, see Figure 2.6) polish the fingernails of her lover and pimp, Dédé. Lang inverts this superficial detail, having Kitty (his version of Lulu) demand that Chris (her helpless would-be lover) do her toenails. He has his female protagonist's flatmate and double, Milly (they share clothes, a flat and a job), claim 'I ache like a dog/*une chienne*', referencing the Renoir title that Lang has changed. Likewise, in Renoir's *La Bête humaine*, Grandmorin greets Séverine with the words 'you have lost weight', while Owens (Lang's

FIGURE 2.6 La Chienne (The Bitch) *(1931, dir. Renoir)*.

version of Grandmorin) greets Vicki (Lang's Séverine) with the phrase 'you've put on a little weight'. Even in his differences from Renoir, Lang returns to him, underlining the formative function of the director not only on his own adaptation but indeed on those which follow it.

But what is particularly intriguing about the directorial interaction between Renoir and Lang is their shared self-reflexivity in their adaptations. Both, in film, reflect on the potency and incapacities of their directorial function and identities. Lang's adaptation of Renoir's *La Chienne* focuses on a tellingly named bank clerk and Sunday painter, Chris Cross. Lang's protagonist's name suggests origin and presence, and that X marks the spot, since crosses have long been used in place of signatures by those who cannot write. However, Chris Cross underlines that in the interpersonal play of adaptations, creative identities are simultaneously present and powerful, and absent and appropriated. Chris Cross copies past masters to train his eye, appropriating their identities on canvas. But his works are then appropriated, signed and sold to others by Kitty March, the woman he keeps as she fabricates an illusory creative personality and signature for herself with the help of her boyfriend Johnny. She steals both Chris's canvases and his words, passing off his statements on art as her own when talking to the art critic Janeway. She claims, like Chris, to 'put a line around what I feel when I look at things', suggesting that painting is like falling in love, as 'every painting, if it's any good, is a love affair'. Chris's painting is critically successful under Kitty's signature and he can admire his success, but only in a form that is both his and not his, bearing as it does the mark of another. Tom Gunning argues that '*Scarlet Street* stands as possibly Lang's Hollywood masterpiece, partly because it offers his most complex view of the process of art-making and the identity of the artist/author.'[71] He suggests such evaluations of adaptive identity are absent in Renoir's earlier version of this film. However, the closing image of Renoir's *La Chienne* questions his claim. While Lang's film closes with Chris Cross unable to paint or to kill himself and haunted by the voices of Kitty and Johnny (he has murdered the couple who appropriated his artistic work and signature), Renoir's film, for all its greater gaiety, closes with a still more striking image of authorial appropriation. A self-portrait by Legrand (Renoir's equivalent of Chris Cross whose name suggests a stature he never achieves in art), already appropriated by Lulu and Dédé (Renoir's equivalent of Kitty and Johnny), moves still further beyond Legrand's grasp as it is sold by an art dealer to a buyer. Legrand neither sees nor recognizes what used to be his mirror reflection despite his proximity to the canvas. The final image of the film depicts the creative identity that once was his, pulling away from both him and the camera in a car. The adaptations of both Renoir and Lang reflect on the loss innate to their directorial identities as they adapt the work of others.[72]

If the close of Renoir's *La Chienne* couches such a reflection in potentially anxious, negative terms, such a vision is perhaps not reflective of the directorial transactions of adaptation, in which Renoir revels, as his adaptation of the Guy de Maupassant short story 'Une partie de campagne' (*A Day in the Country*, 1936) makes clear. Renoir finds a directorial signature for himself by borrowing multiply from elsewhere. Renoir writes thus of the film:

> *A Day in the Country* didn't force anything on me. It only offered me an ideal framework in which to embroider. I truly believe in this idea of a framework in which to embroider. It's a question of plagiarism. I must admit something: I'm absolutely in favor of plagiarism. I believe that if we want to bring about a great new period, a new renaissance of arts and letters, the government should encourage plagiarism. When someone is convicted of being a true plagiarist, we should give him the Legion of Honor straight away. I'm not kidding, because the great authors did nothing but plagiarize, and it served them well. Shakespeare spent his time writing stories that had already been written by little-known Italian authors and by others.[73]

Art, for Renoir, is an adaptive, interpersonal transaction: creative spirits fashion an artistic originality for themselves by adapting from elsewhere. His adaptation of *Une partie de campagne* enacts this philosophy, visibly playing with the textual identities from which it appropriates. That Renoir borrows from Maupassant in this film is clear both from its opening credits – which proclaim the fact – and from the detail and style of the film itself. That Renoir puts his own imprint on the adaptation is equally clear – it features another cameo from the director, this time in the form of the wily innkeeper who mocks Henriette and her family even as he profits from them. Renoir, moreover, borrows copiously and exuberantly from a range of other sources. Jean-Honoré Fragonard, the eighteenth-century painter of *The Swing* (1767), cannot be ignored in *Une partie de campagne*, for Renoir, the son of the famous Impressionist painter, is very direct in his reference to him. The film's heroine, Henriette, swings while in the countryside, enjoying a moment of freedom and flight from the restrictions of her life in her father's shop and the unappealing shop boy destined to be her husband. The joy of this moment of escape is magnified as the camera swings with her, enabling the audience to share her soaring exultation. She is, like Fragonard's painted protagonist, surrounded by desiring gazes. Fragonard's female figure is watched amorously by the man pushing her, who lies beneath her soaring flight on the swing, able to peek beneath her skirts, and by the three stone cupids who apparently turn to gaze on her, such is her sexual appeal. Renoir's film adapts each of these viewers, adding still more – Henriette is propelled on the swing by a male presence. We, the audience, take the place of the lecherous man beneath her as she soars forward, glimpsing beneath her skirts. The stone cupids find a presence both in the priests in training who stop to gaze at her, their head fanning himself in the heat of the desire they seemingly cannot resist, and in the use of four grubby young boys who watch from a wall, who, for all their youth, are not impermeable to Henriette's appeal. Henri, the man who will seduce Henriette, watches too, with his sidekick from the city. That his intended seductions will be successful is confirmed by Renoir's pictorial adaptation of Fragonard. In Fragonard's painting, the female character's shoe flies off as she soars on the canvas, a common pictorial trope for an impending loss of virtue. In Renoir's film, Henriette's hat falls off in a cinematic moment which, like Fragonard's shoe, signals her sexual fall. Adaptation, according to Renoir's *Une partie de campagne*, is an interpersonal creative transaction in which the director draws presence, originality and vitality from the creative identities from whom he/she borrows.

If source authors, stars/actors and directors all visibly shape adaptations between 1927 and 1939, the less visible, but no less powerful, identities engaged in the process also demand attention. Regimes and politicians have a clear impact in the years 1927–39 on the adaptations made. Nazi Germany is a powerful case in point. The regime's impact on adaptive output can be traced in two ways: first, from the rate at which French texts were adapted as it rose to prominence; second, from the form and message that specific adaptations adopted. Adaptations based on French sources diminish in number in Germany in a manner perhaps concurrent with the rise of National Socialism. A comparison of the adaptive output of 1932 and 1933 is revealing in this respect. Numerous French sources were adapted in German-language versions in 1932 and reveal much about trends in the European adaptation of French sources in this era. Seeking to capitalize on their strong market position and cater for French-speaking audiences, German production companies frequently made films in both German and French simultaneously.[74] The German film production company Nero-AG released *L'Atlantide* (1932, dir. Pabst), an adaptation of Pierre Benoit's novel *L'Atlantide*, discussed in Chapter 1. A sound remake of Jacques Feyder's 1921 film, it was shot in three languages (English, French and German) with a view to servicing different international markets and competing specifically with Hollywood. Carl Lamac directed *Kiki* (1932), a musical comedy based on André Picard's 1918 play of the same name. The film was made in German- and French-language versions but had the same star – Anny Ondra – in both. The German production company UFA was particularly prominent in such parallel productions. Carl Boese and Heinz Hille directed *Der Frechdachs* (*The Cheeky Devil*, 1932), an adaptation of a Louis

Verneuil play. A separate French-language version, *Vous serez ma femme* (*You Will Be My Wife*), was released alongside it. UFA also made French and German versions entitled *Mensch ohne namen* (*Man without a Name*) and *Un homme sans nom* (1932, dir. Ucicky), adapting Balzac's work. The same production company made French and German versions of Félix Gandéra's play *Quick* directed by Robert Siodmak (1932). This brief summary of films released in 1932 reflects the frequency and prevalence of French source texts in German-language film.

The contrast between the number of German-language adaptations of French sources in 1932 and 1933, though, is stark. They dwindle to next to nothing in 1933 and remain comparatively sparse for the remainder of the Nazis' time in power. A notable exception comes in the form of Lotte Reiniger's groundbreaking silhouette film adaptation of Mérimée and Bizet's *Carmen* (1933, dir. Reiniger). In a nine-minute piece, Reiniger's animations offer a plot line built around a triumphant gypsy heroine. She wins over three lovers, subdues a bull in a bullfight and closes the story by riding off on a bull with her chosen lover. Reiniger's choice of a French source is far from incidental. A committed opponent of the Nazi regime, Reiniger uses the plot line of the film to speak to the persecution of Roma under National Socialism and the movement's designation of them as 'asocial' and 'criminals'. It was produced in the year in which Reiniger fled Germany, because of her opposition to the Nazis, to ply her trade abroad.[75]

French sources did not disappear entirely from the adaptive output of Germany under the Nazi regime. But those adaptations that did appear were clearly shaped to the needs and messages of the regime. The formative influence of Joseph Goebbels, the Reich Minister of Propaganda from 1933, is tangible. Goebbels shaped the adaptive output of Germany in restrictive ways: the entire film industry was put under complete control of the propaganda ministry, which banned certain films but also pushed for numerous films to be made, notably adaptations of canonical literature. Marc Silbermann writes:

> Goebbels's demand for 'quality' films was prompted by political aims, for films dealing 'filmically' with popular themes would not only fulfil a covert ideological function but would also fill the cinemas, thus strengthening the industry, and act as an instrument to legitimate the 'cultural' credibility of the young state at home and abroad. For Goebbels then, the ideological, artistic, political and economic considerations were intimately linked. ... His insistence on films devoid of obvious stated political messages was part of a general program instituted in 1936–7 to enhance the quality of film art. In particular, a striking number of films based on classical or well-known literary sources was produced in 1937, owing in part to the assumption of

inherent quality in the literary sources and in part to the expectation of absorbing that quality by mere contagion.[76]

Nazi Germany adapted literary sources for political reasons, and politics shaped the cinematic output of the era. The German-Spanish co-production of *Carmen, la de Triana* (1938, dir. Rey) is a case in point. The film, yet another adaptation of Mérimée's *Carmen*, was a Spanish-German joint venture under the name Hispano-Film-Produktion led by the Nazi-controlled UFA Studios in Berlin. The collaborative venture sought to feed the Spanish and German markets and to counter the power of Hollywood, which was 'controlled by Jews' according to anti-Semitic Nazi propaganda.[77] The Spanish-language market was large, with approximately fourteen thousand theatres worldwide, and Germany was, at the time, a market leader in cinema technology. Goebbels invited the famous singer and actress Imperio Argentina and her film-director husband, Rey, to Germany in 1938. Rey pushed for *Carmen* as a suitable star vehicle for Imperio Argentina and it was filmed in German- and Spanish-language versions simultaneously. The same sets and technical team were used but, leading lady aside, both versions had different casts. The German-language adaptation, *Andalusische Nächte* (*Nights in Andalusia*), was directed by Herbert Maisch, an expert in Nazi propaganda military films.[78] Goebbels's imprint on Rey's *Carmen, la de Triana* is less visible than in Maisch's piece, but it remains tangible. The film is, as José Colmeiro argues, 'a propaganda "war film" rather than simply another folkloric film musical'.[79] The film's hero, José, is explicitly told to keep his distance from the locals, but he is tempted away from his military duty by his desire for the exotic, dangerous gypsy Carmen. Ultimately, though, writes Colmeiro, 'José restores the honour of the fatherland by rejecting the association with Carmen and the threat to the nation that she represents'.[80] He saves his former regiment from a brigand ambush and dies in the process before being buried, his rank and military record cleansed of its gypsy blemish. While the film, 'one of the first popular culture by-products resulting from the ideological and political alliance between Nazi Germany and Francoist Spain', reveals much of Franco and his regime, Goebbels's imprint and influence are stronger.[81] His objections to the inappropriate subject of gypsies (Triana was traditionally the gypsy neighbourhood of Seville) were accommodated. The Romani lexicon so prevalent in Mérimée's original story is eradicated in the film. Argentina – clearly a non-gypsy in the lead role – plays a part 'reduced to a collection of token folkloric clichés', a part in any case crushed by militaristic might and duty to the fatherland at the film's denouement.[82] *Carmen, la de Triana* makes visible the invisible presence of Goebbels in the fabric of its fictions.[83]

The most invisible personalities shaping the adaptations of this era, though, come in the form of the censors, shadowy figures whose excisions and actions shaped the adaptations that passed before them in ways we cannot always trace. Christine Grandy refers to the formative power of the censors in Britain.[84] Censorship of films in Britain came under the remit of the British Board of Film Censors (BBFC), which made itself visible in different ways.[85] Its president, Edward Shortt, spoke, for example, to the Cinema Exhibitors Association in the summer of 1935, addressing head-on what he saw as the increasing presence of unacceptable themes in films coming before the censors.[86] That the censors could ban certain films and themes is clear. But their function was formative as well as prohibitive. Annette Kuhn has argued that 'regulation … may be understood not so much as an imposition of rules upon some pre-constituted entity, but as an ongoing and always provisional process of constituting objects from and for its own practices'.[87] Grandy concurs: 'The BBFC and the Home Office also engaged in the equally silent approval of "the same themes repeated over and over again" in fiction and film.'[88] Thus, while the identities of the individual censors are often unknown, accessible only in their handwritten notes on films, their presence can be detected in the common patterns and in the shape and form of adaptations in this era. British adaptations in this era, Grandy argues, do not allow the troubles of the world to have a significant place: they offer an ideological fantasy separate from the reality of interwar unemployment and disillusionment. They produce a reassuring vision of men and women within the social structure – the woman must abdicate all for love, particularly any earning power, to enshrine the hero at the heart of the nation and the economy to dispel the tensions caused by the alteration of women's position after the First World War. They depict Englishness as capable, moral and honourable in a world where foreign villains always get their comeuppance, troublesome women are always contained and male predominance is always preserved.[89] *Mimi* (1935, dir. Stein) may bear the hallmarks of its source author Henri Murger and Puccini's operatic rewrite; it may be shaped by the auteur presence of its actors (Douglas Fairbanks junior, like his father, demanded control of scripts and creative decisions) and of the themes and tropes common in the films of its director, Stein. But *Mimi* fits the pattern outlined above. Mimi relinquishes her earning power with rich protectors to give up all for a penniless playwright whom she propels, through her nurturing of his hard work, to success, thus defeating the foreign-sounding creditors who demand the payment of debts, before conveniently dying to wipe the stain of her love outside of matrimony from Rodolphe's life. In fitting this pattern so closely, *Mimi* demonstrates the formative function of the censors in Britain at the time, shaping itself to their requirements and revealing them as key players in the interpersonal webs of adaptive creation.

The adaptations of French literary sources made between 1927 and 1939 collectively underscore the intriguing interpersonal network of creative identities via which they are refracted and from which they glean their very being. They force us to refocus our quest for the source text via a recognition that adaptation is done by people, for people and is innately interpersonal. Christiane Nord and André Lefevere conceptualize recreative art as interpersonal in its genesis rather than intertextual, urging us to seek the people behind the artefacts and not merely the written text. Their interpersonal dialogue and vision of recreative art is anticipated by the adaptive output of the 1920s and 1930s. The films of this era offer a probing portrait of the people at play in the processes of adaptation. They show the importance of the source author, often placing him/her as personality at the core of their adaptive acts. They explore the complex ways in which different types of actors – heroes, heroines, character actors and villains – impact upon the adaptive works in which they star or feature. They reveal too the ways in which directors negotiate a personal cinematic identity and originality for themselves even as they borrow from an earlier source author. They cast light on the sophisticated acts of adaptation that take place between directors when filmmakers such as Lang adapt other directors. They evaluate the hidden influence of political figures such as Goebbels, whose presence is powerful in its invisibility. They also make clear the powerful impact of the censors, the people whose names we no longer know, but who, despite this invisibility, shaped the type and style of the adaptations made in this era in telling ways. The power of the adaptive output of the years 1927–39 lies in the persuasive portrait it offers us of the multiple, intriguing, overlapping, conflictual and creative interpersonal transactions from which the art of adaptation is made.

Notes

1 See, inter alia, Mansaku Itami's version of Hugo's *Les Misérables*, *Kyojin-den* (*The Giant*, 1938, dir. Itami) for a Japanese market; Ma-Xu Weibang's adaptation of *Le Fantôme de l'Opéra*, 夜半歌聲 (*Song at Midnight*, 1937, dir. Weibang); and Vladimir Vaynshtok's reworking of Verne's *Les Enfants du capitaine Grant*, Дети капитана Гранта (*The Children of Captain Grant*, 1936, dir. Vaynshtok).

2 Christiane Nord, 'Function Plus Loyalty: Ethics in Professional Translation', *Génesis. Revista Científica do ISAG* 6 (2006–7): 7–17 (10).

3 Lefevere, *Translation, Rewriting and the Manipulation of Literary Fame*, 12.

4 Keith Reader, 'Raymond Bernard's *Les Misérables* (1933)', in *Studies in French Cinema: UK Perspectives, 1985–2010*, ed. Will Higbee and Sarah Leahy (Bristol: Intellect, 2011), 233. For a detailed reading of the

adaptive afterlives of Hugo's *Les Misérables*, see *'Les Misérables' and Its Afterlives: Between Page, Stage and Screen* (London: Ashgate, 2015), ed. Kathryn M. Grossman and Bradley Stephens. Grossman and Stephens write: 'On screen, there have been at least 65 different film, television, and animated adaptations, outnumbering screen versions of two other popular nineteenth-century novels – Jane Austen's *Pride and Prejudice* (1813) and Charles Dickens's *Great Expectations* (1861) – by a ratio of at least four to one.' The relationship of Hugo's novel with the medium of film began, as they point out, as early as 1897 with the Lumière brothers' short film *Victor Hugo et les principaux personnages des Misérables* (2–3).

5 It would again be adapted in 1944 in an Egyptian film, *El Boassa*, starring Amina Rizk and Abbas Fares.
6 Delphine Gleizes, 'Adapting *Les Misérables* for the Screen: Transatlantic Debates and Rivalries', in *'Les Misérables' and Its Afterlives*, ed. Grossman and Stephens (London: Ashgate, 2015), 133.
7 Harold Bloom, *The Western Canon: The Books and School of the Ages* (San Diego: Harcourt Brace, 1994).
8 Victor Hugo cited in Michael D. Garval, *'A Dream of Stone': Fame, Vision and Monumentality in Nineteenth-Century French Literary Culture* (Newark: University of Delaware Press, 2004), 110.
9 Kathryn M. Grossman, 'From Classic to Pop Icon: Popularizing Hugo', *French Review* 74.3 (2001): 482–95 (484).
10 Reader, 'Raymond Bernard's *Les Misérables*', 312.
11 Reader, 'Raymond Bernard's *Les Misérables*', 313.
12 Rémi Fournier Lanzoni, *French Cinema: From Its Beginnings to the Present* (New York: Bloomsbury, 2015).
13 Reader, 'Raymond Bernard's *Les Misérables*', 313.
14 Reader, 'Raymond Bernard's *Les Misérables*', 316. Jean-Loup Passek's *Dictionnaire du Cinéma Français* describes his acting thus: 'He acts with all his soul, but also with all his tics, too clearly in evidence in close-up; his wrinkles become deeper, his cheeks tremble; and then his voice becomes insinuating, hissing, shouting and thunderous to break down into sobs as the action requires.' Passek cited in Reader, 'Raymond Bernard's *Les Misérables*', 316.
15 Reader, 'Raymond Bernard's *Les Misérables*', 318.
16 Bloom, *The Western Canon*, 4.
17 Lanzoni, *French Cinema*, 65.
18 Claude Gauteur and Ginette Vincendeau, *Jean Gabin: anatomie d'un mythe* (Paris: Nouveau Monde, 2006), 126.
19 René Barjavel cited in Gauteur and Vincendeau, *Jean Gabin*, 44. My translation. For further discussion on the shaping influence of Gabin as star on this film and its canonicity, see Kate Griffiths, *Émile Zola and the Artistry of Adaptation* (Oxford: Legenda, 2009), 107–30.

20 Michel de Certeau, *The Practice of Everyday Life: Volume One* (Berkeley: University of California Press, 1984), 174. For a fuller reading of Renoir's fascination with the figure of the poacher, see Griffiths, *Émile Zola and the Artistry of Adaptation*, 113.
21 Kauf, '*Unholy Love*', *Variety* (30 August 1932): 21.
22 Bradley Stephens writes of Dumas *père* that his works have 'proven both inspirational and irresistible for adapters across the world, not least those working with live-action film. There are well over 250 cinematic and television versions of Dumas' work, making him one of the world's most adapted writers.' Bradley Stephens, 'Animating Animality through Dumas, D'Artagnan and Dogtanian', *Dix-Neuf* 18 (2014): 193–210 (193).
23 *The Count of Monte Cristo* (1934, dir. Lee), *Le Comte de Montecristo* (*The Count of Monte Cristo*, 1929, dir. Fescourt), *Bosco the Musketeer* (1933, dir. Harman), *I quattro moschettieri* (*The Four Musketeers*, 1936, dir. Campogalliani), *Les Trois Mousquetaires* (*The Three Musketeers*, 1932, dir. Diamant-Berger), *The Three Musketeers* (1933, dir. Schaeffer/Clark), *The Three Musketeers* (1935, dir. Lee), *The Three Musketeers* (1939, dir. Dwan), *The Iron Mask* (1929, dir. Dwan), *The Man in the Iron Mask* (1939, dir. Whale), *The Black Tulip* (1937, dir. Bryce).
24 Théophile Gautier cited in Edmund Birch, '"Les Suites des suites": Alexandre Dumas' *Le Comte de Monte-Cristo* and the News', *Dix-Neuf* 21 (2017): 297–311 (298–9). My translation.
25 Birch, '"Les Suites des suites"', 297.
26 Birch, '"Les Suites des suites"', 297.
27 Bloom, *The Western Canon*, 8.
28 Bloom's comments in *The Western Canon* about modern moves to incorporate writers of different ethnicities into the canon because of their previous visible exclusion resonate with the treatment of Dumas in the nineteenth century (Bloom, *The Western Canon*, 278). Dumas's father, Silvia Marsans-Sakly writes, 'was a half-Haitian and half-French mulatto, born into slavery but freed when his nobleman father took him to France'. He went on to become the first black general in Napoleon's army but his son nevertheless experienced discrimination because of his mixed-race ancestry throughout his career, discrimination he sought to address in his 1843 novel *Georges*, a text about ethnicity and colonialism. Silvia Marsans-Sakly, 'Geographies of Vengeance: Orientalism in Alexandre Dumas' *The Count of Monte Cristo*', *Journal of North African Studies* 24.5 (2018): 738–57 (753).
29 Philip Dunne, *Take Two: A Life in Movies and Politics* (New York: Limelight, 1992), 32.
30 This star/actor divide still persists, according to Anthony Minghella. He claims: 'It's true of all wonderful actors that they somehow are in a complex relationship with stardom, particularly British actors; they think they mistrust it, and they want the regard of their peers. They want to be perceived as actors.' Anthony Minghella quoted in Matt Woolf, 'One Cool Jude', *Observer* (14 December 2003): 5.

31 Caroline Lejeune, 'I Knew Donat When', *Picturegoer Weekly* (28 September 1935).
32 Victoria Lowe, ' "Something That Is US": Robert Donat, Screen Performance, and Stardom in the 1930s', *Journal of Film and Video* 63.3 (2011): 13–29.
33 Lowe, ' "Something That Is US" ', 15.
34 Lowe, ' "Something That Is US" ', 17.
35 Lowe, ' "Something That Is US" ', 17–18.
36 Lowe, ' "Something That Is US" ' 18.
37 Lanzoni, *French Cinema*, 67.
38 *Marius* was released as *Zum goldenen Anker* (*The Golden Anchor*, 1932, dir. Korda) in Germany. Fritz Wendhausen directed a German version of *Fanny* (1934). Mario Almirante directed *Fanny* in a film of the same name for an Italian market (1933). A version of *Topaze* made in the United States and directed by D'Abbadie d'Arrast was released (1933).
39 Lanzoni, *French Cinema*, 72.
40 *Madame Bovary* (1937, dir. Lamprecht), *Bel-Ami* (1939, dir. Forst), *Mensch ohne Namen* (*Man with No Name*, 1932, dir. Ucicky), *Amphitryon* (1935, dir. Schünzel).
41 Alfred Eibel, 'Faut-il oublier Maurice Dekobra', 21 March 2019, http://www.lmda.net/din2/n_egar.php?Eg=MAT03298.
42 Susan McClary traces the prevalence of *Carmen* in film:

> Films of *Carmen* began to appear in 1910 with versions produced by both Pathé and Edison. In 1915 Cecil B. DeMille released a *Carmen* starring the opera-singer Geraldine Ferrar, a casting decision that enhanced the film with Ferrar's prestige alone, since the film was silent; and Fox responded with a version starring Theda Bara, the quintessential 'vamp'. Some of the more illustrious *Carmen* movies that followed include ones featuring Charlie Chaplin and Pola Negri (Lubitsch's *Gypsy Blood*) and Delores del Rio (*The Loves of Carmen*). Technically speaking, all of these were silent films; but in practice the familiar music was ever-present, performed by staff musicians at local cinemas. The first sound version of the opera appeared in 1931 (also titled *Gypsy Blood*) and by 1948 at least sixteen *Carmen* films had been produced. (Susan McClary, *Georges Bizet: Carmen* (Cambridge: Cambridge University Press, 1992), 130)

43 See Jeffrey Vance, *Douglas Fairbanks* (Berkeley: University of California Press, 2008), 251.
44 Julie Sanders, *Adaptation and Appropriation* (London: Routledge, 2016), 33.
45 Leonard Wallace, 'Grand Opera Comes to the Talkies', *Film Weekly* (7 November 1931), https://search-proquest-com.abc.cardiff.ac.uk/docview/1705133197?rfr_id=info%3Axri%2Fsid%3Aprimo.
46 *Film Weekly* (7 November 1931).

47 'Gypsy Blood', *Film Weekly* (27 May 1932): 26.
48 Patrick McGilligan, *Cagney: The Actor as Auteur* (South Brunswick, NJ: A. S. Barnes, 1975), 199.
49 Vance, *Douglas Fairbanks*, 1.
50 The Company's first production made clear, in its opening credits, the extent to which it rested on Fairbanks as persona, on the swashbuckling acrobatic performer so visible collectively in his films. Vance writes:

> The company's inaugural film is marked by a special introduction preceding the film's main title, in which a special title, in simple white lettering on a black background, expresses the sentiments of the newly formed United Artists: 'It is our hope and desire to attain a standard of entertainment that will merit your approval and continued support.' To break the serious tone of the proceedings, an enthusiastic Fairbanks literally rips through the title itself, does a front somersault, and excitedly proclaims to the camera via an intertitle 'Listen folks – they make me start the ball rolling. So here's the first picture – Gee whiz! – I hope you'll like it.' (Vance, *Douglas Fairbanks*, 73–4)

51 Vance, *Douglas Fairbanks*, 113.
52 Vance, *Douglas Fairbanks*, 113.
53 Vance writes, 'Fairbanks was the real force both in front of and behind the camera, and he frequently took charge of the difficult scenes. He was a cinema auteur over thirty years before the concept was developed; he put his own identifiable stamp on his films.' Vance, *Douglas Fairbanks*, 155.
54 Vance, *Douglas Fairbanks*, 117–18.
55 Vance, *Douglas Fairbanks*, 107.
56 Vance, *Douglas Fairbanks*, 111.
57 Vance, *Douglas Fairbanks*, 250.
58 Vance, *Douglas Fairbanks*, 250.
59 Vance, *Douglas Fairbanks*, 250. Irving is clear that Fairbanks senior dominated this production as auteur in all its aspects. He claims that although Dwan was 'nominally director, his contribution was mainly executive, just as Douglas's pseudonym Elton Thomas was a portmanteau title for himself and all those who had elaborated his original treatment of the two novels'. Vance, *Douglas Fairbanks*, 262.
60 Vance, *Douglas Fairbanks*, 120.
61 Vance, *Douglas Fairbanks*, 250–1.
62 Vance, *Douglas Fairbanks*, 253.
63 Several of the original cast members of *The Three Musketeers* repeated their roles in *The Iron Mask*: Marguerite de la Motte as Constance, Nigel de Brulier as Cardinal Richelieu, Lon Poff as Father Joseph, Charles Stevens as D'Artagnan's servant, Planchet, and Léon Bary as Athos. Noticeably absent, however, was the original Aramis, Eugene Palette, who had gained

so much weight in the intervening years that he was replaced by Italian actor Gino Corrado. George Siegmann, the original Porthos, died during the film's preproduction and Stanley J. Sandford, a tall, heavy-set actor best remembered for his work in silent comedies, filled the large shoes (and costume) of Porthos. (Vance, *Douglas Fairbanks*, 251)

64 E. Ann Kaplan, *Women and Film: Both Sides of the Camera* (New York: Methuen, 1983), 45.
65 Kaplan, *Women and Film*, 37.
66 Kaplan, *Women and Film*, 42.
67 Kaplan, *Women and Film*, 46.
68 Christine Grandy identifies a similar pattern in relation to British films of this era, noting that Marguerite's claim to love Armand more than she loves herself, a claim she puts into practice, mirrors trends in British films at the time in which 'women … gave up their own claims to economic and social mobility for the sake of love and did so repeatedly'. Gertrude Lawrence's role as Mimi in the film of the same name (*Mimi*, 1935, dir. Stein) enacts her claim. The film, based on Henri Murger's *Scènes de la Vie de bohème* and the Puccini opera stemming from it, has the heroine eschew her wealthy protectors to nurture the artistry of a penniless playwright with whom she falls in love, before leaving him when voices of authority consider her an impediment to his success. She dies as the play she nurtured him to write is acclaimed on the Paris stage as an overwhelming success. Christine Grandy, *Heroes and Happy Endings: Class, Gender and Nation in Popular Film and Fiction in Interwar Britain* (Manchester: Manchester University Press, 2014), 30.
69 Renoir made *Nana* (1926) from Émile Zola's novel of the same name, *The Little Match Girl* (1928) from the Hans Christian Andersen tale, *La Chienne* (*The Bitch*, 1931) from a novel by Georges de la Fouchardière, *La nuit du Carrefour* (*Night at the Crossroads*, 1932) from a work by Georges Simenon, *Boudu sauvé des eaux* (*Boudu Saved from Drowning*, 1932) from a play by René Fauchois, *Madame Bovary* (1934) from Gustave Flaubert's novel of the same name, *Une partie de campagne* (*A Day in the Country*, 1936) from Maupassant's short story and *La Bête humaine* (1938) from Émile Zola's novel.
70 Tom Gunning writes, 'whereas Hitchcock's appearances emphasized his highly recognisable figure, Lang's appearances remain anonymous. He appears not as a face or a caricature silhouette, but in close ups of hands, standing in for actors playing characters in his films.' Tom Gunning, *The Films of Fritz Lang* (London: BFI, 2000), 2. Moreover, Lotte Eisner claims that the deranged whistle of the child killer in Lang's *M* does not belong to the actor playing the part but rather to his director. Lorre, apparently, could not whistle. Lotte Eisner, *Fritz Lang* (New York: Da Capo Press, 1986), 124.
71 Gunning, *The Films of Fritz Lang*, 324.
72 For a fuller treatment of this theme, see Kate Griffiths, *Émile Zola and the Artistry of Adaptation* (Oxford: Legenda, 2009), 107–31.

73 Jean Renoir, *Renoir on Renoir: Interviews, Essays, Remarks* (Cambridge: Cambridge University Press, 1990), 233.
74 This process of parallel shooting in different languages is far from the preserve of German film. In 1929, some companies made the same films in several different languages, reusing sets and costumes. Although many of these multilingual films were made in Hollywood, Paramount and the German company Tobis-Klangfilm followed a similar pattern in Paris studios. Advances in dubbing made this practice obsolete by 1933. See Elizabeth Ezra, ed., *European Cinema* (Oxford: Oxford University Press, 2004), 6.
75 For more details on Reiniger's groundbreaking work, see Grace Whitney, *Lotte Reiniger: Pioneer of Film Animation* (Jefferson, NC: McFarland, 2017). For a reading of Nazism's stance on the Roma community, see Robert Gellately and Nathan Stoltzfus, *Social Outsiders in Nazi Germany* (Princeton, NJ: Princeton University Press, 2001).
76 Marc Silbermann, *German Film and Literature: Adaptations and Transformations*, ed. Eric Rentschler (London: Methuen, 1986), 91.
77 José Colmeiro, 'Nationalising *Carmen*: Spanish Cinema and the Spectre of Francoism', *Journal of Iberian and Latin American Research* 15.1 (2009): 1–26 (3).
78 Colmeiro, 'Nationalising *Carmen*', 3.
79 Colmeiro, 'Nationalising *Carmen*', 2.
80 Colmeiro, 'Nationalising *Carmen*', 7.
81 For a reading of the imprint of Franco in this film, see Colmeiro's treatment of the focus on the unifying national Spanish identity at the expense of more regional identities as well as the depiction of Catholicism. Colmeiro, 'Nationalising *Carmen*', 8.
82 Colmeiro, 'Nationalising *Carmen*', 5.
83 Rey's film – which adapts Mérimée, the doctrines of German politicians of the era, and the rise of Franco and his vision of Spain, as well as elements of Maisch's German-language version of it – itself has an interesting adaptive afterlife, as Colmeiro makes clear:

> In Fernando Trueba's 1999 film *La niña de tus ojos* (*The Girl of Your Dreams*), a cast featuring Penelope Cruz and Antonio Resines recreate a troupe of Spanish actors and film crew shooting a folkloric variation of 'Carmen' in the Nazi-controlled UFA studios in Berlin. The narrative is loosely based on the real filming of *Carmen, la de Triana* in Germany in 1938 by Spanish film star Imperio Argentina and her husband director Florián Rey. In a frustrated film take, a group of actors dressed in nineteenth-century traditional costumes as Andalusian patrons of a typical flamenco tavern appear lethargic and depressed-looking. … Suddenly the harsh reality of a group of Gypsy and Jewish prisoners brought from a nearby labour camp and forced to work as unpaid extras in the film becomes clear to everyone, including the spectators, and

immediately contaminates the safe folkloric film narrative with the dark spectre of Fascism. (Colmeiro, 'Nationalising *Carmen*', 1)

84 Christine Grandy, *Heroes and Happy Endings: Class, Gender and Nation in Popular Film and Fiction in Interwar Britain* (Manchester: Manchester University Press, 2014).

85 Grandy offers a potted history of the creation and structures of the BBFC:

> The film trade chose to erect the BBFC in 1913 rather than face direct government interference. Representatives of the trade elected the president of the BBFC, although the Home Secretary could nominate a candidate. ... Although no statutory law came into effect for the content of film, in practice and through various rulings of the courts as well as the actions of the Home Office, the BBFC's powers were gradually increased throughout the 1920s and consequently followed as law. The Home Office increasingly deferred concerns and queries about the content of film to the BBFC in this period. Indeed without the direction of the Obscene Publications Act that governed the Home Office, the BBFC created its own list of censorable subjects in a given year and worked from that on a case by case basis. Consequently few cinemas were locally licensed to display films that did not possess a certificate from the BBFC. (Grandy, *Heroes and Happy Endings*, 181–2)

86 Grandy, *Heroes and Happy Endings*, 177.
87 Annette Kuhn cited in Grandy, *Heroes and Happy Endings*, 178.
88 Grandy, *Heroes and Happy Endings*, 178.
89 Grandy, *Heroes and Happy Endings*, 177–211.

3

Politics, propaganda and the censored screen: Adapting French literature during the German Occupation (1940–44)

Andrew Watts

The Second World War marked a boom period for adaptation in France. Of the 220 films made under the German Occupation, no fewer than 106 – 48 per cent of the country's total film production during these years – were reworkings of literary texts.[1] Adaptations proliferated in a variety of genres, from lavish costume dramas to comedies, detective thrillers and fantastical films. In their attempts to avoid censorship, French filmmakers drew inspiration repeatedly from canonical authors whose fiction appeared to pose no threat to the occupying authorities. Having been adapted only once in France during the 1930s, the works of Balzac spawned seven films between 1940 and 1944. The Occupation also saw works of contemporary literature recreated on-screen, in particular the murder-mysteries of Belgian writer Georges Simenon, with nine adaptations, and Pierre Véry, with four films.[2] As well as being produced in large numbers, adaptations enjoyed widespread popularity with audiences in France during this period. For many spectators, cinematic versions of literary texts – particularly those inspired by the writings of culturally prestigious authors such as Balzac and Zola – offered a defiant image of Frenchness and a reassertion of French national identity in the face of Nazi oppression.

The extent to which the fiction films of this period reflect the political context of their production nevertheless continues to provoke fierce scholarly debate. In the extensive body of academic literature devoted to Occupation cinema, the majority of critics have claimed that, in order not to antagonize the Germans or the Vichy government headed by Marshal Pétain, wartime films resolutely avoided any political commentary. 'Films made during periods of high historical trauma', claims Florianne Wild, 'usually do not or cannot reflect the events of the moment in which, as cultural artefacts, they are produced. The French cinema during the German Occupation of France is a case in point.'[3] Filmmakers in France have commonly shared this view. Writing in the introduction to André Bazin's *Le Cinéma de l'Occupation et de la Résistance* (*French Cinema of the Occupation and Resistance*), François Truffaut asserted that 'there was no place for subversion or protest in the films of this period; the sanctions would have gone beyond those of the Commission de Censure'.[4] By contrast, some scholars have argued that the political discourses and ideologies of wartime France do find an expression in film, but only to a very limited degree. Susan Hayward, for example, estimates that only 9 per cent of films made during the Occupation could be seen to articulate different aspects of Nazi and Vichy ideology.[5]

The present chapter challenges these critical perspectives by demonstrating that many adaptations produced in occupied France engage with the political concerns of the time, often in ambivalent and unexpected ways. My concern is not to prove that specific films were collaborationist or resistant, or to identify clues in their production and mise en scène that might identify them as belonging to one or the other of these categories. Scholars, foremost among them François Garçon and Jean-Pierre Bertin-Maghit, have already given plentiful consideration to these issues.[6] This chapter focuses instead on the ways in which French filmmakers dramatized the politics of the Occupation and why adaptations proved especially adept at doing so. In so doing, it builds on and extends the work of Dan Hassler-Forest and Pascal Nicklas, who describe adaptation as an inherently political process. 'Since the act of adaptation by its very definition involves a process of transformation and rewriting,' they explain, 'any adapted text must by necessity also involve the repurposing of ideas that implicitly or explicitly articulate a sense of political engagement.'[7] Hassler-Forest and Nicklas argue that such engagement is particularly visible in the adaptive output of the twenty-first century, in which globalization and the advent of new media technologies have encouraged the use of adaptations for political ends. However, the link between politics and adaptation is not rooted solely in this contemporary context. My analysis of Occupation cinema shows how a much earlier generation of filmmakers responded to the political circumstances of their own time and how questions of political ideology can be seen to have shaped the practice of adaptation during this period.

This chapter explores the relationship between politics and adaptation in occupied France from a variety of artistic and ideological perspectives. First, it considers the representation of resistance and collaboration in *Pontcarral, colonel d'empire* (*Pontcarral, Colonel of the Empire*) (1942, dir. Delannoy) and *La Main du diable* (*Carnival of Sinners*) (1943, dir. Tourneur), respectively. These films illustrate how key adaptors did not simply avoid these subjects for fear of punishment but rather incorporated them into the aesthetic features of their films. Second, this chapter examines the way in which adaptations of French literature during this period reflected on Nazi and Vichy ideology. This section focuses particularly on *Les Inconnus dans la maison* (*Strangers in the House*) (1942, dir. Decoin), a film that can be read simultaneously as an anti-Semitic diatribe and a proclamation of the importance of traditional family values. Third, this chapter uses the concept of occupation – with its connotations of possession and control – to analyse specific ways in which wartime directors and screenwriters approached adaptation as an artistic process. Using as case studies *Le Dernier des six* (*The Last of the Six*) (1941, dir. Lacombe) and its sequel *L'Assassin habite au 21* (*The Murderer Lives at Number 21*) (1942, dir. Clouzot), both adaptations of novels by Stanislas-André Steeman, I argue that these films remodelled their source texts in order to claim the cinematic territory that American detective comedies such as *The Thin Man* (1934, dir. Van Dyke) had occupied in France before the war.

Finally, and most importantly, this chapter reflects on what adaptation can tell us about the wider importance of French cinema during the Occupation. As Hayward has argued, the dual trauma of military defeat and the subsequent years of occupation caused a crisis of national identity for France. Between 1940 and 1944, the country was in the 'invidious position of being "not herself" but "other" and suppressed, and yet, of having the semblance of being herself – a myth sustained by the illusory power wielded by the Vichy government which continued to administer after 1942 even though the Nazi occupation had spread over the whole country'. While for Hayward this sense of 'political and national schizophrenia ... has little to no record in film',[8] this chapter reveals that adaptations readily voiced the crisis of identity that enveloped France during the Occupation. At the level of plot, films such as *L'Assassinat du Père Noël* (*The Killing of Santa Claus*) (1941, dir. Christian-Jaque) and *Le Colonel Chabert* (*Colonel Chabert*) (1943, dir. Le Hénaff) revolve around the themes of collective trauma, mental instability and uncertain identity. In so doing, they echo France's struggle to rebuild her own fractured identity during the war and enable us to situate adaptation at the very heart of this national preoccupation.

Adaptation between resistance and collaboration: *Pontcarral, colonel d'empire* and *La Main du diable*

Before proceeding to an analysis of specific films from the Occupation period, I wish first to explore some of the key developments in French cinema between 1940 and 1944 and how these affected the practice of literary adaptation during this period. As numerous scholars have demonstrated, the Occupation brought mixed fortunes for the film industry. In certain obvious respects, these were bleak years for audiences and filmmakers in France. In the wake of the German invasion and the morale-crushing defeat of June 1940, many of the leading directors of the 1930s fled the country. Julien Duvivier, René Clair and Jean Renoir all departed for Hollywood, where they were joined by some of the most famous French stars of the day, including Jean Gabin and Simone Simon. The Nazis moved swiftly to ban British films and did the same for American productions when the United States entered the war in December 1941. Shortages of film-stock and raw materials severely undermined the country's filmmaking capacity, which declined markedly compared to pre-war levels. Between 1935 and 1939, France produced an average of 120 films per year; between 1940 and 1944, this number fell to an average of 55 films annually.[9]

However, the impact of the Occupation on French cinema was by no means entirely negative. In contrast to the chaotic state of the country's film industry during the 1930s, when a third of production companies went bankrupt every year, the Germans implemented much tighter legal and financial controls which helped to ensure that films were properly financed before production began. During these years of political repression and economic hardship, audiences also flocked to the cinema. 'The Occupation was a period when all films were successful,' recalled director André Cayatte, 'because the cinema replaced everything else: meeting place, heated area, means of escape, weekend outings.'[10] The popularity of cinema as a leisure activity translated into an exponential increase in national box office revenue, which rose from 1.3 billion francs in 1938 to 3.8 billion in 1943.[11] With fewer films competing on the domestic market, each film could now expect to generate between two-and-a-half and four times the revenue it might have earned before the war.[12]

The Nazis readily supported the continuation of a profitable film industry in France and quickly sought to harness its commercial potential. Key to the Germans' strategy in this respect was their creation of a new production company, Continental Films, on 1 October 1940. Funded by Nazi capital and headed by Alfred Greven, a former producer at the German film company UFA, Continental aimed to produce French-language films capable of attracting large audiences and maximizing revenues. In its pursuit of these objectives, the company seized control of the major Paris studios at Neuilly and Boulogne-Billancourt, in addition to key production and distribution facilities including laboratories and cinemas. In seeking to ensure that Continental's output would appeal to French audiences, Greven, who answered directly to Joseph Goebbels, maintained that the company's films should not be vehicles for Nazi propaganda and that they should be free of political bias. As Roy Armes explains, 'the German imperative was commercial not ideological: to foster – or at least do nothing to hinder – the creation of a prosperous French film industry, reflecting French values, but within which German commercial interests would have a considerable share'.[13] However, as this chapter will demonstrate, the fact that Continental tried strenuously to exclude politics from its films did not prevent some of these productions from engaging with the ideological concerns of the time or from incorporating politically subversive material.

Continental was responsible for a significant portion of France's cinematic output during the Occupation and became a key producer of adaptations. Between 1940 and 1944, the company released thirty feature films, more than both Pathé and Gaumont, who made fourteen and eight films, respectively, during the same period.[14] Of the thirty films produced by Continental, fifteen were adaptations of literary texts and included some of the most commercially successful and technically accomplished films of the period. In 1941, Continental's first film was an adaptation of Pierre Véry's 1934 novel *L'Assassinat du Père Noël*, directed by Christian-Jaque. This was followed by versions of three mystery novels, Simenon's *Les Inconnus dans la maison* and Steeman's *Le Dernier des six* and *L'Assassin habite au 21*. Continental's reinvention of two nineteenth-century novels, Balzac's *La Fausse maîtresse* (*The False Mistress*) (1841) and Zola's *Au bonheur des dames* (*The Ladies' Paradise*) (1883), both directed by André Cayatte and released in 1942 and 1943, respectively, also enjoyed considerable popularity with audiences.

That the company established itself as the primary source of literary adaptations in wartime France is not surprising given the financial advantage Continental held over its competitors. As Evelyn Ehrlich points out, the company had an initial operating capital of 200 million francs, a vast sum when one considers that the average cost of a film in 1941 was 3.4 million francs.[15] Greven also ensured that his studios were kept well supplied with film-stock, materials for sets and costumes, and electricity, access to all of which became increasingly limited as the war progressed. For other production companies that did not benefit from the same kind of support, making historical period adaptations, especially, proved a more difficult undertaking. As Edwige Feuillère remembered of her experience of starring in a reworking of Balzac's novella *La Duchesse de Langeais* (*The Duchess of Langeais*) (1941, dir. Baroncelli), 'we had to snatch everything we could by pulling strings or by means of other "fiddles": the permits, licences, tickets, film, wood and paint for the sets, fabric for the costumes'.[16] Such challenges help to explain why no other production company completed as many adaptations as Continental during this period.

Despite the practical and financial difficulties associated with making films in wartime, the Occupation also witnessed a revitalization of French cinema through the emergence of a new cohort of directors, producers and screenwriters. The departure of some of the country's leading filmmakers at the outset of the war created space in the industry for a fresh group of cinematographers to advance their careers. Out of the eighty-one filmmakers who worked under the Occupation, nineteen were first-time directors.[17] The impact of this sudden wave of promotions was clearly felt in the sphere of adaptation, where it resulted in some of the most creative, and profitable, films of the Occupation period. Having worked as an assistant to Jean Renoir in the 1930s, Jacques Becker began directing his own films during the war and garnered critical acclaim for his 1943 version of Pierre Véry's *Goupi Mains Rouges*. Similarly, this period witnessed the rise to prominence of Henri-Georges Clouzot, who joined Continental as a scriptwriter in January 1941. Clouzot went on to write screenplays for two adaptations that year, *Le Dernier des six* and *Les Inconnus dans la maison*, before directing another, *L'Assassin habite au 21*, in 1942. These films enabled him to hone his skills as a director and provided him with a platform from which to embark on the project with which he would eventually become synonymous, *Le Corbeau* (*The Raven*), released in 1943.

The professional advancement that some filmmakers achieved during the war nevertheless contrasts with the experience of Jewish cinema professionals, who under Vichy were excluded from working in any part of the film industry.[18] The ban forced many into hiding in the south of the country, where some continued to work, uncredited, on films produced by studios in Nice and Marseilles. In May 1941, producer Jacques Cohen set up a workshop in Juan-les-Pins with the aim of providing work for Jewish scriptwriters who had fled Paris. This clandestine venture spawned some thirty screenplays, though only one of these, an adaptation of Albert Paraz's novel *L'Arche de Noé*

(*Noah's Ark*), reached the screen in 1947, two years after the war ended.[19] In the north, too, Jews continued to work in the film industry and to contribute to key adaptations produced during this period.

One of the most striking examples of Jewish involvement in the practice of adaptation under the Nazis is that of Jean-Paul Le Chanois. A screenwriter of Jewish extraction, Le Chanois was born Jean-Paul Étienne Dreyfus but adopted a professional name in order to distance himself from any association with France's most infamous case of anti-Semitism, the Dreyfus Affair. Having worked as an actor and studio assistant in the 1930s, he was able to continue his career under the Nazis because he had three Aryan grandparents and had been baptized by the Catholic Church. This allowed him to obtain the professional membership card that was obligatory for working in French cinema during the Occupation. Le Chanois was subsequently – and ironically, given his Jewish background – employed by Continental, where he wrote the screenplays for *La Main du diable*, a modernization of Gérard de Nerval's 1832 novella *La Main enchantée* (*The Enchanted Hand*), and two films based on works by Simenon, *Picpus* (1942, dir. Pottier) and *Cécile est morte!* (*Cécile Is Dead!*) (1944, dir. Tourneur). While working at Continental, he also remained an active member of both the Resistance and the French Communist Party. Le Chanois created two Resistance groups in the studios at Boulogne-Billancourt, and prior to leaving the company in 1943, he stole film-stock that he later used in making *Au cœur de l'orage* (*In the Eye of the Storm*) (1944–5), a clandestine documentary about the *maquis* of the Vercors.

In addition to attempting to force Jews out of the film industry, the German and Vichy authorities sought to exert their control over French cinema through censorship. In the occupied zone, the Propaganda Abteilung oversaw the process of scrutinizing screenplays, which had to be submitted for official approval before a production visa could be granted. A further exhibition visa was issued only after the censorship office, or *Filmprüfstelle*, had reviewed a final edit of the film. In the south, censorship fell within the remit of the Service du Cinéma, though as Colin Crisp points out, in practice the Propaganda Abteilung had final jurisdiction over both zones.[20] At any stage of the process, censors could demand cuts and modifications, or issue a ban (which they did in the case of a number of adaptations, such as Marc Allégret's *Félicie Nanteuil* (1943), based on Anatole France's *Histoire comique*, after the film's male lead Claude Dauphin joined the Free French Forces). Though often inconsistent, censorship had a significant impact on filmmaking practices, including adaptation, during this period. The threat of incurring sanctions meant that screenwriters often vetted their own scripts carefully before submitting them for official review. Thus, when playwright Jean Giraudoux wrote the screenplay for Baroncelli's version of *La Duchesse de Langeais* in 1941, he omitted those scenes and references from Balzac's novella that he considered were likely to antagonize the Germans. More specifically, he chose not to include any of Balzac's frequent comparisons of love to a form of warfare or military conquest.[21] Giraudoux also left out one of the most violent moments in the source text, in which the fictional General de Montriveau threatens to brand the Duchess with a hot iron. Similarly, if some filmmakers hoped that censors would pay little attention to reworkings of literary texts, these hopes were often thwarted. In 1942, the authorities demanded a number of cuts to *Pontcarral, colonel d'empire*, Jean Delannoy's version of the 1937 novel *Pontcarral* by Albéric Cahuet, on the grounds that the film was excessively nationalistic. These included changes to a scene in which King Louis-Philippe tasks the eponymous Pontcarral with leading a regiment in the Algeria campaign of 1830. In particular, the king's assertion that 'it is time to rouse France from her humiliations and return some glory to her flag' was unpalatable to German censors, who demanded that it be cut.

Despite falling foul of censorship, *Pontcarral, colonel d'empire* provides a fascinating starting point for exploring how filmmakers engaged with the political context of the Occupation, not least because of its nationalistic content. The film was made by Pathé at the midpoint of the war in 1942. This was a period in which the Occupation was well established in France, and the tide of the war had yet to turn in favour of the Allies. The timing of *Pontcarral, colonel d'empire* was especially significant for director Jean Delannoy, who wanted to encourage spectators not simply to accept the Occupation as a permanent reality. As he explained after the war, 'I felt the need to make a film that would shake the French out of their apathy, given their growing inclination to compromise with our occupiers, out of indifference, but often because they wanted to serve their own interests by doing business with the Germans.'[22] Delannoy's aim is reflected in the opening titles of the film, which are clearly designed to stir a renewed sense of patriotism in audiences by evoking memories of the Napoleonic Empire. The film's title screen creates this association with Napoleon at the outset. As we read the title *Pontcarral, colonel d'empire*, the shadow of a figure looms upwards from the bottom of the frame. Ostensibly, the shadow is that of Pontcarral, a former army officer who, following the collapse of the Napoleonic Empire in 1815, has chosen to live in semi-retirement rather than serve the restored Bourbon monarchy. However, this shadow, wearing a tricorn hat, unmistakably recalls the figure of Napoleon himself. As the title music rises to a crescendo, the shadow grows ever taller, as if to remind spectators of Napoleon's towering influence over French history. This link to the First Empire is underscored by the next screen, in which the shadow of an imperial eagle appears behind the name of director Delannoy. As the opening titles continue, a further shadow of a group of flag-bearing soldiers prompts audiences to remember the stunning victories fought out by Napoleon's *Grande Armée* on the battlefields of Europe – while casually forgetting the disaster of Waterloo. Even before its first scene, *Pontcarral, colonel d'empire* seeks to fill French audiences with pride in their own national identity.

Not surprisingly, given Delannoy's stated ambitions for the film and the patriotic imagery of its opening titles, the theme of resistance is integral to the plot of *Pontcarral, colonel d'empire*. The first sequence in the film situates the action firmly within the context of 1815 and the return of the monarchy. After tilting downwards from the top of a church tower to reveal a bustling crowd below, the camera switches to focus on a man who sings merrily as he changes the sign on the town square from 'Place Napoléon' to 'Place Louis XVIII'. At the foot of his ladder, a young woman walks past selling *fleurs de lys*, before the camera pans across a banner bearing the words 'Vive le roi Louis XVIII'. As the townsfolk of Sarlat celebrate the arrival of the Restoration, Delannoy introduces a key element of political resistance in this scene by turning to show a hand holding a gun and slowly taking aim from behind the shutters of a stable (see Figure 3.1). The as yet unseen figure shoots down the sign on the town square hung only moments before, then fires a second shot that blows the hat off a local dignitary and causes the terrified crowd to

FIGURE 3.1 Pontcarral, colonel d'empire (Pontcarral, Colonel of the Empire) *(1942, dir. Delannoy)*.

disperse. The theme of resistance remains prominent in the second part of this scene as the authorities attempt to persuade the gunman – soon to be revealed as Pontcarral (Pierre Blanchar) – to give himself up. As in the novel, the former soldier responds to the officers outside the stable with bursts of song, drawing laughter from the crowd. Finally, after the stable is set on fire, Delannoy adds a heroic dimension to Pontcarral's resistance, as the character suddenly bursts through the doors on horseback and jumps through the flames towards the camera. Such an overt portrayal of political rebellion in the opening minutes of the film makes it easy to understand why some critics have interpreted *Pontcarral, colonel d'empire* as carrying a defiant, anti-Nazi message. 'In effect,' writes Pierre Billard, '*Pontcarral* has been perceived as a "Resistance film", or in any case, as an antidote to the poisonous submission associated with this period.'[23]

More difficult to explain is why, given its resistance theme, the Germans allowed *Pontcarral, colonel d'empire* to be released at all. According to Francis Courtade, the fact that the authorities chose not to ban the film entirely suggests that 'they did not suspect that anyone would be so rash as to defy them'.[24] However, in granting an exhibition visa, censors may also have recognized that Delannoy offers a more ambivalent portrayal of the resistant spirit than post-war critics have so often claimed. Most notably, the film can be seen to undermine the notion of Pontcarral as a resistant hero through the representation of his marriage to the aristocrat Garlone de Ransac. Having brushed aside her family's contempt for his Napoleonic past, Pontcarral struggles to win the affection of his new wife, who refuses to consummate the marriage and continues an affair with her lover, Hubert de Rozans. This situation takes a brutal turn after Pontcarral overhears de Rozans boasting of his conquest in public. Enraged, the former soldier returns home, where he rapes Garlone before killing her lover in a duel the next morning. Delannoy invests this sequence with a much more violent edge than the novel does and calls particular attention to Pontcarral's dominance over his wife. Whereas in the source text the characters enter the room together before the rape occurs, in the film Pontcarral is shown breaking down the door to the bedroom. Positioned behind Blanchar, the camera captures Garlone's fear as he advances across the room towards her, forcing actress Annie Ducaux to back away. In further contrast to the novel, which elides the duel between Pontcarral and de Rozans entirely, we then see the two men taking up their pistols and pacing out their steps across a meadow, before the sound of a gunshot reverberates out of frame. For Noël Burch and Geneviève Sellier, this sequence merely confirms that *Pontcarral, colonel d'empire* is a resistant – and indeed deeply misogynistic – film. Delannoy's film 'stands almost completely alone,' they argue, 'in suggesting that in order to retrieve a warlike spirit that was annihilated by the humiliation of the Defeat, the minority of men capable of taking up arms and resisting first needed to reaffirm their imperious virility'.[25] However, the factor that Burch and Sellier omit from their analysis is that such notions of male dominance were also firmly ingrained in fascist ideology, which readily interpreted a soldier's capacity for violence as a powerful sign of virility. Similarly, the Vichy regime advocated male dominance over the marital home as one of the key building blocks upon which a defeated France should found its recovery. Far from serving only as a glorification of the Resistance, *Pontcarral, colonel d'empire* reflects several different ideological currents – fascist, Pétainist and resistant – all of which were circulating during the period of the film's production.

The closing scenes of *Pontcarral, colonel d'empire* further illustrate the way in which this film can be seen to undercut its own resistant message. In the first part of this sequence, Pontcarral resumes the leadership of his regiment and departs on the Algeria campaign. Echoing the opening titles of the film, Delannoy presents another rousing tribute to the French army, as Pontcarral rides out with his men to the sound of trumpets and military fanfare. When the film was released in cinemas, audiences were quick to interpret these scenes as a defiant gesture towards the Nazis, with many spectators breaking into cheers and applause. However, as Hayward has argued persuasively,[26] the resistant connotations of Pontcarral's triumphant return to military service appear much more ambiguous when juxtaposed with the final shots of the film. In this short epilogue, which has no direct equivalent in the novel, we see a group of *Spahis* – North African soldiers trained by the French – riding across the desert and saluting a memorial stone inscribed with the name of Pontcarral. The scene presents – perhaps unintentionally – a reminder of the figure of General Henri Giraud, who with the support of the Allies became high commissioner of Algeria in December 1942, the same month in which *Pontcarral, colonel d'empire* was released. Having made a daring escape from a German prison earlier that year, Giraud was championed as a hero by the Resistance, his exploits leading some spectators to compare him to the fictional Pontcarral (most notably in Lyons, where graffiti proclaiming 'Pontcarral is Giraud' appeared on buildings during the winter of 1942–3).[27] However, Giraud's reputation as a resistant hero by no means reflected the true complexity of his political beliefs. While refusing to cooperate with the Germans, he continued to support the Vichy regime and to apply its policies, including the discrimination against Jews, in North Africa. In evoking the figure of Giraud in its final scene, *Pontcarral, colonel d'empire* thus seemed as attuned to the ideology of Vichy as it did to the spirit of Resistance – a fact which may also help to explain why the film escaped without a complete ban.

While *Pontcarral, colonel d'empire* revolved – albeit somewhat problematically – around the figure of the resistant hero, other wartime adaptations presented a subversive image of the Nazis. One of the most intriguing films of the period in this respect was Maurice Tourneur's *La Main du diable*. Produced by Continental in 1943, this fantasy-horror was loosely inspired by Nerval's *La Main enchantée*, in which an apprentice cloth merchant, Eustache Bouteroue, acquires a magic potion for his right hand in order to transform himself into a skilled swordsman and win a duel. With a screenplay by Le Chanois, *La Main du diable* recreates Nerval's protagonist as a struggling artist, Roland Brissot (Pierre Fresnay), who obtains fame, wealth and a glamorous mistress after purchasing a mysterious, disembodied hand. Moreover, the film updates the historical context of the source narrative to a period that, although it resembles the 1940s, remains vague and unspecified. Coupled with its fantastical plot, *La Main du diable* exploits this vagueness in an attempt to disguise its political satire. Despite appearing disconnected from the era of its production, the film readily parodies the Nazis, most notably in the portrayal of Roland Brissot as a second-rate artist. Brissot's attempts to establish himself as a painter echo the early career of Hitler, who as a young man twice failed to gain entry to the Vienna Academy of Art. For the first part of the film, Brissot remains similarly unable to fulfil his artistic ambitions, which Tourneur and Le Chanois evoke with blistering mockery. In one early scene, the painter's beautiful model Irène is shown sitting for a portrait, before the camera pans around to reveal Brissot slumped at his easel with a vacant expression, his palette resting limply in front of him. The next scene further ridicules his attempts at artistic innovation, as he excitedly tells Irène of his plan to produce a series of paintings of men seen through the eyes of a lark, a horse and a worm. By reinventing Nerval's fictional cloth merchant as a frustrated artist, *La Main du diable* appears to revel in appropriating the source text and using it to poke fun at the Nazis through the conduit of their own production company.

As well as satirizing Hitler, *La Main du diable* can be seen to reflect on the practice of collaboration. The threat of censorship and imprisonment meant that filmmakers were for the most part reluctant to represent this activity on-screen during the Occupation. However, as an active member of the Resistance, Le Chanois delighted in inserting subversive references in his scripts and, despite being employed by Continental, frequently targeted those who collaborated with the Nazis. Following the Liberation in 1944, the screenwriter explained how, for example, he had lampooned the notorious collaborationist politician Marcel Déat in the Simenon adaptation *Picpus*. In preparing his script, Le Chanois decided to call the film's cat Déa, 'so that at a given moment I could say "Déa is done for" '.[28] In *La Main du diable*, the name

'Brissot' carries a similarly playful, anti-collaborationist charge, since it recalls the somewhat ambiguous figure of Jacques Pierre Brissot. One of the leading supporters of the French Revolution, Brissot was an enlightened thinker who argued for the right of individuals to rebel against political despotism and the abuse of royal power. However, his career was also plagued by accusations that he had betrayed his fellow revolutionaries by collaborating as a police spy, and he was eventually guillotined. Echoing the fate of Jacques Pierre Brissot, the fictional protagonist of *La Main du diable* succumbs to temptation and enters unknowingly into collaboration with the Devil, thereby setting himself on his own path towards death.

While Le Chanois's enthusiasm for mocking collaborators appears as a subtle feature of his screenplays, the plot of *La Main du diable* lends itself more obviously to interpretation as an anti-collaborationist allegory. By selling his soul to the Devil (here characterized as a diminutive man in a bowler hat played by Pierre Palau), Brissot can be seen to represent those Frenchmen and women who chose to collaborate with the Nazis. As Bosley Crowther, a reviewer for the *New York Times*, wrote in April 1947, following the release of *La Main du diable* in the United States, 'there may be some hidden significance in this film which is applicable to those citizens of France who bartered their souls during the Nazi occupation'.[29] If the anti-collaborationist resonance of this film has been well documented,[30] such readings have nevertheless paid little attention to the way in which Tourneur uses staging and cinematography to warn against dealing with the Devil/Nazi Germany. *La Main du diable* represents the demonic pact as a source of fear and suffering, as the scene in which Brissot acquires the hand illustrates. In this sequence, which was shot mainly by Tourneur's assistant Jean Devaivre, Brissot and the chef Mélisse retire to an upstairs room of the restaurant to contemplate the mysterious object. As the actors climb the stairs, the voice of the kitchen hand – played by Pierre Larquey and appropriately called Angel – pleads from out of frame 'don't buy it, sir, don't buy it'. Stark, Expressionist lighting projects Angel's shadow onto the back wall of the staircase, where his oversized, silhouetted hand appears as a sinister foreshadowing of the demonic hand that will soon attach itself to Brissot (see Figure 3.2). After the artist agrees to buy the talisman, Tourneur and Devaivre employ a series of rapid cuts which associate this transaction with fear and physical agony. Starting with a close-up of Brissot placing a coin in the chef's hand, the director cuts suddenly to Mélisse as he screams in pain. We then see Brissot's horrified reaction before the camera cuts back again to Mélisse and tilts downwards to reveal a mutilated stump where the chef's hand once was. At the very point in the film at which Brissot purchases the talisman, *La Main du diable* uses a mixture of lighting, shadow and jarring camera movements to present

FIGURE 3.2 La Main du diable (Carnival of Sinners) *(1943, dir. Tourneur).*

this as a cautionary tale in which collaboration with the Devil leads quickly to suffering.

The final part of the film reinforces this warning by representing the demonic pact as ending repeatedly in failure. Having been unable to raise enough money to buy back his soul, Brissot meets the seven previous owners of the hand at a masked banquet, where each recounts how he acquired the talisman. In a series of embedded narratives told using stylized décor and shadow puppetry, Tourneur shows the hand being passed down through history, where each recurrence of the demonic pact brings pain, humiliation and usually death. In the first tale, which recalls the plot of Nerval's story, a musketeer describes how he bought the talisman from an alchemist, only for this to result in him killing his best friend in a duel. The musketeer then sells the hand to a thief who in turn becomes a master-forger, bankrupts the kingdom and is killed in a people's revolt. Eventually, the hand reaches the chef Mélisse, whose thriving restaurant founders when the hand turns against him and he starts to burn the sauces that once made him famous. It is tempting to interpret this sequence as echoing the ideology of the Vichy regime, which blamed France's defeat in 1940 in part on the governments of the Third Republic. According to Pétainist discourse, the Occupation was the price that had to be paid for the moral weakness and political incompetence of earlier generations. The masked banquet sequence in *La Main du diable* can be viewed in similar terms. As Brissot relates his own story, his struggle to reclaim his soul appears as the result of a series of failures that stretches back into the past (an interpretation supported by Tourneur's mise en scène, which shows the actors lined up on a staircase and passing the hand back through the generations). However, when juxtaposed with the film's ending, this sequence can also be interpreted as a call to resist collaboration. After depicting the catalogue of suffering that stems from dealing with the Devil, Tourneur emphasizes the need to put an end to this series of Faustian pacts by having Brissot return the hand to the tomb of its original owner, the monk Maximus Léo. Although he dies in the endeavour, falling from the ruins of an abbey during a climactic fight with the Devil, Brissot completes his own salvation and prevents Satan from claiming another soul. In the closing shots of the film, the artist is shown lying dead with a crowd of onlookers gathered around his body. Such an ending suggests that only by spurning collaboration can one regain one's freedom and restore unity – a hope that, retrospectively, we might see *La Main du diable* as expressing for France in 1943.

Adaptation and political ideology: *Les Inconnus dans la maison*, *Les Roquevillard* and *Goupi Mains Rouges*

In dramatizing the themes of collaboration and resistance, *Pontcarral, colonel d'empire* and *La Main du diable* invite us to consider how adaptations of this period engaged with specific aspects of Nazi and Vichy ideology. Filmmakers by no means ignored issues that featured prominently in the policies of both the occupiers and the Vichy government, such as family life, juvenile delinquency and the social status of Jews. Henri Decoin's 1942 version of Simenon's mystery novel *Les Inconnus dans la maison* brought together these concerns in a film that – alongside *Le Corbeau* – proved one of the most controversial releases of the Occupation period. Scripted by Clouzot and produced by Continental, *Les Inconnus dans la maison* focuses on a group of teenagers who become embroiled in the murder of a minor gangster, Big Louis. One of the members of the group, Émile Manu, stands trial for the crime, but is acquitted when his lawyer, Loursat (Raimu), exposes Manu's jealous friend Luska as the real killer. The representation of Luska warrants particular attention in the context of a political reading of this film, not least because it illustrates how *Les Inconnus dans la maison* engages with Nazi propaganda and racial policy. Published in 1941, Simenon's novel had presented an overtly anti-Semitic portrayal of Luska, whom the narrator describes as belonging to 'that race of men one sees sleeping in the corridors of overnight trains'[31] and as wearing a pungent-smelling jacket that causes others to keep their distance from him. By contrast, in his analysis of the courtroom sequence in the film version of *Les Inconnus dans la maison*, Pierre Billard argues that Clouzot and Decoin carefully elide any reference to Luska's Jewish identity. In the adaptation, Luska, played by French-Algerian actor Marcel Mouloudji, appears before the court and gives his first name as Amédée rather than Ephraïm, the name by which he is known in the novel. Unlike the source text, which traces Luska's parentage to Eastern Europe, the film also makes no mention of how the family came to settle in France. For Billard, this deliberate effacement of the character's Jewishness is entirely in keeping with the usual practice of Occupation filmmakers, who tended to eschew the kind of stereotypical portrayals of Jews that had been common in French films during the 1930s. In 1943, for example, Pierre Billon's *Vautrin* made no reference to the Jewish origins of Balzac's fictional banker Nucingen – an omission that appears all the more noticeable given that Billon had constructed a deeply anti-Semitic portrait of the Jewish financier Gunderman in his 1936 version of Zola's *L'Argent*. 'Far from prompting a wave of anti-Semitism on screen,' Billard summarizes, 'the political and ideological context [of the Occupation], coupled with pressure from the authorities, purged French cinema of its anti-Semitic content.'[32]

This argument nevertheless breaks down in the case of *Les Inconnus dans la maison*, which presents a much more subtle engagement with anti-Semitic stereotypes than Billard acknowledges. Closer analysis of the courtroom sequence reveals, first, that the virulent anti-Semitism of Simenon's text does not disappear entirely in adaptation. In the film, when Loursat begins to elaborate his theory of the motives behind the crime, he makes an implicit reference to Luska's Jewish origins by calling him Ephraïm. As the camera cuts to Luska in the public gallery, we then hear Loursat's voice follow up with the accusation that the shop belonging to Luska's parents – like the character's jacket in the novel – has an unpleasant smell. More significantly, the film's portrayal of Luska echoes Nazi propaganda, which persistently stereotyped Jews as criminals. As numerous scholars have noted, *Les Inconnus dans la maison* was first screened in cinemas as part of a double-bill with a German propaganda film, *Les Corrupteurs* (*The Corrupters*). Produced in 1941 by the Institut de l'Étude des Questions Juives and directed by Pierre Ramelot, *Les Corrupteurs* comprised three sequences in which individuals fall victim to what the film claims is the pernicious influence of Jews on French society.

The joint distribution of *Les Corrupteurs* and *Les Inconnus dans la maison* was clearly intended to create an association in the minds of audiences between the main feature and the propaganda film that preceded it. As Colin Crisp points out, the first sequence of *Les Corrupteurs* presents a situation that is 'recognizably similar'[33] to the plot of *Les Inconnus dans la maison* insofar as it depicts a young man who turns to crime after watching gangster films made by Jewish studios in Hollywood. Almost identically, in *Les Inconnus dans la maison*, Loursat blames the murder of Big Louis partly on the influence of cinema. However, the factor that Crisp overlooks in juxtaposing *Les Corrupteurs* and Decoin's film is that the link between them is made possible by Clouzot's invention of dialogue that does not feature in the source text. In his closing address to the court, Loursat describes how teenagers in the provinces go to the cinema in search of entertainment, only then to imitate the stars they have admired on-screen. 'One fine evening,' the lawyer tells the packed courtroom, 'the spectator, these children, become actors, and cover themselves in blood.' When inserted in the film and viewed in tandem with *Les Corrupteurs*, this rationalization of the crime invited audiences to condemn Jews on two levels: first by showing a murderer, Luska, who is Jewish, and second by suggesting that Jewish-made films have poisoned his mind. Resituated within the context of its original screenings, Decoin's version of *Les Inconnus dans la maison* does not strip Simenon's novel of its anti-Semitism, but rethinks and redeploys it in a manner that proves strikingly consistent with Nazi racial stereotypes.

To consider *Les Inconnus dans la maison* a pro-Nazi film would nevertheless be to underestimate its wider engagement with Occupation politics, most notably through its representation of family life. Decoin's re-imagining of the courtroom sequence, which accounts for almost half the film, foregrounds the involvement of the fictional teenagers' families at the outset. After presenting an overview of the bustling courtroom, the director zooms in on the public gallery and focuses in turn on each of the parents whose offspring are implicated in the case. Echoing Simenon's scathing portrait of a vain provincial bourgeoisie, Pierre Fresnay's voice-over presents the families as being acutely aware that they are being scrutinized in a public drama. Monsieur Destrivaux, for example, sits with his arms folded in an expression of 'anguish and shame', before the camera pans to Madame Manu, who sheds a tear as the voice-over describes her as playing the part of the dignified middle-class woman for the rest of the town. This series of shots recurs much later in this sequence, when each of the teenagers is shown sitting next to their parents and relatives. However, in marked contrast to the source text, Decoin's renewed emphasis on the families is accompanied by a thunderous assault in which Loursat blames the older generation, including himself, for failing to provide their children with proper outlets for their energies. Spoiled, neglected and, in the case of his own daughter Nicole, forced to live with an alcoholic father, these teenagers, he exclaims, have sought entertainment elsewhere, in bars, brothels and the cinema. 'Can you show me the way to the stadium, the velodrome, the swimming pool?' Loursat asks the jury. 'No, there is no stadium, velodrome, or swimming pool.' Loursat's impassioned address further illustrates the way in which adaptations of this period were often used to articulate political arguments. 'When a novel did not contain the right message,' writes Julian Jackson in relation to *Les Inconnus dans la maison*, 'it could be doctored for the purpose.'[34] What Jackson does not elaborate, however, is that whether such messages were considered 'right' or 'wrong' was largely a matter of political perspective. On the one hand, Loursat's warning that parents should better provide for the next generation could be seen as a reflection of Pétainist values, which – in accordance with the Vichy slogan 'Work, Family, Fatherland' – considered the family as one of the fundamental elements of a productive French society. On the other hand, this profoundly negative portrait of dysfunctional family life appears as anti-French propaganda. In the immediate aftermath of the Liberation, the latter view predominated, with the result that *Les Inconnus dans la maison* was banned for presenting what the Resistance considered a damning portrait of French society.

In its sometimes ambiguous reflections on anti-Semitism and parental responsibility, *Les Inconnus dans la maison* – like all of the films discussed in this chapter – raises the question of how French spectators responded to adaptations during this period and, more specifically, whether they viewed them in political terms. Not surprisingly, the repressive climate in which such films were produced meant that published commentaries on them – particularly in the authorized press – were often cautious in reading any political significance into the stories represented on-screen. In the case of *Les Inconnus dans la maison*, press reviews tended to focus on the film's artistic qualities and on its fidelity to the source text. In her review for *Paris-Midi* on 26 May 1942, Françoise Holbane, for example, praised the 'skilful, solid dialogue' provided by Georges Clouzot and lauded the way in which the film had succeeded in capturing the atmosphere of the novel. 'This foggy, small-minded town,' she claimed, 'this big house enveloped in lethargy, are very much those of Simenon.'[35] Most reviewers also marvelled at the performance of Raimu. Writing in *Comœdia*, Audiberti paid an effusive tribute to the actor's ability to create a sense of growing dramatic tension: 'In the courtroom, his [Loursat's] silences during the parade of witnesses, plausible a thousand times over and yet deliciously manufactured, foreshadow the awakening of the old devil.'[36] However, if journalistic responses to *Les Inconnus dans la maison* largely avoided political commentary, the collaborationist critic and virulent anti-Semite Lucien Rebatet was more forthcoming in interpreting the film as a condemnation of bourgeois society. In his review for the journal *Je suis partout* on 23 May 1942, Rebatet described Loursat's courtroom speech as reminding him of Céline, an author whose wartime publications were, like his own, strongly infused with anti-Semitism. 'In passing through the mouth of Raimu,' claimed Rebatet, 'this diatribe against the fetidness of the bourgeoisie has an almost Célinian ring to it … and is marvellously suited to the present day.'[37] While the exact meaning of this reference to Céline remains unclear, it is tempting to speculate that Rebatet saw *Les Inconnus dans la maison* as reflecting a belief he shared with his fellow author, namely that Jews were to blame for many of the social, economic and political problems that had led to France's defeat in 1940.

If *Les Inconnus dans la maison* condemned the provincial middle classes as Rebatet argued, Jean Dréville's 1943 film *Les Roquevillard* depicted family life in a manner that was more closely aligned with Pétainist ideology. Based on Henry Bordeaux's 1906 novel of the same title, *Les Roquevillard* relates the story of a respected Savoyard family whose honour is threatened when the son Maurice elopes with his employer's wife, unaware that she has stolen her dowry in order to fund their affair. Bordeaux's work found a natural home on-screen during the Occupation, spawning two adaptations in addition to *Les Roquevillard*, *La Neige sur les pas* (*The Snow on the Footsteps*) (1941, dir. Berthomieu) and *La Croisée des chemins* (*The Crossroads*) (1942, dir. Berthomieu). These films proved well suited to the context of wartime France, not least because they revolved around the themes of family unity, ancestral tradition and Christian faith that were key tenets of Pétain's National Revolution. Dréville's adaptation of *Les Roquevillard* taps into these conservative values at the outset. In contrast to the first chapter of the novel, in which Bordeaux describes a grape harvest, the film begins by panning along a row of wooden church chairs inscribed with the names of the members of the Roquevillard family. As the camera moves along the line and with organ music playing loudly throughout the sequence, Dréville cuts to show the face of the character to which each chair belongs. After reaching the head of the household, François Roquevillard (Charles Vanel), we see a wide shot of the whole family, which, in a reflection of its togetherness, kneels in unison to pray. As well as serving the practical function of introducing spectators to the key participants in the film, this opening sequence establishes clearly the importance of family to the subsequent plot. Emphasizing the social esteem in which the Roquevillards are held, Dréville then shows them leaving church, where outside the locals are heard sharing stories of their respect for the family and its generosity towards the town. 'They are decent people, the Roquevillards,' one woman declares, to which her friend replies, 'And so united.' Through this short expository sequence, the film presents a vision of traditional family values that is consistent with both the source text and Pétainist discourse.

Les Roquevillard appears to align itself even more closely with Pétainism by juxtaposing the themes of family tradition and commitment to the land. In the sequence that follows their attendance at church, the Roquevillards return to their country estate, La Vigie, where François gives the notary Frasne a tour of the property. Set against lingering shots of the Savoyard mountains, this sequence can be seen to articulate the Pétainist principles that families should continue the work of their forebears and develop the land as a means of strengthening the country for the future. Starting with a slow tracking shot as Frasne and Roquevillard stroll across a field, the sequence calls attention to the way in which La Vigie has been built on the efforts of several generations of Roquevillards. 'Each piece of land has its history,' François explains. Describing himself as a custodian of the land rather than its proprietor, he points to the fields, woods and vineyard that he and his ancestors have acquired for the estate. As he reflects on his duty to continue to expand the ancestral domain, François then looks towards the cemetery, the camera matching his point of view as he declares that previous generations of Roquevillards are buried there so as to keep watch over the property. Writing in the newspaper *Aujourd'hui* on 30 August 1943, in a review that appears to refer directly to this sequence, Hélène Garcin praised Dréville's cinematography for capturing the Savoyard countryside in a manner that she believed surpassed Bordeaux's novel. 'The presence of a stunning mountain range, in the background of the exquisite "Vigie", she claimed, 'makes us understand the character of this region much better than all of the text borrowed from Henry Bordeaux.'[38] However, as this sequence illustrates, Dréville does not simply translate Bordeaux's landscape descriptions into cinematic language; he also invests them with political meaning. By linking this visual emphasis on the countryside with the theme of family tradition, the film can be seen to exploit Bordeaux's text in order to promote a distinctly Pétainist agenda.

The climactic sequence in *Les Roquevillard* reasserts Bordeaux and Pétain's shared belief in the preservation of traditional social hierarchies. Like *Les Inconnus dans la maison*, Dréville's film stages a dramatic courtroom sequence in which Maurice stands falsely accused of stealing 200,000 francs from Frasne's safe prior to eloping to Italy with Édith. Restricted in his defence by Maurice's refusal to accuse Édith of the crime, François evokes the past achievements of his family in an attempt to persuade the jury of his son's innocence. His witnesses, he claims, are those ancestors 'whose names are inscribed in the stones of our region', who gave the town its municipal laws and 'whose dust has made this Savoyard land that we love'. Drawing much of its dialogue directly from the novel, this sequence exploits the formidable screen presence of Vanel, who during the war remained a committed, and very public, supporter of the Vichy regime. In a series of low-angle shots which present the actor as a towering, authoritative figure in the courtroom, François declares that the mere fact of being a Roquevillard should be proof enough of Maurice's innocence. As this impassioned speech reaches its conclusion, the film clearly endorses this argument with an overhead shot that captures the public gallery erupting in cries of 'bravo!', before the camera cuts to the disbelieving Frasne, who realizes that he has now lost the case as well as his wife. This deeply reactionary address proves faithful to the social elitism espoused by Bordeaux, who depicts the Roquevillards as triumphing over Frasne's jealousy and vindictiveness precisely because of their ancestry and historical prestige. However, what is more relevant in terms of the political resonance of the film is that this defence of the ruling class echoes the anti-egalitarianism of the Vichy government. For Pétain, France's great, ancestral families had a fundamental role to play in the country's moral and social regeneration, and their place in the social hierarchy should be respected. In its obvious support for this ideological position, Dréville's reworking of *Les Roquevillard* appears as one of the most overtly Pétainist adaptations of the Occupation period.

In comparison with *Les Roquevillard*, Jacques Becker's 1943 version of *Goupi Mains Rouges* reveals a much more ambiguous engagement with Pétainism. Adapted for the screen by Pierre Véry, the author of the 1937 novel on which the film was based, *Goupi Mains Rouges* proved one of the most successful releases of the Occupation period, both critically and commercially. The film also consolidated Becker's reputation as a director in his own right. 'So much creative artistry', wrote Roger Régent in reference to *Goupi Mains Rouges* in 1948, 'showed us in a stunning way that Jacques Becker was a director who knew how to *make a film*.'[39] Véry's screenplay revolves around the return of Eugène Goupi from Paris to his native Charente, where his family plans for him to marry his cousin, Lily. However, far from being welcomed back into the fold, Eugène (nicknamed 'Goupi-Monsieur' by his provincial relatives) soon becomes the main suspect in the theft of 10,000 francs from the Goupi household and the murder of the family matriarch, Tisane. Apart from its interest as a murder-mystery, *Goupi Mains Rouges* stands out as a film whose portrait of rural France appears to run counter to Pétainist discourse, which preached a return to the land as the first step towards rebuilding the country's moral and intellectual strength. Central to this vision was the figure of the peasant, which the National Revolution characterized as a decent, hard-working citizen. Becker's adaptation of *Goupi Mains Rouges*, argues Jacques Siclier, refused to share this perspective and 'gave the official ideology a good kick'⁴⁰ by representing peasants as insular, prone to violence and, above all, obsessed with money. These negative traits are reflected in the opening sequence of the film, in which the Goupis await the arrival of Eugène. At the outset, Becker warns us not to expect an idealized portrayal of the countryside as the first shot shows the Goupi farmhouse under a menacing sky filled with dark clouds. The director then cuts to the courtyard, where the servant Marie washes bottles, surrounded by chickens and geese. The scene appears as a gentle, pastoral depiction of the daily workings of a farmhouse. However, Becker quickly undermines this impression by cutting to a shot of Tisane, who peers out suspiciously from a nearby window, as if to check that her servant is working. Finally, the camera follows Marie back into the inn run by the head of the household, Moneybags. Emphasizing the Goupis' avaricious nature, Véry's script has Moneybags explain that he did not want to collect Eugène from the station for fear of having to close the inn and losing custom. In representing peasants as individuals who are motivated by money rather than altruism, Becker and Véry seem to delight in undermining Pétain's vision of a morally wholesome countryside.

A closer analysis of the way in which *Goupi Mains Rouges* adapts its source text shows, however, that the film is not the straightforward subversion of Vichy's agrarian ideology that it first appears to be. Through the changes he makes to Véry's text in adaptation, Becker can be seen to make his film conform more closely to the image of the countryside promulgated by the National Revolution. As Gregory Sims has argued in a richly detailed study of the film, this conformist tendency – which was likely to have been driven by Becker's desire to avoid censorship – is most obvious in the scene in which Eugène returns to the stable, where his family has locked him away on suspicion of theft and murder.⁴¹ As he walks back from the farmhouse to his makeshift prison, Eugène loosens his tie, removes his jacket and rolls up his sleeves, as if shedding the outward signifiers of his urban past and embracing his true, rural identity. He pauses to contemplate the landscape, the camera reflecting his point of view with a slow pan from right to left that highlights the beauty of the countryside. As the shot arcs back towards the farm, we then see Lily, who approaches Eugène and smiles warmly as she holds out a packet of cigarettes. Finally, the pair sit down on the hillside, where, in a moment that recalls the biblical paradise of the Garden of Eden, they share an apple (see Figure 3.3). With its emphasis on the natural landscape and the sensuality of the peasant girl Lily, this scene reflects clearly the simple, idyllic image of rural life that was central to Vichy thought. As Sims points out, however, the fact that it does so is very much a product of Becker's adaptation, which attenuates the raw, naturalist depiction of Eugène's imprisonment that Véry presents in the novel.⁴² In contrast to the source text, in which Eugène emerges from the

FIGURE 3.3 Goupi Mains Rouges (It Happened at the Inn) *(1943, dir. Becker).*

stable 'with a four-day-old beard',[43] in the film he is clean-shaven except for his neatly trimmed moustache. By a similar token, the novel does not invest Lily's clandestine visit to the stable with the same Edenic connotations as the film. Instead of offering to share an apple as he does on-screen, in the source text Eugène attempts to persuade his provincial cousin to smoke one of his cigarettes. As his reworking of this sequence illustrates, Becker softens and romanticizes the much harsher representation of rural life contained in Véry's novel and, in so doing, appears to promote rather than subvert Pétain's agrarian discourse.

To interpret *Goupi Mains Rouges* as pro-Vichy in its treatment of the countryside would nevertheless be to oversimplify the way in which the film also revels in its political ambiguity. This ambiguity is illustrated by the final sequence in the film, in which the oldest of the Goupis, nicknamed the Emperor, reveals to Mains Rouges that the family gold is hidden in the weights and pendulum of the grandfather clock. The subsequent scene appears as a homily to Pétainist values, as Mains Rouges (Fernand Ledoux) tells his relatives that he knows where the gold is, but that its location must remain secret, 'because it is found money rather than earned money'. Explaining that the gold can only be used in the event of a financial emergency to protect the Goupis' land, he turns to Eugène and declares that peasants respect money because 'money is work'. This scene, which does not feature in the novel, presents such a glowing tribute to the peasantry that it seems an obvious attempt on the part of Becker and Véry to ensure that the film escaped censorship. However, as Tony Williams observes, the final shot of the film is much more ambiguous in its political resonance.[44] Panning left away from the dinner table, Becker first shows us the Emperor lying in bed in the background of the shot. In the same movement, the camera then pans back right and dollies in to a close-up of the golden pendulum swinging inside the grandfather clock (see Figure 3.4). According to Sims, this closing shot represents an 'unmistakable metaphorical move ... into the sphere of the timeless, or at least a temporality based on an unbroken family line, which is precisely the temporality attributed to the peasantry in the official discourse of the "return to the land" '.[45] Alternatively, for Williams, this final shot could be interpreted as a 'symbol of the economic greed that has characterized the Goupis throughout the film' and as a 'critique of the right-wing materialism behind the veil of Vichy propaganda'.[46] What is intriguing about this shot, however, is not simply that it is ambiguous but that it performs the political ambiguity that runs throughout the film. With a camera movement that moves left, right and then forwards, Becker illustrates

FIGURE 3.4 Goupi Mains Rouges (It Happened at the Inn) *(1943, dir. Becker).*

his reluctance to commit to any one ideological perspective. Like the camera that changes direction several times, his version of *Goupi Mains Rouges* reveals its ambivalence towards Pétainism, resulting in a depiction of rural life that ultimately defies political classification.

Adaptation as Occupation: *Le Dernier des six* and *L'Assassin habite au 21*

In its often ambiguous representation of the politics of the time, the adaptive output of occupied France invites further consideration of the way in which adaptation functioned as an artistic process between 1940 and 1944. The concept of occupation – a concept that revolves around the idea of taking possession of another's space and attempting to impose a new identity on it – appears as an invaluable framework through which to explore some of the key ways in which adaptors reinterpreted literary texts during this period. Analysis of Henri Lacombe's *Le Dernier des six* (1941) and Henri-Georges Clouzot's *L'Assassin habite au 21* (1942) shows in particular how wartime directors and screenwriters often engaged in an aggressive appropriation of their source material that saw them disregard fidelity and promote their own artistic concerns over those of the original author.

Both based on murder-mystery novels by the Belgian writer Stanislas-André Steeman, *Le Dernier des six* and *L'Assassin habite au 21* provided Continental with two of the most profitable releases of the Occupation period. *Le Dernier des six* appears as the less innovative of the two films, both technically and thematically, and as a result has failed to garner as much critical attention as its sequel. However, the film is particularly worthy of interest for the way in which the authorial identity of Clouzot can be seen to impose itself over that of the original author Steeman. The plot of *Le Dernier des six* revolves around six friends who win a bet and agree to go their separate ways for five years, so that each can attempt to grow his initial stake and eventually share the profits with the others. As the time approaches for the supposed friends to reconvene, one of them is murdered, leaving Commissaire Wenceslas Vorobeïtchik (otherwise known as Wens, played by Pierre Fresnay) to investigate the case. In recreating this story for the screen, Steeman worked in collaboration with Clouzot, but later conceded that little of his novel remained in the film version. This was due to the adaptive strategy employed by Clouzot, who would only 'build something', Steeman complained, 'after having *contemptuously* demolished any resemblance to the original, purely for the ambition of *effect*'.[47] Clouzot's determination to stamp his own artistic vision on *Le Dernier des six* is reflected in the extensive changes that he makes to Steeman's plot in adaptation. In several instances, he discards episodes from the source text entirely and replaces them with scenes which better illustrate his own, largely pessimistic, view of humanity. Such pessimism is illustrated by the sequence in which Wens and his fellow officers discover the body of one of the eponymous six, Gribbe, in a hotel room. In contrast to the source text, in which the murdered Gribbe is found in a lift shaft, Clouzot writes a sequence that is populated by the kind of weak, self-serving characters who would become typical of his later films. These include a spineless hotel owner, who after unlocking the door to Gribbe's room tells Wens, 'You go in first'. Upon discovering the body, Wens then reprimands one of his officers for failing to keep Gribbe under surveillance for his own protection. 'You will have that on your conscience,' remarks Wens, with obvious disgust at his colleague's negligence. In rewriting the source text for the screen, Clouzot forcefully appropriates Steeman's work and occupies it with his own, bleak perspective on society.

The manner in which the film version of *Le Dernier des six* imposes its own artistic concerns on the source text is further reflected in Lacombe's cinematography, which clearly exhibits some of the key techniques and characteristics of early film noir. These elements are especially prominent in the closing sequence of this adaptation, which unmasks the killer as Gernicot, who had faked his own death earlier in the film. In the novel, Steeman resolves the mystery in a somewhat conventional manner by describing how Wens and another member of the eponymous six, Perlonjour, lure Gernicot to a meeting in a dark apartment. In a final moment of suspense and revelation reminiscent of the detective novels of Agatha Christie, Gernicot enters the room, where Perlonjour suddenly exposes the killer's identity by shining a torch in his face. As Gernicot attempts to escape down the stairs, Wens follows quickly behind and shoots him dead. Echoing the artistic aggression shown by Clouzot in reworking Steeman's plot, Lacombe transforms this ending into a technically intricate sequence that uses light and shadow in a manner that would become a recurring feature of subsequent noir thrillers. In representing Gernicot's arrival at the climactic meeting, Lacombe shoots actor Lucien Nat from behind, making him appear as a silhouetted – and at this stage still unidentified – figure at the window. After firing a shot and missing his intended targets, Gernicot then flees across a field, pursued by Wens and his men who wear the familiar noir attire of trilbies and brown raincoats. The closing scenes of the film evoke the noir aesthetic even more deliberately, as Gernicot is shown attempting to escape through an underground cave. Lacombe's camerawork creates a disorientating effect, as Gernicot descends ever deeper into the labyrinthine network of tunnels, each of which fails to lead to an exit. Finally, in a moment of entrapment that is equally noir in its resonance, the killer takes the last remaining option of crossing a muddy pool, into which he sinks and drowns. Far from simply transposing Steeman's ending to the screen, Lacombe takes ownership of this sequence and re-imagines it, both visually and thematically, in a distinctly noir style.

As well as reflecting the artistic vision of Clouzot and Lacombe, *Le Dernier des six* illustrates how Continental sought to occupy the cinematic territory that American films had held in France before the war. One of the ways in which *Le Dernier des six* attempted to do this was by evoking the glamour and spectacle of Hollywood musicals of the 1930s. As Evelyn Ehrlich observes, the film contains a notable sequence that draws on the work of American choreographer and musical director Busby Berkeley.[48] During the 1930s, Berkeley had choreographed many of Hollywood's most acclaimed musicals, including *42nd Street* (1933, dir. Bacon) and *The Gold Diggers of 1933* (1933, dir. Le Roy). His musical numbers typically featured a large cast of female dancers performing in geometric patterns whose intricacy was highlighted by the frequent use of overhead shots. Equally characteristic of Berkeley's style were the elaborate sets on which these numbers were often staged. As we saw in Chapter 2, people and personalities can exert a powerful influence on the way in which French literature is reinvented on the screen. Such influence is clear in *Le Dernier des six*, which adapts Berkeley in its own musical number set in Senterre's nightclub. This sequence immediately calls to mind the American choreographer's innovative use of camera angles by showing a group of female dancers reflected in the polished stage, followed by an overhead shot of the dancers twirling in white dresses. Serving as a prelude to the cabaret act of the markswoman Lolita, the number – which has no equivalent in the source text – proceeds to echo Berkeley's artistic enthusiasm for trick shots and visual effects. A double exposure, for example, shows three dancers falling from the tops of water fountains as Lolita shoots the balloons they are holding. A further trick shot then presents a miniature woman frolicking topless in a champagne glass. In her analysis of this production number, Ehrlich points out that director Lacombe lost his job over his refusal to shoot this sequence, which he felt was incongruous with the rest of the film. Continental insisted that the segment should be included, resulting in Lacombe being replaced as director by Jean Dréville.[49] However, the element that is particularly intriguing in this sequence is that it ends with a French can-can. Relocating the dancers from the vast stage, Dréville films them closer to the bar and tables, thus creating a more intimate, French-style cabaret setting. In a series of close-ups of the dancers' high kicks and twirling skirts, the director evokes the energy and excitement of the can-can, before cutting to a shot of the audience as it breaks into rapturous applause. As this sequence stakes its claim to the

FIGURE 3.5 Le Dernier des six (The Last of the Six) *(1941, dir. Lacombe).*

cinematic space previously occupied by Berkeley's musical numbers, so, too, does it appear as a proud reassertion of French culture and a symbol of resistance to the Nazis (see Figures 3.5 and 3.6).

Continental's determination to capture the market share that before the war had belonged to American films is further illustrated by the company's exploitation of the *Thin Man* series. Inspired by Dashiell Hammett's 1934 novel *The Thin Man*, the first in this series of detective comedies was released by MGM that same year and proved so popular with audiences that it subsequently spawned five sequels. Starring William Powell as private detective Nick Charles and Myrna Loy as his wife Nora, the films were based on a formula of fast-paced action and visual gags. A recurring feature of the series was also the comic repartee between Nick and Nora, who seek repeatedly to better each other's capacity for sarcasm and cutting humour. As Ehrlich has argued compellingly, the intertextual presence of the *Thin Man* films is evident in *Le*

FIGURE 3.6 Le Dernier des six (The Last of the Six) *(1941, dir. Lacombe).*

Dernier des six and is particularly obvious in Clouzot's version of *L'Assassin habite au 21*, in which Wens attempts to catch a Paris serial killer who goes by the name of Monsieur Durand.[50] Echoing the slick humour of *The Thin Man*, one of the early sequences in the film shows the order to catch Durand being passed down through the various levels of government and the police, with the minister, prefect and police commissioner each giving the man beneath him an ever-diminishing amount of time to solve the case. Finally, the order reaches Wens, who, in a visual joke that is highly reminiscent of the *Thin Man* series, simply leaves a note on his desk with the words 'understood, if I don't catch Durand in two days, I'm fired'. More obviously, *L'Assassin habite au 21* adapts the *Thin Man* formula by pairing Wens with his endearing but short-tempered girlfriend Mila-Malou (Suzy Delair), neither of whom features in Steeman's novel (see Figure 3.7). The relationship between Wens and the combustible Mila recalls the incisive comic exchanges between their fictional counterparts Nick and Nora, not least in the scene in which Wens is preparing to leave his apartment in order to take up residence at the Pension Mimosas, where he knows that one of the guests is the murderer Durand. Suspicious that Wens may be going to visit another woman, Mila resorts to an array of tactics to prevent him from leaving, from removing his toothbrush from his

FIGURE 3.7 L'Assassin habite au 21 (The Murderer Lives at Number 21) *(1942, dir. Clouzot).*

suitcase to promising to be nice for a week. Finally, as Wens departs, the camera shows Mila following him onto the landing, where, in anticipation of the danger that her partner is about to face, she calls out, 'Did you draw up a will?' In its humour, characterization and rapid-fire dialogue, *L'Assassin habite au 21* readily imposes the *Thin Man* template on Steeman's work in adaptation, resulting in a detective comedy that is heavily Americanized in both style and conception.

While appropriating material from Hollywood cinema and the *Thin Man* series, *L'Assassin habite au 21* simultaneously effaces the British content of its source text. Steeman's novel was originally set in London, and the author hoped that the film would retain this British setting, which he considered integral to the atmosphere and sense of mystery that he wished to evoke. Steeman explained of his novel:

> *L'Assassin habite au 21* took place in London, in the fog, and I would have liked to have made it into a symphony in grey in the style of *Dr Jekyll and Mister Hyde*. But if one thinks back to the events of that time, I was not surprised to learn that the action had to be situated in Paris.[51]

Perhaps not wanting to antagonize his employers at Continental, Clouzot chose not to depict Germany's enemy Britain on-screen and eliminated the British context of Steeman's plot in adaptation. Accordingly, the murderer, who in the novel carries the distinctly British name Mr Smith, becomes Monsieur Durand in the film. Similarly, his address is relocated from number 21 in London's Russell Square to 21 Avenue Junot in Paris. However, if these changes were made in order not to offend the political sensibilities of the Germans, they can also be seen to generate – perhaps inadvertently – a critique of the Occupation. As Colin Crisp observes, 'the (voluntary) suppression of any reference to Britain in the occupation cinema resulted in London's "evil atmosphere" being transferred to France, and implicitly attributed to the German occupation'.[52] In the case of *L'Assassin habite au 21*, the effect of this transferral is illustrated by the opening sequence of the film, in which a drunkard boasts of winning the lottery before being murdered by Monsieur Durand. In the novel, this first murder occurs on a London night so murky, writes Steeman, that Mr Smith's victim 'falls without a cry, and is enveloped by the fog before he hits the ground'.[53] Displaying the same kind of artistic aggression that had characterized his approach to adapting *Le Dernier des six*, Clouzot re-imagines this episode entirely and resituates it in Paris. First, we see the unwitting victim leave a café, having announced his intention to walk across the city towards Jaurès. In a point-of-view shot filmed from the perspective of the killer, the camera then follows the increasingly anxious man along the winding pavement, eventually backing him into a doorway where Monsieur Durand stabs him with a long dagger concealed inside a walking cane. Apart from reflecting Clouzot's cinematic artistry, this sequence appears, retrospectively, to return us to the political context of the war. By moving a Parisian setting into the narrative space that London occupies in the source text, *L'Assassin habite au 21* depicts France as violent and filled with hidden danger – a situation for which the film implies the Nazis are responsible.

In their aggressive approach to recreating their source texts, *Le Dernier des six* and *L'Assassin habite au 21* enable us to align the concepts of adaptation and occupation in a variety of ways. Both films impose a new set of artistic concerns on Steeman's novels, such as the bleak pessimism and film noir style that Clouzot and Lacombe bring to their adaptive process. More broadly, these films show us how Continental extended the German military occupation into the cinematic sphere by appropriating key techniques from Hollywood musicals and detective comedies. In enabling us to rethink adaptation as a form of occupation, *Le Dernier des six* and *L'Assassin habite au 21* ultimately point back to the atmosphere of fear and anxiety that enveloped France during this period. In so doing, they encourage us to consider the way in which filmmakers used adaptation to explore the effects of the Occupation on French national identity.

Adaptation, ambiguity and the representation of national schizophrenia (1941–3)

Despite their engagement with artistic representations of Britain and America, it was to the political situation at home that French wartime adaptations remained most sensitive. In the final part of this chapter, I want to examine two films, René Le Hénaff's *Le Colonel Chabert* (1943) and Christian-Jaque's *L'Assassinat du Père Noël* (1941), focusing on how these adaptations can be seen to reflect the crisis of national identity that France faced under the Occupation. These films place questions of collective trauma, uncertain identity and mental instability at the heart of their aesthetic concerns. In so doing, they reveal the creative dexterity with which adaptations dramatized the country's wider struggle to rebuild and redefine itself during this period.

The theme of fractured identity plays a prominent role in Le Hénaff's version of Balzac's 1832 novel *Le Colonel Chabert*. Like its source text, the film recounts the tale of a Napoleonic veteran who, having been declared dead at the Battle of Eylau in 1807, returns to Paris ten years later to find his wife remarried and his fortune gone. Le Hénaff's reworking of this plot was based on a screenplay by Pierre Benoit, who as an established novelist and member of the Académie française was well equipped to lend the film the kind of artistic prestige befitting of Balzac. His involvement nevertheless failed to translate into critical or commercial success for *Le Colonel Chabert*, which received a lukewarm reception upon its release in 1943. Writing in *Je suis partout* on 10 December, Lucien Rebatet claimed that the canonical status of Balzac's text had prevented Le Hénaff from exploiting fully the possibilities of his own medium. 'Balzac went much higher and much further in this novella,' Rebatet declared. 'But it [Balzac's work] is too illustrious to enable one to change anything about it.'[54] In addition to Rebatet's disappointment at what he viewed as the overly literary style of the production, Max Bihan, film critic for the newspaper *Comœdia*, questioned the wisdom of casting the portly Raimu as a haunted military veteran. 'M. Raimu is bursting with good health,' Bihan complained, 'the fat leaps out through his make-up from every pore, a defiant pot-belly goes before him everywhere. Chabert was a ghost, he is a hippopotamus.'[55]

That scholars have remained similarly unimpressed by this film is, however, surprising given the specific resonance that the plot of *Le Colonel Chabert* acquires within the context of the Second World War. As James Travers observes, 'it is possible to interpret the film as a subtle allegory of France under occupation. Colonel Chabert, a supporter of the republican ideal and loyal follower of Napoleon, personifies the nation that has had her identity stolen.'[56] As is so often the case in scholarly discussions of wartime adaptations, such casual comparisons nevertheless fail to consider how the film actively resituates its source material within a contemporary context. One of the ways in which Le Hénaff does this in his version of *Le Colonel Chabert* is by highlighting the collective nature of the eponymous soldier's experience. Whereas the novel had explored the private, domestic implications of Chabert's struggle, the film presents his crisis of identity as a form of shared, and indeed national, trauma. This sense of collective crisis starts to build in a sequence that has no direct equivalent in the novel, in which Chabert narrowly escapes being imprisoned in an asylum. At the level of both plot and mise en scène, Le Hénaff underscores how Chabert's situation quickly embroils those around him, as one after another characters are sucked into its orbit. Moments of shared crisis abound in this sequence. The first of these occurs between Chabert and his driver, who exchange a hard stare as the old soldier realizes that he is about to be locked away and then flees into the woods. Chabert's escape triggers a full-blown manhunt, represented by a series of shots which become progressively more overcrowded as the asylum owner and his orderlies join the search. As the uniformed orderlies track Chabert through the bushes, we see them first in pairs and threes, and then, as their search becomes increasingly desperate, in a group of four. Cutting between shots of Chabert and his dogged pursuers, Le Hénaff reinforces the sense of collective crisis that envelops the characters in this scene by showing them all being soaked by a torrential storm. As this sequence illustrates, Chabert's battle to reclaim his identity does not end with him, but spreads through an ever-widening sphere of his compatriots.

In extending Chabert's crisis from the private to the collective domain, Le Hénaff can be seen to link this struggle to the national crisis of identity faced by occupied France. The sequence in which Chabert recounts his story to the lawyer Derville deserves special attention in this regard, since it appears to contain an implicit reference to this wartime context. As Anne-Marie Baron points out, this scene is notable for its vivid special effect, in which Chabert's eyes glow with the memory of Murat's cavalry charge at Eylau.[57] Less obvious, however, is the way in which Le Hénaff adapts the narrative perspective of the novel in order to emphasize the shared nature of Chabert's experience. In Balzac's text, the Napoleonic veteran describes his memories of Eylau in a stirring first-person address that privileges his own viewpoint. Le Hénaff retains much of this personal perspective in adaptation but at the same time highlights its collective resonance by dissolving into images of the cavalry charge. This flashback – which was filmed using officers and horses from the Paris cavalry regiment – appears, in the words of Véronique Monteilhet, as a 'depersonalization' of Chabert's story which removes the protagonist from his own tale and underscores that there were thousands of other soldiers like him.[58] What is significant about this subtle loosening of the first-person perspective, however, is that it also invites contemporary spectators to identify with Chabert's plight. As the old soldier prepares to leave Derville's office, he summarizes his situation by declaring that he is not alone in suffering the consequences of Napoleon's defeat. 'Our sun has set,' he sighs, 'we are all cold now.' For Chabert, the collapse of the Empire has deprived him of his former identity and France of strong, authoritarian government. Within the context of the Occupation, these words nevertheless carry a different political charge. Transposed directly into the film from Balzac's text, this sentence – which also found its way into the screenplay of *Pontcarral, colonel d'empire*[59] – can be interpreted as a coded reference to France's situation under the Germans. By retaining the phrase in this sequence, Le Hénaff and screenwriter Benoit appear – perhaps unwittingly – to encourage spectators to compare Chabert's loss to that of wartime France. Chabert's crisis, the film suggests, is also 'ours'. Instead of the glories of empire, France has Nazi oppression. Similarly, rather than an energetic leader such as Napoleon, France has the aged Pétain. By guiding the audience towards a collective viewpoint, the film can be interpreted as an attempt to transform Chabert's private struggle into a bitter lament at the national trauma of defeat and occupation.[60]

The notion of collective crisis proves similarly important to the plot of Christian-Jaque's 1941 film *L'Assassinat du Père Noël*. Inspired by Pierre Véry's 1934 novel of the same title, the film was the first production released by Continental in the wake of the German restructuring of the French film industry. Adapted for the screen by Charles Spaak, who worked with Pierre Véry in writing the screenplay, *L'Assassinat du Père Noël* is a murder-mystery that revolves loosely around the theft of a valuable diamond from a small Savoyard church on Christmas Eve. Among the first to fall under suspicion is Père Cornusse (Harry Baur), a globe-maker who every year delights in playing the role of Santa Claus for the village children. As Crisp has noted, Christian-Jaque's adaptation belongs to an unusual category of rural gothic films which during the Occupation tended to feature eccentric characters and fantastical themes. 'Never less than weird, and often, as their titles suggest, rather sinister, these films', writes Crisp, 'focus on remote provincial regions preferably cut off temporarily from all contact with urban France.'[61] *L'Assassinat du Père Noël* appears as a model of the genre in these respects. Faithful to Véry's conceptualization of murder-mysteries as fairy tales for adults, the film presents a strange, fantastical netherworld populated by eccentric characters. The central figure in this cast is Cornusse, who revels in telling the village children stories about a fictitious Chinese outlaw, Fi-Zhou, but admits that he has never left the confines of his own region. The globe-maker's daughter Catherine, meanwhile, lives in her own fairy-tale world, in which she makes dolls and refuses to marry the local schoolteacher, Villard, because he does not carry a sword or ride past her window on horseback. As befits its fantastical aesthetic, this cast also includes a mysterious Baron, who feigns leprosy in order to keep his curious provincial neighbours at a distance. In depicting a community that appears so disconnected from reality, *L'Assassinat du Père Noël* provides the earliest reflection of Continental's aim to produce non-political films that were far removed from the ideological debates of the time.

If *L'Assassinat du Père Noël* appears as one of the strangest films of the Occupation, it nonetheless speaks powerfully to the sense of 'national schizophrenia' that Hayward claims is largely absent from the French cinema of this period.[62] One of the elements of the film that is particularly significant in this respect is its representation of the village as a community riven by mental illness, moral degeneracy and physical malady. These aspects are prominent in Christian-Jaque's portrayal of the local madwoman, La Mère Michel, and her determination to expose the pharmacist Ricomet as the architect behind the crime. In contrast to the novel, in which La Mère Michel is never identified explicitly as suffering from madness, the film dwells repeatedly on her mental instability and obsessive behaviour, as she wanders the village searching endlessly for her cat, Mitsou. This search culminates in a sequence in which she interrupts a town council meeting and vents a series of accusations which threaten to expose the corruption behind Ricomet's outward image of bourgeois respectability. These accusations range from theft ('he stole my savings') to sexual deviancy ('he wears women's stockings') and criminal malpractice ('he puts arsenic in all his medicine'). Quickly turning defence into attack, Ricomet responds by arguing that La Mère Michel's home should be searched. In the next scene, we see the men from the town council breaking down the door of the madwoman's home, where they find not the missing diamond but Mitsou, stuffed, inside a cupboard. This sequence invites allegorical interpretation on a number of levels. Most obviously, the madness of La Mère Michel, coupled with the accusations she hurls at Ricomet, echo the Pétainist notion of France as a morally degenerate society that had sown the seeds of its own defeat in 1940. Equally, the pharmacist's contradictory behaviour can be viewed as reflecting that of the Vichy government. In a manner reminiscent of Pétain, who advocated the need for a moral regeneration of France while sacrificing the country to his collaborationist policies, Ricomet claims to be caring for his patients while simultaneously undermining their well-being. In his portrait of a corrupt, diseased community, Christian-Jaque invites spectators to reflect on the political schizophrenia of a government that is torn between protecting and persecuting its citizens.

Despite this bleak depiction of a corrupt, crisis-stricken community, *L'Assassinat du Père Noël* ends more optimistically by emphasizing the triumph of traditional values in the face of adversity. In the closing sequence of the film, we see Père Cornusse, duly restored to his role as Santa Claus, marching through the snow followed by a group of village children. The camera then cuts to him entering the bedroom of Christian, a young boy previously struck down by an illness that throughout the film has prevented him from walking. Holding up one of his globes, Cornusse invites the child to walk across the room to claim his gift, which, after climbing tentatively from his bed, he does (see Figure 3.8). Moving to a close-up of the Christmas tree, Christian-Jaque proceeds to pan through the branches, bringing us ultimately to a shot of Catherine and the Baron, who delicately attaches a pair of earrings to his beloved's ears. The voice of Cornusse links these two scenes, as we hear him tell Christian that Catherine has been 'sleeping for so, so long', and that 'she dreamt of a Prince Charming who would come one day to wake her'. Though steeped in melodrama, this sequence lends itself readily to a political reading. For Travers, the return of Cornusse as Santa Claus can be interpreted as a gesture of defiance towards the Nazis, one which proves

FIGURE 3.8 L'Assassinat du Père Noël (The Killing of Santa Claus) *(1941, dir. Christian-Jaque).*

that ideals and traditions cannot be killed.[63] At the same time, this sequence contains a double awakening – that of Christian from illness and Catherine to love – which could be seen to articulate the hope that France would one day be awakened from the slumber of occupation. Such a reading must nevertheless be treated with caution, for as Ehrlich warns, 'the expectation or hope of eventual liberation was a rarely expressed sentiment in 1941. Far more common was an incipient reappearance of French nationalism, which was discreetly encouraged by Vichy.'[64] It is impossible to know whether contemporary spectators interpreted the film in these terms. This ending nevertheless presents a positive counterweight to the film's representation of a degenerate society and, in the final images of Christian and Catherine, highlights the promise of recovery, renewal and enduring happiness.

The adaptive output of occupied France proves a compelling case study through which to explore the relationship between politics and adaptation. Despite the practical and political difficulties that weighed upon the French film industry between 1940 and 1944, adaptations featured among the most commercially successful and critically acclaimed films of this period. Far from being immune to the politics of the time, adaptations were acutely sensitive to the political and ideological context of their production. Whether engaging with the theme of resistance in *Pontcarral, colonel d'empire*, or collaboration in *La Main du diable*, filmmakers developed innovative ways of circumventing censorship to dramatize political arguments. However, analysis of French literature films produced under the Occupation illustrates that they are often politicized in ambivalent, ambiguous ways. In its treatment of family life, for example, *Les Inconnus dans la maison* can be seen to conform to aspects of both Nazi and Pétainist ideology, and ultimately complicates its own political message. In so doing, such films appear not merely as politicized artefacts but as works that actively perform their ideological ambiguity – a feature reflected most obviously in *Goupi Mains Rouges*, in which the changing direction of Becker's camera in the final shot of the film signals the director's ambition to transcend simple ideological boundaries. If politics is a recurring feature of these films, it also suggests a framework for understanding how cinematographers approached the practice of adaptation during this period. In their attempts to fill the void left by Hollywood films, *Le Dernier des six* and *L'Assassin habite au 21* show that adaptation can be viewed as a form of occupation in which a new, often politicized identity is imposed on the source text. Despite the ostensibly innocuous entertainment that such films provided, they can be seen to reflect, finally, on the crisis of national identity that France experienced under the Occupation. In *Le Colonel Chabert* and *L'Assassinat du Père Noël*, we find echoes of this national trauma in the representation of collective crisis and mental instability, both elements of a broader, political schizophrenia that scholars have thus far been reluctant to discern in the French cinema of this period. The capacity of adaptations to engage with the national context of their production would remain a key factor in post-war cinema, as reworkings of literary texts assumed a key role in the country's attempts to reconcile itself with the painful and problematic legacy of the war years.

Notes

1. Jean-Pierre Bertin-Maghit, '*L'éternel retour:* un choix idéologique', in *Cinéma et histoire: autour de Marc Ferro*, ed. François Garçon (Courbevoie: CinémAction-Corlet, 1992), 143.
2. Jacques Siclier, *La France de Pétain et son cinéma* (Paris: Henri Veyrier, 1981), 117, 124.
3. Florianne Wild, 'The Case of the Undead Emperor: Familial and National Identity in Jacques Becker's *Goupi Mains Rouges*', in *France in Focus: Film and National Identity*, ed. Elizabeth Ezra and Sue Harris (Oxford: Berg, 2000), 157.
4. François Truffaut, 'André Bazin, the Occupation, and I', in *French Cinema of the Occupation and Resistance: The Birth of a Critical Esthetic*, ed. André Bazin; intro. François Truffaut; trans. Stanley Hochman (New York: Frederick Ungar, 1984), 18.
5. Susan Hayward, *French National Cinema* (London: Routledge, 1993), 192–3.
6. See, for example, François Garçon, *De Blum à Pétain: cinéma et société française (1936–1944)* (Paris: Du Cerf, 1984); and Jean-Pierre Bertin-Maghit, *Le Cinéma français sous l'Occupation: le monde du cinéma français de 1940 à 1946* (Paris: Perrin, 2002).
7. Dan Hassler-Forest and Pascal Nicklas, eds, *The Politics of Adaptation: Media Convergence and Ideology* (London: Palgrave Macmillan, 2015), 1.
8. Hayward, *French National Cinema*, 140.
9. François Garçon, 'Ce curieux âge d'or des cinéastes français', *Politiques et pratiques culturelles dans la France de Vichy* (special issue of *Cahiers de l'Institut d'Histoire du Temps Présent*), 8 (June 1988): 193–206.
10. Cited by Colin Crisp, *The Classic French Cinema, 1930–1960* (Bloomington: Indiana University Press, 1993), 54.
11. Garçon, 'Ce curieux âge d'or', 202.
12. Crisp, *The Classic French Cinema*, 54.
13. Roy Armes, 'Cinema of Paradox: French Film-making during the Occupation', in *Collaboration in France: Politics and Culture during the Nazi Occupation,*

1940–1944, ed. Gerhard Hirschfeld and Patrick Marsh (Oxford: Berg, 1989), 134.

14 Françis Courtade, 'La Continental', in *Tendres ennemis: cent ans de cinéma entre la France et l'Allemagne*, ed. Heike Hurst and Heiner Gassen (Paris: L'Harmattan, 1991), 224.

15 Evelyn Ehrlich, *Cinema of Paradox: French Filmmaking under the German Occupation* (New York: Columbia University Press, 1985), 44.

16 Edwige Feuillère, *Les Feux de la mémoire* (Paris: Albin Michel, 1977), 137.

17 Garçon, 'Ce curieux âge d'or', 201.

18 Alan Riding indicates that at the start of the war, 15 per cent of workers in the French film industry (approximately nine thousand individuals out of sixty thousand) were Jewish (*And the Show Went On: Cultural Life in Nazi-Occupied Paris* (London: Duckworth, 2011), 189).

19 Stéphanie Corcy, *La Vie culturelle sous l'Occupation* (Paris: Perrin, 2005), 106.

20 Crisp, *The Classic French Cinema*, 56.

21 Honoré de Balzac, *La Comédie humaine*, ed. Pierre-Georges Castex, Roland Chollet and Rose Fortassier, 12 vols (Paris: Gallimard, Bibliothèque de la Pléiade, 1976–81), v. 5, 967–8.

22 Guy Paqui, *Jean Delannoy: ses années lumière, 1938–1992* (Toulon: Presses du Midi, 2010), 76.

23 Pierre Billard, *L'Âge Classique du cinéma français: du cinéma parlant à la Nouvelle Vague* (Paris: Flammarion, 1995), 393.

24 Francis Courtade, *Les Malédictions du cinéma français: une histoire du cinéma français parlant, 1928–1978* (Paris: Alain Moreau, 1978), 210.

25 Noël Burch and Geneviève Sellier, *The Battle of the Sexes in French Cinema, 1930–1956*, trans. Peter Graham (Durham, NC: Duke University Press, 2014), 122.

26 Hayward, *French National Cinema*, 197–8.

27 Colin Crisp, *French Cinema: A Critical Filmography*, 3 vols (Bloomington: Indiana University Press, 2015), v. 2 (1940–58), 59.

28 Cited by Christine Leteux, *Maurice Tourneur: réalisateur sans frontières* (Hellenvilliers: La Tour verte, 2015), 451.

29 Cited by Harry Waldman, *Maurice Tourneur: The Life and Films* (Jefferson, NC: McFarland, 2001), 164.

30 On the anti-collaborationist undertones of *La Main du diable*, see, for example, David Hanley, 'Serial Killers, Deals with the Devil, and the Madness of Crowds: The Horror Film in Nazi-Occupied France', in *Recovering 1940s Horror Cinema: Traces of a Lost Decade*, ed. Mario DeGiglio-Bellemare, Charlie Ellbé and Kristopher Woofter (Lanham, MD: Lexington, 2014), 191–2.

31 Georges Simenon, *Les Inconnus dans la maison* (Paris: Gallimard, 1941), 225.

32 Billard, *L'Âge classique du cinéma français*, 385.
33 Crisp, *French Cinema: A Critical Filmography*, 38.
34 Julian Jackson, *France: The Dark Years, 1940–1944* (Oxford: Oxford University Press, 2001), 320.
35 Françoise Holbane, '*Les Inconnus dans la maison*', *Paris-Midi* (26 May 1942): 2.
36 Audiberti, '*Les Inconnus dans la maison*', *Comœdia* (23 May 1942): 5.
37 Lucien Rebatet, *Quatre ans de cinéma (1940–1944)*, ed. Philippe d'Hugues, Philippe Billé, Pascal Manuel Heu and Marc Laudelout (Pardès: Grez-sur-Loing, 2009), 92.
38 Hélène Garcin, '*Les Roquevillard*', *Aujourd'hui* (30 August 1943): 2.
39 Roger Régent, *Cinéma de France de 'La Fille du Puisatier' aux 'Enfants du Paradis'* (Paris: Bellefaye, 1948), 133–4.
40 Siclier, *La France de Pétain et son cinéma*, 216.
41 Gregory Sims, 'Returning to the Fold: Questions of Ideology in Jacques Becker's *Goupi Mains Rouges* (1942)', *French Cultural Studies* 13 (2002): 5–31 (16–17).
42 Sims, 'Returning to the Fold', 24.
43 Pierre Véry, *Œuvres complètes*, ed. Jacques Baudou, 3 vols (Paris: Éditions du Masque-Hachette Livre, 1997), v. 3, 104.
44 Tony Williams, '*Goupi Mains Rouges*', *Senses of Cinema*, November 2014, http://sensesofcinema.com/2014/cteq/goupi-mains-rouges/.
45 Sims, 'Returning to the Fold', 18.
46 Williams, '*Goupi Mains Rouges*'.
47 Cited by Susan Hayward, '*Les Diaboliques*' (London: I.B. Tauris, 2005), 3.
48 Ehrlich, *Cinema of Paradox*, 48–9.
49 Ehrlich, *Cinema of Paradox*, 34.
50 Ehrlich, *Cinema of Paradox*, 48–9.
51 Cited by José-Luis Bocquet and Marc Godin, *Henri-Georges Clouzot cinéaste* (Sèvres: La Sirène, 1993), 28.
52 Crisp, *French Cinema: A Critical Filmography*, 50.
53 Stanislas-André Steeman, *L'Assassin habite au 21* (Paris: Poche, 1939), 5.
54 Rebatet, *Quatre ans de cinéma*, 244.
55 Max Bihan, '*Le Colonel Chabert*', *Comœdia* (11 December 1943): 5.
56 James Travers, '*Le Colonel Chabert* (1943)', 2007, http://www.filmsdefrance.com/review/le-colonel-chabert-1943.html.
57 Anne-Marie Baron, *Romans français du XIXe siècle à l'écran: problèmes de l'adaptation* (Clermont-Ferrand: Presses universitaires Blaise Pascal, 2008), 40.
58 Véronique Monteilhet, 'Les adaptations balzaciennes sous l'Occupation', *L'Année balzacienne* 3.1 (2002): 327–47 (345).

59 Garçon, *De Blum à Pétain*, 114–15.

60 For an alternative reading of *Le Colonel Chabert* which juxtaposes Benoit's collaborationist leanings with the pacifist resonance of the film, see Max Andréoli, 'Place de Balzac dans le cinéma français sous l'Occupation', in *Balzac à l'écran*, ed. Anne-Marie Baron, *CinémAction*, 173 (2019), 67–8.

61 Crisp, *French Cinema: A Critical Filmography*, 30.

62 Hayward, *French National Cinema*, 140.

63 James Travers, '*L'Assassinat du Père Noël* (1941)', 2002, http://www.filmsdefrance.com/review/l-assassinat-du-pere-noel-1941.html.

64 Ehrlich, *Cinema of Paradox*, 53–4.

4

The formative function of the dominant film poetics: The impact of film movement, moment and genre (1945–70)

Kate Griffiths

Having explored the currency in and of adaptation in Chapter 1, the interpersonal transactions of the people shaping it in Chapter 2 and the political forces impacting upon it in Chapter 3, this chapter considers the ways film movements and genres shape the adaptations made within them. It does so with a focus on the years between 1945 and 1970 as this offers an expanse of time large enough both to house multiple prominent movements and to permit the tracing of their interaction in a global context. Different film movements and genres in this era rework the same French texts, producing starkly divergent versions of them. This chapter will thus trace the adaptation and readaptation of core French literary sources within different movements and genres, assessing the impact and influence of those movements and genres. It will consider the French *tradition de qualité* (Tradition of Quality), the French New Wave which countered it, US musical films of this era, Italian Spaghetti Westerns, popular cinema from the golden age of Indian film and the British epic cinema of David Lean. It will do so via the prism of André Lefevere's contention that the dominant poetics of an era shape a work at least as much as its source text does. Collectively, the case study movements and genres of this chapter highlight that to seek only the source text in an adaptation is to miss the core formative function of the dominant film poetics at the time in which they were made.

Lefevere's concept of the 'dominant poetics' forms the theoretical framework through which this chapter seeks to evaluate adaptations made between 1945 and 1970. Lefevere argues that when we remake a source text for a new time and context, we shape that source text for the 'dominant poetics' of the target culture, accommodating it to the culture's tastes, values and politics.[1] He argues that we often recast the original to resonate with the poetics of our era simply to make it pleasing to the new audience and ensure that our audience engages with it both commercially and creatively.[2] Lefevere's value to adaptation studies is pronounced. His work offers a means to map the power and influence of film movements and genres on the source texts they remake. It underlines that those who seek just a source text in the adaptations made between 1945 and 1970 ignore powerful formative forces in their genesis in the form of the film poetics within which they were made.

Lefevere's theoretical framework demonstrates that movements matter and that the conventions of film genre impact upon the source text being adapted. For Lefevere, poetics, however dominant, are shifting in their power, as movements and genres mutate, evolve and endlessly react against each other. Movements in film between 1945 and 1970 enact his vision of poetics, defining both themselves and their approach to the French source texts they adapt in relation to each other. So too, Lefevere argues, are poetics geographically diverse. Hence, in order to do justice to Lefevere's vision, this chapter analyses the influence of film movements in diverse geographical contexts – France, the United States, Italy, India and the UK – in relation to its control texts: French literary sources from any era of publication.

The formative function of the French Tradition of Quality

The adaptation of French literary texts, particularly canonical ones, lies at the heart of the French Tradition of Quality. This film movement dominated French cinema prior to and in the 1950s. It cherished craft, established directors and the adaptation of classic works. Though critically and commercially dominant in its era, this movement is conspicuous in its near absence from the landscape of film criticism. So successful were the attempts of its cinematic successor in France, the New Wave and particularly filmmaker François Truffaut, to denigrate the Tradition of Quality that, Bill Nichols writes, 'most of the films [associated with this movement] are virtually unmentioned in recent film histories and seldom exhibited in English-speaking countries'.[3] Rodney Hill notes that in 2006, of the nineteen films written by Jean Aurenche and Pierre Bost, the scriptwriters whom Truffaut held up as the whipping boys for the Tradition of Quality, only three were available on home video in the North American market.[4]

The very existence of the Tradition of Quality and its determined attachment to the adaptation of canonical French literary sources stem from specific ideological and economic forces triggered in the aftermath of the Second World War. Building on the former Comité de l'Organisation de l'Industrie Cinématographique (COIC), the Centre National de la Cinématographie (CNC) came into being in post-war France. While the CNC continued, as Alan Williams points out, to 'control French cinema very much as the COIC had, through essentially the same regulatory mechanisms',[5] Susan Hayward proposes that the CNC marked a break from the past, from the institutions of the Occupation and a commitment to a resurgent, distinctly French national film industry.[6] The CNC was key to the generation of the term 'Tradition of Quality' and, in part, the ideology behind it. Rodney Hill writes:

> 'Tradition of Quality' originally was used by the Centre National de la Cinématographie (CNC), an arm of the French Ministry of Culture dedicated to maintaining a coherent national cinema strategy, to describe the kind of filmmaking that the French government wanted to promote in the postwar era.[7]

The genesis of the Tradition of Quality was not just ideological but also economic. France needed to compete with the powerhouse that was Hollywood. Hill underlines the way in which the Blum–Byrnes agreement (1946) lifted the restrictions on Hollywood films in the French market in return for a loan. It enabled Hollywood films to flood the market, posing a significant threat in economic terms to the French film industry. Of these Hollywood works, Hill claims: 'In the first half of 1947, 388 such films were exhibited in France.'[8] France and the CNC responded by turning to the greats of French literature and adapting them into cinematic form. Williams explains the core values of the Tradition of Quality, which were shaped by political and economic forces:

> Because of the American menace, it was assumed that successful French films needed high budgets for popular stars, attractive costumes, elaborate sets, and so on. ... The kind of cinema which emerged largely as a result of these strategies is often called the Tradition of Quality – though it was a 'tradition' at best only a few years old. 'Quality' meant, first of all, that the

films could not be inferior to the best American products, either technically ... or materially. ... Quality cinema attempted to meet the American threat in two ways: by beating it at its own game (making expensive movies with mass market appeal) and by emphasizing its home-court advantage, its Frenchness. ... But Frenchness alone could not guarantee mass market appeal. For that, the Tradition of Quality relied on production values, and above all on *stars*.[9]

In their bid to sell Frenchness and specifically quality, the CNC and the filmmakers working with it turned to the classics of the national canon. Claude Autant-Lara's 1954 version of Stendhal's 1830 novel *Le Rouge et le Noir* (*The Red and the Black*), an adaptation scripted by Truffaut's nemeses Jean Aurenche and Pierre Bost, is a case in point.

The core values of the Tradition of Quality shaped the adaptation which Autant-Lara, Aurenche and Bost crafted from Stendhal's *Le Rouge et le Noir*. The novel has become something of a literary and canonical monument, its author, as Claire Deslauriers points out, reputed for his high-culture value as a result of his obscure, allusive and elitist approach.[10] The adaptation makes much of the monumentality of its literary source, emphasizing its equivalence to that source. The adaption opens with a shot of an edition of Stendhal's novel, lingering in an extended close focus on the red leather cover of the book. The distance and angle of the shot cast the audience as readers rather than viewers. When the book opens, the film's opening credits are superimposed onto its pages. Autant-Lara's name, as well as those of Aurenche and Bost, sit like palimpsests on the book of which their adaptation presents itself as an extension. The literary nature of Autant-Lara's adaptation permeates the film. Stendhal used epigraphs to mark chapter starts. Autant-Lara's adaptation does likewise as the director inserts pages of text with isolated epigraphs in scene breaks throughout his film. While this is reminiscent of the intertitles used in silent film, the technique is literary rather than cinematic for it breaks the illusion of cinema with the pages of a book, relentlessly sending the viewer back to the book to which this film seeks to be equivalent. The adaptation, though, is literary in other ways. Its use of inner monologue is key to my line of argument here. Literature, an intimate medium, can delve easily into the deepest recesses of characters' thoughts, dreams and minds. Film, while it can dip fleetingly into the intimacy of these recesses through a point-of-view shot or a flashback, struggles to offer us sustained and natural access to the intimate workings of its characters' minds, to the thoughts they never voice. Autant-Lara's adaptation offers the viewer this sustained access but on a literary model. The adaptation features prolonged and extensive voice-overs which convey the inner thought processes, secret conflicts and private urges that drive Julien Sorel; sharing, in the voice of the actor playing the part, the hidden recesses of Sorel's mind. Mathilde invites Julien to scale a ladder under cover of darkness to come to her room. The adaptation dramatizes for the audience the twists and turns of Julien's consciousness as he debates in voice-over whether this is a Machiavellian trap or an irresistible sexual offer. He decides to take up the challenge based on how handsome and romantic he will appear while ascending the dangerous ladder. This adaptation constructs itself around core literary techniques and potentialities, privileging the canonical literature so dear to the Tradition of Quality.

The adaptation is not just shaped by the Tradition's belief in the monumentality of literature; it is also indelibly marked by its monumentalization of the stars so dear to the movement. The adaptation is a star vehicle for its male lead, Gérard Philipe, the actor whose death, David Thompson points out, coincided 'with the seismic arrival of the New Wave, [ensuring that Philipe was] instantly condemned to be associated with the old guard, the "tradition of quality" or "le cinéma de papa" '.[11] Philipe had already achieved star status by the time of his role in *Le Rouge et le Noir*, due in no small part to his breakthrough success in Autant-Lara's *Le Diable au corps* (*Devil in the Flesh*, 1947) and the even more successful adaptation of Stendhal's *La Chartreuse de Parme* (*The Charterhouse of Parma*) (1948, dir. Christian Jaque). In technical terms, Autant-Lara's *Le Rouge et le Noir* plays on the monumental status of Philipe as male lead, underscoring his association with quality. But it does so in complex ways. The dominant camera angle of the production is actually an extreme high-angle shot that entraps and diminishes characters, a shot which, for Janey Place and Lowell Peterson, is 'an oppressive and fatalistic angle that looks down upon its helpless victim to make it look like a rat in a maze'.[12] This high-angle shot characterizes the court scene in which the protagonist, Julien Sorel (played by Philipe), is doubly trapped: first in the social structures from which he has had the temerity to try to break free, and second in the court proceedings for murder which will condemn and execute him. So too does it characterize the scene in which Julien shoots his first lover. The camera surveys from on high the chaos below in the aftermath of the shot. In its telling use of symmetrical high-angle technique, the adaptation links the scenes, marking them as cause and effect. Such camera angles underscore Julien's entrapment, filming him from above. Yet if Autant-Lara's adaptation diminishes and entraps Julien, it monumentalizes the actor playing him, Gérard Phillipe, the performer on whose status this adaptation draws (see Figure 4.1). This is most noticeable in the scenes in which Julien play-acts, scenes whose inner monologue marks him as an actor, metatextually referencing the real actor playing him. Julien enters Madame de Rénal's room, driven, his dramatized inner monologue makes clear, not by love or desire but by a need to capitalize on the personal advancement that

FIGURE 4.1 Le Rouge et le Noir (The Red and the Black) *(1954, dir. Autant-Lara)*.

playing the part of a lovelorn hero offers. A skilled actor, he stage-manages his actions. Madame de Rénal kneels at his feet, kissing them, idolizing him as the film does Gérard Philipe in the low-angle shot which he dominates. In the film's second scene, Julien travels in a carriage with his father, play-acting obedience to the clerical career his father wishes for him. The scene is shot in a slight low angle, which elevates Julien above his father and the life he has planned for him. An analogous low-angle shot features in the scene in which Julien stares, with far more fervour than he initially did at Madame de Rénal, at the comparably performative bishop whom Julien identifies as an aspirational role model. The bishop stands before a mirror practising and acting out the ceremony in a shot that emphasizes his dominance of the scene – he points out to the congregation that the most mighty monarch has come to kneel before the power of God incarnated in him. In a complex play of identification, Julien identifies with the play-acting bishop whom he resembles in age and attractiveness and whose future he seeks.[13] Julien Sorel may repeatedly be trapped in high-angle shots, but the adaptation aggrandizes Gérard Philipe in financial, cultural and creative terms in keeping with the Tradition of Quality's need for culturally ratified stars.

If this Tradition of Quality film seeks monumentality, New Wave film director and critic François Truffaut works in print to deny it. Truffaut's famous

1954 essay 'A Certain Tendency of the French Cinema' is, in the words of Charles Drazin, a prolonged, angry 'assault against the whole "tradition de la qualité" of the French cinema'.[14] Truffaut's criticisms are wide-ranging and they cut to the heart of debates on what adaptation should be and how it should represent its source text. Truffaut's core criticism of the Tradition of Quality is that in its quest for equivalence, its mission to approximate literature and film, it undervalues film as a medium, neutralizing its creative potentialities. For Truffaut the work of Autant-Lara and Aurenche and Bost moves too close to its literary sources and the structures of their medium. Truffaut writes:

> I consider an adaptation of value only when written by a *man of the cinema*. Aurenche and Bost are essentially literary men and I reproach them here for being contemptuous of the cinema by underestimating it. They behave, vis-a-vis the scenario, as if they thought to re-educate a delinquent by finding him a job.[15]

For Truffaut, a critic flying against the current of fidelity theorists, the adaptations of this creative team and the Tradition of Quality are not original enough in film to merit acclaim. They monumentalize literature too much. Whatever one thinks of Truffaut's 'A Certain Tendency of the French Cinema', its efficacy in all but removing the Tradition of Quality from the annals of cinema criticism cannot be denied.[16] If, as this chapter has already suggested, comparatively little is written on this movement – which commercially and creatively dominated large parts of a decade in French cinema – next to nothing has been published on Autant-Lara's *Le Rouge et le Noir*.[17] The Tradition of Quality, as a movement, not only shaped *Le Rouge et le Noir*'s aesthetics but has also permanently affected the film's availability and status, or lack thereof, in the history of film criticism.

Truffaut's reading of the Tradition of Quality, though, does Autant-Lara's film a disservice. Autant-Lara's *Le Rouge et le Noir* gestures towards the need for a re-evaluation of the movement with which it is associated and, importantly, the need to recognize the core questions it asks of adaptation studies. Truffaut criticizes the Tradition of Quality for seeking cinematic equivalence to both its source texts and their medium. But Autant-Lara's adaptation repeatedly and insistently dismantles the very possibility of equivalence to a source text. It asks us to reconsider what adaptation is and the frameworks via which we judge it. It does so by adapting a text that plays with and ultimately refuses access to its sources. Stendhal's epigraphs at the head of each chapter and Autant-Lara's adaptation of them are key in this respect. Stendhal's novel promises to give truth and reality as its source. Sandy Petrey reads the novel's opening as 'language that has stood as a faithful description of reality for more than a hundred and fifty years ... [It offers] the classic realist narrative of human experience in a precise socio-historical milieu.'[18] However, Stendhal's novel undercuts its adaptive endeavour by underlining that the source and the truth or reality it proffers are innately inaccessible. The novel shows that truth is not a stable, graspable, deliverable source text. Equivalence to it is not possible. Stendhal offers an epigraph attributed to Danton: 'Truth, bitter truth.' This epigraph, which promises truth, denies it on two levels. First, as Petrey points out, Danton never actually said this.[19] And second, it appears in a novel whose driving force, Julien, demonstrates the impossibility of truth. He lies incessantly both to those around him and to himself. Julien believes himself to be driven by truth. Shortly before being executed he grandly claims: 'I have loved truth.' But truth is alien to him. He speaks these words in a scene in which he revels in his dramatic role, playing the part of a maligned and misunderstood man, heroically crushed by the society against which he has railed. That he is play-acting a role rather than inhabiting the truth of his identity is perhaps acknowledged in his statement, 'two steps away from death, I am still a hypocrite'.[20] In an extended destabilization of source texts, some of the epigraphs Stendhal uses to open chapters are either very loose versions of quotations or outright fabrications. They destabilize, question and undo the very sources they purport to offer. They point to source texts which simply are not there. Stendhal's text constructs itself around both an inability and a refusal to give the reader the source texts it offers. It refuses equivalence.

Autant-Lara's adaptation does likewise. It promises, as this chapter has already suggested in its images of Stendhal's printed book, *Le Rouge et le Noir* as its source, but makes clear its inability to offer the truth of that source. It does so, like Stendhal, via its use of epigraphs. Scene transitions in Autant-Lara's film are often punctuated with screenshots of epigraphs on a page of the novel itself. Certain of these epigraphs replicate those of Stendhal. Autant-Lara duplicates, for example, the Danton epigraph about the need to be true. He, like Stendhal, uses it to destabilize the sources he purportedly offers. It appears prior to a scene where Madame de Rénal writes a letter confessing her affair with Julien; a letter that will disgrace him in his house of employment and lead to his murderous actions. The letter is at once true (it recounts a liaison that did take place) and false (it is dictated by Madame de Rénal's confessor, who shapes it to his own tone and purpose, having burned Mathilde's version). Sources and their truth, Autant-Lara's film suggests, are complex things. Subsequent to Madame de Rénal's initial sexual interlude with Julien, the adaptation offers the following epigraph: 'The perversity of woman! What pleasure, what instinct leads them to betray us?' The epigraph is again true (Madame de Rénal has just duped her husband). It is simultaneously false, for Julien has actually duped Madame de Rénal, professing a false love to which his inner monologue gives the lie. Julien's false love contrasts starkly with the truth of the real love Madame de Rénal feels, a love for which she sacrifices her marriage, standing and children. Madame de Rénal is unable to settle to read while, in a symmetrical scene, Julien lies untroubled and absorbed entirely in his book. Equivalence, it appears, does not exist either between sexual partners or between source and adaptation. Autant-Lara's film thus pushes for the viewer to question and distrust its epigraphs. It is profoundly significant therefore that it uses Stendhal's novel itself as epigraph. Autant-Lara's film cites Stendhal in epigraphs which simultaneously make the source author present in his film and force the viewer to question not only the adaptation's equivalence to said source author but also the very possibility of equivalence itself. Autant-Lara's adaptation both monumentalizes its source text and questions and destabilizes the film's relationship with it. Autant-Lara's *Le Rouge et le Noir* poses key re-evaluative questions about whether equivalence is possible, what it might mean in adaptive terms, offering a vision of adaptation which is far more complex than Truffaut allows for the Tradition of Quality. Autant-Lara's *Le Rouge et le Noir* underscores the unexplored adaptive self-reflexivity of the Tradition of Quality and its unsuspected importance to adaptation studies.

Adaptation and the French New Wave: Revolutionary reworkings of French literature

The French New Wave which supplanted the Tradition of Quality and dominated the 1950s and 1960s may have rejected, as Truffaut made clear, the ideology and aesthetics of the Tradition of Quality, but it did not reject the adaptation of French source novels.[21] Eleven out of the twenty films which Truffaut himself made were, Erica Sheen points out, adaptations.[22] But the New Wave, as *Jules et Jim* (*Jules and Jim*) (1962, dir. Truffaut) shows, adapted different texts from the Tradition of Quality in starkly different ways, shaping them to its revolutionary intent. Driven by a belief that cinema had failed as a medium, that it had become static, key New Wave filmmakers reworked French texts with the intention to transform both cinema and the society around it. Truffaut's *Jules et Jim* is a case in point. In stark contrast to the canonical novelists so dear to the Tradition of Quality, Truffaut's film adapts a little-known source text, Henri-Pierre Roché's novel of the same name (1953). Roché (1879–1959) was a journalist, art collector/dealer and, late in his life, a novelist. He published just two novels – the first was *Jules et Jim* at the age of 74. A semi-autobiographical work, it allegedly depicts the love triangle between Roché, the German writer Franz Hessel and Helen Grund, who ultimately married Hessel. Truffaut's immediate attraction to the novel when he first read it is well documented – he sought Roché out and asked to be able to adapt it, before putting the project on hold for several years.[23] This attraction stems, arguably, from the social and artistic revolution which the novel seeks, a social and artistic revolution which Truffaut's novel enacts in film, for it tallies with the core transformative ideology of the New Wave.

The New Wave, as a movement, shaped Truffaut's *Jules et Jim* by creating a cinematic environment thirsty for the creative revolution Roché's novel propounds. Roché's novel and Truffaut's film of it seek to revolutionize society, transforming the ways in which we live and love. They focus on a three-way friendship which underlines that social laws repress our instinctive urges and are consequently unnatural, urging us to break free of them. They push us to live and love following our animal desires, regardless of their impact on others. The love triangle at the heart of novel and film is sexual but not sexualized (no sex is ever visible and the lovers are depicted in childlike, innocent terms) (see Figure 4.2). The three protagonists depict their relationship as a social experiment, quantifying their emotions in mathematical and scientific language as they seek 'to rediscover the laws of human life'.[24] Novel and film drown out the rules and voices of society to offer an alternative, natural, truthful world order in which happiness results from the satisfaction of personal desires. The vocabulary of the natural world is relentlessly applied to the novel's protagonists. Kathe (Catherine in Truffaut's film) is thus a 'tortured lamb', a 'queen bee', a 'dazzling comet' lighting up the sky.[25] This natural vocabulary implicitly pitches society beyond the lovers and its constructed laws as unnatural, perverted and repressive. Roché's novel exists in film because it shares the New Wave's intent to trigger revolution.

FIGURE 4.2 Jules et Jim (Jules and Jim) *(1962, dir. Truffaut).*

But Roché's novel and Truffaut's film not only propose a social experiment, they also test and evaluate it, assessing the limits of their proposed revolution. That the social revolution they set out fails is clear. The protagonists' pursuit of their individual desires inevitably brings them into conflict with each other, rendering them incapable of living together collectively. Recognizing this failure, Kathe/Catherine deliberately kills herself and Jim in a car accident. Both Roché and Truffaut contrast the destructive horror of her actions with the continued childlike depiction of her vocabulary and being. Like a child appealing to a parent for attention, she shouts to Jules 'Watch me!' before cruelly killing herself and his best friend before his gaze. The social experiment dies with Kathe and Jim, for they leave no offspring to continue it. The sole member of the social experiment left alive, Jules, feels nothing but 'relief'.[26] The adaptation is perhaps more emphatic than the novel in its annihilation of the experiment. It depicts the containment of these social pioneers in coffins, their destruction by cremation flames, the pulverization of their charred bones into ash and the enclosure of their ashes in the small memorial lockers characteristic of French crematoria. These multiple acts of containment take place in a scene with a narrator's voice-over delivered at such speed that it will not allow us to grieve for, mark or fully process their lives' end. Both novel and adaptation state of the ashes that 'Kathe [Catherine] had always wanted hers to be scattered in the wind on a hilltop. But that was against the regulations.'[27] In both novel and film the society which the lovers seek to evade and redefine ultimately comes back to contain them. But, importantly, social laws do not prevail before the novel and adaptations have encouraged us to reconsider them as an artificial construct rather than an immutable and eternal given. Roché's novel caters to the New Wave urge to revolutionize society but also reflects the self-consciousness of the New Wave about the limits and impossibilities of its proposed revolution. Roché's novel and the movement remaking it speak powerfully to each other.

The revolution proposed by Roché and Truffaut and the New Wave, though, is not just social, it is also artistic. Collectively they seek to reconfigure what art is. Roché's novel challenges art in aesthetic terms. It presents a sophisticated sociological experiment in simple, childlike language. Not only is the novel's title reminiscent of a child's first reader, but its prose reads as though drawn from one. Roché's use of this innocent, childlike vocabulary is multilayered. It supports the presentation of the protagonists as childlike and innocent, refusing to allow us to write off their love triangle as sordid and sexual. The novel's simple style and the short telegraphic sentence structure couch the social experiment with a simplicity, straightforwardness and logic which both reel the reader in and imply the obviousness of the alternative social structure the novel proposes. The novel, though, disconcerts beyond language and sentence structure. It refuses its heroine Kathe any narrative coherency. She drives the narrative and the social experiment in it, despite being absent from the novel's title. Yet she functions as a disconcerting void within both novel and experiment. For all his/her overarching knowledge, the novel's narrator asks questions of Kathe and is unable ultimately to answer them: 'Kathe, with her eyes lowered, was smiling her archaic smile. What was she thinking?'[28] Roché uses this quotation to link Kathe to the stone statue in his novel, the bewitching antique carving which no man can resist. In so doing, he carves out an intertextual reference between his heroine and the murderous statue in Prosper Mérimée's short story 'La Vénus d'Ille' ('The Venus of Ille', 1835). Roché's intertextual allusion is complex, though. It does not help define the character; rather it makes her more elusive. Mérimée's female protagonist is a mysterious statue of unknown and unknowable origins believed to come to life to kill her metaphorical husband (a real man who slips his wedding ring on the statue's finger while playing tennis). Above and beyond this allusion to Mérimée's unknowable heroine, Roché multiplies the textual allusions surrounding Kathe in dizzying, contradictory terms. Kathe is at once Napoleon, Manon Lescaut and Botticelli's Venus (in a washbasin rather than a mythical shell).[29] Roché's intertextual references are so plural and contradictory as to be non-referential. We lose ourselves in them, sharing Jules's and Jim's fascination for the heroine they do not understand, the heroine who is everywhere and ultimately nowhere in the novel. Roché's novel is aesthetically subversive in its refusal to allow us to situate its anchor character.

Aesthetic disconcertion in Roché's novel, a lure for the insurrectional intent of the New Wave as a movement, becomes an attempt at full-scale artistic revolution in Truffaut's adaptation of it. The relentless pace and number of kaleidoscopic scenes packed into the opening sequence overwhelms the viewer's sensibilities. At increasing velocity, jump cuts and hurried voice-over narration bounce the viewer between the childlike male protagonists who dress up, play piggyback games, talk abstract philosophy and visit prostitutes. With a wink to the censorship the film would inevitably face and the abbreviation that characterizes this film – which proceeds almost in shorthand, refusing to provide its viewer with full narrative coherency – the prostitutes are not depicted in full but metonymically. We glimpse only a watch comically strapped to a dainty female ankle, indicating that this woman's lovers are on the clock. The camera revels in its capacities as Truffaut basks not in the literary nature of his source but in his adaptation's ability to be film. The film's opening is frenzied in its editing, the jump cuts bouncing the viewer between scenes with highly visible editing techniques, forcing the viewer to contemplate the machinery of film itself. The director's use of fleeting freeze-frames works in a similar vein. Truffaut pauses his own action, at times fully and at others only very slightly. He refuses to naturalize the story and instead insists on the mechanics of the medium in which it is created. Truffaut, in keeping with the New Wave, exploits the freedom and technical innovation which can come with a handheld camera, filming Thérèse in a dizzying 360-degree rotational shot as she plays the train game, turning on the spot and breathing out cigarette smoke. In technical terms, Truffaut's film exploits to the full the New Wave's intent to be revolutionary and insurrectionary. Yet intriguingly, in its opening sequence, Truffaut's film wryly pokes fun at the very possibility of the insurrection his own film and movement proposes. An anarchist paints a revolutionary slogan on a wall. Having unexpectedly run out of paint, he slaps the girlfriend with him, upset at the idea that people will say that anarchists do not know how to spell. Comedy stems from the fact that spelling is a form of governing authority. It is precisely the type of thing anarchists propose to abolish. Truffaut's film proposes aesthetic revolution, but it does so in surprisingly measured ways, weighing, in its images, the limits of revolution. The French New Wave is attracted to Roché's *Jules et Jim* for its revolutionary content. Truffaut both amplifies his source novel's revolutionary intent under the aegis of the movement within which he works as director and simultaneously weighs its limitations.

Adapting in and against genre: French source texts in musical film

If Truffaut adapts Roché's *Jules et Jim* because it resonates with and is receptive to the revolutionary intent and imprint of the New Wave movement, Otto Preminger's 1954 *Carmen Jones*, in contrast, adapts against many of the conventions of the cinematic genre in which it works: musical film. Having rapidly established itself as a genre with the onset of sound in the late 1920s and early 1930s, musical film flourished in the studio system of the 1940s and early 1950s, the timeframe of this chapter, after which its popularity waned. While musicals were the signature genre of Metro-Goldwyn-Mayer, as Steven Cohan points out, other studios continued to produce them and musicals 'often single-handedly made up a company's annual profits, as Betty Grable's musicals did for Twentieth Century Fox throughout the 1940s, and the Fred Astaire–Ginger Rogers series did for RKO Radio Pictures throughout the 1930s'.[30] Musicals allowed studios to offer escapist entertainment while earning maximum commercial profit in star vehicles that enabled the companies in question to showcase the latest technological innovation and special effects. The genre, within this studio system, had strict narrative and aesthetic conventions, which were arguably set out in Fred Astaire's cycle of musicals for RKO. Cohan argues:

> The scores, written by leading Broadway talents such as Irving Berlin, were likewise composed to repeat similar functions and through a similar sequence: Astaire in a solo, the two stars in a challenge dance, Astaire in a speciality dance, the two stars in a romantic duet, the two stars in a novelty dance incorporating them into a big production number.[31]

'So formulaic does the pattern become,' Rick Altman observes of the numbers' sequencing, 'that ... a routine is established which is rarely varied.'[32] Not only does the order and rhythm of a musical film often follow a highly conventionalized form, it also, as a genre, has specific aesthetic and production conventions which shape the texts it adapts. While characters obey the rule of the fourth wall when acting, creating a world in which they do not acknowledge our presence as audience, they break it to turn to address us while singing. According to Thomas Schatz, whenever musical performers do a number they usually 'shift their identities from being actors in a drama to entertainers addressing the audience directly'.[33] There is thus, he argues, an intriguing slippage between fictional character and star persona as a result of the conventions of the genre. Moreover, as Cohan points out, because musicals tended to be large, costly productions with elaborate sets and costumes, extensive orchestras and a huge off-screen personnel, to save the cost of bringing a complete orchestra back to set for a new scene or shoot, soundtracks were pre-recorded as an industry standard. Such pre-records were edited, often more than once, in order to achieve the best vocal performance and then played back on set for the singer to lip-synch or to sing along with.[34] This genre convention is visible in Preminger's *Carmen Jones* as characters' sung words often do not synchronize fully with the lips of the actor playing them, making the industry conventions of this genre and their impact visible on this adaptation of a French source. Both the musical film genre's direct-address moments and its visible disconnect between singer and song fracture our ability to believe in the reality of what we watch. But musical films, as Cohan argues persuasively, are not about reality; rather, they revel in their escapism, running entirely counter to the realist discourse of commercial narrative film.[35] Musical films have their own set of creative and technical conventions which shape the French literary texts they adapt.

Preminger's *Carmen Jones* is both shaped by those conventions and adapts them, while simultaneously working to subvert them. It may follow much of the structural rhythm of the musical film genre and many of its industrial practices, but it probes, questions and partially breaks free from the

THE FORMATIVE FUNCTION OF THE DOMINANT FILM POETICS   161

genre's escapist bent. It does so by updating *Carmen*'s nineteenth-century plot to contemporary North America, using an entirely black cast in a musical vehicle that delves into the racial history of the United States. Set during the Second World War, the plot focuses on femme fatale Carmen Jones, who works in a parachute factory in North Carolina. When she is arrested for a fight with her co-worker, the army assigns Corporal Joe to deliver her to the civilian authorities fifty miles away. She seduces and beguiles Joe away both from his love, Cindy-Lou, and his military duty. He deserts, following her to Chicago while she indulges in an affair with champion boxer Husky Miller. Unable to control and own her, Joe strangles Carmen at one of Husky's fights. Preminger's piece breaks the escapist conventions of the musical genre to intervene politically in debates on North American ethnic history.[36] It does so in a number of ways. First, in its selection of an entirely African American cast, it makes a political statement on racial exclusion in the genre in which it works, building on the success of the tiny number of previous all-black musicals. While elements of racial diversity are visible in the history of musical film prior to *Carmen Jones*, they often appear in highly segregated inserted solos (see Figure 4.3). Preminger's film adapts Bizet's *Carmen* into Second World War America, offering its leads a star vehicle. Second, Preminger's adaptation structures itself around songs that contemporary critics hailed as using African American vernacular, which was marketed as authentic. Carmen, having had her cards read and feeling the spectre of death hanging over her, sings the following lyrics:

> It ain't no use to run away from dat old boy if he is chasing you.
> It's best to stand right up and look him in de face when he is facing you.
> So I won't fill my pretty eyes with salty tears cos I ain't got the time.
> I gonna run out every second I got left before he trows me down.

FIGURE 4.3 Carmen Jones *(1954, dir. Preminger)*.

Third, and perhaps most importantly, Preminger's adaptation engages in an in-depth exploration of whether freedom is truly possible for any of its African American cast within its fictions. Carmen, the eponymous heroine, is a case in point. Throughout the adaptation she proclaims her need for freedom at all costs. Her morning-after note to Joe, having seduced him, reflects this: 'Sorry honey, like I told you, couldn't stand being cooped up in jail. I gotta be free to come and go. I'd just die. Don't hate me. Cos I love you Joey like I loved no man before.' She flees the love-nest she shares with him in Chicago, a room shot in enclosed close to mid-length shots to emphasize its claustrophobia, for similar reasons. She aids and abets Joe's escape from the military police even after she has fallen for another man, 'Cos I can't stand nobody being cooped up.'

Carmen's quest for freedom may drive her, but it is an illusory, impossible quest for, in ways which Preminger relates to her status as an African American, she is multiply trapped. First, this film filled with tarot readings, omens and portents makes clear that Carmen is fated for death. Immediately after we see a sign outside Carmen's house – 'Have your fortoon told. Palm readings. Asterlogie. 25c' – Carmen's grandmother tells her that trouble is coming Carmen's way due to the buzzard feather which appears on her doorstep. The appearance of the nine card in Carmen's hand confirms that death seeks her. Knowledge of this triggers her relationship with Husky and her intent to live every second she has. Carmen is trapped by the fates. A second level of entrapment encloses the adaptation's heroine in the form of Joe's love for her. He may meet her and fall in love with her in the wide open spaces of the journey between the parachute factory and the offices of law enforcement, but the spaces to which Joe takes her become progressively smaller and more constraining. They culminate in the tiny storeroom at the boxing match where Joe makes good on his threat that if he cannot possess Carmen then she will die at his hands. Joe's murderous actions bring him no freedom, though; as contemporary critic Nora Holt pointed out, in relation to Hammerstein's work, they gesture to the absolute entrapment of the African American population in North American history, a past which Holt argues has not yet been shaken off. She writes:

> I rather take exception to the dramatic last words of Joe, who accepts with fatalistic philosophy the doom that faces him as a murderer. His final words are:
> String me high on a tree
> So dat I soon will be
> Wid my darling! my baby!
> my Carmen!

The first line is all too reminiscent of atrocities committed in the South when lynching parties occur ever and again to arouse us to shame, hatred and finally acceptance, but never forgetfulness.[37]

A third level of entrapment encloses Carmen in visual terms. Preminger's film repeatedly shoots her in elevated high-angle shots that enclose her in the action, trapping her beneath the dominating gaze of the camera which dissects her life, giving the lie to the freedom she claims so vociferously to seek. The scene in Billy Pastor's club is emblematic in this respect. Carmen vehemently professes her right to choose her own destiny in a scene in which the music and drums gesture towards African heritage. Yet the camera films Carmen from on high, denying the freedom her words and musical beats claim.[38] In its triple entrapment of Carmen as an African American woman, Preminger's film breaks the conventional escapist entertainment conventions of the musical film genre to adapt politics and ask probing questions of the very possibility of freedom for African Americans in his contemporary era.

If Preminger's reworking adapts against certain of the conventions of musical film, it is shaped by, plays on and amplifies others. When musical films break the fourth wall to have their characters sing directly to the audience, the star persona of their actors becomes distinctly visible. Preminger's film offers the audience the characters of Joe and Carmen as they act, his version of Bizet's José and Carmen. These characters give way to the stars performing them in the song numbers. Carmen becomes more visibly the actress and singer Dorothy Dandridge as she sings, and Joe recedes in place of the star persona of actor and singer Harry Belafonte. Yet though both had starred together previously in *Bright Road* (1953, dir. Gerald Mayer) and were potentially visible and accessible to the audience as actors (and in Belafonte's case as a singer), *Carmen Jones*, rather than capitalizing on their star currency, built it for them. Dandridge was nominated for an Academy Award for Best Actress, becoming the first African American nominated for a leading role for her part as Carmen Jones. Moreover, on the back of the film's success – it was one of the highest-earning of its year of release – she secured a three-movie deal with Twentieth Century Fox for a minimum of $75,000 per film. The adapted identities in Preminger's film, though, are not just dual. Though both his lead actors were singers, Preminger wanted operatic voices, so both Dandridge and Belafonte were dubbed by other singers (Dandridge's songs were overlaid by vocalist Marilyn Horne and Belafonte's by LeVern Hutcherson).

Preminger's film pushes the genre's tension between star and character still further in its images. Joe and Carmen, as well as the actors who play them, are joined and perhaps overshadowed by the weighty star status of the adaptive parts they play; by the legions of versions of the same characters which precede them. That Carmen is a canonical figure is clear from, if nothing else, the sheer profusion of Carmen adaptations in film which feature in this book. Each of these adaptations, in their own way, gestures towards their operatic forebear, acknowledging her presence in the essence of their very being. Preminger's Carmen Jones is no different. A 1950s African American, she opens the film in a red and black swirling dress which references both the Spain of her forebear and its flamenco tradition as she dances with a red flower. Such is the dominance and canonicity of Bizet's Carmen that she makes Carmen Jones always already known. Thus, when champion boxer Husky Miller (Preminger's version of Escamillo the Toreador) tries to sweet-talk her, Carmen replies 'You talk like you know me already.' He does, we all do, so indelible is the identity of the character whom she reincarnates, so known is her fate. Carmen Jones, may be, as this chapter has suggested, trapped in the adaptation's camera angles, in the racial politics of contemporary America, but she is also trapped in the destiny of her adaptive forebear, an ending the vast majority of viewers know before the film's opening credits so much as roll. Carmen's conviction that death tracks her, shown by tarot cards, buzzard feathers and the number nine, is correct. But it is not fate that tracks her down, but the weight of her source text in its known-ness and canonicity. Thibaud Leplat argues that the principle of 'the classic' is that we know the ending of a work, yet watch/read/consume it anyway.[39] *Carmen Jones* harnesses the known-ness of its source both to trap its heroine and in order to push the viewer to contemplate the play of sameness in difference that is adaptation as a genre. The film's musical numbers are important in this respect. Preminger keeps the melody of some of Bizet's most famous songs from the opera. The toreador song is a notable example. His adaptation nudges us to remember the skill and music of an earlier source author (who himself borrowed the work from Mérimée). But to the melodies of the canonical Bizet opera he puts new words. The boxer Husky Miller, Preminger's version of the bullfighter, sings to the toreador melody:

> Stand up and fight until you hear the bell
> Trade blow for blow
> Keep punching till you make your punches tell.

What Preminger's piece offers, in a musical moment which takes us to the heart of adaptation, is difference in sameness as he weaves new lyrics and creation into a narrative and inescapably canonical melody of the past. Preminger's film asks us to contemplate the marriage of old and new, replication and creation, in the complex artefact that is adaptation. Highlighting the multiplicity of identities at play – character, star, canonical forebear – Preminger's film is not only shaped by the conventions of the musical film genre, it also uses them to ask probing questions about what adaptation actually is and our impossible demand that it be both original and replicative.

Complex freedoms: The space of adaptation in the Italian Spaghetti Western

Such is the lure of Carmen as both a character and an adaptive source text that Mérimée's novella and Bizet's adaptation of it were remade in a starkly contrasting genre, the Italian Spaghetti Western, in the same era. It appeared as *L'uomo, l'orgoglio, la vendetta* (*Man, Pride and Vengeance*) (1967, dir. Luigi Bazzoni), starring Franco Nero. Bazzoni's film, in a very different genre, offers a very different *Carmen* from that of Preminger. Bazzoni's adaptation is clearly shaped by the Spaghetti Western genre, which flourished in the mid-1960s before petering out in the mid-1970s. It earned its name from American critics because, while borrowing and adapting American Western models, its films were produced and directed by Italians.[40] In terms of output and commercial takings, Spaghetti Westerns occupy a comparatively large place in cinema history.[41] And yet, in critical terms, comparatively little is written about them. This near-silence stems, perhaps, from the critical perception of Spaghetti Westerns as highly commercial, low-budget productions seeking quick-hit box office takings by imitating the plots, methods and acting cast of Spaghetti Western hits such as *A Fistful of Dollars* (1964, dir. Leone).[42] The Spaghetti Western genre in general and Bazzoni's film in particular occupy comparatively little space in the critical canon on adaptation and indeed cinema more broadly.

But Italian Spaghetti Westerns should not be written off, for they are works that push us, in their transnational existences, to contemplate the borders and boundaries of adaptation. They adapt and relocate the North American Western tradition, moving it to Europe, playing with its certainties and spaces. They destabilize the myths of origin, foundation and fixity in the Hollywood Westerns which sought, in André Bazin's view, to offer themselves as the founding myth of the United States.[43] Spaghetti Westerns were, as the paragraph above shows, given their name by American critics because they were produced and directed by Italians. The term, though, is misleading. The majority of the films made under this banner were international co-productions between a combination of nations: Italy, Spain, France, Portugal, Spain, the United States, Yugoslavia, Greece and Israel. They were, in any case, designed to meet an international market and often featured multilingual casts, having their sound post-synched after production so that they could be released in different world markets. Dimitris Eleftheriotis is incisive on this point. He argues:

> It is useful to understand the Spaghetti Western ... as a phenomenon closely linked to the process of globalization ... [that] also highlights the accelerated mobility of cultural products around the world and their increasing detachment from national contexts. Such a model ... perceives cultural production as operating not on a national but on a transnational, even global level.[44]

According to Eleftheriotis, the hero of the Spaghetti Western takes the audience 'beyond the boundaries of the nation' by erasing and playing with the markers of national identity.[45] Spaghetti Westerns visibly and concurrently adapt themselves for multiple national contexts. *Carmen* is thus an ideal source text for the genre, sharing as it does its spatial and national hybridity. Mérimée, as influenced by the literary movement of Romanticism as Bazzoni was by that of the Spaghetti Western, constructed his novella around the thirst for nature, local colour and exoticism that drove much of the Romantic movement contemporaneous to him. He situated his French-language text in southern Spain in a work clearly geared to the needs of its French national market. The complex spatial hybridity of Mérimée's work, which is only amplified by its adaptation and readaptation in diverse national contexts all over the world, resonates with the spatial hybridity of the Spaghetti Western movement.

That the spatial hybridity characteristic of the Spaghetti Western genre shapes Bazzoni's *Man, Pride, and Vengeance* is clear. Space is as complex in the film as it is for the genre in which it situates itself. The film's cast is international and multilingual, and this adaptation of *Carmen* was released in various dubbed languages under different titles in multiple countries. The action opens with long shots and extreme high-angle establishing shots that seek to fix and offer the spatial expanse in which we find ourselves, running with protagonist José in arid, immense, rugged terrain. These establishing shots, though, establish only the impossibility of the very space they offer. They reference, despite their Spanish contextualization, the North American Wild West of the Hollywood Westerns their Italian counterparts seek to reinvent. This Wild West, a brave new world to which José dreams of escaping with Carmen ('let's go away together and begin all over again, Carmen. A new life, a clean one'), is an impossible one. It is ever beyond his reach for Carmen, despite her false promises, will not board the boat to leave for it with him (see Figure 4.4). That he remains trapped in these expanses is made clear by the prevalence of extreme high-angle shots, like those in Autant-Lara's *Le Rouge*

FIGURE 4.4 L'uomo, l'orgoglio, la vendetta (Man, Pride, and Vengeance) *(1967, dir. Bazzoni).*

et le Noir, trapping him in a towering and overbearing verticality, emphasizing his insignificance in the vastness of the landscape he inhabits. Indeed, the expanses and freedom of the opening sequence are illusory in another respect, for the film opens with its conclusion – José being tracked by the forces of law and order for his crimes – before working back to explain how he gets there. In a bold acknowledgement of its own adapted status, *Man, Pride, and Vengeance* starts with the canonical ending which its audience is, in all likelihood, awaiting, knowing perhaps the Mérimée source text, or its more canonical Bizet adaptation, or indeed one of the legion of adaptations which both have triggered. If José is trapped in the vast expanses of the desert, his entrapment is all the more pronounced in the cityscape in which he meets Carmen, the cityscape that leads to his desperate desert run from the forces of law and order and their guns. Almost entirely using close to mid-length shots, the camera insistently films José and Carmen in barred, blocked images. This shows both the impossible space their relationship occupies, and the literal and metaphorical imprisonment to which it will inexorably lead for José. Their first discussion takes place through the bars of a gate. When Carmen dances for José's officer's party as a demoted José stands on sentry duty below, they talk again through the bars of a window. Numerous scenes are accompanied by clocks ticking or chiming in shots that trap them temporally as well as in the small spaces of the city. Bazzoni's adaptation will not allow Carmen and José to escape from their pre-written, canonical narrative.

However, in Bazzoni's Spaghetti Western, entrapment brings a measure of freedom. José's incarceration for dereliction of military duty under the pull of Carmen's powerful sexuality rips him from the enclosed spaces of the city and the claustrophobic technique with which it is filmed. It transports him to the comparative freedom of life as a renegade criminal in the lawless expanses of the desert. The freedom José gains in the arid vastness of the desert is more expansive than that which the character achieves in other comparator Carmen adaptations: Joe in Preminger's *Carmen Jones* remains claustrophobically contained in the four walls of a cheap room for rent; José in Malcolm Sargent's *Gypsy Blood*, the adaptation explored in Chapter 2, has little more space in the house and compound courtyard in which he hides for Carmen. José's complex freedom in Bazzoni's film, and indeed that of his director, stems precisely from the Spaghetti Western genre and its established trope of vigilantes in the lawless expanses of the wilderness. That the film adapts the conventions and tropes of the Spaghetti Western as well as its source text is clear, and the film finds a freedom in so doing. The heroine is of core importance here. Carmen dominates the Mérimée source text, and indeed many of its recreations in adapted form. Yet the Spaghetti Western genre allows Bazzoni to erase her in complex ways in *Man, Pride, and Vengeance*, wresting a space for himself and his cinematic narrative. Women in Spaghetti Westerns are, Russ Hunter argues, either prostitutes, or angels tragically erased too soon.[46] Writing on what he sees as 'the lack of romance-driven narratives' in Spaghetti Westerns, he claims that 'Female characters do not "exist" for their male counterparts in any meaningful sense beyond being objects to be tussled over, whores in saloons or painful distant memories alluded to in flashback.'[47] It is thus far from insignificant that Carmen, in Bazzoni's film, is tellingly erased from the film's title. That Carmen drives the action is clear – José's love for her overrides everything, pulling him away from his military career and sense of duty and into the criminal gang so characteristic of the Spaghetti Western genre. But she is fundamentally absent even in her presence, refusing to be pinned down in any comprehensible way. She endlessly professes and then recants her love for José before beginning the cycle anew. She lies in her professions of truth (when she claims to work in a respectable aristocratic house) and tells the truth in her tangible lies: 'And one day when I do begin to tell you lies I'm sure you'll believe it's the truth.' Such is her contradiction that she begins to cancel herself out, erasing herself in a film that is supposedly driven by her. She is both angel (she appears before a draped image of the Virgin Mary in a similar pose and costume) and whore. If Carmen's erasure from the film – she disappears for long passages of the action – bears witness to the influence of the Spaghetti Western genre on this adaptation, so too does the monetary narrative which comes to replace her. Money is, Bert Fridlund argues, the driving force of the Spaghetti Western, both within its plots and as a commercial film genre.[48] Bazzoni's *Man, Pride, and Vengeance* intriguingly confirms this. José and Carmen's husband put aside their desire for her and join forces in a renegade band to liberate a crate of gold from a travelling dignitary in a plot which goes awry. They fight over money rather than Carmen. Money and Carmen, though, have much in common and the adaptation monetarizes Carmen. What love exchanges there are between José and Carmen are strikingly financial in their vocabulary and transactions. Carmen sends José bread and a means of escape in prison, writing 'I always pay my debts.' Following his imprisonment for her actions, Carmen states: 'Oh I know we have some accounts to settle.' Attempting to end their liaison later in the action, she says, 'You're still here Sergeant, go away. I've paid my debts and we're all square now aren't we?' She re-engages his affections later in a transaction that is both sexual and financial, paying him in kisses to turn a blind eye: 'Would you like to earn a little money on the side? Then let some of my friends pass tonight.' Carmen comes to represent money, circulated in an adaptation that is powered by the very exchanges that erase her as a protagonist. Bazzoni wrests a complex freedom for himself and his film from his canonical source by adapting the tropes and conventions of his target genre: the Spaghetti Western.

Multiple adaptations: Flaubert's *Madame Bovary* in the golden age of Indian film

If Bazzoni's *Man, Pride, and Vengeance* adapts the conventions of the Spaghetti Western at least as much as his source text, Hrishikesh Mukherjee's *Anuradha* (1960) works within the norms of his film moment to such an extent that the French source text hidden behind his adaptive endeavour becomes all but invisible. Mukherjee's film was based on a short story written by Sachin Bhowmick first published in the Bengali monthly magazine *Desh*; a story adapted loosely, his autobiography claims, from Gustave Flaubert's *Madame Bovary*. That Mukherjee's film does adapt elements of Flaubert's novel indirectly is clear – Anuradha, a celebrated radio singer and dancer, gives up her rich family and nascent fame to marry Nirmal Chowdhary, a doctor who has decided to live in hardship, serving the poor in the isolated village of Nandagaon in memory of his mother (who died without medical help). Following her heart, Anuradha rejects an arranged marriage (to Deepak) set up by her father to follow her love, Chowdhary. Sacrificing all for Chowdhary, who is consumed by his work, Anuradha gives up her music, takes on all the household chores which were previously alien to her rich existence, and is increasingly ignored by the husband, who is more devoted to the poor than to her. Resisting her father's urgings to return to him, Anuradha is then confronted by her lovelorn suitor Deepak's urgings to return to her music, a

God-given talent, and, implicitly, to him. More faithful than Flaubert's heroine, Anuradha does resist the call to renege on her marriage vows, staying with the husband for whose success she sacrifices all. Neither an avowed adaptation, nor one that is instantly recognizable as such, *Anuradha* occupies an intriguing adaptive space as it adapts Bhowmick's short story and the canonical Flaubert novel behind it.

Mukherjee's film enjoys an intricate relationship with Flaubert's text. Anuradha, in keeping with the conventions of popular film of the Nehruvian era, sings in special numbers which permeate the film (see Figure 4.5). Intriguingly, though, unlike the musical film conventions highlighted above, her songs do not break the film's diegesis or the fourth wall for they are part and parcel of the action. Anuradha's songs reference the Flaubert novel overwritten by the Bhowmick short story. Lamenting, like her Flaubertian predecessor, her dissatisfaction in marriage, she sings of fire, stating 'My garland of dreams is withering', referencing the marriage bouquet Emma throws onto the fire in Flaubert's novel. Both Emma and Anuradha sit, bored, at windows, staring down at the world neither can fully access. Anuradha's windows are, if anything, more blocked than those of her nineteenth-century predecessor. Frequently shuttered and barred, the windows by which Anuradha sits underscore her lack of freedom of movement. In stark contrast to Emma, who circulates comparatively freely in Flaubert's novel, the rural setting and social system in which she lives confine Anuradha to her house, and the film never allows her to venture beyond it without her husband or

FIGURE 4.5 Anuradha *(1960, dir. Mukherjee)*.

father. Both Emma and Anuradha seek cures for their melancholia: Emma from the priest, and Anuradha from her husband himself. Both couch their request in medical terms. Anuradha states: 'You cure everyone else. Have you ever given a thought to my illness? ... I am left alone all day. Who do I talk to? The walls.' Performing the melancholia of her French forebear, Anuradha stages a charity dance performance for flood victims early in the film, starring as the princess whose melancholia prevents her from smiling, a melancholia that foreshadows both her own marriage and that of Flaubert's heroine. At the height of her performance, a coin is thrown to a beggar, echoing, for the viewer who knows Flaubert's text, the money Emma hurls at the destitute blind man who haunts the action, mocking and doubling her in many ways. The princess in Anuradha's performance of her is brought back to life by music, returned to happiness by the travelling musician who brings melodies to her existence. Emma, in Flaubert's novel, feels herself brought back to life and joy by her adulterous affair with Léon, an affair that music makes possible. Emma tells Charles she is travelling to have music lessons as cover for her illicit liaison. As transtextual as Bazzoni's adaptation was transnational, Mukherjee's *Anuradha* simultaneously points to the Bhowmick short story it adapts and the Flaubert novel that lies behind it. It underscores the complex literary geographies of its own adaptive existence.

Mukherjee's film makes Flaubert visible in the very things it changes from Flaubert's novel, affording it a complex space and voice in its cinematic fictions. It does so in a series of deliberate inversions of and allusions to Flaubert's novel. Charles's incompetence as a doctor strained his marriage, while Chowdhary's excellence in the field has the same impact on his relationship with his wife. Charles botches Hippolyte's club-foot operation, triggering Emma's contempt and subsequent affairs. Chowdhary is hugely successful in the plastic surgery he undertakes on the rich society woman whose car has crashed near his rural village. Her father works to reconcile him with his wife, overcoming her contempt and forcing her husband to see her as the foundation on which his success depends. In a knowing reference to the Flaubert source text, an admiring doctor early in the action acclaims Chowdhary's skill in terms that take us directly back to Charles, his bungling counterpart in Flaubert. Such is Flaubert's Charles's mismanagement of the club-foot operation that ultimately another professional has to step in to amputate the foot. In Mukherjee's film, such is Chowdhary's legendary skill that when Anuradha's father tries to consult the family doctor in relation to her sprained ankle, that doctor declares his blind faith in Chowdhary, teasingly referencing Flaubert's Charles in his imagery: 'Give her 101 injections, even amputate her leg, you have my permission.' Mukherjee's film not only voices key elements of Flaubert's source, it also gives voice to what it has changed, most notably in relation to its ending. Flaubert's novel famously ends with Emma dying at her own hand, leaving a bereft, distraught Charles wishing he could have done things differently. Mukherjee's film offers an alternate ending in which Anuradha refuses to leave her doctor husband for her romantic, dashing, would-be lover Deepak, embracing instead the self-abnegation and anonymity of her marriage in order that her husband serve humanity and the Indian nation. However, it is, adaptation critic Millicent Marcus suggests, not unusual for adaptations to voice what they have changed in relation to their source, inscribing those changes into their plot and paradoxically giving space to the elements of the text they have amputated.[49] Mukherjee does precisely this in a scene which is, to use Marcus's terminology, 'umbilical' in its profession of a link to a source text which it has altered. Mukherjee may change Flaubert's ending but he does not omit it, for he displaces it onto a subplot in which a work-obsessed rural peasant neglects his wife, who dies (not by her own hand) in his absence and as a result of his unknowing neglect. The voices of Flaubert's text whisper through Mukherjee's film and it is entirely appropriate that they do so, for Flaubert's novel is a text precisely about displaced, disjointed, adapted voices. Flaubert's Emma adapts the Romantic literature on which she gorged as a convent girl, singing Lamartine's canonical poem 'The Lake' as she trysts with her lover Léon on a comparable lake. She relocates Lamartine's words to her own situation, adapting his vision and love for a dead muse to her own nascent love affair. Emma's borrowed voice finds compelling counterparts in Mukherjee's film. The adaptation's song numbers are significant here. Anuradha sings at key points in the film, and her song numbers are always evocative of her inner state of mind, of the thoughts that often do not leave the confines of her consciousness. The songs represent Anuradha's most intimate words. And yet, in the film, they are ultimately not her own. Anuradha was played by Leela Naidu, a former Miss India, in her first film part. In keeping with conventions in Indian film of the time, Naidu did not sing her own numbers. M. K. Raghavendra writes of Hindu films of this era:

> Playback singers are always used to render songs but few attempts are made to 'match' the voice of the actual singer with that of the actor/actress singing it on-screen. ... Neepa Majumdar notes the very small number of singing stars actually providing playback. For almost five decades, every major film actress borrowed from the same singing voice, that of Lata Mangeshkar.[50]

Mangeshkar sings the song to which Naidu as Anuradha mimes, as the film plays back an identity which aurally reassures the audience that this film fits the conventions of Indian popular film in the Nehruvian era. Anuradha's voice in the adaptation, like Emma's in the novel, expresses itself by ventriloquizing another. Mukherjee's film speaks Flaubert's novel, but it speaks it differently.

The film's difference, a visible and audible difference, stems precisely from the influence of its moment. Mukherjee's *Anuradha* stems from the golden age of Indian cinema, which was both prolific and successful from the 1940s to the mid-1960s. While this golden age was characterized by diversity, Mukherjee has been hailed as creating a 'middle cinema' of India, carving 'a middle path between the extravagance of mainstream cinema and the stark realism of art cinema'.[51] For all its diversity, Indian cinema of this Nehruvian age was, Jyotika Virdi argues, characterized by core tropes.[52] These tropes clearly shape Mukherjee's adaptation. He adapts his cinematic moment, a time that has a far more formative influence than Flaubert's novel. That Flaubert's bumbling, substandard doctor becomes a pioneering expert, fighting poverty and developing new techniques and cures in his backwater laboratory with the aid of foreign medical journals, is unsurprising for, Virdi argues, 'In the 1950s the hero in Hindi films was a crusader for the nation and optimistic about its future, notwithstanding his critical appraisal of problems besetting the nation.'[53] Mukherjee's Dr Chowdhary fights not just illness but also the poverty that triggers it. His response to his young daughter's question 'Why are people poor? Is it an illness?' is revealing. He states: 'Yes dear. Poverty is a very bad illness.' It is an illness he seeks to fix at the expense, if necessary, of his own marriage and family. He isolates, neglects and renders his wife unhappy in ways he deems inevitable in his mission to serve his nation and its poor. His wife sits at their window watching the world in which he is so active, the camera's elevated high shot emphasizing both her social class – which prevents her from mixing in this rural backwater – and her lack of freedom as a woman to access the spaces her husband traverses so freely. Faced with her unhappiness, he only replies 'I am a doctor after all. My first duty is towards my patients.' The conventions of the golden age of Indian cinema command that it be so. Vridi writes:

> Hindi cinema positions itself as a national cinema ... by naturalizing and idealizing the nation's imagined community as one that commands fierce love and loyalty. It also narrates the nation's problems, which the hero single-handedly solves by displaying physical and moral courage.[54]

The price for the hero's heroism and success is, Virdi points out, female happiness. The gender dynamic in films of this golden age of Indian cinema is 'exceptionally powerful'.[55] Virdi writes, 'When women are afforded centrality, they suffer: their sacrifice, restraint, forbearance, chastity, and stoicism strengthen and ennoble them in the face of hardship.'[56] Thus, Mukherjee's film may place its heroine in the foreground, naming itself after her, but the plot line and the mechanics of its mise-en-scène reflect her self-sacrifice, making clear that she must give up all for the good of her husband and, as a consequence, that of the Indian nation. Thus, in physical terms, Anuradha's world becomes tangibly smaller as the adaptation progresses. The daughter of a wealthy man, she has the luxury of space in literal and metaphorical terms, living in plush surroundings, enjoying the freedom both to move freely about the city and to make choices about her life as a celebrated performer and potential marriage partners. Marriage restricts her space, confining her to interior, largely static shots in the rural backwater to which her husband moves her. Her elevated window shots offer her a powerful view of this backwater but prevent any access to it. Music, song and performance disappear from her world as her instruments gather dust and her husband asks her to switch off a record, which distracts him from his work. The adaptation clearly formulates Anuradha's erasure as an individual in the world, which she makes possible. When hosting a dinner guest, the father of the woman whose life her husband has saved, Anuradha explains that she has given up music. The man bows before her and offers her, and not her husband, the cheque for his daughter's treatment, stating that 'Nirmal is here because of her sacrifice. Her voice is lost today … To give life to others she gave up her music.' He continues:

> Your husband will become a very renowned man one day, he will make headlines. People will welcome him. They will sing his praises, honor him. But no one will realize that far away, behind all this applause was a voice that got lost. There was a flower that withered away. A light that blew off. … These are our daughters, sisters, mothers who no one knows.

Mukherjee's adaptation makes clear Anuradha's annihilation within her marriage, but it is no feminist piece for, while recognizing her sacrifice, it offers no real alternative or solution. Invited to leave her husband by her father and later tempted to do so by Deepak, who urges her to be true to herself and to God in her divine talent, Anuradha does not do so, choosing husband and nation over herself. Such, Virdi argues, is the inevitable fate of women in Indian cinema of this golden age. She writes:

> The time-honored love story formula, the benighted love triangle, always shows a woman torn between two men. Narratives of love foreground women caught in dramatic moments of conflict with their conscience: they wrestle with love, desire, and duty. Men do not face conflicts in love: their universe expands beyond love into lofty struggles against society, for social

justice, and against evil forces. The male hero wins the woman he wants, while she struggles within her narrow moral universe to make the 'right' choice – choosing the hero.⁵⁷

Mukherjee's adaptation adapts its cinematic moment and movement more than the Flaubertian source text which, in complex ways, lies behind it.

Epic adaptations: *Madame Bovary* and David Lean's *Ryan's Daughter*

David Lean's 1970 adaptation of Flaubert's *Madame Bovary* is starkly different from Mukherjee's take on the novel. Lean, like Mukherjee, is influenced by the film genre within which he works at least as much as by Flaubert's novel. Lean's genre is epic film. Lean's *Ryan's Daughter* does not acknowledge the novel or its author in the film's opening credits. But Lean and the film's writer, Robert Bolt, weave implicit acknowledgements to both throughout the adaptation. The plot parallels are stark. Lean's heroine is a pampered, spoiled Rosy who has read too many novels and goes in quest of the impossible romanticized life they promise by marrying a well-meaning but sexually unexciting school teacher, Charles. Charles, as well as sharing the name of his Flaubertian predecessor, will, like him, share his wife with a dashing Romantic hero, Major Doryan (Lean's version of Rodolphe): an act which will lead to their combined social ruin rather than the financial ruin they experience in Flaubert's novel. Flaubert's hapless curate becomes a far more incisive social commentator in Lean's piece, predicting Emma's ruin at her father's hands. The curate struggles to hold together the warring factions of this rural Irish town as Lean and Bolt relocate Flaubert's nineteenth-century French setting to the First World War era in an Ireland contemptuous of and rising up against the British troops policing it while also fighting in the trenches. Flaubert's Hippolyte, the stableman whose operation Charles botches, crippling both Hippolyte and Charles's own marriage to Emma, becomes the limping village idiot Michael (played by John Mills). Michael is no less damaging to Rosy than Hippolyte was to Emma for, driven by his love for Emma and his will to impress her, he dresses up as the military man Doryan with whom she is having an affair, inadvertently alerting the priest and the village to her infidelity. For all Lean and Bolt's careful reworking of Flaubert's source novel, and the range and depth of their literary allusions to it, many critics did not realize that Lean's film was an adaptation. Pauline Kael, panning the film, was one of the few critics to make the association:

Bolt and Lean have given us Flaubert's *Emma Bovary*. ... At the beginning we see the dreamy Rosy reading a cheap romance. [... There is] illicit bliss with a classy lover; ruin and suffering; forgiveness from the devoted, betrayed husband.[58]

Lean's film is an adaptation, but it is one in which Flaubert's novel is overshadowed by other factors, most notably the genre of filmmaking with which Lean is associated.

Lean's association with the genre of the 'epic' in film is, Andrew Collins writes in a retrospective of the director's film, clear. '[I]t will always be impossible', Collins writes, 'to use the word "epic" and not immediately think of him [Lean].'[59] What is less clear is what specifically might be meant by 'epic' cinema. Though the term has shifted in its use over time, epic films are generally held to be works with a sweeping scope and scale, often created with a big budget and focusing, like the literary form from which they derive, on the deeds and adventures of a heroic character. They may be literary adaptations and/or period pieces that showcase the expanse of a known historical era. Lean's *Ryan's Daughter* is epic in its use of scale and space. Lean's films habitually open with bold, wide-screen establishing shots. Such shots, in their vastness, fill *Ryan's Daughter*, a film which turns away from the interiority of Flaubert's novel as he dissects characters' thoughts and urges at such close and ruthless focus (see Figure 4.6). The adaptation does allow its viewer two telling point-of-view shots in the film's two sex scenes from Rosy's perspective – the first a static, short, abrupt shot of the ceiling as she lies, unsatisfied, in her marital bed; the second a blissfully hazy euphoric shot of the forest canopy as she lies, sated, with Major Doryan. But the rest of Lean's film is relentlessly exterior in its focus. Emma's urges, half formulated

FIGURE 4.6 Ryan's Daughter *(1970, dir. Lean)*.

and then silenced by the priest, go unexplored, and those of her handsome but damaged First World War hero and lover, Major Doryan, though hinted at in fragmentary flashback, are relentlessly quashed and silenced by the man himself. The adaptation will not allow us into the personal and private spaces of its characters' minds. Instead, echoing the spatial paradox at the heart of Flaubert's novel as Emma feels suffocated in the endless expanses of the rural locations in which she lives, Lean's film traps its characters in panoramic spaces. Characters are repeatedly filmed in an extreme high-angle shot as they walk the empty expanse of the isolated Irish beaches where they live. Lean's shots are panoramic in all that they encompass but bear down inexorably on the characters inhabiting them, underlining the entrapment of characters in their lives as well as their social and political situations. Rosy's hat blows away in the sea wind as she walks to meet Charles when he returns from his teaching conference in Dublin. So too does his hat. Their actions as they retrieve each other's hats pair them to each other, but they also link these characters in their isolation. Their finances, education and social standing set them apart from the village they inhabit, a village they will flee at the adaptation's close. Broken by their experiences in the village, they escape to seek the space and anonymity of Dublin. The space of Lean's film is epic in its vastness, but that vastness maintains the ability to stifle those who live in it.

If notions of the epic shape Lean's film and his interpretation of the source text, so too does his film subvert key elements of its genre, notably in relation to heroism. Rather than constructing itself around a clear and incontrovertible notion of the heroic, Lean's film intriguingly asks what heroism actually is. It posits but then destabilizes the potential heroes at the heart of its plot. The film's potential heroes are numerous. Most visible among them is the celebrated war hero Major Doryan, who arrives in Kirrary as a decorated war veteran. He mockingly hails himself 'a crippled bloody hero'. The film contrasts his wartime bravery with the avowed cowardice of the trembling British officer who asks Doryan, having read about his heroics in the paper, for advice as he prepares to be sent to the front:

> I'm a coward you see – always have been. I hate it. The ruddy thought of it gives me the shakes. That's my nightmare. The shakes. I don't mind dying. Not if it's quick. I wouldn't mind a gammy leg like you. I'm going to disgrace myself.

The film immediately questions the apparent clear distinction between coward and hero, as Doryan claims he would repeat none of his heroism should the same situation arise, before trembling at the bursts of sound from the generator. He situates cowardice at the heart of his bravery while the justly petrified officer departing for the front leaves as commanded, heroic in his very fear. Lean's film also questions heroism in the form of Rosy's father, who sets himself up as a hero of the Irish cause, talking its talk, while simultaneously informing against the rebels and standing mutely as his daughter is wrongly punished, his acts of treachery attributed by the village folk to her. Heroism again proves a thorny, relative concept with regard to the Irish Republican Brotherhood (IRB) leader Tim O'Leary, who erupts into the adaptation's storyline. Seeking to recover a shipment of arms being floated from a ship to the shore, the whole village turns out to help O'Leary, their hero, in his mission. He brings the whole village together behind a cause and his heroic persona. A hero for the village, he is, however, a criminal to the British forces in the film, having killed, earlier in the action, a police constable. Heroism, Lean's film suggests, depends entirely on your geographical borders. Lean plays with the heroic conventions of the genre his film inhabits.

Epic films are often literary adaptations and frequently monumentalize their source. Lean's film may approach Flaubert's source text only obliquely in its references and plot allusions, rather than monumentalizing it per se, but it is monumental in its determined characterization of itself as literary in stature. Flaubert, as a writer, was renowned for the painstaking graft he put in as a wordsmith, torturously and repeatedly polishing his prose, testing its rhythms and artistry on his literary colleague Louis Bouilhet. 'Every sentence, every paragraph, it seemed, would have to be forged painfully, read aloud, and worked over again and again, like lines of verse; the book could advance only at a snail's pace; it would take years!'[60] The parallels between this literary collaboration and that of Lean and his writer Robert Bolt are, Park-Finch argues, telling. Park-Finch writes of Lean and Bolt, detailing the ten months of daily collaboration in which they argued over every line of dialogue:

> This process has been well-documented elsewhere, albeit with little or no comment on the fact that the authors were already walking in Flaubert's footsteps and beginning an unconscious mimesis that would continue throughout [the project's creation].[61]

Park-Finch continues with the comparison:

> When Flaubert finally began, he found the new style increasingly difficult to master, particularly since Bouilhet subjected every page to close scrutiny. They would meet in the evenings or the weekends, when Bouilhet would make him re-read the latest sentences and paragraphs and help to rework them until they described the events simply, clearly, and devoid of the flowery lyricism and embellishments of the romantics.[62]

Comparably, Lean would start each day with 'criticisms of what they had done the day before', giving Bolt no option but to 'put another sheet of paper into the typewriter'.[63] For Park-Finch, Lean and Bolt's film monumentalizes itself in other ways. It borrows extensively and intensively from Thomas Hardy's *Far from the Madding Crowd* (1874). Doryan owes much to Hardy's Sergeant Troy, who lures Rosy/Bathsheba away from her respectable husband, makes love to her after a horse ride in a bluebell wood and commits suicide in an act that recalls Troy's assumed drowning and self-destructive behaviour.[64] But Lean and Bolt's film monumentalizes itself too, in its determined and deliberately literary nature. Malcolm Bowie draws attention to Flaubert's penchant for 'assonance, alliteration, rhyme, and near-rhyme'.[65] Finch-Park argues that there are clear stylistic parallels in Bolt's screenplay, a screenplay that works hard to mark itself as literature:

> 'The shadow seagull is swallowed up in the colder light' (Bolt 12) and 'A salmon flings itself at the fall of water' (Bolt 101) are examples of an extensive use of poeticism, designed perhaps to convey a romantic or even elegiac atmosphere to the cameraman and crew. The recurring 's' sounds hint at the sea as it ebbs and flows in the background, while 'shadow' becomes 'swallow' and finally 'colder', the main vowels being linked by repeated 'l's. In the second sentence, alliteration again suggests water, but this time the 'f' sounds conjure up rapids and waterfalls in a mountain stream. Elsewhere, clashing consonants convey a more austere feeling, as in: 'This is Killin's Cross where the third-class coast road strikes inland' (Bolt 12). In this sentence, the hard 'k's and 'c's combine with the 't's and 'd's, denoting sparse scenery and harsh conditions. Such pictorial language appears again [in] the screenplay: 'It is a piled-up bright red tinker's cart trotting towards us between jolly little hills where beechwoods stand bare.' Once more there is a conscious articulation of strong 'p's and alliterated 'b's, helping the sound of the horse's hooves to be heard in the repeated 't's of the 'tinker's cart trotting towards us'. ... [W]hen Rosy is hiding from the sun in a cleft of rocks, prior to being interrogated by Father Collins about her disappointed marital expectations, she has 'a coil of seaweed like wet yellow satin round her wrist. As it slithers off she coils it again' (Bolt 67). The repeated 'w's and the half-rhymes of 'weed', 'wet', 'sat', and 'wrist' vividly portray Rosy as a sea-wraith in her cave, with a coiling, snake-like piece of seaweed evoking the biblical temptation of Eve as it 'slithers' around, hinting at Rosy's state of mind before her fall from innocence.[66]

Literature, in the form of poorly digested Romantic novels and poetry, may destroy Emma Bovary and, to a lesser extent, Rosy Ryan, but Robert Bolt creates his work from Flaubert as literature, marking his screenplay both with the plot and detail of his source and with the style and literary rhythms of its genre. Lean and Bolt's film marks itself as epic in its literary nature.

History, as a source text, is the frequent focus of epic film as a genre. Lean's film is both shaped by that convention – it relocates Flaubert's plot to Ireland in the First World War era – and interrogates it, probing what history is and how we construct it in film. *Ryan's Daughter* both reflects Irish history and, in some small measure, altered it for one small village. It pumped huge amounts of money into a small Irish town, Dunquin. Finch-Park writes:

> Suddenly, young men who had been thinking of emigrating to the United States found themselves paid large sums on a regular basis as part of an influx of money that transformed the lives of the 1,300 inhabitants. Such was the immense impact on the community that a local teacher composed a song (*God Save our Lean*) that was published in the *Kerryman* … while local factories, garages, and businesses were co-opted into the day-to-day business of making props, costumes, sets, and equipment, as well as driving the 104 vehicles and feeding everyone involved.[67]

The adaptation helped transform the area into a key tourist destination, stimulating the hospitality sector, which it continues to sustain today via paratextual documentaries – the BBC's *Rosy Ryan Returns* (2000) and the independent *A Bit of a Fillum* (2009) – and a festival called '*Ryan's Daughter* Revisited'.

Lean's film not only altered a small section of Irish history, it also pushes its viewer to interrogate the history which epic film so often takes as a source. History, as it is recorded in *Ryan's Daughter*, is visibly factually incorrect. Rosy is hounded out of the village for informing on the IRB to the British forces. Her act of treachery goes down in village history. Yet she is innocent, and the truth of her father's perfidy – he volubly and falsely describes his history as an Irish Republican hero at the drop of a hat – goes undetected and unrecorded. History is also, Lean's film emphasizes, geographically and politically conditioned. Its truth depends on the national and political mindset within which you find yourself. Tim O'Leary, the IRB leader, has a heroic past for the Irish Republican community, a criminal one for the British Unionists. Rosy's father's acts of informing are treacherous for the Irish Republicans yet dutiful to the mind of the British forces. That they never come to light and remain silent is key to the film, which has its own silences. The film depicts Irish Nationalists as allies of Germany, receiving arms shipments from them and resolutely opposing the British forces and their endeavours. Yet the film makes no mention of the 210,000 Irish soldiers, many of them committed

Republicans, who fought with the British forces in the trenches. They fought on the urging of the Nationalist leader John Redmond, who argued that the freedom of small invaded nations like Belgium or Serbia was analogous to that of Ireland. Their fight, he argued, was one and the same. If Redmond depicted their endeavour as heroic, Irish history has not recorded it as such. Irish survivors of the war came home not to a hero's welcome but to a more resolutely nationalist political scenario in which they met with hostility and even violence for fighting on the side of the British oppressors. Keith Jeffery writes, 'For all of them the high public honour and celebration with which they had departed contrasted sharply with the changed circumstances of their return.'[68] History, Lean's film demonstrates in its silence, shifts and mutates.

Lean's film underscores the complexity of history as source in the epic genre for it is influenced not only by the past but also by its historic present. Contemporary history certainly shapes Lean and Bolt's creation of *Ryan's Daughter*; as they worked on their screenplay in 1968, the Provisional Irish Republican Army (IRA) began a paramilitary campaign, triggering a new set of Troubles fuelled by their importing of weapons – reminiscent of the gun-running scenes in *Ryan's Daughter*. Historical frames and moments blur and merge in other ways in Lean's adaptation. Accused of betraying the IRB and the villagers to the British forces by informing to her lover Major Doryan, Rosy is stripped and shorn of her hair for collaborating with the enemy. The scene harks visibly back to the Second World War and *les femmes tondues* – the women publicly shorn of their hair for sleeping with the German occupying forces in France. History, the basis of the epic film, is, Lean's adaptation suggests, more mobile, multiple and fluid than it would have us think. It is, in that very mobility, unknowable and unfixable; hence, perhaps, the adaptation's close. Rather than definitively reuniting or separating the battered and broken pairing of Rosy and Charles, the adaptation has them leave for Dublin, perhaps as a couple, perhaps as individuals going their own way. When Charles admits to the priest that he is thinking of leaving Rosy, the priest replies thus: 'Mebbe you're right. Mebbe you ought. But I doubt it. And that's my parting gift to you. That doubt. God bless.' Walking back to the village, Father Collins offers the film's final judgement: 'I don't know … I don't know at all …' History, whether the personal history of Rosy and Charles or the political history of the Irish struggles against which their story is set, proves to be shifting and refuses to be absolute. Lean's film plays with the historical conventions so key to the epic genre of his work.

While source texts matter to the adaptations made of French texts studied in this chapter, so too do the dominant poetics in film in the era 1945–70. Each of the adaptations studied in this chapter demonstrates the complex mix of ingredients in the adaptive artefact, for they are composite pieces which adapt both a source piece of literature and the movement or genre with which they associate themselves. The way these films adapt movements and genres is complex. They work both within and against conventions in key places, visibly inverting them in ways that ask probing questions of their borders and boundaries. Autant-Lara's *Le Rouge et le Noir* monumentalizes both the literary source behind it and itself as a culturally high creative artefact performed by quality actors and production techniques, in keeping with the French Tradition of Quality with which it aligned itself. But it also pushes its viewer to question the truth of its literary source and its ability to capture that source, asking difficult questions about the adaptive process. The French New Wave – which categorically rejected the central tenets of the Tradition of Quality – did not reject its focus on adaptation, which its filmmakers continued, albeit in a very different vein. Truffaut's *Jules et Jim*, shaped by both its source text and the New Wave urge to revolutionize art and life, adapts a socially and artistically iconoclastic text in cinematographically iconoclastic ways in its bid to change the world. If Truffaut adapts in keeping with the conventions of his movement in this instance, Preminger's *Carmen Jones* moves powerfully to subvert the escapism of the musical film genre within which he works, using his film to question the essential freedoms of African Americans in contemporary North American society. Playing on the weight of the *déjà connu* of his canonical text's ending, he traps his protagonists both in their creative fate and in their sociocultural situation. Bazzoni's *Man, Pride, and Vengeance* crafts a creative freedom for itself by adapting its film genre, the Spaghetti Western, as well as the *Carmen* source text that lies at its heart. His adaptation foregrounds the geographical complexity of the adaptive artefact as it moves the space of the source text across era, medium and nation. It does so in one of the most spatially complex film genres, the Spaghetti Western, in which multiple locations and target nations are referenced and encompassed. The conventions of the film moment within which Mukherjee's *Anuradha* is made, the golden age of Indian cinema, shape his film almost to the exclusion of its source text, *Madame Bovary*. Source texts, the film makes clear, are multiple and shifting even before they pass through the prism of the dominant aesthetics of the adapting film's time. Lean, as a director, came to define epic film as a genre in his era, yet his *Ryan's Daughter* interrogates the very conventions of that genre, questioning the heroism, literary stature and history on which it was based. In their parallel adaptations of *Carmen* and *Madame Bovary*, Preminger, Bazzoni, Mukherjee and Lean show the powerful formative influence of the dominant poetics within which they each work. They are all shaped by and invert key tropes of this dominant poetics. They cast valuable light on the complex cultural composite that is adaptation. They require us, as film critics and viewers, to go in quest of more than just source texts when we watch literature remade as film.

Notes

1. Lefevere's core interest is in translation, but he extends his theoretical model to include other art forms, including film adaptation. He suggests: 'The same basic process of rewriting is at work in translation, historiography, anthologization, criticism, and editing', before allying it with 'adaptations for film and television'. André Lefevere, *Translation, Rewriting and the Manipulation of Literary Fame* (London: Routledge 2017), xii.
2. André Lefevere, ed., *Translation, History, Culture: A Sourcebook* (London: Routledge, 1992), 26.
3. Bill Nichols, ed., *Movies and Methods* (Berkeley: University of California Press, 1976), 224.
4. *La Symphonie pastorale* (*Pastoral Symphony*) (1947, dir. Delannoy), *Jeux interdits* (*Forbidden Games*) (1952, dir. Clément) and *Gervaise* (1956, dir. Clément). Various attempts to rehabilitate the Tradition of Quality have been made. Rodney Hill writes, 'In all fairness, Richard Neupert and others have suggested that such a harsh assessment of the "Tradition of Quality" overlooks a very real quality cinema to be found in that period, now somewhat neglected, of French film history.' Rodney Hill, 'The New Wave Meets the Tradition of Quality: Jacques Demy's *The Umbrellas of Cherbourg*', *Cinema Journal* 48.1 (2008): 27–50 (29–30). However, where the Tradition of Quality does feature in the landscape of film movements and their evolution, it does so largely as a backdrop to the development of the New Wave, as the moribund movement against which they reacted.
5. Alan Williams cited in Hill, 'The New Wave Meets the Tradition of Quality', 32.
6. Susan Hayward cited in Hill, 'The New Wave Meets the Tradition of Quality', 32.
7. Hill, 'The New Wave Meets the Tradition of Quality', 30.
8. Hill, 'The New Wave Meets the Tradition of Quality', 33.
9. Williams cited in Hill, 'The New Wave Meets the Tradition of Quality', 33.
10. Claire Deslauriers, 'Démodé et indémodable: Enjeux contemporains d'un style stendhalien', *Dix-Neuf* 19.1 (2015): 22–32 (22–23).
11. David Thompson, 'Three Films with Gérard Philipe', *Sight & Sound* 26.4 (April 2016): 100–1.
12. Janey Place and Lowell Peterson, 'Some Visual Motifs of *Film Noir*', in *Film Noir Reader*, ed. Alain Silver and James Ursini (New York: Limelight Editions, 1996), 68.
13. Play-acting forms the crux of Julien's identity. Peter Brooks writes:

    > Julien continually sees himself as the hero of his own text and conceives of that text as something to be created, not simply endured. … His scenarios make him not only the actor, the feigning self, but also the stage manager of his own destiny, constantly projecting the self into the future on the basis of hypothetical plots. One of the most

striking examples of such hypotheses occurs when, after receiving Mathilde's summons to come to her bedroom at one o'clock in the morning, he imagines a plot – in all senses of the term, including plot as machination, as complot – in which he will be seized by Mathilde's brother's valets, bound, gagged, imprisoned, and eventually poisoned. So vivid is this fiction that the narrator tells us: 'Moved like a playwright by his own story, Julien was truly afraid when he entered the dining room.'

Peter Brooks, 'The Novel and the Guillotine; Or, Fathers and Sons in *Le Rouge et le Noir*', *PMLA* 97.3 (1982): 348–62 (352).

14 Charles Drazin, *The Faber Book of French Cinema* (London: Faber and Faber, 2011), 280.
15 Truffaut cited in Bill Nicholls, ed., *Movies and Methods: Volume One. An Anthology* (Berkeley: University of California Press, 1976), 229.
16 Writing on Truffaut's article, Rodney Hill suggests it has had 'a disproportionate level of influence over scholarly opinion of the "Tradition of Quality" in the intervening half-century since it first appeared in the pages of *Cahiers du cinema*'. Hill, 'The New Wave Meets the Tradition of Quality', 30.
17 See Maria Scott, 'Acts of Suppression: Adapting *Le Rouge et le Noir*', *Literature/Film Quarterly* 3.35 (2007): 237–43.
18 Sandy Petrey, *Realism and Revolution: Balzac, Stendhal, Zola and the Performances of History* (Ithaca, NY: Cornell University Press, 1988), 150.
19 Petrey, *Realism and Revolution*, 149.
20 For a compelling reading of Julien's play-acting and duplicity, see Pierre Dubé, 'Reflections on Chapter Titles in *Le Rouge et le Noir*', *Dalhousie French Studies* 30 (1995): 45–54. Stendhal, *The Red and the Black*, trans. Roger Gard (London: Penguin, 2002), 522–3, 524.
21 While Rodney Hill points out that defining 'New Wave' precisely is a rather slippery enterprise, largely because its members did not conceive of themselves as a movement, he cites Michel Marie's identification of eight broad characteristics of the New Wave. Hill writes:

> For Marie, a New Wave film is made by an *auteur*-director (who ideally is also the screenwriter). New Wave films often use nonprofessional actors or newcomers, and they evince an improvisational approach to the script and acting. They privilege location-shooting over studio sets, make use of small crews, and utilize rudimentary lighting and direct sound, as opposed to post-production dubbing of dialogue (we might broaden this, allowing for other innovative uses of sound and music in Demy's films). Finally, New Wave films are concerned with contemporary cultural issues, everyday life, and ordinary characters. (Hill, 'The New Wave Meets the Tradition of Quality', 28)

22 Erica Sheen, 'Anti-Anti-Fidelity: Truffaut, Roché, Shakespeare', *Adaptation* 6.3 (2013): 243–59 (256).

23 Antoine de Baecque and Serge Toubiana, *Truffaut: A Biography* (Berkeley: University of California Press, 2000).
24 Henri-Pierre Roché, *Jules et Jim*, trans. Patrick Evans (London: Penguin, 2011), 126.
25 Roché, *Jules et Jim*, 178, 169, 170.
26 Roché, *Jules et Jim*, 185.
27 Roché, *Jules et Jim*, 185.
28 Roché, *Jules et Jim*, 86.
29 Roché, *Jules et Jim*, 87, 208, 121.
30 Steven Cohan, *Hollywood Musicals: The Film Reader* (London: Routledge, 2002), 3.
31 Cohan, *Hollywood Musicals*, 9.
32 Rick Altman, *The American Film Musical* (Bloomington: Indiana University Press, 1987), 164.
33 Thomas Schatz, *Hollywood Genres: Formulas, Filmmaking and the Studio System* (New York: Random House, 1981), 217.
34 Cohan, *Hollywood Musicals*, 13.
35 Cohan, *Hollywood Musicals*, 2.
36 The film is an adaptation of Oscar Hammerstein's all-African American Broadway musical and the Bizet text behind it (Preminger was unhappy with large sections of Hammerstein's piece and commissioned a rewrite of it). Hammerstein's adaptation is as revisionary in racial terms as its subsequent film adaptation. Hammerstein, as Annegret Fauser makes clear, was a founding member of the Hollywood Anti-Nazi League in June 1936 'which clearly addressed US racial politics as much as German fascism in its revised mission statement of 1937 requiring its members to "combat racial intolerance and thus combat Nazism, which uses intolerance as a weapon to attain power" '. Annegret Fauser, 'Dixie Carmen: War, Race and Identity in Oscar Hammerstein's *Carmen Jones* (1943)', *Journal of the Society for American Music* 4.2 (2010): 127–74 (137–8). Hammerstein supported African American causes financially and in non-monetary ways: as he was completing the third act of *Carmen Jones* in July 1942, he wrote to the National Urban League in light of its call for equal access to defence work for African Americans:

> Due to pressure of other causes being made upon me, the enclosed check is all I can afford at the moment. Later in the year, however, I hope I will be able to augment this by a larger one. Meanwhile, I am so interested in the philosophy behind the movement of your League that I would be delighted to help you in other ways, if you can point out to me what I can do. (Hammerstein cited in Fauser, 'Dixie Carmen', 138)

37 Nora Holt, cited in Fauser, 'Dixie Carmen', 153.

38 Preminger's number owes much to Hammerstein's adaptation, of which Fauser writes thus:

> In the 1942 opening of Act 2 – the scene at Billy Pastor's – Hammerstein describes the dancers as whirling 'in a wild series of varied evolutions combining jive, jitters and African frenzy', a reference deleted in the revised version. What remains of the African allusion, however, are Carmen's lyrics in 'Beat out dat rhythm on a drum', which have her sing 'feel it beatin' in my bones, / It feel like twen'y millyun tomtoms. / I know dere's twen'y millyun tomtoms / Beatin' down deep inside my bones!' The musical effect was accentuated by the on-stage presence of renowned drummer Cozy Cole, who turned this sequence into a virtuoso showpiece, and whose increasingly dominant use of the bass drum throughout that number – sonically prominent even in the number's truncated version on the original-cast album – mimicked the sonorities of the tom-toms. According to Naomi André, Harlem Renaissance authors in the 1920s and 1930s had coded the sound of the tom-toms as embodying the essence of Africa to the point that William Grant Still opened his composition *Africa* with it. (Fauser, 'Dixie Carmen', 155–6)

39 Thibault Leplat, 'Quel rapport entre un match de foot et *Hamlet*', *Le Nouvel Observateur*, 18 March 2019. https://bibliobs.nouvelobs.com/screenshot/20190318.OBS1980/quel-rapport-entre-un-match-de-foot-et-hamlet.html.

40 Italian Westerns were not born with the Spaghetti Western genre in the 1960s and go back to the earliest days of film. Arguably the first Italian Western film was made by the key Spaghetti Western director Sergio Leone's father, Vincenzo Leone, in 1913: *La Vampira Indiana* (*Indian Vampire*), with Sergio Leone's mother in the title role. While Spaghetti Westerns proliferated in the 1960s and were a box office success story, Bert Fridlund points out that by 1969, Italian Westerns were in stark decline: seventy-one were produced in 1968, a figure which fell to twenty-six in 1969. Their share of total Italian production fell from 30 per cent to 11 per cent. While there was a brief revival as a result of some soul-searching and innovative departures on the part of the movement, it proved short-lived, as by 1973 production was down to eighteen, soon, as Fridlund puts it, 'to dwindle into practically nothing'. Bert Fridlund, ' "A First Class Pall-Bearer!"': The Sartana/Sabata Cycle in Spaghetti Westerns', *Film International* 6.3 (2008): 44–55 (55).

41 On the transnational affiliations of this genre, see David Martin-Jones, 'Transnational Allegory/Transnational History: *Se sei vivo spara/Django Kill … If you Live, Shoot!*', *Transnational Cinemas* 2 (2012): 179–95.

42 Russ Hunter writes:

> Despite (or perhaps because of) this popular success, studies of Italian cinema history generally ignored the Spaghetti Western, instead valorizing and focusing upon Italian neo-realism as a perceived

manifestation of what an Italian cinema *should* be: engaged, political and above all else an art cinema. A more general move towards the study of popular culture has seen a welcome growth of studies exploring the political economy of the Spaghetti Western and the dynamic impact it had upon 1960s Italian cinema and its audiences. Moreover, recent work around the Spaghetti Western has built upon earlier, more fragmented accounts and begun to operate on a more detailed textual level, exploring both the thematic and conceptual concerns central to the sub-genre as well as identifying the often complex political allegories at play in many later 'Zapata' Westerns.

Russ Hunter, 'The Ecstasy of Gold: Love, Greed and Homosociality in the Dollars Trilogy', *Studies in European Cinema* 9.1 (2012): 69–78 (71).

43 For a fuller reading of this concept, see Martin-Jones, 'Transnational Allegory/Transnational History', 184.
44 Dimitris Eleftheriotis, *Popular Cinemas of Europe: Studies of Texts, Contexts and Frameworks* (London: Continuum, 2001), 97–8.
45 Eleftheriotis, *Popular Cinemas of Europe*, 126.
46 Hunter, 'The Ecstasy of Gold', 73.
47 Hunter, 'The Ecstasy of Gold', 73.
48 Fridlund, ' "A First Class Pall-Bearer!" '.
49 Millicent Marcus, *Filmmaking by the Book: Italian Cinema and Literary Adaptation* (Baltimore: Johns Hopkins University Press, 1993), 140.
50 M. K. Raghavendra, *Seduced by the Familiar: Narration and Meaning in Indian Popular Cinema* (Oxford: Oxford University Press, 2008), 52.
51 Ajit Duara, 'A Touch of Realism', *The Hindu*, 3 September 2006, n.p.
52 Jyotika Virdi, *The Cinematic ImagiNation: Indian Popular Films as Social History* (New Brunswick, NJ: Rutgers University Press, 2003).
53 Virdi, *The Cinematic ImagiNation*, 92.
54 Virdi, *The Cinematic ImagiNation*, 94.
55 Virdi, *The Cinematic ImagiNation*, 121.
56 Virdi, *The Cinematic ImagiNation*, 122.
57 Virdi, *The Cinematic ImagiNation*, 127.
58 Pauline Kael cited in Heebon Park-Finch, 'From *Madame Bovary* to *Ryan's Daughter*: Literary, Cultural, and Historical Palimpsests', *Adaptation* 10.1 (2017): 51–72 (54).
59 Andrew Collins, 'The Epic Legacy of David Lean', *Guardian*, 4 May 2008, https://www.theguardian.com/film/2008/may/04/features.
60 Francis Steegmuller, cited in Park-Finch, 'From *Madame Bovary* to *Ryan's Daughter*', 56.
61 Park-Finch, 'From *Madame Bovary* to *Ryan's Daughter*', 55.
62 Park-Finch, 'From *Madame Bovary* to *Ryan's Daughter*', 55–6.

63 Adrian Turner cited in Park-Finch, 'From *Madame Bovary* to *Ryan's Daughter*', 56.
64 Park-Finch, 'From *Madame Bovary* to *Ryan's Daughter*', 57.
65 Malcolm Bowie, 'Introduction', in Gustave Flaubert, *Madame Bovary: Provincial Manners*, trans. Margaret Mauldon (Oxford: Oxford University Press, 2004), xiii.
66 Park-Finch, 'From *Madame Bovary* to *Ryan's Daughter*', 60.
67 Park-Finch, 'From *Madame Bovary* to *Ryan's Daughter*', 61.
68 Keith Jeffery, 'Ireland and World War One', BBC, 3 October 2011, http://www.bbc.co.uk/history/british/britain_wwone/ireland_wwone_01.shtml.

5

The history of adaptation/ adaptation and history (1970–2004)

Kate Griffiths

This book, as its title suggests, charts the history of French literature in film. But history is not something merely to be reconstituted from these adaptations. Rather history, as the chapters of this book have argued, is an active force shaping adaptations in myriad ways as directors adapt for the target time, values and politics of their historical moment. But what this book has not yet considered is the fact that history is not just a shaping force in the adaptive process. It also functions, at times, as a source text in its own right. Directors, in complex ways, adapt both a historical era and a literary source text written in it for cinematic release. History as a source text presents difficult questions for adaptation studies. How fixed is it a source? How graspable is it in film? Intriguingly, the case study films of this chapter do not shy away from such questions. Rather, in complex and self-reflexive ways they engage with the difficulties of adapting history as source. They craft complex adaptive artefacts which contemplate their limits and incapacities. They find a potent creative power and presence in so doing.

The case study films of this chapter are intentionally diverse. They range from porn to children's animation, encompassing heritage film along the way. Their association stems from the way in which each turns to a different history, seeking not only to capture it in film but also evaluating its success in so doing. Just Jaeckin's 1974 soft-porn film *Emmanuelle* adapts the sexual revolution of the 1960s and 1970s in society, literature and film, pushing up against the limits of what it can show. The *Black Emanuelle* unauthorized spin-offs of this film undertaken by a variety of directors, but most often associated with Joe d'Amato, adapt Italy's complex relationship with its colonial pasts and peoples, using their exotic spaces to challenge the borders of porn history in their topics and style. The British *Carry On* spin-off of the *Emmanuelle* franchise, the disastrous *Carry On Emmanuelle* (1978, dir. Thomas), adapts British social and class history of the era. It also adapts the history of the *Carry On* franchise for which it was one of the death knells, anthologizing the British film phenomenon which it was bringing to an end. Janet Perlman's animation *The Tender Tale of Cinderella Penguin* (1981) underlines that when you adapt, part of what you adapt is the history of adaptation. Working from Charles Perrault's fairy tales, Perlman's piece also adapts the multiple adaptations accreted onto the surface of said fairy tales. Perrault's tales, far from being a point of origin, are in any case the latest retelling of age-old stories which, like the animations made of them, circulate in new forms for new eras, nations and contexts. The heritage films which flourished in this era adapt history even more directly. Claude Berri's *Germinal* (1993), epic in its scale and commitment to history, echoes the intention of its source author, Émile Zola, to capture the past as source. Zola's novel questions its ability to grasp history as/in text. Berri's film quietly does likewise, exploring the multiple voices of the past which both inform and ultimately escape it. If Berri's film is quietly self-reflexive, Baz Luhrmann's *Moulin Rouge!* (2001) deconstructs the historical genre it ostensibly inhabits, revitalizing and reinventing said genre in so doing. Luhrmann's film exuberantly proffers and refuses both its source history and a range of French literary texts. It whets the viewer's appetite for a return in history and literature to a source. But it ultimately circles and recircles back on itself in an adaptive narrative which counters the very possibility of such a return. Jean-Pierre Jeunet's *Un long dimanche de fiançailles* (*A Very Long Engagement*) (2004) closes this chapter's case study years in which heritage adaptations are so prominent. An adaptation of a historical era, the First World War, and Sébastien Japrisot's novel based on it (1991), Jeunet's adaptation, in ways which speak to Luhrmann's *Moulin Rouge!*, deconstructs the heritage adaptation genre to which it nevertheless belongs. Jeunet adapts in his film a history which he makes clear he cannot grasp in any tangible way. History, Jeunet's film suggests, is a personal, subjective, multiple and at times false thing. It is a created and creative entity, an adaptation. History, be it in pornography, heritage film, *Carry On* films or children's animation, is a complex concept and source text in the film adaptations of this era.

Adapting the history of sex, film and society: The *Emmanuelle* brand

The histories which Just Jaeckin's 1974 soft-porn film *Emmanuelle* adapts are as multiple and diverse as the lovers the eponymous heroine takes in the course of the film. The wife of a French diplomat in Bangkok, Emmanuelle embarks on a voyage of sexual self-discovery and experimentation. She explores sex with her husband, other women, sex in public and threesomes, discussing her explorations with her mentor.

Emmanuelle clearly adapts the history of film in France. Seeking to work in the fertile philosophical vein opened by the French New Wave discussed in Chapter 4, a movement waning when *Emmanuelle* broke, Jaeckin's film is experimental both in its sexual content and in its philosophical message. As Chapter 4 argued, Truffaut's New Wave powerhouse *Jules et Jim* seeks to question and deconstruct the social conventions which govern human relationships, casting them as unnatural. Emmanuelle Arsan's novel *Emmanuelle* does likewise in extensive philosophical musings about the nature of humanity, society and the rules within which people love.[1] Citing philosophers, critical theorists and literary writers throughout, Arsan writes:

> Love is always unnatural. It's the absolute anti-nature. It's the crime, the insurrection par excellence against the order of the universe, the false note in the music of the spheres. It's man escaping from the Garden of Eden with a burst of laughter.[2]

While Truffaut's film pushes a reading of social and sexual laws as unnatural, Arsan's novel and Jaeckin's adaptation of it push their respective heroines into apparently 'unnatural' sex acts. They do so as a means to defy and deconstruct the social structure which defines and sets the parameters of the natural. Jaeckin's film may cut the vast majority of Arsan's philosophical musings, focusing on the aesthetics of the sexual body in their place, but it retains the novel's experimental structures, which hark back to the previously discussed scientific language and experimental approach of *Jules et Jim*. Garrett Chaffin-Quiray characterizes the novel as something of a Bildungsroman, arguing: '*Emmanuelle* is reducible to three movements of experimentation, reflection and conquest.'[3] Emmanuelle, under the guidance of her mentor, the ageing lothario Mario, experiments, testing the social laws and mores which the New Wave sought to explode, before quashing them with her new world order. *Emmanuelle* is, Chaffin-Quiray argues: 'a complicated palimpsest of cheap thrills and lofty ambitions. ... Firstly concerned with carnal pleasure, it turns into a lengthy treatise on bourgeois morality before exploding that morality through drug use, paedophilia and sexual orgy.'[4] *Emmanuelle* adapts elements of the New Wave's subversive intent, but it does so in the context of sex.

But ultimately, the way *Emmanuelle* films sex neutralizes its subversive intent, moving it away from the New Wave. *Jules et Jim* subsumes sex to philosophy, hiding it from view, Jaeckin's film does the inverse, putting sex centre stage in order to shock and titillate its audience. But Jaeckin's filmic form is, in stark contrast to the New Wave, recuperative in its aesthetics of sex. Jaeckin applies fashion lighting to his shots, accompanying them with pop music and, in Chaffin-Quiray's words, 'suggestive sexual coupling'.[5] He shows shocking sexual subject matter but in aesthetically unexceptional ways. Chaffin-Quiray argues:

> Professional lighting and recorded, or dubbed, sound is standard. Outdoor scenes and controlled backgrounds are commonplace and camerawork is static, editing seamless. Long takes are the rule with performances punctuated by awkward dialogue. In short, *Emmanuelle* is the obverse of the New Wave style and its return to a traditional production standard is what causes the film to sputter.[6]

Emmanuelle's aesthetic neutralizes some of the impact of its sexually shocking source. Jaeckin, a former fashion photographer, offers a series of almost photographed pornographic *tableaux vivants* which aestheticize the female body in static, ultimately contained and choreographed ways (see Figure 5.1). With the abolition of the source novel's philosophical content and intent, the

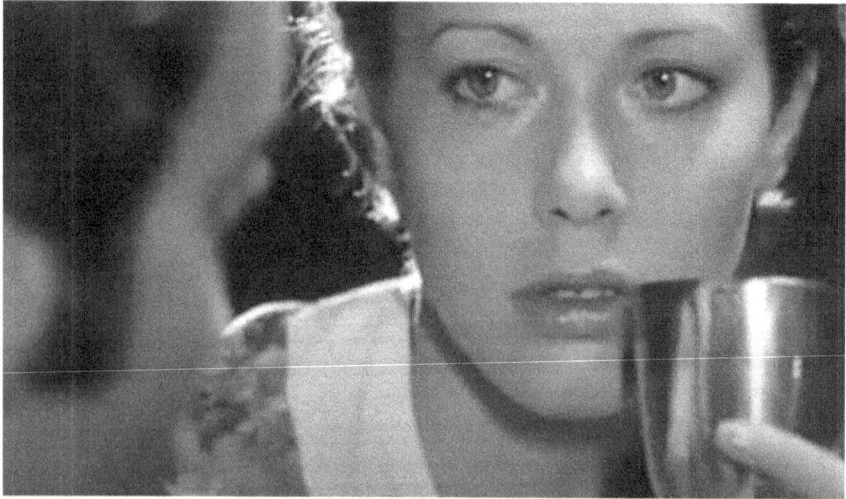

FIGURE 5.1 Emmanuelle *(1974, dir. Jaeckin)*.

links between these filmed sexual pornographic *tableaux vivants* feel flimsy to say the least. In its aesthetic and overarching narrative editing, Jaeckin's film refuses its heroine the sexual freedom its content and genre promises, trapping her instead as the latest descendant in the long line of photographed pornographic tableaux from the nineteenth century on. Picking up precisely on *Emmanuelle*'s pictorial, static photography, Pierre Schneider writes:

> One is reminded of the exotic backgrounds chosen by fashion magazines to present the new couture collections. Indeed, Mr Jaeckin's astuteness has been to realise that these magazines are the rightful heirs to the publications specialising in artistic nudes, popular and even acceptable in France around the turn of the century. It takes money to achieve this kind of artistic quality in a movie. One definition of the difference between pornography and eroticism might therefore be: the size of the budget.[7]

Jaeckin's *Emmanuelle* adapts elements of the history of the New Wave in its content, though not in its form.

Jaeckin's film also adapts the history of pornography as a genre and the historical trends which make it boom in certain eras. Porn had been feature of the cinematic landscape since the silent era, but the 1970s represent something of a golden age of cinematic porn for social, economic and legal reasons. The social movements and events of the 1960s, with their intent to undermine conservative values relating to the human body, sexuality and love, created a cultural space and a public more open to the soft-core porn of the 1970s. Porn cinemas previously, in the United States for example, had not published viewing times, as small cohorts of hard-core porn fans dropped in and out of cinemas which showed films on loop.[8] But, sensing a lucrative new market as a result of bringing soft-core porn into the mainstream, the cash-hungry and at times financially strapped film industries around the world turned to erotic film releases, screening them like they did mainstream features.[9] They were aided by the fact that by the mid-1950s, pornography had been decriminalized in many European nations and in the United States where box office successes like *Last Tango in Paris* (1972, dir. Bertolucci), *Emmanuelle* (1974, dir. Jaeckin) and *Deep Throat* (1972, dir. Damiano) proliferated. So close to the mainstream did soft-core porn come that Jon Lewis suggests there was a crucial point in the early 1970s when porn features did so well in *Variety*'s list of top grossing films that Hollywood even contemplated moving into porn production.[10] Though eventually Hollywood turned away from such an initiative, the influence of Hollywood on Jaeckin's *Emmanuelle* is clear in its push for glossy, slick, high-end production values. Jaeckin's film adapts the social, legal and commercial frameworks shaping pornography in the 1970s.

Jaeckin's *Emmanuelle* not only reflects the history of porn, it is also entwined with the historical and technological evolution of the genre. Jaeckin's film, though critically panned, was a huge commercial success and has become something of a cinematic monument in the history of porn films. Such was its success in the cultural and cinematic landscape that hosts of spin-offs – some authorized, many not – adapted its legacy.[11] The loosest of adaptations, these spin-offs take the Emmanuelle character and relocate her to new national contexts, new plots and new tales. Through these adaptations, which all rework, in some form or another, Arsan's novel and the accreted adaptations which lie on its surface, it is possible to reconstitute a history of porn in different technological eras. Jaeckin's film, with its comparatively high budget and high production values, apes, as this chapter has suggested, mainstream Hollywood cinema in its production, aesthetic and distribution. When the *Emmanuelle* brand hits the 1980s, video recorders and cameras had entered the home market. As Chuck Kleinhans points out, the effect of this new technology was dramatic.[12] X-rated home video rentals swelled, and by 1987 there were just 250 cinemas in the United States screening porn, a decline of 500 in just five years.[13] The home video camera meant that porn versions of *Emmanuelle* changed in their budgets, production and aesthetics. Aimed often at the home market, they eschewed cinema production values. Porn in the 1970s often took the form of feature-length, dramatic narratives shot on film in classical style at the hands of largely accomplished directors. Porn in the 1980s was starkly different. It could now be made at home (*Playboy* had an advertising section just for home productions). And those who made it professionally often now made back-to-back features, with slashed budgets, the new technology allowing them to produce more quickly, more cheaply than their 35 mm theatrical precedents. These new-technology porn films pushed budget thrills with little character development over narrative development and high production values. Lehman concludes: 'If one measures them against the hard-core feature, they show a loss of both production values (such as lighting) and narrative development.'[14] Kleinhans adds:

> The narrative in porn features tends to move 'back' to the more aesthetically primitive stag film or episodic series. Similarly the acting changes from a style that calls for more character development and some psychological realism to a skit or cartoon-style simplicity.[15]

The evolutions of *Emmanuelle* in different eras, technologies and aesthetics collectively construct a history of the porn genre.

The histories with which the *Emmanuelle* adaptations are entwined are not merely cinematic and technological, though. So too are they colonial. The *Black*

Emanuelle series, made by a variety of directors but most often associated with Joe D'Amato, is key to my line of argument here.[16] The series, starring the Indonesian actress Laura Gemser as a globe-trotting photo-journalist uncovering violence and injustices against women in narratives which simultaneously objectify her as sex object, draws freely on Jaeckin's *Emmanuelle*, avoiding legal action for its infringements only by spelling its protagonist's name with one less 'm'. Gemser starred in sixteen *Black Emanuelle* films as well as working with D'Amato on some similar erotic dramas such as *Eva Nera* (*Black Cobra Woman*) (1976), which were subsequently retitled as 'Emanuelle' adventures for sale in foreign territories, Xavier Mendik points out. D'Amato's *Black Emanuelle* films, in Mendik's words, situate

> the heroine in repeatedly ghoulish, violent and grisly situations. By pitching his heroine against rapists, cannibals and snuff movie directors as well as slave traders and manipulating mystics, D'Amato constructed a series of narratives more befitting a horror 'Scream Queen' than a porn diva. As Gemser's deathly status was often conflated with her blackness, D'Amato's films provide a way into understanding the very specific European fears and contradictions around black sexuality and savagery underpinning this cycle of 'exploitation' cinema.[17]

These *Black Emanuelle* films not only underscore the history of the *Emmanuelle* brand based on the Arsan novel, but also interact with and magnify the colonial history which troubles Arsan's source novel, Jaeckin's adaptation of it and, finally and most indelibly, D'Amato's reworking of both.

Written by Marayat Bibidh under the pen name of Emmanuelle Arsan, the novel *Emmanuelle* is penned by a writer born in Bangkok of mixed Thai and French descent. In much the same manner as the canonical French travel writing of the eighteenth century, it sends an implicitly white French woman to exotic, oriental climes to explore her sexuality and amorous freedoms in escapades in which she could not/does not engage in mainland France. Mendik, working from ideas propounded by Anne McClintock, argues:

> The principles of oppression that underpinned European expansion and colonisation into non-Western lands until the late nineteenth century were often coded as an erotic and yet monstrous journey into the unknown. Part of the appeal of foreign exploration was the idea that European 'adventurers' would come into contact with exotic and unusual forms of sexuality. Western impressions of these locales as sites of physical excess reflect the levels of sexual repression and morality that dominated Europe at the time.[18]

The same Orientalist dynamic lies at the core of Jaeckin's adaptation, which functions as a glossy travelogue with picturesque documentary shots of landscape interspersed with the stylized, simulated sex scenes which they render possible. In both Arsan's novel and Jaeckin's adaptation the heady, exciting sexual freedoms and explorations of the Orient are used to critique the repression of the European homeland. But these freedoms and explorations remain curiously separated and insulated from the Western world in a narrative which refuses to let said freedoms and explorations seep beyond the confines of the exotic. Arsan's heroine is liberated by the exotic, finding her own sexual pleasure in it. But she is also scared by it and repulsed by its monstrosity. She is horrified by the Orient ('Everything here is disgusting'), by men urinating in the river, by the landscape she cannot know or master and which she traverses only with a guide, taken aback by its monstrosity.[19] Steeped in age-old stereotypes about the cleanliness of the locals, when Mario commands her to drink from the penis of a native, Emmanuelle struggles with nausea not at the sex act with a stranger but solely in relation to the Oriental body:

> It was not that she felt it was degrading, in itself, to perform that act of love with an unknown boy. The same game would have pleased her greatly if Mario had imposed it on her with a blonde, elegant boy who smelled of *eau de cologne* in the bourgeois drawing room of a Parisian friend ... but with this [boy] it was not the same. He did not excite her at all. On the contrary, he frightened her. Furthermore, she had been at first repelled by the thought that he might not be clean.[20]

The Orient, in Arsan's novel, is a space of sexual freedom and a space of monstrosity and fear.

If Arsan and Jaeckin replicate the Orientalist mindset, D'Amato's films amplify it and blur it. They amplify the monstrosity of the colonial or oriental other. *Emanuelle e gli ultimi cannibali* (*Emanuelle and the Last Cannibals*) (1977, dir. D'Amato) is a case in point. In this film the heroine investigates the existence of cannibals in the Amazon jungle, after discovering ancient tribal markings on the vaginal lips of a white female mental patient. Gemser subsequently watches a ritualistic tribal execution in a sequence which, Mendik argues,

> conflates colonial fears about sexuality and death (via the punishment of a couple's illicit relationship), [and] features the graphic castration and consumption of a man's penis. These acts, as well as the savage butchering of a European couple that Emanuelle photographs during the climax of the

film once more confirm [Fatimah] Tobing Rony's claim that anthropological cinema represented 'a science strewn with corpses, one obsessed with origins, death and degeneration'.[21]

Gemser represents the Western voice of reason, investigating and offering the truth in her analysis of the Orient she traverses. But D'Amato's films also destabilize the Orientalist framework. For Gemser simultaneously represents the West and the dangerous Orient. Her ethnic difference is emphasized. It is not only part of her sexual attraction but also part of the danger she poses. Gemser, as Emanuelle, traverses West and East, home and Orient, uncovering both (as well as herself). She threatens the poles on which the Orientalist framework rests. As Mendik points out, in '[Alderberto] Albertini's *Black Emanuelle*, Gemser is asked by a young African boy "why are we the colour we are", to which the heroine replies "let's tell people that we never wash" '.[22] In *Emanuelle and the Last Cannibals* Emanuelle disguises herself as a native water goddess to rescue her white female lover from sacrifice. She explains: 'As I look very much like them, they will believe their water god has come to receive their sacrifice.' The colonialist history of the cycle of the Black Emanuelles is complex. The films at once magnify the monstrosity of the other within the colonialist, Orientalist discourse, and destabilize the very benchmarks of said discourse via a heroine who refuses to be either self or other.

If the *Black Emanuelle* series adapts the complexities of European colonial history, the adaptation of the *Emmanuelle* brand into English in the form of *Carry On Emmanuelle* (1978) adapts British social history, drawing its potency as much from its study of British class as from its seductive source. As a largely British phenomenon, the *Carry On* franchise needs some introduction. Steven Gerrard, in his compelling book on the franchise, sums the films up as a 'series of 31 low-budget, ribald and innuendo-laden comedies that have remained at the cornerstone of British film comedy since [they] marched into view in 1958'.[23] Though they were generally panned in critical terms, the public loved them. *Carry On Up the Khyber* (1969, dir. Thomas) and *Carry On Camping* (1969, dir. Thomas) held the top two positions at the British box office in 1969. Featuring a revolving troupe of well-known comedy actors – Bernard Bresslaw, Peter Butterworth, Kenneth Connor, Jim Dale, Charles Hawtrey, Hattie Jacques, Sid James, Joan Sims, Kenneth Williams and Barbara Windsor – the series developed its own aesthetic, its own set of in-jokes as well as its own brand. That this brand turned to Arsan's and Jaeckin's versions of *Emmanuelle* is perhaps not surprising given the fact that saucy, ribald, sexual innuendo and humour lay at its core from the outset; a sexual humour which became slightly bluer as the series evolved throughout the swinging sixties and faced competition from British 'glamour' films and their sexual content. Film parody and pastiche was also core to the *Carry On* franchise, as a survey of the titles made in the 1960s makes clear. Gerrard writes:

> *Carry On Spying* (1964) … ridiculed James Bond, *Carry On Cleo* (1964) mocked the Burton-Taylor farrago of *Cleopatra* (1963), *Carry On Screaming* (1966) out-hammered Hammer's horrors and *Carry On Don't Lose Your Head* (1967) was a parody of Gainsborough's 1940s melodramas.[24]

The *Emmanuelle* brand offered sexy, well-known grist for the *Carry On* team's racy, innuendo-filled mill. Both the title and the opening scene of the film clearly set the piece up as a reworking of Jaeckin's *Emmanuelle* in visual terms. The opening credits riff off Jaeckin's lingering leg shots of Sylvia Kristel on a plane as she travels to a new life of sexual exploration. It does so accompanied by a catchy pop song by Masterplan entitled 'Love Crazy', whose lyrics educate the viewer about their *Carry On* heroine's intent:

> The woman is love crazy, she's out on her own,
> The woman is love crazy, I work so hard sometimes I wish she'd leave me alone.

Obeying the character description offered by the lyrics, Emmanuelle seduces a bespectacled, geeky virgin, still living with his devoted mother, in the plane toilet, comically initiating him into the mile-high club.

Carry On Emmanuelle uses laughter to critique contemporary class history and its structures. While much of the plot has little to do with its *Emmanuelle* sources, cutting the visible sex and nude bodies as well as the core novel's philosophy almost in their entirety, it does share something of the Orientalist structures of its forebears. But, importantly, it redeploys them in the context of the British class system. Both Arsan's novel and Jaeckin's adaptation of it take a European character to the Orient, using the space of the Orient to explore a new sexual philosophy and freedom, which implicitly criticizes the conventions and restrictions of Europe. *Carry On Emmanuelle* works in the other direction. It brings an exotic, sexual French other to a sexually repressed Britain and uses her to critique British society. Such a critique is not solely the preserve of *Carry On Emmanuelle*, but characterizes the series as a whole, a series which Gerrard argues uses its laughter to 'form … critiques against those in positions of authority, where the utopian collective of the masses almost always conquered the stiff, sexually inept and socially awkward ruling class'.[25] A seemingly class-less sexual being as a result of her foreign status,

Emmanuelle comes to Britain and undoes British class rules. They bewilder her, and her bewilderment urges the contemporary audience to question their validity. Married to a diplomat, Emmanuelle sleeps with all social classes, moving between servants and ambassadors, moving metaphorically and literally between the upstairs and downstairs domains of both. The working-class servants embrace their sexuality with her, sharing their best sexual moments with each other and the viewer in flashback with frank and comic enjoyment. The upper-class guests at the ambassador's dinner party hide their sexual arousal under the table, subsuming it in ridiculous ritual and social niceties. Emmanuelle sleeps with each of the upper-class male guests (lesbianism does not feature in the film), but she does so in private, in scenes barred from the viewer's gaze. Each such scene is metaphorically represented by the hanging on a hook of the symbol of each upper-class man's profession (in the case of the high-ranking Navy admiral, his wooden leg) as they undress and have sex behind closed doors. *Carry On Emmanuelle* adapts and assesses British class history far more than it reworks Arsan and Jaeckin as source texts.

Carry On Emmanuelle's exploration of British class history draws on multiple British sources. It reworks, as Gerrard emphasizes, the British music hall traditions of a rotating cast, bawdy jokes and the stereotypes of 'the skinny, bespectacled man, the buxom maid, the harridan, the ridiculed figure of authority, ... storylines that openly mocked and satirized British .... government and ways of life'.[26] It also adapts, sometimes in straight transpositions, Donald McGill's saucy British seaside postcards and their focus on caricatures of 'drunken husbands, harridan wives, comedy vicars, blond and buxom young women and naïve brides'.[27] Its focus on the history of British class dominates as the film deconstructs the British social system with laughter and snide innuendo just as its sexual forebear, *Emmanuelle*, deconstructed the history of sex and the sexual mores which would contain her (see Figure 5.2). *Carry On Emmanuelle*, though, does not ultimately propose revolutionizing the class structure. It may mock it in its progression, but it does not dismantle it. The threat Emmanuelle poses is ultimately temporary, for the class system within which she lives recuperates her. She is driven to sexual profligacy as a result of her husband's disinterest in sex as a result of being impaled on a French church spire. Emmanuelle, however, closes the film vowing fidelity to her husband and ecstatically pregnant with his multiple children following a doctor's confirmation that he may resume full marital relations. *Carry On Emmanuelle* may explore and question the British class system and its history in its adaptive recreation of Arsan and Jaeckin, but it does not overthrow it. It offers us an intriguing reading of British class history.

FIGURE 5.2 Carry On Emmanuelle *(1978, dir. Thomas)*.

Adapting the history of adaptation: Janet Perlman's *The Tender Tale of Cinderella Penguin* (1981)

If *Carry on Emmanuelle* adapts the history of class, animations like Janet Perlman's 1981 Canadian animated short, *The Tender Tale of Cinderella Penguin*, survey, rework and analyse the history of adaptation itself. Perlman's adaptation problematizes the linear, binary conceptualizations of the relationship between adaptations and their source text. It does so by recognizing that adaptations of canonical sources adapt each other, referencing each other as they rework their source text. Adaptations often adapt the adaptive history of their source texts, interacting with the afterlives of said source text.

Perlman adapts into animation the fairy tale *Cinderella*, a fairy tale perhaps best known for the version offered by French writer Charles Perrault in his 1697 *Histoires ou contes du temps passé* (*Histories or Tales of Past Time*). Perlman adapts the well-known fairy tale into a ten-minute reworking which transposes the action into a world of penguins. That her version adapts Perrault's version of the tale is clear, for Perrault was responsible for the addition of the pumpkin with which Perlman's animation opens – Cinderella penguin unzips it to step out and commence the action. Perrault was also responsible for the fairy godmother and the glass slippers. Perlman's Cinderella wears webbed flipper shoes, and the fairy godpenguin turns penguin mice into penguin horses. Perlman relies on her audience's knowledge of her source text to enable comprehension, for her animation is truncated to just ten minutes, has no words and is interpreted solely by penguins. So embedded is Perrault's fairy tale and its reworkings, filmed or animated, in our consciousness, so monumental is it, that the animation is able to work almost in shorthand, confident of its viewers' comprehension. We suspend our disbelief and buy into a text which, if watched without pre-knowledge of its source, would make little sense. The animation offers us a point-of-view shot as Cinderella penguin waltzes in her ragged apron, moving us to share the forlorn dance as she twirls with a mop to the cruel merriment of her ugly stepsisters. And it is our pre-knowledge of the text which makes the penguin ugly sisters actually ugly. Animation, as Perlman points out, cannot quantify characters in terms of aesthetic beauty or the lack thereof when transposing them to the animal kingdom.[28] Perlman's adaptation only works because the canonicity of its source text in its various incarnations is so strong in historical terms as to be imprinted on our consciousness (see Figure 5.3).

Though Perlman's reliance on Perrault's source text is clear, she adapts more than Perrault as source text. She adapts the adaptive history of Perrault as source text, working from the adaptations made of him. Perrault's tale,

FIGURE 5.3 The Tender Tale of Cinderella Penguin *(1981, dir. Perlman)*.

as the compendium in which it was published indicates, was his adaptation of an age-old story, his version of a tale told and retold for new moments and contexts over the centuries. As it had multiple adaptive precursors prior to Perrrault's version of it, so too did it have multiple adaptive afterlives as writer after writer returned to and retold it, most notably the Brothers Grimm in their 1812 version of the tale, a version which they subsequently revised in 1819 with different plot elements. Perlman's adaptation adapts not just Perrault as source text, it also references the Grimm brothers' rewriting of it, incorporating the cumulative history of fairy tale as a source. The penguin prince desperate to find the foot which fits the glass slipper visits the house of the ugly step-penguins. The ugly step-penguins file their feet desperately, apparently trying to reduce them in size. Their actions are a clear reference to the Grimm version of the tale in which the stepsisters gruesomely cut off part of their feet at their mother's bidding to try to cram them into the slipper the Prince holds. As Julie Sanders persuasively points out, fairy tales function as something of a metaphor for the history of the adaptive process, as tales are told and retold in new contexts and incarnations for new eras and media, pointing both to a distant but ultimately ungraspable source and to the series of adaptations made and remade which have come to lie on its surface.[29] In her ten-minute animated short Perlman both relies on the monumentality of her source and questions its fixity, adapting the cumulative history of its adaptation. Her film both adapts and urges us to consider the history of adaptation.

History as source text: The heritage genre: *Germinal* (1993, dir. Berri)

Emmanuelle and *The Tender Tale of Cinderella Penguin* adapt different histories, but they do so tangentially. The heritage films made of French texts in the same timeframe adapt history head-on, taking it as a source text almost as much, if not more so, than the literary works on which they are based. Claude Berri's 1993 *Germinal* is a powerful case in point. Berri's film is based on Émile Zola's 1884 mining novel of the same name, which traces the rise, fall and rise of a would-be trade unionist, Étienne Lantier, in a mining village in Northern France as he leads his comrades through a disastrous strike. Berri's film does adapt Zola as source text. But it does so in some ways quite freely. In relation to the source novel, he cuts the uncomfortable sexual bartering of the source text as the shop owner trades goods for the sexual favours of prepubescent miners' daughters, and he cuts the ménage à trois as the Maheu family's neighbour sleeps with her husband and lodger on shift rotation, not out of sexual desire but merely for expediency, servicing the men on whose wages she depends.[30] Berri makes the working-class miners more appealing to increase his contemporary viewer's ability to empathize with them. Berri cuts much of the Zola novel, arguably to make space for the historical era he seeks also to adapt.

But if Berri is free with his literary source, he is as free with his historical moment. His film pushes not for the temporal specificity of the Second Empire in which Zola's novel is based, but rather a historic and monumental nineteenth-century past characteristic of so many heritage films. Donald Reid writes:

> Berri was not seeking to re-create a specific historical reality; he rejected out of hand the idea of bringing a historical consultant on board. Although the film is clearly set in the past, Berri went out of his way to assure that the viewer could not situate the period in which the action took place. Great effort was taken to see that the costumes looked right, not that they were specific to an era. ... Berri set out to make a *Germinal* free of the weight of contemporary events and history, the better to work it into his mythopoeic world.[31]

Berri's film adapts not a specific history quantifiable in date and detail. It adapts history as a broad expanse. It moves to encapsulate it in a film which clearly belongs to the heritage genre and its aesthetic tropes. Andrew Higson defines the heritage film thus:

> Narratively, the films move slowly and episodically rather than in a tightly causal manner; they demonstrate a greater concern for character, place, atmosphere, and milieu than for dramatic, goal-directed action. There is also a preference for long takes and deep focus, and for long and medium shots, rather than for close-ups and rapid cutting. The camera is characteristically fluid, but camera movement is dictated less by a desire to follow the movement of characters than by a desire to offer the spectator a more aesthetic angle on the period setting and the objects that fill it. Self-conscious crane shots and high-angle shots divorced from character point of view, for instance, are used to display ostentatiously the seductive mise-en-scène of the films.[32]

Berri's film enacts Higson's definition of the genre *à la lettre*. Pictorialist in its approach, it favours long, wide shots of landscape and exterior scenes which showcase a landscape marked as 'the past'. Berri's panoramas mirror Zola's Naturalist desire to show all in fiction; a desire which translates into vast frescoes of the northern mining landscape. Berri's film moves slowly, offering a series of connected tableaux rather than proceeding in a tightly causal manner. He uses heritage space to show history as time. Heritage space for Berri comes to represent time, revolving as his plot does around a tight nexus of geographic spaces: the Maheu house, the pit and Rasseneur's inn. These geographical spaces acquire a temporal capacity as they are spaces from which his beleaguered miners cannot escape, spaces which have entrapped their ancestors for centuries, spaces in which their descendants are doomed to toil, living through exactly the same torment as their forebears. This space of history dominates the plot to such an extent that the characters are secondary to it. Consequently, close-focus shots are comparatively rare in this film as characters are dwarfed by the landscape they inhabit, by the weight of history which bears down upon them. Extreme high-angle shots are frequent in this adaptation, shots which survey the characters from on high, trapping them in their geographical and historical fate. They occur most wrenchingly in the scenes in which the miners attack the mine, surveyed from on high by the elevated camera. The miners' words and actions proclaim their bid for freedom, their mission to wrest a financial, social and political space for themselves through collective violence. The camera angle, as it bears down on them, minimizing and entrapping them, emphasizes the futility of their bid. Berri's film adapts history as its source text just as his characters rework, relive and adapt the lives of their forebears in narratives ceaselessly revisited.

Berri's film, like Zola's novel, may take history as its source text, but history, Zola makes clear, is no easy thing to capture as source. History drives Zola's plot as Étienne looks to the past to power his present, drawing on the eternity of oppression of the Maheu family and their co-workers within the capitalist structure. He seeks to craft a narrative which will liberate them and him. He seeks revolution, in the form of a definitive break from the past, trying to build a new world order. But instead he falls into the revolutions, into the circles and cycles of history, repeating and re-enacting the past which he seeks to harness and from which he is so desperate to break. His rousing speech in the wood, urging the miners to continue striking, is an example of this. He sets out the ills of the past, of the centuries-old entrapment of the workers, of 'the old rotten society'.[33] He uses this past to make the case for 'the future humanity, [for] the edifice of truth and justice rising in the dawn of the twentieth century'.[34] He promises the workers 'our turn is come' but his words are no more than the latest turn and re-turn in the endless revolutions and rotations of history. The aged miner Bonnemort is clear on this point. Étienne uses him as a symbol of the past from which his speech seeks to break. Yet Bonnemort's words reinforce that Étienne is already re-enacting the past. Bonnemort makes clear that he has heard such words and plans of revolution many times over in the strikes that have permeated the circles and cycles of his misery; circles and cycles from which he sees no break:

> [Bonnemort] kept to his main idea, however: things had never gone well and never would go well. Thus in the forest five hundred of them had come together because the king would not lessen the hours of work; but he stopped short, and began to tell of another strike – he had seen so many! They all broke out under these trees, here at the Plan-des-Dames, lower down at the Charbonnerie, still farther towards the Saut-du-Loup. Sometimes it froze, sometimes it was hot. One evening it had rained so much that they had gone back again without being able to say anything, and the king's soldiers came up and it finished with volleys of musketry. 'We raised our hands like this, and we swore not to go back again. Ah! I have sworn; yes, I have sworn!'[35]

Étienne's attempt in the novel to capture and harness the past, breaking from it, captures and traps him precisely in the circles and cycles of said past.

The past is no less complex a source for Étienne's maker, Zola. Zola adapts the Second Empire era in France (1852–70) in a novel actually written in 1884, in the early years of the Third Republic. Zola's historical research for the novel was detailed and the effort he put into it well documented, as his visits to mines and preparatory work books show. A variety of critics have drawn attention to the historical and contemporary events that found their way into Zola's pages. Zakarian describes Zola's fictional strike as a 'mosaic of Anzin, 1884, Aubin and Ricamarie, 1869, with an occasional reference to Fourchambault, 1870'.[36] When taken to task for the outlandishness of his novel's ending, Zola himself pointed to his work as an adaptation of reality: 'It is simply the adaptation of a well-known event in mining history – the catastrophe which took place in the Marles pit in the Pas-de-Calais region.'[37] Zola adapted not just events but people. In the quest to identify models for Germinal's labour leaders, critics have suggested Basly (whom Zola met), Assi and Rondet as possible models for Rasseneur, Étienne and potentially Souvarine.[38] If Zola adapts these men, he does so partially and in a mobile form. Zakarian writes:

> It is only exceptionally that Zola finds all the material for a dramatic incident or technical fact in one reading. More often than not he synthesises several accounts ... found in three or four different sources, or he compresses several facts into one fictional incident.[39]

The same is true of Zola's character studies. Elements of the description Zola made of Basly feed into Rasseneur and Étienne, men who echo and replace each other in the novel. Moreover, Zola gave voice to the stereotype of the labour leader voiced by Leroy-Beaulieu:

> Speech always comes easily to them ... They are the curious product of an era in which ambition has seeped into and motivated all classes, where a superficial education sharpens and polishes minds.[40]

Zola offers his reader history, but he also refuses his reader history as a fixed, graspable entity. Like his character Étienne in his speech in the clearing in the wood, Zola collapses different eras, personalities and events into one compelling, creative, powerful narrative which deforms, fictionalizes and questions the truth of what it presents as the past.

If Zola's reading of history is a complex palimpsest of eras, personalities and perspectives, that of Berri in his film is no less labyrinthine. The film offers us not history as a set, static thing but an interweaving of multiple histories which collectively push the viewer to contemplate history as a plural, shifting and ultimately subjective thing, rather than a monolithic, ontological fact. Berri's motivations for making the film were starkly subjective, as he made clear in numerous interviews, driven as he was by his father's history and left-wing politics. His *Germinal* adapts not just Zola's nineteenth-century era but, concurrently, that of Berri's father and Berri's childhood memories of tales of it. He states:

> I was born in the Faubourg-Saint-Denis, in a working-class neighborhood of Paris. As far as I can remember, my father, a modest furrier, always talked to me about the world's injustice. He went through the Popular Front in 1936. He must have dreamed of a 'better world', before becoming disillusioned. After the war, he voted Communist. I was about ten years old when he began taking me to demonstrations which rallied tens of thousands of people. I can still hear the crowds' enthusiastic cheering, and I remember what hope Communism represented at that time for millions of honest and sincere people.[41]

But the personal pasts woven into Berri's *Germinal* are not just those of Berri and his father. Publicity for the film played on its cast's working-class roots, which shaped Berri's casting choices. Renaud, the singing star who played Étienne, came from a mining family on his grandfather's side. Maximilien Regiani, who plays Pierron, had himself been a miner. Gérard Depardieu, who took the part of Maheu (Figure 5.4), came from sheet-metal worker stock on his father's side while Miou Miou, who plays la Maheude, came from a line of fruit and vegetable sellers in Les Halles on her mother's side. As Donald Reid

FIGURE 5.4 Germinal *(1993, dir. Berri).*

points out, 'In interviews, these actors spoke freely of calling upon memories of their past to do the film.'[42] And the complex subjective histories adapted in Berri's film do not stop here. Hundreds of locals, miners, ex-miners or their offspring were hired to work as extras on the film. 'Their participation in this affair', Pierre Assouline argues, 'was a question of fidelity to their memory, to that of their fathers and grandfathers.'[43] Into these personal and family memories, Berri wove the star personae and industry memories of his cast in the minds of the audience, as shown by his choice of Renaud as the actor to play Étienne. Synonymous with May 1968 and its insurrectionary spirit, Renaud had been active in anarchist groups in this era, subsequently building a cult following as a socially and politically engaged singer-songwriter. His words of insurrection in Berri's *Germinal* are thus both Zola's and his own, speaking as they do both to Zola's class struggle and those which circled and recircled in the twentieth century, and to Renaud's own engagement with said struggles. Just as Étienne's rousing speech in the clearing in the woods borrows from political thinkers whose tracts Étienne had digested badly, from the people who precede and surround him, so the memories and speech of Berri's protagonists draw on their own shifting range of subjective sources and perspectives. History, Berri's film underlines, is not a static, absolute source text to be adapted in easy, graspable ways. Rather, Berri's *Germinal* implicitly dramatizes a reading of history as personal, subjective, multiple and messy. It adapts multiple pasts and multiple people in creatively complex and compelling ways, a little like its source author.

Deconstructing history and the heritage genre: The dizzying adaptive circles and cycles of *Moulin Rouge!* (2001, dir. Luhrmann)

Berri's *Germinal* gently questions the heritage genre it inhabits, probing the complexities of what it means to adapt history as a source. Baz Luhrmann's *Moulin Rouge!* (2001) blows the genre to pieces, paradoxically reinvigorating it in so doing. The layers of history and historical literary texts which *Moulin Rouge!* adapts as source are dizzying in their multiplicity and plurality. In Luhrmann's film they sit in the past but are impossibly of our present as well. The exuberant proliferation of sources behind Luhrmann's film ask difficult questions of the heritage genre and indeed of adaptation studies more generally. This film will not offer a source text in the singular; instead it problematizes and pluralizes the concept in intricate ways. Luhrmann's multiple sources, then, merit further attention.

Like Berri, Luhrmann's film is visibly based on an earlier source; a source, interestingly, made canonical by its subsequent adaptations: Henri Murger's *Scènes de la vie de bohème* (1851). Murger's little-studied text became Giacomo Puccini's much-lauded and adapted *La Bohème* (1896), an operatic work which has a complex adaptive afterlife in film, evaluated in Chapter 2's assessment of Paul L. Stein's 1935 *Mimi*. As Grace Kehler points out, Luhrmann's film adapts both Murger and Puccini as source.[44] The film borrows from *La Bohème*'s anti-establishment approach, featuring penniless artists, sensual women and tangled love affairs. Luhrmann, as Kehler underlines, literally places his protagonist Christian under 'a huge, lipstick-red, neon sign announcing L'Amour'.[45] Affixed to the façade of Christian's Parisian boarding house, this sign is a recreation of one that Luhrmann used when he directed a Sydney opera production of *La Bohème*.[46] *La Bohème*'s narrative maps onto *Moulin Rouge!*: as Puccini's writer Rodolfo falls for consumptive seamstress Mimi, so Luhrmann's aspiring writer Christian falls for Moulin Rouge performer Satine. Both Rodolfo and Christian surround themselves with poverty-stricken but talented bohemians who inspire their art. In both the lovers separate, albeit for different reasons, and in both the heroine returns to her lover to die. Luhrmann uses specific scenes to riff off his textual predecessors. In *La Bohème* the bohemian artists comically distract the landlord when he comes to demand rent. In *Moulin Rouge!* they lurk in a slapstick manner, distracting the audience as Satine seeks to distract the Baron both from his intent to extract sexual payment from her and from the presence of Christian in her room. Katherine Larson writes:

> Luhrmann and Pearce quote and expand Mimi's famous faint from Act 1 of *La Bohème*. Shortly after her first appearance, Satine faints twice, first falling from her trapeze into a throng of dazzled men and then swooning into Christian's arms in the elephant boudoir.[47]

Larson finds further parallels in relation to the bird imagery which clusters around Luhrmann's Satine. In *La Bohème* Mimi describes her life before Rodolfo as a 'solitary nest', contrasting this loneliness with a life with Rodolfo when '[a] gentle chirping comes from the nests'.[48] Rodolfo returns to this imagery in the last scene of the opera in which he announces in relation to Mimi, 'The swallow has come back to its nest and sings.'[49] Luhrmann adapts this imagery in *Moulin Rouge!* The shots in Satine's dressing room repeatedly focus on a birdcage in shots which reflect the heroine's entrapment in the world she inhabits. She talks to the bird which represents her, uttering her wish to fly far away from the Moulin Rouge. Her wish, which will be transferred into the version of 'Someday I'll Fly Away', she sings from the roof of the elephant (see Figure 5.5). Her wish will go unrealized and, in the scene where Zidler, the Moulin Rouge boss, commands her to end her liaison with Christian, the birdcage, as Larson points out, 'sits slightly blurred, in the foreground of the shot as if to remind her of her own caging. Later Zidler announces Satine's death in terms that recall Rodolfo's imagery: "My little sparrow is dying." '[50] In

FIGURE 5.5 Moulin Rouge! *(2001, dir. Luhrmann)*.

the last shot of the film, the camera zooms in on Christian's garret and on the tiny birdcage which hangs from its eaves as he writes a creative masterpiece made possible and inspired by his doomed love. Luhrmann's film adapts *La Bohème* in intricate ways.

But Luhrmann's is not a film with a single source. It is a multiple adaptation and insists on the multiplicity of competing, clashing texts behind its historical images. *Moulin Rouge!* may adapt *La Bohème* but it simultaneously adapts Giuseppe Verdi's 1853 *La Traviata*, itself an operatic reworking of Alexandre Dumas *fils*'s *La Dame aux camélias* (*The Lady with the Camellias*) (1852). The adaptive afterlife of both Verdi's and Dumas's tale is no less complex and well known than that of *La Bohème*, as my exploration of its incarnation as George Cukor's *Camille* (1936) in Chapter 2 makes clear. Luhrmann is well acquainted both with the source texts of Dumas and Verdi and with the adaptations which have come to lie on their surface. Satine, like the heroine of Dumas and Verdi, is a famed courtesan who sells her favours to survive, and not a seamstress. Like her predecessors, she falls for a less-than-rich man, then repudiates him for his own good, finding herself entrapped by the financial structures of her world and its male protectors. In both the texts of Verdi's opera and Luhrmann's film, as Elizabeth Hudson points out, the repudiated true love returns to throw money at the courtesan figure, offering, in his hurt, insulting payment for the love she gave both freely and truly.[51] According to Kehler, '*Moulin Rouge!* repeats *La Traviata*'s intent scrutiny of a woman whose sexual employment and cultural identity have been conflated, focusing on the prostitute as a means to interrogate contemporary society's fraught treatment of the commercial.'[52] And Satine's prostitution is important. She is required to sleep with the Baron to save Christian, her infidelity driven paradoxically by her fidelity. If infidelity becomes anathema to Satine, causing her to turn her back on her very profession, it is at the heart of Luhrmann's film, which skips as joyfully, playfully and visibly between sources as Satine formerly did with her lovers.

In its promiscuous play of historical sources, *Moulin Rouge!* adapts Bollywood film and its complex cinematic history. Sangita Gopal and Sujata Moorti note Luhrmann's trip to a Bollywood film:

> We went out one night and there was a big poster up for a Bollywood movie. I said 'Let's go see that'. We did – 2,000 audience members, high comedy, high tragedy, brother kills brother, [they] break out in some musical numbers, all jumbled up together in four hours of Hindi. We thought that was amazing. So our question was, 'Could we create a cinematic form like that? Could a musical work?'[53]

Gopal and Moorti are clear that *Moulin Rouge!* 'draws on Bollywood's affective economy, generic idioms, and performance traditions', integrating them into their adaptation of Puccini and Verdi *et al*.⁵⁴ It is far from insignificant that when the Duke scoffs at Christian's pitch to stage a musical set in Switzerland based on the concept of 'love overcoming all obstacles', Christian's eyes fall on a statue of the elephant god Ganesh in a 'point of view shot accompanied by a sitar chord'.⁵⁵ Thinking on his feet, he changes his proposed show's setting to India and the show, *Spectacular, Spectacular*, metamorphoses into a love triangle featuring a courtesan, a sitar player and the evil Maharaja. Gopal and Moorti write:

> This plot clearly references the 'real-life' situation developing between Satine, Christian, and the Duke, but it is also strikingly similar to the Sanskrit drama *Mrichhakatika* (*The Clay Cart*). The Duke is taken with this change of locale, and, encouraged by his response, Christian, Satine, Zidler, and the bohemians launch into an energetic song-dance medley that imagines *Spectacular, Spectacular* as an Orientalist fantasy involving magical sitars, tantric cancan, a replica of the Taj Mahal, juggling bears, fire-eaters, intrigue, danger, and romance staged with the help of the latest theatrical technology, including machinery and electric lights.⁵⁶

They make a compelling case that *Moulin Rouge!* adapts a subgenre of Hindi popular cinema, the tawaif or courtesan film, which mobilizes the figure of the courtesan to reflect on the 'historical transformations unleashed by modernity'.⁵⁷ In its mixing of multiple generic threads, with chase scenes, sentimental romance and tragic melodrama, *Moulin Rouge!* follows the narrational protocols of the Bollywood masala movie, adapting Luhrmann's reaction to his Bollywood film trip.⁵⁸ Moreover, Gopal and Moorti argue that the consumptive heroine Satine's death scene in her lover's arms is Bollywood through and through. They write:

> [I]n exquisite slow motion, surrounded by her tearful 'family' at the Moulin Rouge, … the camera sharply cranes back to an overhead shot of a shower of rose petals. Her last words are 'Tell our story… That way I'll always be with you'. This use of slow motion and the extended death scene in which the dying heroine elicits promises from her lover are old-school Bollywood.⁵⁹

Luhrmann's turn to Bollywood in some senses takes us back to the nineteenth-century context of Murger and Dumas *fils*, to the century characterized by the exotic fascination of Romanticism and the vogue for Orientalism. Luhrmann inscribes this vogue into his film with his focus and research on the historical figure Chocolat, a famous performer in the nineteenth century. Luhrmann writes Chocolat into his fictional narrative, situating him as the man saving Satine from the rampaging Baron and delivering her to the safety of Christian's arms. Gopal and Moorti note:

Footit and Chocolat were perhaps the most famous interracial slapstick duo in nineteenth-century France. Footit was quick and clever, while Chocolat – of Afro-Cuban origin – was a dim-witted simpleton with formidable acrobatic skills. Toulouse Lautrec was a big fan and painted Chocolat many times, in many formats (just as he did the female dancers of the Moulin Rouge). He was widely used in advertising – for bananas, coffee, soap, shoe polish, and chocolate – and James Small has suggested that his blackness played a central role in his commodification, even as he helped draw racial Others into a Western market economy. He was part of the influx of performers of color in fin de siècle France who helped transform racial difference into 'performative and commodified modes of spectacle and consumption'.[60]

Luhrmann's *Moulin Rouge!* turns to the exoticism and history of Bollywood just as nineteenth-century French culture turned to that of the Orient.

At the heart of the fluid sources between which *Moulin Rouge!* moves so deliberately sits nineteenth-century history, and specifically that of the Moulin Rouge itself. Like Berri, and as is characteristic of heritage filmmakers, Luhrmann and his team undertook in-depth historical research into both the people and the artefacts of the era. The film adapts real personalities. Toulouse-Lautrec is a case in point. Luhrmann explains in his commentary to the film the importance of the historical truth of his presentation of this nineteenth-century artist. Lautrec's history is intricately entwined with that of the Moulin Rouge. He was commissioned to design posters for its opening, his works were displayed in the venue, and he painted a range of its key performers and personnel. Luhrmann not only weaves Lautrec through his film but crafts his dialogue from snippets of Lautrec's letters: letters the writers of the film researched and adapted in their quest for historical veracity. Luhrmann uses people as markers of historical truth. So too does his film mobilize objects in the same way. Luhrmann explains: 'Whenever we had a chance to take something from the nineteenth century and eulogize it, it was a really good thing.'[61] The jewellery the Baron gives Satine as a down-payment on her sexual favours is an example. Art designer Catherine Martin states: 'We had a great jewellery catalogue [from the era] and these were jewellery items, all the garter clips and garter holders were jewellery items at the time and sometimes bejewelled so we copied them and used them.'[62] Painstakingly, and at times expensively, *Moulin Rouge!*, in keeping with the heritage genre, researches and recreates the historical past as source as accurately as it can.

But *Moulin Rouge!* does not sit easily within the heritage genre and indeed pushes its viewer to question the history it claims to proffer. In aesthetic terms *Moulin Rouge!* contravenes the majority of aesthetic tropes which Andrew Higson argues, as we saw earlier in this chapter, characterize the heritage film.⁶³ Instead of moving slowly and episodically, *Moulin Rouge!* is causally packed and kaleidoscopic, so teeming with events, actions and characters that they spill beyond the confines of the screen and at times our understanding, overwhelming and confusing us even as they draw us into their colour and exuberance. Luhrmann describes the film's kaleidoscopic and confusing opening thus: 'Don't be passive. You've got to keep up with this. You've got to be involved. It's almost daring you to give up on it.'⁶⁴ The long takes and deep focus of heritage film are dramatically reduced in *Moulin Rouge!*, a film whose editing is frenetic, visible and draws attention to itself. In the world of the Moulin Rouge, with its showy commercial performance, rapid cutting underscores the cheap thrills and quick-hit intent of the spectacle, as spectacle follows spectacle. The short depth of the shots often reflects the false, foreclosed truth of this world, a truth allowed more space and camera depth when the camera goes backstage to witness the dirt, illness and poverty on which the illusion of the Moulin Rouge is based. Luhrmann's film is not a naturalistic piece of heritage filmmaking. For all its documentary research of real figures and objects, it has no intention of persuading us that it is real, that it is history. In the opening sequences of the film Kylie Minogue appears in a cameo role as a Disney-like animation against the CGI mocked-up skyline of nineteenth-century Paris. She appears as a green fairy of absinthe, beckoning Christian into the Underworld of the Moulin Rouge. This is a film which, far from hiding its status as a performance of history, foregrounds it, revelling in its special effects and self-reflexively drawing attention to its camera screen, editing and trickery. As the plot deconstructs the glossy façade of the Moulin Rouge performances, the film itself deconstructs the performance of history in the heritage genre. Andrew Higson's work is key to my argument here. Higson persuasively argues that heritage films take us back to a past conditioned, shaped and formed by the needs of our present.⁶⁵ They offer a false antique, a modern version of a world long gone. Luhrmann's film engages with and enacts Higson's view of heritage film by underscoring that the past it offers is of our present. The characters and objects who/which surround Christian may be painstaking recreations of a nineteenth-century world, but the lyrics of this Orphean poet with the power to move all around him (Satine resists him until she hears him sing) are drawn almost uniquely from, in Luhrmann's words, 'the greatest love songs of the twentieth century'.⁶⁶ Christian, a figure of the past, sings the words of our present, merging temporal eras as the characters draw on canonical songs from some of the most canonical artists or art works of the twentieth century: Elton John, Madonna, Marilyn Monroe, David Bowie, Freddie Mercury, Sting, *The Sound of Music*. Luhrmann's film makes visible the hidden Janus-like temporalities of the heritage genre as it offers a past of and for the present.

But the temporalities or histories of *Moulin Rouge!* are not just dual. Rather, Luhrmann's film adapts multiple eras and moments, pushing us to view history as a cumulative, messy, multiple series of overlapping moments, rather than a distinct, delineated time which may easily be grasped. Discussing his film's use of twentieth-century classic pop songs in a clearly nineteenth-century narrative, Luhrmann reminds us that the process is nothing new. Judy Garland did it, he explains, in *Meet Me in St Louis* (1944) when she sang 'The Trolley Song', a song clearly of her era with its Big Band radio music, in a film set in the 1900s.[67] Luhrmann's reference to the films of the 1940s and 1950s is far from incidental, for *Moulin Rouge!* repeatedly and insistently cites them in both its aesthetic and content. Describing Satine's entrance into the film and the Moulin Rouge on a trapeze, Luhrmann is vocal on this point: 'Throughout the film we're constantly quoting the world of movies so that you the audience are conscious that you're making these very extreme gear changes.'[68] He makes clear that Satine's outfit, with its tail suit, is historically inaccurate but that 'we're clearly quoting [a] Vincent Minnelli musical look. … It really looks like a musical number from the 40s or the 50s.'[69] This palimpsest-like approach to history is clear throughout the film. For *Moulin Rouge!* gives us multiple moments, engaging in the adaptation of history as a complex, continual and convoluted flow, rather than a moment which may be abstracted out of time and offered in film. To this end, *Moulin Rouge!* mixes Sting's canonical 'Roxanne' with a classical tango called 'Tangera' as the theatre performers sit idle, waiting to see if Satine's unseen prostitution of herself upstairs with the Duke will succeed in liberating the patronage they need in order to return to work. In a complicated, multiple act of displacement they dance a jealous, sexual tango. It points to the displaced sexual action between the Duke and Satine, to the multiple, contradictory displaced times which this historical film makes impossibly and simultaneously present, and to the new resonances it wrings from the association and relocation of multiple artists and timeframes. History, *Moulin Rouge!* makes clear, is a messy, complex thing, and its adaptation into film a compelling and creative process.

How true is history? *Un long dimanche de fiançailles* (*A Very Long Engagement*) (2004, dir. Jeunet)

If Luhrmann's *Moulin Rouge!* asks when history is, playing with its multiple temporalities and how they can be adapted to film, then Jean-Pierre Jeunet's *Un long dimanche de fiançailles*, another heritage film, pushes things a step further. It asks how true history is as a source, unpicking the complexities of its creation in a powerful deconstruction of the very genre it inhabits. The film features a young unmarried couple, Mathilde and Manech, in the north of France. Sent to fight in the First World War, Manech is presumed dead. Mathilde takes it upon herself to investigate, finding out that he was court-martialled for self-mutilation with four other men and sent over the top. The film traces her quest to find out whether he survived.

The deconstructive intent of this adaptation, a reworking in film of Sébastien Japrisot's 1991 novel focusing on the First World War, is not immediately evident. The film appears to sit squarely within the heritage genre, not posing the visible aesthetic challenge immediately discernible in Luhrmann's kaleidoscopic, chronologically challenging images. Jeunet's adaptation, like the quintessential heritage film, is carefully researched and makes much of period detail. The film's opening sequence demonstrates this. The piece opens on a shot of a shattered Christ, swinging in the rain in an elevated shot which dwarfs the trenches, entrapping the conscripted men in them, ant-like in their historically known fate (see Figure 5.6). Jeunet, in his Christ, offers us history in film, for the image is drawn from a photograph of the First World War, as is the dead horse in a tree which follows soon after. Jeunet adapts not just photographs from the era but postcards and film footage too. He sets a bustling scene featuring Jodie Foster in the marketplace of Les Halles in Paris, a marketplace which no longer exists. But Jeunet's film recreates it using CGI from contemporary postcards of the era. Jeunet also inserts snippets of contemporary film footage. Mathilde, an orphan who has suffered from polio, lives with her aunt and uncle, her parents having been killed in a tram accident. Jeunet inserts near-contemporary footage of both the polio virus and a tram accident. He does something comparable in relation to the execution

FIGURE 5.6 Un long dimanche de fiançailles (A Very Long Engagement) *(2004, dir. Jeunet).*

of the prostitute Tina Lombardi, the girlfriend of one of the other condemned men. Jeunet found near-contemporary footage of an execution, but was unable to use it. Consequently, he mocked up the footage in his twenty-first-century film for the duration of the execution, aping the look and techniques of what he had seen in the archive by filming in black and white, slowing his film and making his images grainy. The aesthetic disjunction between these inserted film clips and the rest of Jeunet's film is pronounced. It shows, in its visibility, that Jeunet's film is not history; it cannot give us the past. It is a modern recreation and uses the full battery of modern cinematic weapons, paradoxically, to take us back to a past in which they did not exist. Jeunet's film expresses a core tension at the heart of the heritage adaptation genre.

Jeunet's deconstruction of history as a source and his film's ability to be faithful to it permeates the film, forming the bedrock of *A Very Long Engagement*'s plot. Mathilde is presented with history as fact. Five men, her fiancé among them, were condemned and thrown into No Man's Land for self-mutilation. None survived. Yet history proves to be untrue; to be an unstable, shifting narrative which Mathilde revises and corrects. A historian figure of sorts, Mathilde goes to the official war archive and finds it barred to her, the historical documents about Manech's fate missing, incomplete and inaccurate. Armed with the historical objects the intriguingly named Esperanza gives her (he is dying and has no hope, though he gifts her some) – the men's last letters and objects they wished to leave to their nearest and dearest – Mathilde sets to work. She tracks down witnesses, extracting oral and written testimony to investigate the history presented to her as fact. She and the film ultimately show it to be false. The film does this by constructing itself in a structurally risky manner. The whole of the plot revolves around the throwing of these men over the top into No Man's Land, a scene which the film replays repeatedly in the course of the narrative. Jeunet's film eschews tight, teleological narrative causality to turn and re-turn around one event. Each reincarnation of the central scene in which the men go over the top is shot from a different perspective, a different angle, offering different testimony about what happened. The first version of it is short, filmed from the trenches where Esperanza stands. His sight, and consequently ours, is obscured by the trench defences, the rain and his point of view. Each time we watch the scene, we do so from the perspective of different eyewitnesses (Esperanza, the cook Célestin Poux, a German in the trenches, the farmer from the Dordogne). We are offered diametrically different readings of it and contrasting conclusions about who survived. Mathilde discovers early on that two men may have survived, but her belief in which two men changes with each testimony she receives. Through his return to the same story, the same fictional piece of history, Jeunet powerfully demonstrates the malleability of history as source.

It is written by the victors. The official documents in the army archive impose their meaning on what actually happened. History is subjective, reconstructed from the multiple, often contradictory memories of different participants. It is sometimes false. Mathilde ultimately discovers that her fiancé Manech has survived, albeit in amnesiac form, along with the farmer from the Dordogne. But she cannot correct history. To do so would be to retrigger the army's need to punish and kill both men. Both men live under the assumed names they took on when they switched dog tags on the battlefield, fabricating the evidence of their own death by placing Manech's red glove and the farmer from the Dordogne's German boots on dead men. They fabricate history and succeed. History, Jeunet's film suggests, is a problematic, shifting source.

If Jeunet's film shows that history is an unstable, untruthful source, so too does it show that film is, in any case, not a neutral screen on which to capture it. *A Very Long Engagement* makes clear that its cinematic gaze on history is filtered through and adapted via the cinephilia of its director; by the images and history of the films in which he is steeped. The film's cinematic references and allusions are numerous. Jeunet compels us to trace the history of film in his images as well as that of the First World War. Manech, dangerously injured and in No Man's Land, waves to one of his fellow condemned men, appealing for help. He stands against the grainy, grimy colours of the trenches. The hand he uses to call for attention stands out in the colours of the landscape as a result of the vibrancy of the red mitten he wears. The importance of the mitten is twofold. An example of an item associated with children, the mitten underscores both the tragedy of this barely adult man being thrown into the horrors of war and the childlike state to which his mind had been forced to revert in order to survive. The film makes much of the childlike politeness of Manech in the most horrific of circumstances. He addresses the man to whom he appeals for help as 'Sir' and addresses him with the formal French '*vous*'. He also plays like a schoolboy when his captor's weapon falls into his hands. But Manech's red mitten is also important because it serves as a direct reference to *Schindler's List* (1993, dir. Spielberg), another war film in which the sole flash of colour comes in the form of a childlike figure dressed again in red and brutally attacked in an act of war. Spielberg's film forces its viewer to watch as a little girl in a red coat wanders through the black and white atrocities of Nazi soldiers rounding up and killing Jews. The camera later comes, in a horrific flash of colour, to rest on the splash of her red-coated body in a black and white pile of corpses. Jeunet's colour scheme alludes to other Spielberg films, most notably *Saving Private Ryan* (1998). As Spielberg's Second World War film differentiates between the time at war and the time at home by using different colour schemes, so Jeunet's *A Very Long Engagement* films its trench scenes in greys and mucky blues, and its scenes away from the trenches in sepia yellows and browns. Jeunet's film allusions extend beyond Spielberg. When Ange Bassignano knifes a man in the backside in Corsica, he does so in dapper Mafioso clothes, sepia colours and mise-en-scène reminiscent of the 1970s, which compels the audience to associate him with *The Godfather* (1972, dir. Coppola). The exuberant postman with his morning acrobatics when delivering the post to Mathilde makes little sense unless read as a direct allusion and homage to Jacques Tati. Moreover, as Jeunet's Tina Lombardi pursues her mission to avenge her Corsican lover Ange by shooting an army officer in a closed, dark tunnel with a mechanism designed to trigger her weapon, there is an unmistakable reference to an analogous tunnel in *The Third Man* (1949, dir. Reed), as Jeunet dips into both its imagery and its shadowy, film noir, claustrophobic environment. Film, Jeunet's *A Very Long Engagement* makes clear, is no neutral screen on which history can be captured and adapted unproblematically. Cinema comes with its own history, with its own conscious and subconscious memories which shape the creative products its produces.

The case study films of this chapter reflect important trends in the history of adaptation between 1970 and 2004, contemplating the adaptive reworkings of French source texts in a variety of genres: porn, comedy, animation and heritage film. But they do not merely construct a history of what was adapted in this era. Instead, they actively contemplate the formative function of history on the cinematic works produced as well as the creative challenges of taking history as one's source text. Adaptations like those of the *Emmanuelle* franchise and its authorized and unauthorized spin-offs reveal much about the time and culture of their making as well as the predilections, real or supposed, of their target audience. But adaptations also, in this era, contemplate whether history can be captured in film. Berri's *Germinal* underscores the multiplicity of the heritage it seeks to memorialize in film; a heritage national, industrial and personal. Luhrmann's *Moulin Rouge!* pushes harder against the confines of the heritage genre it inhabits, showing history as a complex, mercurial source with a foot in the past and in the present. Luhrmann's kaleidoscopic narrative both breathes new life into the heritage genre and fractures it irrevocably in his recognition of history as multidirectional entity which film can never truly tame. Luhrmann's film may question whether history can be captured by film as source, but Jeunet's *A Very Long Engagement* takes things a step further by urging its viewer to ask how true history actually is as source, embracing a disconcerting vision of it as an adaptive, shifting narrative whose truth depends on your time and your perspective. The multiplicity of versions of the past found in Jeunet's film resonates with the multiplicity of textual precursors adapted in Janet Perlman's *The Tender Tale of Cinderella Penguin*. Perlman's source, Perrault's 'Cendrillon; ou la petite pantoufle de verre' (Cinderella; or the little glass slipper) is as monumental and culturally recognizable as that of Jeunet: the First World War via Japrisot's retelling of it in literature. Both Perlman and Jeunet rely on the known-ness of their source; on its status as a cultural and historical monument. But both deconstruct the fixity of said source, adapting multiple versions of it in creative artefacts which emphasize both the creative power of the past and its shifting nature. History, the adaptations in these case study years suggest, is no simple thing in the world of adaptation.

Notes

1 Emmanuelle Arsan, *Emmanuelle*, trans. Lowell Bair (London: Harper Perennial, 2009).
2 Arsan, *Emmanuelle*, 143–4.
3 Garrett Chaffin-Quiray, 'Emmanuelle Enterprises', in *Alternative Europe: Eurotrash and Exploitation Cinema since 1945*, ed. Ernest Mathijs and Xavier Mendik (London: Wallflower, 2004), 136.
4 Chaffin-Quiray, 'Emmanuelle Enterprises', 137.
5 Chaffin-Quiray, 'Emmanuelle Enterprises', 139.
6 Chaffin-Quiray, 'Emmanuelle Enterprises', 140.
7 Pierre Schneider, 'Paris: Surprise Garden at Les Halles', *New York Times*, 11 December 1974. Also cited in Chaffin-Quiray, 'Emmanuelle Enterprises', 140.
8 For a history of porn prior to *Emmanuelle*, see Chuck Kleinhans on the context in the United States:

> In the 1950s, 60 to 70 theaters nationally, mostly in large urban areas, showed soft-core films. In the 1960s, driven by simple economics existing burlesque houses converted completely to film or had 'nudie cuties' replace the traditional live music and comedians who filled in between the strippers. In the early 1970s, following the Supreme Court's ruling that local community standards should set the norm, thus changing local censorship laws, essentially legalized hardcore – explicit genital sexuality. In the 1970s a peak of 780 theaters regularly showed hardcore films. A typical budget of $100,000 to $150,000 paid for the production of a feature-length drama shot on 35mm film.

Chuck Kleinhans, 'The Change from Film to Video Pornography: Implications for Analysis', in *Pornography: Film and Culture*, ed. Peter Lehman (New Brunswick, NJ: Rutgers University Press, 2006), 156.
9 For full details, see Peter Lehman, ed., *Pornography: Film and Culture* (New Brunswick: Rutgers University Press, 2006).
10 Jon Lewis cited in Lehman, 'Introduction', in Lehman, ed., *Pornography: Film and Culture*, 15.

11 For details of these spin-offs and film afterlives, see Mick Brown:

> Emmanuelle has continued to thrive. In the flood of films that have been released to capitalise on the name, she has popped up in Denmark, America and Japan, met wife-swappers, white-slave traders and cannibals, had a daughter and become a nun. There have been Black, Yellow, even Pink Emmanuelles [sic]. Any resemblance between the original Emmanuelle and her successors is usually purely accidental – the single 'm' or 'l' in the Emmanuelle of most titles avoids any breach of copyright. The majority of films are made in France, Germany and Italy, often under a title which has nothing to do with anybody called Emmanuelle whatsoever.

Mick Brown, 'Carry On (and On) *Emmanuelle*', *Sunday Times Magazine* (21 November 1980): 21.

12 In the 1980s the videocassette recorder entered the home market in a big way. In 1978 15,000 households had VCRs. In 1980 1 per cent of US households had VCRS; by the decade's end 70 percent of all households had them – a rate of introduction that exceeds any other consumer communication appliance, including phone, record player, video, radio, TV and color TV to that time.

Chuck Kleinhans in Peter Lehman, ed., *Pornography: Film and Culture*, 157.

13 Writing on the context in the United States, Kleinhans underlines: 'the X-rated rental market swelled to an estimated 1,000,000,000 rentals in 1987: this was the same number of rentals as admissions to adult theaters four years earlier', Kleinhans in Lehman, ed., *Pornography: Film and Culture*, 157.

14 Peter Lehman, 'Revelations about Pornography', in *Pornography: Film and Culture*, 91.

15 Kleinhans in Lehman, 'Revelations about Pornography', 158.

16 On this suite of films, see Xavier Mendik, 'Black Sex, Bad Sex: Monstrous Ethnicity in the Black Emanuelle Films', in *Alternative Europe: Eurotrash and Exploitation Cinema since 1945*, ed. Ernest Mathijs and Xavier Mendik (London: Wallflower, 2004), 146–59.

17 Mendik, 'Black Sex, Bad Sex', 147.

18 Mendik, 'Black Sex, Bad Sex', 146–7.

19 Arsan, *Emmanuelle*, 194.

20 Arsan, *Emmanuelle*, 216–17.

21 Mendik, 'Black Sex, Bad Sex', 156. Fatimah Tobing-Ronay, *The Third Eye: Race, Cinema and Ethnographic Spectacle* (Durham, NC: Duke University Press, 1996), 46.

22 Mendik, 'Black Sex, Bad Sex', 155.

23 Steven Gerrard, *The Carry On Films* (London: Palgrave Macmillan, 2016), 1.

24 Gerrard, *The Carry On Films*, 4.

25 Gerrard, *The Carry On Films*, 5.
26 Gerrard, *The Carry On Films*, 14–15.
27 Gerrard, *The Carry On Films*, 9.
28 'On the Tender Tale of Cinderella Penguin and When the Day Breaks', https://www.youtube.com/watch?v=KAlwUmd3XAU (accessed 29 July 2019).
29 Sanders, *Adaptation and Appropriation*, 45.
30 For a full exploration of the excisions Berri made to Zola's novel, see Alison Murray. She argues:

> Berri's *Germinal* was stripped of the disturbing elements that might have allowed the film to make a powerful comment on social injustice in contemporary French society. Gone, for example, are images from the novel of youngsters who are brought up in the poverty of the mines and turn to delinquency and alcohol abuse. Gone, therefore, from the contemporary overtones of the film is any possible comment on marginalized youth in contemporary France and the potential influence of a generation raised in poverty. Berri simplifies the characters, too, so that the viewer's sympathy is uncomplicated. In the novel, the miners' wives lend their daughters to Maigrat for an extension of credit; la Maheude treats her children roughly; Jeanlin is cruel and abusive to Lydie and ends up murdering a soldier. None of these problematic details appear in the film. Lantier's seduction by La Mouquette is cut out as well; Lantier's love affairs, in fact, are reduced to a completely chaste admiration for Catherine. On the other hand, the bourgeois characters such as the Hennebeau and Grégoire families receive just enough screen time to appear rich and uncaring, without any of the psychological complexity they have in the novel. We learn nothing, for example, of Mr Hennebeau's inner torment concerning his wife, or of the reasons for her growing disdain for him, although we do, of course, learn of her infidelity, as it adds to the cursory characterization of the bourgeois.

Alison Murray, 'Film as National Icon: Claude Berri's *Germinal*', *French Review* 76.5 (2003): 906–16 (910–11).

31 Donald Reid, 'Claude Berri's *Germinal*', *Radical History Review* 66 (1996): 146–62 (148–9).
32 Andrew Higson, 'Re-Presenting the National Past: Nostalgia and Pastiche in the Heritage Film', in *Film Genre Reader*, ed. Barry Keith Grant (Austin: University of Texas Press, 2012), 602–27 (610–11).
33 Émile Zola, *Germinal*, trans. Havelock Ellis (London: Dent, 1885), n.p.
34 Zola, *Germinal*, n.p.
35 Zola, *Germinal*, n.p.
36 Richard Zakarian, *Zola's Germinal: A Critical Study of Its Primary Sources* (Geneva: Droz, 1972), 161.

37 Zola cited in Elliott M. Grant, *Zola's Germinal: A Critical and Historical Study* (Leicester: Leicester University Press, 1970), 120. My translation.
38 For an overview of work on the potential identities behind Zola's characters, see Henri Marel, 'Étienne Lantier et les chefs syndicalistes', *Cahiers naturalistes* 50 (1976): 26–39.
39 Zakarian, *Zola's Germinal*, 51.
40 Leroy-Beaulieu cited in Zakarian, *Zola's Germinal*, 153–4.
41 Berri cited in Reid, 'Claude Berri's *Germinal*', 149.
42 Reid, 'Claude Berri's *Germinal*', 150.
43 Pierre Assouline cited in Reid, 'Claude Berri's *Germinal*', 150.
44 Grace Kehler, 'Still for Sale: Love Songs and Prostitutes from *La Traviata* to *Moulin Rouge!*', *Mosaic: A Journal for the Interdisciplinary Study of Literature* 38.2 (2005), 145–63.
45 Kehler, no pagination in online version.
46 Kehler, no pagination in online version.
47 Katherine Larson, 'Silly Love Songs: The Impact of Puccini's *La Bohème* on the Intertextual Strategies of *Moulin Rouge!*', *Journal of Popular Culture* 42.6 (2009): 1040–52, no pagination in online version.
48 See on this point Larson's reading of Giacosa and Illica, no pagination in online version.
49 See on this point Larson's reading of Giacosa and Illica in Larson, no pagination in online version.
50 Larson, no pagination in online version.
51 Elizabeth Hudson, '*Moulin Rouge!* and the Boundaries of Opera', *Opera Quarterly* 27.2 (2011): 256–82 (260).
52 Kehler, no pagination in online version.
53 Luhrmann cited in Sangita Gopal and Sujata Moorti, 'Bollywood in Drag: *Moulin Rouge!* and the Aesthetics of Global Cinema', *Camera Obscura* 25.3 (2011): 29–67 (29).
54 Gopal and Moorti, 'Bollywood in Drag', 30–1.
55 Gopal and Moorti, 'Bollywood in Drag', 37.
56 Gopal and Moorti, 'Bollywood in Drag', 45.
57 Gopal and Moorti, 'Bollywood in Drag', 49.
58 Gopal and Moorti, 'Bollywood in Drag', 41.
59 Gopal and Moorti, 'Bollywood in Drag', 54.
60 Gopal and Moorti, 'Bollywood in Drag', 55–6.
61 Baz Luhrmann, *Moulin Rouge!* DVD commentary.
62 Catherine Martin, *Moulin Rouge!* DVD commentary.
63 Higson, 'Re-presenting the National Past'.

64 Baz Luhrmann, *Moulin Rouge!* DVD commentary.
65 Higson, 'Re-presenting the National Past', 610.
66 Baz Luhrmann, *Moulin Rouge!* DVD commentary.
67 Baz Luhrmann, *Moulin Rouge!* DVD commentary.
68 Baz Luhrmann, *Moulin Rouge!* DVD commentary.
69 Baz Luhrmann, *Moulin Rouge!* DVD commentary.

6

Textual migration and adaptive diaspora: French literature adaptations beyond France (1996–2016)

Andrew Watts

On 5 December 2012, British director Tom Hooper's film adaptation of *Les Misérables* premiered in London. Based on the musical first staged in 1980 by Alain Boublil and Claude-Michel Schönberg, whose production had been inspired by Victor Hugo's 1862 novel *Les Misérables*, the film was the result of an international collaboration that extended from Britain and France to the United States. Produced by a combination of British and American studios, it featured a multinational cast led by Hugh Jackman, Russell Crowe and Anne Hathaway. Despite garnering a mixed response from critics, the film would prove popular with audiences worldwide, generating global box office receipts of more than $440 million.

Hooper's reworking of *Les Misérables* appears as one of the most recent and striking examples of the way in which French literature continues to travel beyond France through the process of adaptation. Between 1996 and 2016, cinematic versions of French literature proliferated across a wide spectrum of countries, including China, Germany, Spain, Turkey, South Korea, the United Kingdom and the United States. During this period, filmmakers in these countries drew inspiration time and again from canonical French literature, as evidenced by films such as the 2012 version of Maupassant's *Bel Ami* (1885) by British directors Declan Donnellan and Nick Ormerod, and *Thirst* (2009, dir. Park), a re-imagining of Zola's *Thérèse Raquin* (1867) produced in South Korea. Equally, the late 1990s and early 2000s saw cinematographers outside of France adapt works of contemporary French literature such as Michel Houellebecq's *Les Particules élémentaires* (*The Elementary Particles*) (1998), which Oskar Roehler recreated as a German-language film called *Atomised* in 2006. The new millennium has spawned big-budget Hollywood spectaculars such as *Planet of the Apes* (2001, dir. Burton), and a more recent trilogy of *Planet of the Apes* films (2011–17), whose origins can be traced to Pierre Boulle's 1963 science-fiction novel *La Planète des singes*. Finally, the period has encompassed adaptations of French literature by respected auteurs such as Pedro Almodóvar, whose 2011 film, *The Skin I Live In*, reinterpreted Thierry Jonquet's 1984 novel *Mygale* (*Tarantula*) for a Spanish-speaking audience. As the cinematic production of this period testifies, French literature continues to migrate on a truly global scale, inspiring filmmakers in numerous countries and exhibiting a relentless mobility and adaptability that have enabled it to reach new national and international audiences.

This chapter introduces the original concept of 'adaptive diaspora' to describe and understand how French literature has been adapted beyond France. The notion of diaspora appears as a compelling lens through which to examine this form of artistic migration, not least because the term 'diaspora' reflects the kind of dispersal that French literary texts continue to undergo as a result of their adaptation across numerous different cultures and geographical territories. Originally derived from the Greek term 'διασπορά', or 'scattering', the word is most commonly used to describe the mass dispersal of peoples from their homeland, such as the Jewish diaspora from Israel during the first century BC and the subsequent regrouping of those exiles in foreign lands. More recently, film scholars have adopted the term to refer to cinematographers who have moved from their native countries to establish or continue their careers elsewhere. As Hamid Naficy explains in his seminal study of exilic and diasporic filmmaking, *An Accented Cinema*, displacements of this kind have occurred particularly among Asian and Middle-Eastern filmmakers such as Palestinian director Michel Khleifi and Iranian cinematographer Amir Naderi, who relocated to Belgium and the United States, respectively, in pursuit of greater artistic freedom and better filmmaking resources than had been available to them in the countries of their birth.[1]

My own analysis presents adaptive diaspora as a new critical framework through which to explore the migratory movement of artistic works themselves, rather than of individuals and communities. Built around four key elements – reconfiguration, blending, reinforcement and cross-cultural mobility – the concept shows what happens when French texts are adapted into new cultural contexts and how they are transformed during this process. The first part of my discussion focuses on the idea of reconfiguration and the way in which diasporic adaptations remodel their source materials. Using as case studies two Hollywood films – *Planet of the Apes* and *Diabolique* (1996, dir. Chechik) – this section argues that such adaptations can bring new meanings and resonances to their literary sources, even while appearing to distance themselves from them. Second, I consider how adaptive diaspora revolves around the intricate blending of material drawn from different cultural contexts. E. J-yong's *Untold Scandal* (2003) exemplifies this practice by combining its recreation of Laclos's *Les Liaisons dangereuses* (*Dangerous Liaisons*) (1782) with key elements of South Korean costume drama and traditional Japanese theatre. Third, I turn to the way in which diasporic adaptations can both reinforce and rethink specific aspects of their source texts, as illustrated by the German-language films *Atomised* and *Phoenix* (2014, dir. Petzold), and their engagement with the themes of self-deception and social fragmentation in Houellebecq's *Les Particules élémentaires* and Hubert Monteilhet's *Le Retour des cendres* (*Return from the Ashes*) (1961), respectively. Finally, I examine three films – *Bel Ami*, *Suite française* and *The Skin I Live In* – in order to show how diasporic versions of French literature can dramatize their own cross-cultural mobility. In particular, these films can be seen to play in a self-conscious manner on their connections to cinematic works produced outside of France such as *Vertigo* (1958, dir. Hitchcock) and, more recently, the vampire series *Twilight* (2008–12).

In exploring these four elements of adaptive diaspora, I contend that French literature has been actively reinvigorated by its migration to new cultural contexts. Not all of the adaptations discussed in this chapter received critical acclaim or were major box office attractions. Analysis of these films nevertheless reveals their capacity to bring fresh perspectives to their source material and to foreground aspects of it that have been persistently overlooked or obscured by the passage of time. As Jørgen Bruhn, Anne Gjelsvik and Henriette Thune have argued, 'traits of the adapting text infer upon the adapted text and the other way around in a process that may be termed chiasmic, or, perhaps more relevantly, *dialogic* in Bakhtin's understanding of the word'.[2] My model of adaptation extends this perspective by demonstrating how filmmakers have continued to re-energize the French works that have inspired them and, in so doing, enable us to read those texts differently and more profoundly.

The enthusiasm of filmmakers for adapting French literature outside of France is not, of course, a new phenomenon. As we showed in the first chapter of this book, cinematic versions of French literary texts have been produced in other countries since the silent era, when studios in Italy, Germany and the United States in particular readily appropriated novels, plays and short stories from abroad in an attempt to satisfy the new medium's demand for narrative material. If French literature has circulated internationally on film since the earliest days of cinema, the historical context around this movement has nevertheless changed immeasurably. The late twentieth and twenty-first centuries have seen the film industry become globalized in myriad new ways. Notably, this period has witnessed the rise of production centres which have begun to challenge the hegemonic status of Hollywood. In 2012, China, for example, became the second highest-grossing cinema market in the world. By 2025, it is expected to generate over $22 billion in box office receipts, more than double the revenue of North American cinema.[3] Together with the growth of filmmaking outside of Europe and the United States, new technologies have facilitated what Sean Cubitt describes as a 'radical globalization' of methods of film production. Advances in digital software and broadband technology have enabled film producers to work increasingly across different time zones and geographical territories. 'Compositors match location dailies from one city', explains Cubitt, 'with effects footage from another and send results back to producers in a third, often using differences in time-zones to create a 24-hour production process.'[4] Once films enter distribution, many are no longer released exclusively in cinemas or on DVD and Blu-Ray but made available to an ever-widening international audience through online viewing platforms such as Amazon Prime, Netflix and YouTube. If filmmaking has always been a global enterprise, the cinematic works of the twenty-first century now disperse across geographical borders with striking facility.

By situating French literature adaptations within the context of this globalized film industry, this chapter makes a key contribution to our understanding of the way in which different nations and cultures interact with each other. Scholars have previously studied the nature of this interaction using a range of critical and theoretical approaches. Transnational theory has long been concerned with the way in which people, finance, media and cultural artefacts cross national borders. Elizabeth Ezra and Terry Rowden's *Transnational Cinema: The Film Reader* remains a pivotal reference in this regard. According to Ezra and Rowden, globalization has eroded such boundaries to the extent that the international film industry is now more interconnected than it has been at any previous point in its history.[5] Similarly, cross-cultural mobility is a key preoccupation of memory studies. As researchers including Astrid Erll, Lucy Bond and Jessica Rapson have argued persuasively, memories – such as those relating to the Holocaust or more recent events such as 9/11 – are rarely tied to any one geographical location but more often transcend national, political, ethnic and religious boundaries.[6]

Adaptation studies has certainly not remained indifferent to these debates. Writing in her seminal *Theory of Adaptation*, Linda Hutcheon, for example, characterizes adaptation as a transcultural activity predicated on the movement of stories across media, time and place. 'Adapting from one culture to another', she observes, 'is nothing new: the Romans adapted Greek theatre, after all. But what has been called "cultural globalization" has increased the attention paid to such transfers in recent years.'[7] Research in this area of the discipline has nevertheless focused predominantly on the adaptation of individual works into specific national and regional settings. Moreover, scholarship on cross-cultural adaptation tends to rely heavily on the ideas of 'domestication' and 'indigenization', emphasizing how texts are modified to suit the values and sensibilities of the adapting culture but often neglecting the ongoing relationship between the adaptation, its source material and the culture in which this material originated.[8] My concept of adaptive diaspora offers a new perspective on these issues by considering adaptation not in terms of one-off movements of texts between countries or regions but as a practice that spreads across multiple borders and geographical territories. More importantly, this analysis shows how cross-cultural adaptations – like diasporic communities – are not seamless hybrids. Instead, they reflect a partial integration into their new homeland, not only retaining links to their source texts but also undergoing changes in response to their host culture. Theorizing adaptation as a diasporic process enables us to see how literature can migrate internationally and to understand better the artistic metamorphosis that occurs during that transition.

Diasporic reconfigurations in Hollywood cinema: *Planet of the Apes* and *Diabolique*

The Hollywood film industry provides a natural starting point for analysing the diasporic spread of French fiction, most notably because its studios remain prolific importers of source material from abroad. French cultural products have traditionally featured strongly among these imports, as evidenced by the long-standing enthusiasm of Hollywood studios for remaking French films such as *Les Diaboliques* (*The Devils*) (1955, dir. Clouzot) and *Le Miroir à deux faces* (*The Mirror Has Two Faces*) (1958, dir. Cayatte). As well as importing material internationally, Hollywood continues to dominate the overseas market in cinematic products. As Geoffrey Nowell-Smith explained in 1998, 'the American film industry is a massive exporter, and at various times over the past fifty years the share of box-office acquired by Hollywood has ranged from 30 per cent to 80 per cent in the majority of European markets'.[9] More recently, Hollywood production companies have sought to extend their commercial reach beyond Europe by widening the promotion and distribution of their films in the vast potential markets of Asia and Latin America. This strategy has clearly paid substantial dividends for the major American studios, which according to the Motion Picture Association of America generated 71 per cent of their box office revenues abroad in 2016.[10]

Hollywood's ubiquitous presence in the international film market has contributed significantly to the global diaspora of French literature adaptations. Hollywood studios have continued to draw on the works of canonical French authors, particularly on stories of excitement and swashbuckling adventure which have the potential to attract large worldwide audiences. In 1998, for example, *The Man in the Iron Mask* (dir. Wallace) loosely adapted *Le Vicomte de Bragelonne ou dix ans plus tard* (*The Viscount of Bragelonne or Ten Years Later*) (1847–50), the last of Alexandre Dumas *père*'s novels recounting the adventures of the fictional D'Artagnan and the three musketeers. Capitalizing on the success of *Titanic* the year before by casting Leonardo DiCaprio as both Louis XIV and his twin brother Philippe, the film garnered box office receipts of $183 million, $126 million of which came from overseas sales. However, not all of Hollywood's recent attempts at adapting French literature have found favour with spectators, either domestically or abroad. In 2013, *In Secret* (dir. Stratton), based on Zola's story of adultery and murder *Thérèse Raquin*, proved a commercial disaster for its producer LD Entertainment. Following the withdrawal of actresses Kate Winslet and Glenn Close from their respective roles as Thérèse and Madame Raquin, the film recouped only $652,228 in domestic and foreign sales and fell notably short of covering its modest budget of $2 million.

Despite commercial catastrophes such as *In Secret*, Hollywood retains a pivotal role in the production and global distribution of French literature films by virtue of its partnerships with studios outside the United States. Co-production and co-distribution arrangements of this kind have become an increasingly common feature of the international film industry during the first two decades of the twenty-first century. As well as enabling studios to share the financial risks involved in filmmaking, such partnerships have allowed producers to access larger funding streams and distribution networks than might otherwise be available to them if they were operating alone. French literature adaptations have benefited directly from collaborative agreements of this kind. In 2011, for example, the crime thriller *Unknown* (dir. Collet-Serra), based on Didier Van Caulwelaert's novel *Hors de moi* (*Enraged*) (2003), stemmed from a co-production between Dark Castle Entertainment, an affiliate of Universal Studios, and three German companies including Babelsberg Studios. More recently, in 2013, Beverly Hills-based studio Relativity Media collaborated with its French counterpart EuroCorp in co-distributing *The Family* (dir. Besson), a recreation of French crime writer Tonino Benacquista's Mafia-themed novel *Malavita* (2004). With its cast of established Hollywood stars including Robert De Niro and Michelle Pfeiffer, the film was subsequently distributed to forty-five countries worldwide, with foreign sales accounting for 53 per cent of its total gross of $78.4 million. As *Unknown* and *The Family* illustrate, Hollywood's involvement in cross-continental partnerships has underpinned the global diaspora of French literature adaptations by enabling such films both to be made and to be presented to an international audience.

Hollywood's key position in world cinema nevertheless has significant implications for the way in which it adapts and ultimately circulates French literature films in the American and international market. On the one hand, American production companies must seek to cater for the tastes and demands of domestic audiences. On the other, they must attempt to ensure that their films appeal to spectators across the widest possible spectrum of countries and national cultures. Hollywood has traditionally responded to these pressures by Americanizing imported material, for example, by producing English-language versions of foreign films. In the domestic market, such measures have the advantage of circumventing the well-known resistance of American audiences to non-Anglophone cultural products (as reflected in the widespread unpopularity of foreign and subtitled films in the United States, where in 2013 the combined box office receipts for the top five foreign-language releases amounted to just $15 million.[11] Internationally, Hollywood's strategy of Americanizing its source material has also served as a means of conveying notions of 'Americanness' to overseas spectators. 'Hollywood films seeking an international audience', explains Tom Brook, 'are a form of soft diplomacy through which America presents itself to the rest of the world. They peddle American concepts of success, romance and heroism through stories of individual triumph in the face of adversity, tales of redemption and fantastic battles of good versus evil.'[12] As we shall see, however, this process of Americanization does not simply obliterate the connections between French literature adaptations and their source texts. On the contrary, one of the key features of these diasporic films is that they can often be seen to reconfigure their source material and to highlight its artistic and ideological subtleties in sometimes unexpected ways.

Among this corpus of Hollywood adaptations of French literature, Tim Burton's 2001 version of *Planet of the Apes* appears as a fascinating example through which to begin to elaborate my concept of adaptive diaspora, not least because of the way in which it simultaneously Americanizes its literary source and reconnects with it. Inspired by Pierre Boulle's 1963 science fiction novel *La Planète des singes* and the 1968 film *Planet of the Apes* directed by Franklin J. Schaffner, Burton's adaptation presents itself – superficially, at least – as the archetypal Hollywood blockbuster which foregrounds images of Americanness at the outset. Following a short prologue in which a trained monkey pilot struggles frantically to avoid crashing in a simulated space flight, the film introduces us to a space station which an on-screen caption identifies as the USAF Oberon. Having established that this is an American craft, the sequence then cuts inside to reveal members of the crew, each of whom – including the monkey pilot Peracles – wears a uniform emblazoned with a modernized version of the Stars and Stripes flag. Moreover, this sequence mobilizes the familiar figure of the Hollywood action hero in the form of astronaut Leo Davidson, played by Mark Wahlberg. After seeing Peracles lost during an attempt to investigate a mysterious electrical storm, Davidson defies his commanding officer by leaping into a space capsule and taking off in search of his simian colleague. Davidson's explosive display of masculinity evokes memories of a long line of Hollywood action heroes including John Wayne, Charlton Heston and Arnold Schwarzenegger, as does his casual disrespect for authority as he blasts away from the Oberon and tells the station commander bluntly, 'never send a monkey to do a man's job'. With its emphasis on American imagery and presentation of Davidson/Wahlberg as an all-American action hero, Burton's version of *Planet of the Apes* appears as a distinctly Hollywood production that seems far removed from the story's French origins.

To view *Planet of the Apes* purely as an Americanized film would nevertheless be to underestimate the way in which this adaptation also reconfigures Boulle's novel, most notably through its ending. In the final sequence of Burton's film, Davidson succeeds in returning to what he believes is Earth, crash landing his space capsule on the steps of the Lincoln Memorial in Washington DC. However, after clambering from the wreckage of the pod and entering the memorial, he discovers that the statue of Abraham Lincoln has been replaced by one of the ape leader, General Thade, and that the crowd of police and curious onlookers outside is also made up of apes (see Figure 6.1). Not surprisingly, audiences and critics declared themselves baffled by this ending, which many saw as lacking the clarity and emotional power of the 1968 film, in which astronaut George Taylor (Charlton Heston) discovers the Statue of Liberty buried waist-deep in the sands of a post-apocalyptic Earth. Writing in the *Guardian*, Peter Bradshaw described the conclusion to Burton's film as 'laughable, anti-climactic, and almost scandalously nonsensical'.[13] In his commentary for the DVD release of the film, Burton himself, meanwhile, suggested that the ending had been conceived as a lead-in to a possible sequel. 'I planned the ending out,' the director claimed, '[so that] if they [producers Twentieth-Century Fox] wanted to do other movies, they could track this.'

FIGURE 6.1 Planet of the Apes *(2001, dir. Burton)*.

However, the factor that Burton omitted from this explanation was that his ending also reworked the conclusion of the source text. In the final pages of the novel, Boulle's protagonist Ulysse Mérou returns to Paris after an absence of 700 years and is initially comforted to see familiar sights such as the Eiffel Tower. Yet his delight at being home quickly evaporates when a police officer approaches him and his fellow astronauts as they climb out of their ship. 'He takes a few steps towards us,' reads Mérou's narrative, 'emerges from the grass, and finally appears in front of me in the full light. ... He's a gorilla.'[14] The 2001 version of *Planet of the Apes* clearly recreates this final plot twist, but there is more at stake here for Burton than simply reviving a fragment of the source text. By choosing not to reveal why apes have once again taken control of the planet, the film powerfully reformulates Boulle's earlier vision of humanity as facing an inevitable decline which cannot be explained. In contrast to Schaffner's 1968 film, in which the fall of mankind is attributed to a nuclear holocaust, 'the book', observes Clément Peyrie, 'is more a reflection on how all civilizations are doomed to die. There has been no human fault. It is just that the return to savagery will come about anyway. Everything perishes.'[15] Far from merely appropriating the ending of *La Planète des singes*, Burton sacrifices a clear resolution to his film in favour of an ending that adapts and redeploys Boulle's original message in a vivid, cinematic form.

Like Burton's version of *Planet of the Apes*, *Diabolique* illustrates how diasporic adaptations can engage closely with their French sources, even while appearing to distance themselves from them. Chechik drew inspiration from two works, Boileau and Narcejac's novel *Celle qui n'était plus* (*She Who Was No More*) (1952) and – more problematically – its 1955 adaptation *Les Diaboliques*, directed by Clouzot. Retaining the central plotline of this earlier film, *Diabolique* relates the plan hatched by two women, Mia Baran (Isabelle

Adjani) and Nicole Horner (Sharon Stone), to murder Mia's brutish husband Guy, the headmaster of a boys' boarding school. Following common practice in Hollywood remakes, which often resituate the action of foreign films in the United States, Chechik transposed the setting of his two sources from France to rural Pennsylvania. In so doing, the director described his aim not as being to Americanize his source material but rather to present the fictional boarding school as a kind of 'no place' that existed independently of a specific time or geographical location. 'I didn't want the school to be gritty and real,' Chechik explained, 'and yet I didn't want it to fall into fantasy. I was trying to capture a place that was its own specific world, but that could conceivably exist in reality.'[16] The production team sought to realize Chechik's vision of this self-contained environment using a variety of practical techniques. Houses adjacent to the school were hidden behind large swathes of camouflage netting, while the crew took further measures to block out the sun, flying 60' × 40' scrims over the school in order to invest key scenes with a dark, oppressive atmosphere. 'I really wanted to keep them [Mia and Nicole] in a sombre, claustrophobic world,' added Chechik. 'They're almost like vampire characters. Even though they're out in the country, both women are in a sense caged up in their own prisons.'[17] In displacing its source materials from their original French setting, *Diabolique* resituates them in a location that is at once America and nowhere.

However, if Chechik sought to create a feeling of temporal and geographical isolation in *Diabolique*, his film by no means detaches itself entirely from its French origins. Instead – like all of the diasporic adaptations discussed in this chapter – it establishes an artistic dialogue with the material that inspired it. The interplay between *Diabolique* and its literary and cinematic sources is reflected in the film's title, which gestures towards the French resonance of the story at the outset. Moreover, the title *Diabolique* appears as a variant of Clouzot's title *Les Diaboliques*, of which Chechik denied – initially, at least – that his film was a remake. The relationship between these two films would prove to be one of the most controversial aspects of *Diabolique*, which borrows heavily from its French cinematic source. As Raphaëlle Moine observes, 'the screenplay of *Diabolique* is disconcertingly faithful to Clouzot's version, to the extent that it is difficult to list all of the sequences that are transposed in their entirety from one film to the other'.[18] Clearly derived from Clouzot's film, for example, is the scene in which Guy humiliates Mia in the school dining room by forcing her to eat rotten fish and the iconic sequence in which the supposedly dead headmaster rises out of the bath, his eyes covered by white contact lenses (see Figure 6.2). Chechik's flagrant appropriation of these key scenes triggered a fierce critical and legal backlash against *Diabolique*, the ramifications of which were felt on both sides of the Atlantic. Having

FIGURE 6.2 Diabolique *(1996, dir. Chechik)*.

learned that the film was in production, Clouzot's widow Inès sued its parent studio, Morgan Creek, for breach of copyright, eventually winning 750,000 francs (approximately £100,000) in compensation. Audiences and film critics showed similar hostility towards Chechik's remake, with many deriding it as a pale imitation of Clouzot's masterpiece. 'Film lovers should study the two "Diaboliques" side by side', advised Roger Ebert, in a particularly scathing review, 'in order to see how the Hollywood assembly line trashed its treasure from the past.'[19] In remaking *Les Diaboliques*, Chechik was widely perceived not as reinventing his source material in a new cultural context but as exploiting it shamelessly in the interests of mass entertainment.

Such negative appraisals nevertheless overlook the way in which *Diabolique* reconfigures its French sources by adding new layers of artistic depth and meaning to them in adaptation. Chechik's ability to create such resonances within his film is reflected most obviously in the performance of Isabelle Adjani, whose casting as Mia can be viewed as an attempt to play on our memory of the actress's early career in French cinema. As Moine points out, Adjani's screen persona is linked inextricably to her talent for playing anxious, fragile women.[20] In her breakthrough role in *L'Histoire d'Adèle H.* (*The Story of Adèle H.*) (1975, dir. Truffaut), for example, Adjani starred as Victor Hugo's youngest daughter, who becomes romantically obsessed with a British officer, Lieutenant Pinson, and eventually suffers a complete mental and physical breakdown when he does not reciprocate her love. The opening sequence of *Diabolique* invites us to trace a connection with this earlier film by emphasizing Mia's own weakened state of health. In this first scene, we see Adjani's character rising from her bed during the night and stumbling towards the bathroom, past a cabinet littered with bottles of pills. Alternating between shots of the bathroom and a boy who watches voyeuristically from another part of the school, Chechik proceeds to show Mia undressing before suddenly she gasps for air and clutches at her chest, as if suffering a heart attack. As she lurches desperately towards the sink, she collapses, having failed to reach her medication in time. In highlighting Mia's physical frailty, this sequence can be seen to evoke the intertextual presence of *L'Histoire d'Adèle H.*, in which the heroine passes out first in the streets of Halifax, Nova Scotia, and then again in Bridgetown, where her condition grows so severe that she wanders the port dressed in rags, oblivious to her surroundings. In linking his film to Adjani's debut in French cinema, Chechik emphasizes that *Diabolique* does not so much imitate its French sources as it does inscribe them in a network of new meanings and resonances through the process of adaptation.

As we have argued throughout this book, adaptations often draw on multiple sources rather than existing in a straightforward, hierarchical relationship with one text. In *Diabolique*, Chechik extends the plurality of his sources by blending his adaptation with references to other Hollywood films and genres. The influence of this wider cinematic context is reflected in one of the director's principal ambitions for the film, which was to explore the possible lesbian relationship between Lucienne and Mireille, the female protagonists of *Celle qui n'était plus*. In an interview at the time of *Diabolique*'s release, Chechik claimed that the restrictive moral context of 1950s France had prevented Clouzot from developing this relationship fully in his own adaptation. 'I just felt that [we had the opportunity] to stay emotionally truer to the book', Chechik explained, 'and do a much more complex version.'[21] The casting of Sharon Stone as the seductive vamp Nicole can clearly be interpreted as an attempt to suggest a sexual attraction between the film's female conspirators, not least because it recalls Stone's earlier performance as the bisexual murderess Catherine Tramell in *Basic Instinct* (1992, dir. Verhoeven). However, Stone's involvement in *Diabolique* also points to the way in which this film intersects with key genres in 1990s Hollywood cinema. The climactic sequence of the film represents one such point of intersection by aligning *Diabolique* explicitly with the genre of the female buddy film that enjoyed significant mainstream popularity during this period. In this final scene, Mia and Nicole bludgeon and then drown Guy before private investigator Shirley Vogel (Kathy Bates) – here replacing the detective Alfred Fichet (Charles Vanel) of *Les Diaboliques* – helps them to cover up the crime and claim self-defence. As Lucy Mazdon has argued, this ending reflects the changing status of female actors in 1990s American cinema. By creating what Mazdon describes as an 'all-action sisterhood' between its three female protagonists, *Diabolique* 'recalls the trajectory from victim to victor through female bonding in other Hollywood films of the period (notably *Thelma and Louise*) and the gradual progress of women's roles from subsidiary characters to central action heroine'.[22] In setting out to highlight the implication of lesbianism in Boileau and Narcejac's novel, Chechik situates *Diabolique* within a web of intertextual connections which radiate across 1990s American cinema.

Cross-cultural blending in South Korean cinema: *Untold Scandal* and *Thirst*

While Hollywood remains a key driver behind the global diaspora of French literature adaptations, its cultural and commercial dominance has been challenged increasingly in the late twentieth and early twenty-first centuries by other production centres, not least in Asia. South Korean cinema, in particular, has grown exponentially since the late 1980s, a fact that can be attributed largely to the country's gradual move towards democracy, which began with the election of Roh Tae-woo as president in December 1987. Although a former member of the military, Roh came to power promising democratic reform, including a new constitution and free presidential elections. Crucially for the development of the South Korean film industry, the election of Roh also signalled a weakening of the censorship that had previously prevented cinematographers from making films that did not conform to the ideology of the ruling government. The result, as Darcy Paquet summarizes, was that over the next decade, 'Korea's film output began to diversify in terms of subject matter, scale and genre. A new generation of directors started creating films that marked a clear break from the past and were popular with young viewers.'[23]

The continued growth of South Korea cinema during the 1990s – under the heading of the Korean New Wave and, more recently, New Korean Cinema – was aided significantly by the country's newfound openness to globalization. Under the leadership of Kim Young-sam, who succeeded Roh as president in 1993, South Korea pursued a policy known as 'segyehwa', meaning 'turning towards the rest of the world'. This globalization strategy, which the country embraced in an attempt to strengthen its domestic economy, had a significant positive effect on its film industry. In 1994, Kim was particularly impressed by a report produced by the Presidential Advisory Council on Science and Technology, which showed that the 1993 Hollywood blockbuster *Jurassic Park* (dir. Spielberg) had generated the same amount in profit as Korean car manufacturer Hyundai had received in revenue from the sale of 1.5 million motor vehicles. This compelling evidence of the vast commercial gains that could be made from film prompted a wave of government initiatives aimed at supporting the South Korean film industry. Notably, these included a Film Promotion Law which enabled producers to distribute their films internationally without prior approval from the Ministry of Culture and Sports and to finance their films via co-production agreements with foreign companies. By the end of the 1990s, these measures had helped to transform South Korean cinema into a major industry whose films accounted for 36 per cent of domestic box office sales, compared to just 15 per cent earlier in the decade.[24]

South Korea's globalization policy would also play a key role in shaping the aesthetic features of New Korean Cinema, including adaptations. Since the late 1990s, Korean filmmakers have shown particular enthusiasm for blending elements of their own national culture with artistic materials drawn from other countries and cultural contexts. As Jeeyoung Shin explains, New Korean Cinema has used this process of hybridization to present itself as a culturally diverse, rather than purely local, movement. Moreover, such blending has enabled Korean directors to showcase their ability to adapt and reinvent the conventions of Western cinema as opposed to simply imitating them. 'These hybrid cultural forms provide an important means for their self-definition,' writes Shin of this new generation of filmmakers, 'a self-definition that not only distances itself from a xenophobic and moralizing adherence to local cultural "tradition" but also challenges Western cultural hegemony.'[25] Cross-cultural blending of this kind can be observed in numerous South Korean films since the late 1990s. Among the most notable examples of this trend is *Shiri* (1999, dir. Kang Je-gyu). With a plot that revolves around two South Korean secret agents as they pursue an assassin from the North, the film combines the fast-paced thrills of both Hollywood and Hong Kong action cinema with elements of romantic melodrama designed to appeal to the tastes of South Korean audiences. The formula proved a major success at the Korean box office, where *Shiri* attracted 5.78 million spectators and, in so doing, broke the domestic attendance record previously held by *Titanic* (1997, dir. Cameron), with 4.7 million ticket sales.[26]

Cross-cultural blending has been a key feature of South Korean adaptations of French literature since the early 2000s, as *Untold Scandal* (2003, dir. E. J-yong) illustrates clearly. Inspired by Pierre Choderlos de Laclos's 1782 novel *Les Liaisons dangereuses*, this film is invaluable as an example of diasporic adaptation, especially since it delights in the blending of different national and cultural identities that is one of the central tenets of New Korean Cinema. In the case of E. J-yong, this process of blending was rooted in his long-standing ambition to produce a Korean costume drama, an ambition which only began to crystallize when he heard a piece of music by Bach and conceived the idea for a film that would bring together elements of both

Eastern and Western culture. 'At one point', he recalled in an interview in 2003, 'an image came into my mind – the image of people wearing *hanbok* [traditional Korean clothing] combined with Bach's music. I was curious about how it would look on screen.'[27] Searching for a plot around which to build a cross-cultural drama of this kind, E. remembered Stephen Frears's *Dangerous Liaisons* (1988), which he had watched while travelling around Australia in 1988, and decided to purchase a copy of the original novel. The director's subsequent reading of the text quickly alerted him to the way in which *Les Liaisons dangereuses* deals with themes which resonate across temporal and geographical borders. 'It contains every human emotion,' he explained later of his decision to adapt Laclos's work. 'Love, revenge, hate, betrayal, separation, death ... it has everything in it. Even though it's a French novel, it's a timeless story, like Greek tragedies. I also enjoyed adapting things into different cultural contexts, so I decided to use this story for my film.'[28] Aided by the depoliticization of the South Korean film industry, E. sought to capitalize on what he viewed as the cross-cultural flexibility of Laclos's novel and its capacity to be reworked in a Korean context.

Untold Scandal transposes the geographical setting of *Les Liaisons dangereuses* from late-eighteenth-century France to Korea during the reign of King Jeongjo (r. 1776–1800), the twenty-second ruler of Korea's Chosun Dynasty (1392–1897). In E.'s version, which retains much of the basic structure of the source plot, the fictional Lady Cho challenges her cousin Sir Cho-wan to seduce and impregnate her husband's new concubine and promises to reward his success by allowing him into her bed. Not surprisingly, given E.'s stated aim of producing a cross-cultural adaptation, scholarly discussions of *Untold Scandal* have approached the film primarily as an example of cinematic transnationalism that inserts French cultural material into a Korean setting. The transnational resonance of the film, argue Hye Seung Chung and David Scott Diffrient, is evident from the opening sequence.[29] Beginning with a shot of a hand opening a copy of Cho-wan's diary, the director proceeds to show us a series of paintings of female subjects, culminating in an image of a naked woman who looks over her shoulder with her back towards the artist. As the camera zooms out, we then see the hand of the artist and, over the top of his work-in-progress, the naked model herself. As Chung and Diffrient observe, this image gestures towards the cross-cultural nature of the film at the outset by recalling Édouard Manet's nude painting *Olympia* (1865), in which a Parisian courtesan reclines on a bed, her servant standing next to her holding a bouquet of flowers.[30] The intertextual presence of Manet's work – whether intended or not – can be seen to reflect the cultural hybridity that E. strives to achieve in *Untold Scandal* and for which the film's prologue subtly prepares us. Moreover, it calls attention to the way in which the film both returns to

French sources – from the visual arts as well as literature – and reinvigorates them within a new cultural context.

Chung and Diffrient's transnational reading of *Untold Scandal* nevertheless overlooks the extent to which this film blends its Korean setting with a much deeper exploration of Laclos's writing. One of the most notable features of the film in this respect is E.'s recurring interest in the theatricality of *Les Liaisons dangereuses*. As Simon Davies has pointed out, Laclos's novel draws extensively on the artistic resources of the theatre.[31] At the level of plot, Valmont and Merteuil often compare themselves to actors, playing roles and donning masks as each situation demands. Laclos himself, meanwhile, was an enthusiastic admirer of the work of Racine and readily appropriated the conventions of classical tragedy in his own fiction.[32] *Untold Scandal* can be seen to re-imagine the theatricality of its source text without simply turning it into what Chung and Diffrient have described as a romantic melodrama designed to appeal to the cultural tastes of Korean audiences.[33] References to the theatre feature prominently in this film, as illustrated by the sequence in which Cho-wan breaks off his affair with Lady Chung, the equivalent of Laclos's heroine Madame de Tourvel. Having gained entry to the courtyard of Cho-wan's home – a flat, open space reminiscent of a stage – the virtuous noblewoman sees her former lover sitting at his window (see Figure 6.3). Elevated above the courtyard, Cho-wan's position recalls that of a spectator in a theatre box as he listens to Lady Chung ask why they cannot leave for Beijing together. In a reinvention of the corresponding passage in the novel, in which

FIGURE 6.3 Untold Scandal *(2003, dir. E. J-yong)*.

Valmont breaks with Tourvel by repeating the phrase 'it's not my fault',[34] Cho-wan responds to each of Lady Chung's pleas with the assertion that he 'cannot help it', as if delivering his own, pre-rehearsed script. The sequence ends in a dénouement that appears similarly theatrical, as Lady Chung collapses in the centre of the courtyard, prompting her servants to rush to her aid and escort her out of the side door as stagehands might help an exhausted actress into the wings. E.'s recreation of this episode illustrates that the adaptive process involves more for him than moving his source material mechanically from one cultural context to another. In amalgamating *Les Liaisons dangereuses* with a Korean setting, the director adapts the theatrical underpinnings of the novel, incorporating them into his film in a manner that both highlights and re-energizes Laclos's own artistic fascination with the stage.

E.'s ability to blend theatrical references into his film nevertheless extends beyond his engagement with Laclos's text. In this pivotal scene between Cho-wan and Lady Chung, the filmmaker can also be seen to draw on a much wider range of cultural material, most notably the ancient Japanese tradition of Noh theatre. Originating in the fourteenth century, Noh is a highly codified form of dramatic expression performed on a small open stage without curtains or a proscenium arch. In Noh plays, the actors wear wooden masks carved from Japanese cypress wood. Traditionally, these masks are expressionless, meaning that the performers must convey emotions by tilting their head and allowing light to fall upon the mask at different angles. *Untold Scandal* can be seen to gesture towards the conventions of Noh theatre in several respects. Most obviously, the house from which Cho-wan informs Lady Chung of the end of their affair recalls the straight, geometric lines of a Noh stage, while the courtyard below evokes the unadorned emptiness of this traditional performance space. Similarly, Cho-wan's cold expression as he recounts his reasons for abandoning Lady Chung can be compared to the blankness of a Noh mask – a mask that, in his case, slips only towards the end of the scene, as his eyes appear rimmed with tears.

However, E.'s most intricate borrowing from Noh theatre can be observed in the structure of this scene. As Minae Yamamoto Savas explains in her reading of *Throne of Blood* (1957, dir. Kurosawa), a Noh performance comprises three steps or phases, which were themselves adapted from ancient Chinese court music.[35] The first of these steps is *jo* (a slow, preparatory step towards the subsequent action), followed by *ha* (corresponding to a moment of crisis or rupture) and finally *kyu* (a rapid, concluding phase). E. subtly adapts this structure in *Untold Scandal*, beginning with the slow tempo of *jo* as Lady Chung arrives at Cho-wan's home and enquires as to his whereabouts. The director proceeds to build towards *ha* and the key moment of rupture in the scene, as we see Cho-wan sitting at his window before the adjacent shutter opens to reveal that he has a new mistress. As Lady Chung demands to know why Cho-wan no longer loves her, the pace of the scene becomes more urgent in a manner reminiscent of *kyu*, before culminating in the heroine's collapse. By appropriating key conventions of Noh theatre, *Untold Scandal* illustrates its status as a cross-cultural artefact that blends together material not merely from France and South Korea but also from Japan.

In contrast to the lavish costume drama of *Untold Scandal*, *Thirst* reflects the blending of Eastern and Western culture in the very different genre of vampire romance. Loosely adapted from Zola's 1867 novel *Thérèse Raquin*, *Thirst* revolves around the story of a Catholic priest, Sang-hyun, who contracts vampirism during a medical trial to eradicate a deadly virus. After being released from the trial, Sang-hyun begins an affair with Tae-joo, a repressed young woman who works in a clothing shop owned by her mother-in-law, Mrs Ra. The couple subsequently murders Tae-joo's sickly husband Kang-woo, plunging them into a state of torment that leads to Tae-joo's own conversion to vampirism. In choosing to reinvent *Thérèse Raquin*, director Park Chan-wook set out to combine specific elements of Western culture – in particular vampirism – with a Korean context. Park stated at the time of *Thirst*'s release:

> When you consider the concept of vampirism, it is inherently part of a Western culture. ... So you can say also that my film is about things that are coming from the outside and entering in, such as the virus that enters into the priest, changing him. So we're looking at things from the exterior entering into the interior and whether our inside can accept this thing that has entered from the outside or whether it will reject it.[36]

Park's conceptualization of *Thirst* as a film that brings 'outside' elements into a new cultural setting – a description which resonates strongly with the theme of this chapter – is reflected in the film's plot. In his treatment of vampirism, especially, the director was determined to avoid the kind of clichés and stereotypes that Western cinema has done much to popularize. Rejecting the image of vampires as creatures with elongated canine teeth who are afraid of crucifixes, Park made his own protagonist Sang-hyun a vampire who refuses to kill on moral grounds and who supplies himself with blood from a coma patient.[37]

Alongside the film's treatment of vampirism, Park's enthusiasm for blending different cultural materials underpins his approach to adapting *Thérèse Raquin*, in particular the novel's Naturalist content. *Thérèse Raquin* was the first work in which Zola applied Hippolyte Taine's theory that individuals are governed by the variables of 'race', 'milieu' and 'moment'. Following a preface in which he insists on the importance of heredity in shaping the personalities of his characters

Thérèse and Laurent, Zola proceeds to explore the influence of the physical environment on their behaviour. Situated in a damp, narrow passageway in Paris, the haberdashery shop owned by Madame Raquin, especially, appears as an oppressive, tomb-like space from which the passionate Thérèse longs to escape. 'The thick atmosphere of the dining-room suffocated her,' Zola writes of the eponymous heroine and her surroundings. 'The shivering silence, the yellowish gleams of the lamp pierced her with vague terror, and indescribable anguish.'[38] In *Thirst*, Park focuses his attention similarly on the representation of space and uses the techniques of his own medium to adapt the powerful sense of claustrophobia that Zola creates in the source text. The suffocating effect that Mrs Ra's shop has on Tae-joo is illustrated by a sequence early in the film, in which the family is joined by friends for a weekly game of mahjong. As the visitors arrive, we see Tae-joo retreat first to the bathroom, a space that affords her little privacy as Kang-woo can still be heard outside, complaining that he has caught a cold. After the young woman returns to the kitchen, a series of close-up shots of the guests around the table emphasizes the proximity of the actors to each other and the confined nature of the space around them. A further close-up then shows Tae-joo loosening her blouse in an attempt to counteract the stifling heat and, metaphorically, her own sense of entrapment. As this sequence shows, Park does not transfer the Naturalist impulses of *Thérèse Raquin* to the screen in an imitative manner. Instead, he adapts and renews Zola's interest in spatial constriction through the close, claustrophobic style of his own camera work.

As well as engaging with the theoretical dimensions of *Thérèse Raquin*, Park's recreation of the novel in a Korean context can be seen to expose the blending of literary genres that lies behind Zola's earlier claims to Naturalist objectivity. Despite describing *Thérèse Raquin* as 'an exact and meticulous copy of life',[39] Zola drew extensively in this novel on the resources of Gothic horror. Fantastical, nightmarish imagery abounds in this text, not least in its depiction of the mental and physical turmoil experienced by Thérèse and Laurent following their murder of Camille. 'When the two murderers laid down under the same sheet, and they closed their eyes', writes Zola, 'they believed they could feel the damp body of their victim stretched out in the middle of the bed.'[40] Park's blending of *Thérèse Raquin* with the vampire horror genre reanimates the supernatural elements of the source text, transforming them into integral features of the film's plot and cinematography. The director's recourse to images of horror and the supernatural is illustrated with particular clarity by the sequence in which the dead Kang-woo, his body bloated and soaking wet, reappears in Tae-joo's bedroom (see Figure 6.4). As Tae-joo and Sang-hyun attempt to continue their affair in the wake of the murder, Park shows droplets of water falling onto them from the ceiling above the bed. In a

FIGURE 6.4 Thirst *(2009, dir. Park)*.

further allusion to Kang-woo's earlier drowning, the camera then cuts to a shot of a wardrobe lying on its back in a boiler room, its doors weighted down with a large stone as Kang-woo struggles to escape from inside. As Darcy Paquet observes, the 'blending and bending of old genres' – reflected here in the combination of vampire horror with a French Naturalist novel – represents one of the key ways in which South Korean filmmakers have sought to create a new identity for their national cinema that distinguishes it from the propagandistic filmmaking of the country's pre-democratic past.[41] However, as this sequence illustrates, *Thirst* reveals as much about its French source as it does about the evolution of Korean cinema. In blending material from different genres and cultures, Park reformulates Zola's own ability both to meld Gothic horror with Naturalist theory and to combine creative artistry with his scientific ambitions.

Reinforcing and rethinking diasporic French texts in German cinema: *Phoenix* and *Atomised*

If Hollywood and South Korea have both exerted a powerful influence on the global diaspora of French literature films, so, too, have some of the traditional filmmaking centres in Europe. This is particularly true of German cinema, which since the late 1990s has shown renewed interest in adapting works of French fiction. Following reunification and the fall of the Berlin Wall in 1989, German audiences, writes Jaimey Fisher, had tended to favour 'lighter fare, largely geared to distract from the anxieties that would accompany (yet) another fundamental transformation of state, economy, and culture'.[42] This vogue for undemanding entertainment nevertheless began to wane towards the end of the 1990s, its demise coinciding with the emergence of a new emphasis on realism in German cinema. One of the leading figures in the ongoing development of this realist aesthetic is Christian Petzold, the most prominent member of the group of socially and politically engaged German filmmakers known collectively as the Berlin School. Since embarking on his career in the early 1990s, Petzold has established his reputation as a director whose films probe the complexities of human relationships, often against the backdrop of German history during the second half of the twentieth century. More importantly in the context of the present discussion, many of Petzold's films also reflect his fascination with recreating earlier artistic works and genres in order to bring new perspectives to them in adaptation. His 2007 film *Yella*, for example, is a remake of the 1962 American horror film *Carnival of Souls* which can be seen to allegorize the difficulties of German reunification through its portrayal of a young woman's struggle to escape the former East Germany and make a new life for herself in the West. Similarly, in *Jerichow* (2008), Petzold reworks James M. Cain's 1934 novel *The Postman Always Rings Twice*, using the love triangle at the heart of the original plot as a conduit through which to reflect on questions of immigration and identity in recent European history. As the director explains of his enthusiasm for rediscovering the works of his artistic predecessors, 'it is a kind of archaeology. [There is] newness when we tell the old stories and tales.'[43] In adapting these earlier narratives, Petzold not only reinforces sometimes understated aspects of their themes and plotlines but also rethinks his source material and invites us to contemplate it in new ways.

This dual process of reinforcement and reinterpretation – which I wish to explore here as the third key element of adaptive diaspora – is reflected strikingly in *Phoenix*. Inspired by Hubert Monteilhet's novel *Le Retour des cendres*, *Phoenix* revolves around the story of the fictional Nelly Lenz (Nina Hoss), a Jewish singer who is severely disfigured by a bullet wound shortly before her liberation from a concentration camp in 1945. Transposing Monteilhet's plot from Paris to Berlin, the film follows Nelly as she undergoes reconstructive surgery and then reunites with her husband Johnny, who initially fails to recognize her. However, Johnny does see in this stranger – who tells him her name is Esther – a close resemblance to the wife he remembers and so persuades her to impersonate Nelly so that they might claim the latter's inheritance and share the proceeds. As the title of the film suggests, *Phoenix* provides an excellent illustration of Petzold's ability to resurrect earlier artistic materials and to emphasize specific aspects of those sources while at the same time refitting them for a new cultural context. The film's representation of Johnny warrants particular attention in this regard, not least because of the way in which it re-imagines Monteilhet's own interest in the figure of the schemer. A writer often described by French critics as the Laclos of crime fiction, Monteilhet shares with the author of *Les Liaisons dangereuses* an enthusiasm for creating seductive, Machiavellian characters. In *Le Retour des cendres*, Stan – the character reinvented by Petzold as Johnny – fits squarely into this libertine mould. In a manner reminiscent of Laclos's Valmont, Stan prioritizes pleasure over love and readily concocts the scheme to access his wife's inheritance in the hope that it could buy him 'a whole stable of sports cars'.[44] In *Phoenix*, Petzold can be seen to foreground the theme of manipulation through Johnny's own calculating behaviour. Upon meeting Nelly in the Phoenix nightclub, Johnny wastes little time in identifying her as a suitable accomplice in his plan to secure his wife's inheritance. 'We'll split it,' he tells her coldly, before instructing her to call him by his full name, Johannes, in order to maintain the sense of a business partnership between them.

However, Petzold does not restrict himself merely to underscoring the key role that manipulation plays in the source text. On the contrary, *Phoenix* also focuses our attention on the extent to which Johnny may be deceiving himself and how his behaviour, in turn, might be viewed as representative of German society more generally in the immediate aftermath of the Second World War. The theme of self-deception features strongly in *Phoenix*, most notably in the sequence in which Johnny returns to his apartment to find Nelly wearing make-up and a red dress that had belonged to her before the war. As we hear the sound of Nelly's footsteps on the stone floor, Petzold's camera remains fixed on Johnny and the stunned expression on his face, tantalizing us with the possibility that he will at last recognize his wife. Yet just as he appears on the brink of conceding the truth of Nelly's identity, Johnny seems instead to want to reassure himself that she is merely an impersonator. 'The eye make-up is wrong,' he declares, fighting to regain control of his emotions. 'Your walk, too. Everything.' Johnny's apparent determination to deceive himself that his wife is dead – coupled with Nelly's own willingness to convince herself that Johnny still loves her – can be interpreted as a metaphor for Germany's own struggle to face up to the atrocities that the country had perpetrated under the Third Reich and in particular during the Holocaust. As Geoffrey Macnab observed in his review of *Phoenix* in the *Independent* on 7 May 2015, 'there are obvious allegorical elements here: *Phoenix* can be read as a cautionary tale about German bad faith and self-deception in the post-war era'.[45] As well as highlighting the importance of manipulation to Monteilhet's plot, Petzold adds new meaning to the story in adaptation by rethinking it within a specifically German context.

Like the work of Petzold, the films of Oskar Roehler reflect a fascination with history and the way in which individuals are sometimes damaged by historical forces beyond their control. Roehler began his career as a director in the 1990s, making low-budget films such as *Gentleman* (1995), a loose adaptation of Bret Easton Ellis's 1991 novel *American Psycho*. It was his semi-autobiographical film *No Place to Go* (2000), however, that brought him to wider attention both in his native country and internationally. Based in part on the experiences of Roehler's mother, the novelist Gisela Elsner, the film represents a female writer who struggles to come to terms with the profound social and cultural changes triggered by the fall of the Berlin Wall. *No Place to Go* proved a major critical and commercial success and helped to establish Roehler's reputation as one of the leading filmmakers of post-reunification Germany. Significantly, it also set a thematic precedent for many subsequent films, which have often focused on the anxiety and personal traumas induced by living in a capitalist society. One of the recurring features of Roehler's work in this respect is his interest in troubled romantic relationships. As Marco Abel explains, his films commonly reflect on the difficulty of sustaining a loving partnership in the face of the multiple pressures of contemporary social life.[46] The plot of *Angst* (2003), for example, revolves around Robert, a film director whose relationship with his girlfriend Marie disintegrates after his father is diagnosed with a terminal illness, causing Robert to console himself by visiting prostitutes. Similarly, *Agnes and His Brothers* (2004) portrays the marital disharmony that exists behind the outwardly successful political career of one of the eponymous siblings, Werner. As Abel summarizes Roehler's films, 'all of them depict (especially, though not exclusively) male characters who experience great anxieties from the imposing demands of modern romantic relationships'.[47]

Such anxieties are a key feature of Roehler's 2006 film *Atomised*. Adapted from Michel Houellebecq's controversial novel *Les Particules élémentaires*, the film relates the story of half-brothers Michael and Bruno, whose childhood abandonment by their hippie mother has an enduring impact on their adult lives, in particular on their very different attitudes towards love and sexual relationships. Whereas Michael is a gifted molecular biologist who avoids romantic attachments and physical intimacy, Bruno becomes a teacher whose relentless obsession with sex leads him to depression and to the brink of suicide. Like *Phoenix*, *Atomised* transposes the geographical setting of its source text from Paris to Berlin. In so doing, however, the film also adapts some of the themes that underpin Houellebecq's view of the postmodern world. Central to these themes is the novelist's concern with the isolation of individuals in an increasingly fragmented, capitalist society. As Richard Holloway observes of *Les Particules élémentaires*, 'the title of Houellebecq's book says it all: we are atomised. Like colliding billiard balls, there is little to hold us together, no common identity that can integrate us into the community and its responsibilities.'[48] Houellebecq's notion that society lacks a sense of cohesion, causing individuals to lead isolated and often lonely lives, is one that Roehler's film taps into at the outset by means of a prologue in which Michael outlines his decision to resign from his post at the Berlin Biotechnology Institute. As Michael's voice-over explains his wish to return to his earlier research on the possibility of achieving reproduction without sex, we see the character – played by Christian Ulmen – sitting alone at a computer. Following this initial sequence, Roehler continues to emphasize the solitary nature of Michael's life, as we see the young scientist return home to his apartment. Interspersed with shots of Bruno teaching a class on Baudelaire, these short scenes – which themselves appear isolated in depicting a series of unconnected happenings – show Michael first finding the canary that was his only domestic companion dead in its cage. Further shots see him gently closing his balcony door to block out the noise of a party in another apartment and ultimately consuming a ready meal for one. As this opening sequence illustrates, Roehler clearly reinforces Houellebecq's vision of a world in which communities are breaking down, yet simultaneously employs his own fragmented shot-making to reinterpret that vision in cinematic terms.

Houellebecq and Roehler's shared interest in the theme of social isolation is closely aligned in the novel, and subsequently the film, with the representation of dysfunctional and barely existent family relationships. 'Houellebecq's work', writes Douglas Morrey, 'repeatedly stresses the declining influence of the family. The family, he argues in *Les Particules élémentaires*, was the last bastion of communitarianism separating the individual from the brutal laws of market forces.'[49] According to Bernd Eichinger, the producer of *Atomised*, this view of the family as a fast-disintegrating institution is an aspect of the novel that Roehler was determined to explore in his film. 'There's now more of a tendency', Eichinger claims, 'for people to split up, or for couples to split than there used to be. Families fall apart or lovers split up and look for new partners. ... Houellebecq is onto these things. So is the novel.'[50] *Atomised* clearly underscores this aspect of Houellebecq's sociological vision, not least in its portrayal of Bruno's troubled family life and background. In two scenes, the director shows Bruno first meeting Michael in a bar, where Bruno's seemingly upbeat mood soon gives way to the revelation that his wife wants a divorce. 'She's moved out with the baby,' he tells Michael, before declaring that he 'really wanted to be a good father'. The next sequence expands on this theme of inadequate paternity, as Roehler adapts Houellebecq's earlier notion that breakdowns in family relationships are often passed down from one generation to the next. Cutting to a shot of Bruno as he climbs the stairs of an apartment building to visit his own father, the director shows Klement senior opening the door to his son and mistaking him for a salesman. As the camera follows Bruno inside the dark room littered with empty bottles and glasses – reminders of the older man's alcoholism – Roehler makes clear that the pair are rarely in contact, as Klement senior casually enquires of his son, 'you got married, right?'. However, any concern that Bruno's father has for him is shown to be fleeting, as he first launches into a tirade about the failure of his cosmetic surgery business and then ushers his son towards the door, pausing only to ask if Bruno can lend him some money. The idea that 'history repeats itself' – a phrase that Klement senior utters in the novel[51] – is one that *Atomised* both emphasizes and rethinks in its depiction of broken family relationships. In juxtaposing Bruno's feelings of paternal inadequacy with his own father's indifference towards him, the film does not merely replicate Houellebecq's social vision but instead uses the pairing of these scenes to re-imagine it in a visually potent way.

In exploring the reasons for such dysfunctional relationships, *Atomised* also invites us to think differently about Houellebecq's deep-rooted pessimism towards postmodern society and to recognize the blistering humour that often underpins his work. In *Les Particules élémentaires*, Houellebecq blames the erosion of family life and traditional moral values on the near-revolution of May '68 and on the spirit of personal and sexual liberation that surrounded it. As Carole Sweeney explains, 'Houellebecq's writing suggests, indeed asserts, that May '68 was not primarily an emancipatory and political moment but one of damaging antinomianism that emphasized transgressive desire and egotistical individualism. Arguing that 1968 marked the point at which France began its slide into moral and political decline, Houellebecq's view of '68 is unwaveringly negative and antagonistic.'[52] *Atomised* both perpetuates and rethinks the novelist's contempt for this period in its representation of the New Age camp where Bruno pitches his tent in the hope of indulging in the kind of easy, uncommitted sex that he craves (see Figure 6.5). In reviewing *Atomised* for the *Guardian*, Peter Bradshaw appeared to be thinking of the depiction of this hippie commune when he compared the film to a 'Euro-hardcore version of *Carry On Camping*, with lashings of miserablism, redundant TV movie emotion and scandalously mediocre acting'.[53] Despite its scornful tone, Bradshaw's comparison of *Atomised* to *Carry On Camping* also pinpointed one of the key aspects of Roehler's film, namely its capacity to reformulate the mixture of humour and vitriol with which Houellebecq treats the '68 generation. The New Age sequence balances these elements by showing Bruno attending a massage class, where he is excited by the prospect of being able to touch naked female flesh. Adapting the equivalent

FIGURE 6.5 Atomised *(2006, dir. Roehler)*.

passage in the novel, in which Bruno instead finds himself partnered with a hairy, overweight man, Roehler evokes the comic undercurrent of the situation as Bruno looks around enviously at the other, mixed-sex couples, his growing frustration reflected in a series of close-up and point-of-view shots which show breasts and female torsos being massaged by the other male participants in the group. Far from merely revelling in bleak pessimism, *Atomised* reinforces the humour that resonates through *Les Particules élémentaires* and, in so doing, posits comedy as a key element of Houellebecq's more well-known antipathy towards New Age culture.

As both *Atomised* and *Phoenix* show, the diasporic spread of French literature does not result in it being absorbed wholesale into different national and cultural contexts. Rather, the adaptation of this material outside of France leads to specific aspects of it being retained, reinforced and presented in new ways. *Atomised*, for example, foregrounds the themes of loneliness and social fragmentation that underpin *Les Particules élémentaires*. In tandem with this process of reinforcement, however, diasporic adaptation also involves a rethinking of the source text. Such reinterpretation is particularly clear in *Phoenix*, in which Petzold reshapes the theme of self-deception that is already present in Monteilhet's novel and juxtaposes it with Germany's denial of the full horrors of the Second World War. In adapting their French sources in a German context, Petzold and Roehler show how these works are not simply transformed beyond recognition but are instead realigned with new artistic, cultural and ideological concerns.

Dramatizing diasporic mobility: *Bel Ami*, *Suite française* and *The Skin I Live In*

While diasporic adaptations often focus on reconnecting with their French sources, others can be seen to dramatize their movement towards other cultures by engaging with a much wider array of intertexts. In the final part of this chapter, I want to consider the ways in which three films – *Bel Ami*, *Suite française* and *The Skin I Live In* – invite us to recognize them as diasporic artefacts by playing on their connections to cinematic works produced outside of France. The intertextuality of adaptations is, of course, a subject to which scholars have devoted considerable attention. Most notably, Robert Stam, whose research draws on the theories of Bakhtin, Kristeva and Genette, has explored adaptation as a dialogic practice that thrives on reinventing multiple sources. 'Film adaptations', writes Stam, 'are caught up in the ongoing whirl of intertextual reference and transformation, of texts generating other texts in an endless process of recycling, transformation, and transmutation, with no clear point of origin.'[54] More recently, Stam has reflected on how this dialogism operates in a cross-cultural context. In particular, he argues that adapting works outside of their native culture often results in an 'indigenization' of the source material, for example, the Indian film *Maya Memsaab* (1993, dir. Mehta), which re-imagines its primary intertext – Flaubert's *Madame Bovary* (1856) – as a Bollywood-style production.[55] My own analysis seeks to build on and extend this concept of dialogism by illustrating how diasporic adaptations use intertextuality to highlight their cross-cultural mobility. By calling attention to their intertextual exchanges with films produced in a variety of national and cultural contexts, these adaptations actively perform their movement across different geographical locales. Moreover, these exchanges often appear playful and highly self-conscious, as filmmakers encourage spectators to participate in a game of identifying the intertexts that are being adapted.

This playful self-consciousness appears as a key feature of the 2012 version of Maupassant's 1885 novel, *Bel Ami*. The first feature film made by British theatre directors Declan Donnellan and Nick Ormerod, *Bel Ami* revolves around the story of the fictional Georges Duroy, a former French soldier who attempts to establish his career in Paris as a journalist writing for the newspaper *La Vie Française*. However, when his lack of talent becomes obvious to his employers, Duroy resolves to continue his social rise by seducing a series of influential women, including Madeleine, the widow of his former comrade Forestier, and Madame Rousset, the wife of the newspaper's owner. Despite featuring a high-profile cast led by Robert Pattinson, Uma Thurman and

Christina Ricci, *Bel Ami* received a decidedly mixed response from critics, some of whom accused the film of failing to weave the different strands of its plot into a coherent whole. '*Bel Ami* stutters rather than glides,' wrote Mark Adams for the website *Screen Daily*, 'and while punctuated by some impressive performances and a fine sense of design it can never quite find the right balance between its twin storylines of seduction and politics.'[56] Other critical reactions to the film were more hostile, particularly in their appraisal of Pattinson's performance as the unscrupulous *arriviste* Duroy. 'It's one thing to embody a moral void,' claimed Justin Chang in *Variety*, 'quite another to look merely vacant, and in scene after scene, Pattinson registers a visible strain in negotiating the character's shifts from slick, droll charm to animal-like desperation and thwarted rage.'[57] Describing the film as having 'an utterly blank leading man', Elizabeth Weitzman of the *New York Daily News* went further still in claiming that Pattinson had been miscast. 'Pattinson is an actor of limited range but expansive potential,' Weitzman observed. 'When he's cast in the right roles, he's able to make the most of his brooding beauty. So the fault really lies with the filmmakers, who were more interested in his name and fan base than his suitability.'[58]

The factor that critics surprisingly neglected at the time of *Bel Ami*'s release, however, was that the film juxtaposed the ruthlessness of Georges Duroy with Pattinson's recurring role in the *Twilight Saga* (2008–12). Based on the series of novels by American author Stephenie Meyer, the five *Twilight* films featured Pattinson as Edward Cullen, a vampire who retains the physical appearance of a 17-year-old and who falls in love with a human, Bella (Kristen Stewart). Released in the UK in March 2012, eight months before the final instalment of *Twilight, Breaking Dawn – Part 2* appeared in British cinemas, *Bel Ami* exploited the vampiric resonance of Pattinson's screen persona at the level of both plot and cinematography. The opening sequence of the film plays on this association at the outset. In the first shot in which Pattinson appears on-screen, we see him with his back to camera, a silent, sinister figure dressed in a long black coat and hat as he gazes enviously at the diners in an expensive restaurant. Following the title screen, a further short sequence creates an obvious visual link with *Twilight*, as Duroy is shown slumped in a chair in his threadbare apartment, his body partially illuminated by moonlight in a manner that recalls the pale complexion of Edward Cullen (see Figure 6.6). The second part of this sequence proves similarly, if subtly, replete with references to vampirism, as Donnellan and Ormerod emphasize the predatory nature of Duroy's behaviour. Leaving his apartment under the cover of darkness, Duroy heads to a bawdy cabaret club where he orders a beer before bumping into his old friend Forestier (Philip Glenister). The subsequent conversation between the pair reveals Duroy's willingness to exploit others, as he informs Forestier

FIGURE 6.6 Bel Ami *(2012, dir. Donnellan/Ormerod)*.

that he has no social connections or dinner clothes, prompting the older man to give him two gold coins. In a further illustration of his predatory instincts, Duroy then uses one of the coins to acquire the services of a prostitute whose stark white make-up and red lips give her, too, the appearance of an undead figure. In showing the eponymous protagonist stalking the streets of Paris at night in order to satisfy his desire for drink, money and women, *Bel Ami* revels in layering the predatory Duroy onto the vampiric persona that Pattinson had acquired through the *Twilight* films.

While echoing Pattinson's role in the *Twilight Saga*, *Bel Ami* also adapts and reconfigures the actor's screen persona in a way that differs significantly from the representation of Edward Cullen. Like the South Korean film *Thirst* discussed earlier in this chapter, the *Twilight* novels and their film adaptations avoided many of the clichés – such as elongated canine teeth – associated with Western representations of vampirism. Throughout the series, Edward appears as an unorthodox vampire who consumes the blood of animals rather than humans. He also shows no interest in seducing and enslaving women for his own pleasure but instead falls in love with Bella and feels deeply protective of her. Pattinson's performance in *Bel Ami* encourages spectators to recall the chasteness of this earlier character while simultaneously foregrounding Duroy's relentless sexual appetite. 'In a way', observed film critic Stephanie Bunbury following the release of *Bel Ami*, 'Georges is the opposite of *Twilight*'s fastidiously moral Edward Cullen, whose lesson to every teenage fan is the virtue of holding back. Georges will sink his fangs into anything.'[59] Duroy's readiness to prey on women, and to use sex to advance his career, is reflected particularly clearly in his seduction of Madame Rousset (Kristin Scott Thomas). Having followed his intended target to church, the young man positions himself in the pew behind her as she kneels at prayer. The subsequent mise en scène of this sequence underscores how Duroy stalks women like a poacher hunting game. Having made clear to Madame Rousset that his visit to the church was not an accident, he then blocks her exit as she attempts to flee the building, cornering her in a side chapel where she eventually succumbs to his pursuit and kisses him clumsily. The directors cut then to the inside of Duroy's love nest, where he tugs with increasing ferocity at Madame Rousset's clothes, the camera circling around actress Kristin Scott Thomas in a movement which highlights her character's position as Duroy's latest prey. As this sequence shows, *Bel Ami* does not so much imitate Pattinson's *Twilight* persona as it does remodel it, overwriting the sexual self-restraint of Edward Cullen with the capacity for seduction through which Duroy nourishes his social ambitions.

If *Bel Ami* plays on the vampire thematics of *Twilight*, Saul Dibb's 2015 adaptation of *Suite française* aligns itself more closely with British and American cinematic representations of the Second World War. A co-production between Britain, France and Belgium, *Suite française* was based on elements of the novel of the same title by Irène Némirovsky, a Ukrainian Jew who had emigrated to France prior to the German invasion of 1940. Written between 1940 and 1942, Némirovsky's work recounts life in the small town of Bussy, on the eastern outskirts of Paris, during the Occupation, focusing in particular on the fictional love affair between a French woman, Lucile Angellier, and a German officer, Bruno von Falk, who is billeted to the home that Lucile shares with her overbearing mother-in-law. The unfinished manuscript, which had lain undiscovered in a suitcase for almost sixty years following Némirovsky's death in the Auschwitz concentration camp in 1942, was published in 2004 and quickly became an international bestseller. Over the next four years, *Suite française* sold 2.5 million copies worldwide and was translated into thirty-eight languages, prompting French media company TF1 to secure the rights to adapt the novel in 2007. The subsequent film version nevertheless failed to replicate the commercial and critical success of the source text. At the box office, Dibb's recreation of *Suite française* generated only $9.3 million against its budget of $15 million. Despite TF1's attempt at reaching the widest possible audience by adapting the novel in English, many critics also found the film's resultant 'Britishness' incongruous with its French setting. Writing in *Variety*, Guy Lodge claimed that 'the title is the most authentically French thing about *Suite française*, a fusty but enjoyably old-fashioned WWII soap that, notwithstanding its Gallic locale, is otherwise characterized by a distinctly British brand of plumminess'.[60] In his own review for London's *Evening Standard*, David Sexton argued that TF1's preference for an English-language adaptation, which furthermore mixed British and German accents, had ultimately compromised the artistic integrity of the film. 'There's a long history of dodgy British renderings of France,' wrote Sexton disparagingly, 'from 'Allo! 'Allo! to the clunker that was *Charlotte Gray* – and *Suite française* turns out to be a surprise addition to them.'[61]

To deride the 'Britishness' of Dibb's version of *Suite française* is nevertheless to underestimate the complexity of the film as a diasporic artefact. In its interaction with British and, more widely, American cinema, this adaptation extends Némirovsky's work into an anglophone context in a manner which echoes the novel's earlier dispersal across different languages and cultures. Especially notable in this respect is the way in which the film can be seen to reference other cinematic depictions of the Second World War. The scene in which the farmer Benoît escapes on a motorcycle after murdering a German officer, for example, recalls the memorable sequence in *The Great Escape* (1963, dir. Sturges) in which Steve McQueen's Captain Hiltz leads his own Nazi pursuers on a two-wheeled chase across the Bavarian countryside (see Figure 6.7).

In addition to this brief allusion to *The Great Escape*, Dibb can be seen to construct a more sustained intertextual parallel with British director Anthony Minghella's 1996 adaptation of *The English Patient*. Based on the novel of the same title by Michael Ondaatje and set between the late 1930s and the end of the Second World War, *The English Patient* revolves around the love affair between a Hungarian cartographer, Count László de Almásy (Ralph Fiennes), and a married British woman, Katharine Clifton (Kristin Scott Thomas). As the illicit relationship between the couple intensifies, the film reflects the risks they take in order to be together, culminating in a scene in which they make love in a small storage room during a Christmas party for British servicemen in North Africa. In a series of close-ups, Minghella shows Almásy contemplating and slowly caressing Katharine before the camera cuts outside to a shot of

FIGURE 6.7 Suite française *(2015, dir. Dibb)*.

their intertwined bodies through a frosted glass window. The scene concludes in a moment of high dramatic tension, as Almásy, still beaded with sweat from his amorous encounter, meets Katharine's husband (Colin Firth) in the lobby and lies that he is unaware of Katharine's whereabouts. Dibb's recreation of *Suite française* invites us to trace a connection to this earlier sequence as Bruno and Lucile finally succumb to their own passion for each other. In a manner reminiscent of Minghella's close-ups, Dibb focuses on the faces and limbs of Bruno and Lucile as they feverishly push aside each other's clothes. In a further echo of the equivalent scene in *The English Patient*, the figure of Madame Angellier (Kristin Scott Thomas) then looms towards the frosted glass of the front door, her interruption of the couple's tryst playfully adapting the earlier lovemaking scene in which Scott Thomas's Katharine narrowly avoids her affair being discovered. By engaging with both *The Great Escape* and *The English Patient*, *Suite française* inscribes itself within a corpus of British and American war films and, in so doing, emphasizes the adaptability of the story beyond its French origins.

While cinematic representations of the Second World War appear as key references in *Suite française*, Dibb also reaches more deeply into British cinema and exploits the artistic resources of wartime filmmaking itself. One of the film's most visible intertexts from this period is *Brief Encounter* (1945, dir. Lean), in which a married woman, Laura (Celia Johnson), recounts her experience of falling in love with a stranger, Alec (Trevor Howard), after they meet by chance at a railway station. Upon the release of the film adaptation of *Suite française*, some reviewers were quick to draw unflattering comparisons with *Brief Encounter* and to accuse Dibb of borrowing cinematic techniques from Lean's film that by 2015 seemed both dated and excessively melodramatic. 'As we hear Lucile's emotional voiceover', wrote Geoffrey Macnab in his review for the *Independent*, 'or see shots of her with the sunlight glistening in her hair while elegiac music plays on the soundtrack, the film skirts close to *Brief Encounter*-style melodrama.'[62] Listing what he viewed as the key shortcomings of *Suite française*, Guy Lodge, meanwhile, described Lucile's voice-over as 'intrusive' and 'wholly dispensable'. 'Like a longer *Brief Encounter*', Lodge claimed in his review for *Variety*, 'the love affair under examination is powerful for its necessarily tacit exchanges of feeling. The same can't be said for the film.'[63] Such derisive critiques nevertheless failed to take account of the way in which Dibb adapts and uses *Brief Encounter* to enrich his own creative practice. His dexterity in reworking Lean's film is neatly illustrated by the ending of *Suite française*, in which Lucile agrees to transport Benoît to Paris, where he intends to join the Resistance. Following a shoot-out at a military checkpoint on the outskirts of Bussy, in which Benoît kills two German soldiers, the final shots of the film show Lucile driving into the distance and wiping away tears as her voice-over laments that 'hardly a word of [the] true feelings' between her and Bruno had ever been spoken. This closing monologue is clearly reminiscent of Laura's voice-over in *Brief Encounter*, in which she frequently expresses her emotional turmoil over her affair with Alec. However, in contrast to the ending of *Brief Encounter*, in which Laura returns to her husband and children, Dibb juxtaposes Lucile's voice-over with a moment of emancipation in which she leaves behind her lover, her marriage and the narrow provincial world of Bussy. Unlike Laura, whose narrative is ultimately silenced by her husband Fred, who with the last words of the film thanks her for returning to the marital home, Lucile is empowered by the experience of her relationship with Bruno, becoming what Dibb has described as 'a mouse that roars'.[64] As this final sequence in the film illustrates, *Suite française* does not imitate *Brief Encounter* but rather delights in its artistic movement towards British cinema and in the transformation of Lean's film that it achieves during this process.

The artistic exuberance with which diasporic adaptations can often be seen to dramatize their dispersal across different cultures is reflected strongly in *The Skin I Live In*. Written by Pedro Almodóvar and his brother Augustín, *The Skin I Live In* was inspired by Thierry Jonquet's 1984 crime novel *Mygale*. In the film version, Antonio Banderas plays Robert Ledgard, a world-renowned plastic surgeon who develops a new form of synthetic skin after his wife is badly burned and ultimately commits suicide following a car accident. Racked with grief, Ledgard continues his experiments by kidnapping Vicente, a young man he believes to have raped his daughter, and through a series of operations transforms him into a woman he names Vera (Elena Anaya). As Darren Waldron and Ros Murray have argued, *The Skin I Live In* is a highly intertextual adaptation in which references to other cinematic works feature prominently.[65] In particular, the film can be viewed as a loose remake of the French cult horror *Les Yeux sans visage* (*Eyes Without a Face*) (1960, dir. Franju), in which the fictional Dr Génissier kidnaps young women from the streets of Paris and removes their faces in order to transplant them onto his daughter Christiane, who has been disfigured in a car crash. At the level of plot, Almodóvar plays repeatedly on the connection between his own work and this earlier film. Like his cinematic predecessor Génissier, Ledgard conducts his experiments in an isolated country house/clinic, which Almodóvar transposes from the outskirts of Paris to Toledo in his native Spain. The meticulous care with which Ledgard prepares Vicente for surgery, drawing lines across his body against which to position the grafts of new skin, proves similarly reminiscent of Franju's film, in which Génissier draws around the face of his own victim before removing it. According to Waldron and Murray, this re-imagining of both *Les Yeux sans visage* and *Mygale* 'gives a French inflection to one of Spain's most iconically transnational directors'. *The Skin I Live In*, they claim, 'exemplifies cross-cultural border crossings in which a French novel and French film are transformed to align with the style and preoccupations of Spain's best-known filmmaker'.[66] However, as this final section will show, *The Skin I Live In* does not reflect a simple or slavish recreation of French artistic materials in a Spanish context. By also engaging with films produced in Spain and the United States, Almodóvar reveals how his adaptation spreads and layers itself over a variety of cultures and earlier cinematic works.

American cinema plays a key role in the process of cultural dispersal that can be seen to operate in *The Skin I Live In*. American films have remained a rich source of inspiration for Almodóvar throughout his career. As the director explained in 2008, 'before achieving my success in the United States, American culture and cinema had already influenced my films, always from the perspective of a Manchegan'.[67] Almodóvar's enthusiasm for Hollywood cinema extends in particular to the films of Alfred Hitchcock, on which he has continued to model many of his own cinematic practices. References to Hitchcock's work abound in *The Skin I Live In*. As Pedro Lange-Churion has observed, Ledgard's voyeuristic contemplation of Vera through a closed-circuit monitor echoes the plot of *Rear Window* (1954), in which the wheelchair-bound protagonist develops a fixation with spying on the other residents of his apartment building.[68] More obviously, *The Skin I Live In* adapts specific elements of *Vertigo* (1958), which was itself inspired by the novel *D'entre les morts* (*Among the Dead*) (1954) by French crime writers Boileau and Narcejac. Almodóvar's depiction of Ledgard and his attempts to mould Vera into a recreation of the wife he has lost clearly recall the character of Scottie Ferguson, who in *Vertigo* transforms a woman, Judy (Kim Novak), into the living image of his former love, Madeleine. The artistic parallels between the two films nevertheless run deeper, as both directors reflect on the brutal obsessiveness with which their male protagonists live out their fantasies of creating the ideal woman. In a key sequence in Hitchcock's film, Scottie forces Judy to undergo a makeover so that she resembles Madeleine as closely as possible, unaware that they are in fact one and the same person. Ignoring Judy's demands to know why he wants so desperately to change her, the retired detective insists on buying her the same grey suit as Madeleine had worn, before a series of close-ups show her nails being painted and her hair dyed blonde. *The Skin I Live In* adapts Scottie's cruel indifference to Judy's distress through a scene in which Ledgard checks on how well Vicente has healed following the initial sex change surgery. As Vicente remains strapped to the operating table, Ledgard appears unmoved by his pleas to know what else the surgeon is going to do to him, and why. Almodóvar's mise en scène presents a further nod to Hitchcock in this sequence, as we see Vicente's face through the circular window of the operating theatre, a shot which subtly evokes the swirling circular patterns in the opening titles of *Vertigo*. Finally, after Ledgard has informed Vicente that he is exacting revenge for his daughter's presumed rape, the camera dissolves into a further sequence in which Vera, now fully transformed into a woman, carefully pushes her fingers and toes into a black body suit, movements that Almodóvar shoots in close-up in a manner that echoes the representation of Judy's makeover in *Vertigo*. In both its plot and cinematography, *The Skin I Live In* pays self-conscious homage to Hitchcock, as Almodóvar encourages us to recognize that he has fuelled his own creativity with American cinematic material.

As well as exposing the connections between Almodóvar's own work and that of Hitchcock, *The Skin I Live In* mobilizes the artistic resources of Spanish cinema. As Waldron and Murray point out, the first shot of the film situates this adaptation within the broader context of Spanish cinematic history by opening with a panoramic view of Toledo, the same shot with which Luis Buñuel had begun his 1970 version of the Benito Pérez Galdós novel *Tristana*.[69] By evoking the intertextual presence of Buñuel's film, Almodóvar playfully juxtaposes the story of Tristana, a young woman who yearns for independence from her elderly guardian Don Lope, with the imprisonment that Vicente/Vera suffers at the hands of Ledgard. Having gestured towards one of the leading Spanish filmmakers of the past, Almodóvar proceeds to reveal the manner in which *The Skin I Live In* intersects with his own work and with some of the thematic concerns that have shaped his career. The film is notable particularly for the way in which it articulates his recurring fascination with the strength and permanence of individual identity. *The Skin I Live In*, explains Francisco Zurian, 'recounts the story of someone who, despite all the violent and barbaric acts to which he is subjected in an attempt to erase who he once was, clings to his life in the only way possible, by refusing to forget who he is. The plastic surgeon's scalpel can transform the body but it cannot touch an individual's memory.'[70] The notion of Vicente as an individual who retains an unshakeable sense of self is reflected clearly in the closing scenes of the film, in which he escapes his captivity and returns to the clothing shop in which he once worked. Unlike Jonquet's novel, in which Vincent eventually reconciles himself to his new gender identity, the ending of Almodóvar's adaptation sees Vicente explain to his former colleague Cristina that he was kidnapped and forced to undergo a sex change, before declaring to her and his mother 'soy Vicente' ('I am Vicente') (see Figure 6.8). The factor that scholars have consistently neglected in their analyses of this ending, however, is that in tandem with his serious exploration of the fixity of individual identity, Almodóvar also presents us with a ludic inversion of the ending of his 1990 film *Tie Me Up! Tie Me Down!* In this earlier work, the fictional porn star Marina (Victoria Abril) falls

FIGURE 6.8 The Skin I Live In *(2011, dir. Almodóvar)*.

in love with former mental patient Ricky – also played by Antonio Banderas – after he kidnaps her and holds her prisoner in her own apartment. Vicente, by contrast, feels no such devotion to his captor and, in a departure from the source text, shoots Ledgard dead just as the surgeon was about to fulfil his hope of consummating their relationship. By incorporating this reversal into its adaptation of *Mygale*, *The Skin I Live In* illustrates how Almodóvar not only reconfigures material from different cultures and cinematic traditions but returns ultimately to the cinema of his homeland, and to the reinvention of his earlier films through his new work.

The two decades between 1996 and 2016 proved a period of striking geographical mobility for cinematic adaptations of French literature. Under the influence of an ever more globalized film industry, French literature films proliferated beyond the borders of metropolitan France in countries as diverse as Germany, South Korea and the United States. My concept of adaptive diaspora provides an invaluable framework within which to explore and understand how literary texts are transformed by their migration into new cultural contexts. Hollywood's ongoing appropriation of French literature illustrates, first, how such works are reconfigured by this diasporic process, not least in the case of the 2001 version of *Planet of the Apes*, in which Tim Burton's apparently nonsensical ending presents a vivid reformulation of Pierre Boulle's view that all civilizations must inevitably, and often inexplicably, come to an end. Theorizing adaptation as a form of artistic scattering also enables us to consider how French literature films blend material from different cultures in a manner that can shed new light on their source texts. This process of blending is particularly evident in South Korean films such as *Thirst*, in which Park Chan-wook delights in amalgamating Naturalist fiction with the genre of vampire romance and, in so doing, re-energizes the interest in claustrophobia that underpins Zola's *Thérèse Raquin*. Moreover, in blending different artistic and cultural materials, diasporic adaptations reveal their capacity to reinforce and rethink them. In *Phoenix*, for example, Petzold emphasizes the theme of self-deception that is already present in Monteilhet's *Le Retour des cendres* and uses this to allegorize Germany's own denial of responsibility for the horrors of the Second World War and the Holocaust. Finally, the concept of adaptive diaspora exposes the way in which French literature adaptations are often self-consciously aware of their own status as diasporic artefacts and, by playing on their connections to cinematic works produced outside of France, actively demonstrate their dispersal across a wide spectrum of countries and cultures. The combination of these four elements – reconfiguration, blending, reinforcement and cross-cultural mobility – establishes my model of adaptive diaspora as a flexible and nuanced instrument with which to explore what happens to literary texts when they travel across national borders. In particular, this chapter has shown that the diasporic spread of French literature does not produce works that are perfect hybrids of different national and cultural identities. Cross-cultural adaptation proves instead to be a fractured, fragmented process in which artistic works move imperfectly between geographical territories, undergoing a partial transformation as they do so and retaining often surprising connections to the homeland in which they originated.

Notes

1 Hamid Naficy, *An Accented Cinema: Exilic and Diasporic Filmmaking* (Princeton, NJ: Princeton University Press, 2001), 58–60 and 244–5.

2 Jørgen Bruhn, Anne Gjelsvik and Henriette Thune, 'Parallel Worlds of Possible Meetings in *Let the Right One In*', *Word & Image* 27.1 (2011): 2–14 (9).

3 Research and Markets, 'China Cinema Market to Surpass $22 Billion by the End of 2025 – China's Tightening Censorship Is Making a Bad Box Office, Challenging Growth', 5 March 2020, https://www.globenewswire.com/news-release/2020/03/05/1995612/0/en/China-Cinema-Market-to-Surpass-22-Billion-by-the-End-of-2025-China-s-Tightening-Censorship-is-Making-a-Bad-Box-Office-Challenging-Growth.html.

4 Sean Cubitt, 'Digital Cinemas', in *The Routledge Companion to World Cinema*, ed. Rob Stone, Paul Cooke, Stephanie Dennison and Alex Marlow-Mann (London: Routledge, 2018), 437.

5 Elizabeth Ezra and Terry Rowden, eds, *Transnational Cinema: The Film Reader* (Abingdon: Routledge, 2006), 1–2.

6. For further discussion of cross-cultural movements of memory, see, for example, Astrid Erll, 'Travelling Memory', *Parallax*, 17.4 (2011): 4–18 and Lucy Bond and Jessica Rapson, eds, *The Transcultural Turn: Interrogating Memory Between and Beyond Borders* (Berlin: De Gruyter, 2014); Chiara De Cesari and Ann Rigney, eds, *Transnational Memory: Circulation, Articulation, Scales* (Berlin: De Gruyter, 2014).
7. Linda Hutcheon with Siobhan O'Flynn, *A Theory of Adaptation*, 2nd edn (London: Routledge, 2013), 145.
8. For further background on the concept of indigenization in an adaptive context, see Hutcheon with O'Flynn, *A Theory of Adaptation*, 148–53.
9. Geoffrey Nowell-Smith and Steven Ricci, eds, *Hollywood and Europe: Economics, Culture, National Identity, 1945–1995* (London: BFI, 1998), 1.
10. Motion Picture Association of America, 'Theatrical Market Statistics (2016)', https://archive.org/details/MPAATheatricalMarketStatistics2016/page/n5.
11. Anthony Kaufman, 'The Lonely Subtitle: Here's Why US Audiences Are Abandoning Foreign-Language Films', 6 May 2014, https://www.indiewire.com/2014/05/the-lonely-subtitle-heres-why-u-s-audiences-are-abandoning-foreign-language-films-27051/.
12. Tom Brook, 'How the Global Box Office Is Changing Hollywood', 21 October 2014, http://www.bbc.com/culture/story/20130620-is-china-hollywoods-future.
13. Peter Bradshaw, '*Planet of the Apes*', *Guardian*, 17 August 2001, https://www.theguardian.com/film/2001/aug/17/1.
14. Pierre Boulle, *La Planète des singes* (Paris: Julliard, 1963), 190.
15. Peyrie quoted in Hugo Schofield, 'The French Spy Who Wrote *The Planet of the Apes*', 4 August 2014, https://www.bbc.co.uk/news/magazine-28610124.
16. Quoted in Chris Pizzello, 'Bringing the Dark Side of Character to Light in *Diabolique*', *American Cinematographer* 77.4 (1996): 36–44 (39).
17. Quoted in Pizzello, 'Bringing the Dark Side', 39.
18. Raphaëlle Moine, *Remakes: les films français à Hollywood* (Paris: CNRS, 2007), 24.
19. Roger Ebert, '*Diabolique*', 22 March 1996, https://www.rogerebert.com/reviews/diabolique-1996.
20. Moine, *Remakes*, 136.
21. Quoted in Pizzello, 'Bringing the Dark Side', 37.
22. Lucy Mazdon, *Encore Hollywood: Remaking French Cinema* (London: BFI, 2000), 116.
23. Darcy Paquet, *New Korean Cinema: Breaking the Waves* (London: Wallflower, 2009), 3.
24. Darcy Paquet, 'Genrebending in Contemporary Korean Cinema', 6 July 2000, http://koreanfilm.org/genrebending.html.
25. Jeeyoung Shin, 'Globalisation and New Korean Cinema', in *New Korean Cinema*, ed. Chi-Yun Shin and Julian Stringer (Edinburgh: Edinburgh University Press, 2005), 51–62 (57).

26 Shin, 'Globalisation and New Korean Cinema', 56.
27 Darcy Paquet, 'An Interview with E. J-yong', 10 October 2003, https://koreanfilm.org/ejyong.html.
28 Paquet, 'An Interview with E. J-yong'.
29 Hye Seung Chung and David Scott Diffrient, *Movie Migrations: Transnational Genre Flows and South Korean Cinema* (New Brunswick, NJ: Rutgers University Press, 2015), 131.
30 Chung and Diffrient, *Movie Migrations*, 131.
31 Simon Davies, *Laclos: 'Les Liaisons dangereuses'* (London: Grant & Cutler, 1987), 61–3.
32 For further discussion of Laclos's borrowings from classical tragedy, see, for example, Elizabeth J. MacArthur, 'Trading Genres: Epistolarity and Theatricality in *Britannicus* and *Les Liaisons dangereuses*', *Yale French Studies* 76 (1989): 243–64.
33 Chung and Diffrient, *Movie Migrations*, 143.
34 Choderlos de Laclos, *Les Liaisons dangereuses*, trans. Douglas Parmée (Oxford: Oxford University Press, 1995), 315–16.
35 Minae Yamamoto Savas, 'The Art of Japanese Noh Theatre in Akira Kurosawa's *Throne of Blood*', *Bridgewater Review* 30.2 (2011): 19–23 (22–3).
36 Mekado Murphy, 'Faith and Fangs: An Interview with Park Chan-wook', 30 July 2009, https://artsbeat.blogs.nytimes.com/2009/07/30/faith-and-fangs-an-interview-with-park-chan-wook/. For further discussion of Park's artistic interest in blood and *Thirst* as a cross-cultural production, see, for example, Elli Mastorou, *Les Adaptations d'Émile Zola au cinéma: étude transnationale* (Saarbrücken: Éditions universitaires européennes, 2016), 70.
37 On the representation of vampirism in *Thirst*, see, for example, Antoine Coppola and Lee Ji-soon, 'L'adaptation transculturelle de *Thérèse Raquin* de Zola dans *Thirst*, film coréen', *French Forum* 40.2–3 (2015): 141–55 (142–3); and Kyu Hyun Kim, 'Park Chan-wook's *Thirst*: Body, Guilt and Exsanguination', in *Korean Horror Cinema*, ed. Alison Peirse and Daniel Martin (Edinburgh: Edinburgh University Press, 2013), 206–8.
38 Émile Zola, *Thérèse Raquin* (Paris: Gallimard, 1970), 82.
39 Zola, *Thérèse Raquin*, 60.
40 Zola, *Thérèse Raquin*, 186.
41 Paquet, 'Genrebending in Contemporary Korean Cinema'.
42 Jaimey Fisher, *Christian Petzold* (Urbana: University of Illinois Press, 2013), 9.
43 Quoted in Fisher, *Christian Petzold*, 154, 156–7.
44 Hubert Monteilhet, *Le Retour des cendres* (Paris: Fallois, 1991), 50.
45 Geoffrey Macnab, 'A Berlin Thriller with Hints of Hitchcock and Plenty of Plot Twists', *Independent*, 7 May 2015, https://www.independent.co.uk/arts-entertainment/films/reviews/phoenix-film-review-a-berlin-thriller-with-hints-of-hitchcock-and-plenty-of-plot-twists-10233527.html.

46. Marco Abel, 'Failing to Connect: Iterations of Desire in Oskar Roehler's Postromance Films', *New German Critique* 37.1 (2010): 75–98 (77).
47. Abel, 'Failing to Connect', 77.
48. Richard Holloway, *Looking in the Distance* (Edinburgh: Canongate, 2004), 96.
49. Douglas Morrey, *Michel Houellebecq: Humanity and its Aftermath* (Liverpool: Liverpool University Press, 2013), 57.
50. Interview with Bernd Eichinger, *Atomised* [on DVD].
51. Michel Houellebecq, *Atomised*, trans. Frank Wynne (London: Vintage, 2001), 84.
52. Carole Sweeney, *Michel Houellebecq and the Literature of Despair* (London: Bloomsbury, 2013), 91.
53. Peter Bradshaw, '*Atomised*', *Guardian*, 14 July 2006, https://www.theguardian.com/film/2006/jul/14/comedy.worldcinema.
54. Robert Stam, 'Beyond Fidelity: The Dialogics of Adaptation', in *Film Adaptation*, ed. James Naremore (London: Athlone Press, 2000), 66.
55. Robert Stam, 'Revisionist Adaptation: Transtextuality, Cross-Cultural Dialogism, and Performative Infidelities', in *The Oxford Handbook of Adaptation Studies*, ed. Thomas Leitch (New York: Oxford University Press, 2017), 244.
56. Mark Adams, '*Bel Ami*', *Screen Daily*, 17 February 2012, https://www.screendaily.com/bel-ami/5038235.article.
57. Justin Chang, '*Bel Ami*', *Variety*, 17 February 2012, https://variety.com/2012/film/markets-festivals/bel-ami-1117947114/.
58. Elizabeth Weitzman, 'Robert Pattinson Falls Short as French Social Climber in *Bel Ami*', *New York Daily News*, 7 June 2012, https://www.nydailynews.com/entertainment/tv-movies/movie-review-robert-pattinson-falls-short-french-social-climber-bel-ami-article-1.1091551.
59. Stephanie Bunbury, 'In Search of Fresh Blood', *Sydney Morning Herald*, 18 May 2012, https://www.smh.com.au/entertainment/movies/in-search-of-fresh-blood-20120517-1yrtp.html.
60. Guy Lodge, '*Suite française*', *Variety*, 10 March 2015, https://variety.com/2015/film/global/film-review-suite-francaise-1201447199/.
61. David Sexton, '*Suite française*', *Evening Standard*, 13 March 2015, https://www.standard.co.uk/go/london/film/suite-francaise-film-review-michelle-williams-touching-in-poor-adaptation-of-ir-ne-n-mirovsky-s-10105862.html.
62. Geoffrey Macnab, '*Suite française*', *Independent*, 12 March 2015, https://www.independent.co.uk/arts-entertainment/films/reviews/suite-fran-aise-film-review-a-romantic-but-discordant-dispatch-on-love-and-war-10104994.html.
63. Lodge, '*Suite française*'.
64. Claire Black, 'Saul Dibb on Shooting His New Film *Suite française*', *Scotsman*, 10 March 2015, https://www.scotsman.com/arts-and-culture/film-and-tv/saul-dibb-on-shooting-his-new-film-suite-francaise-1-3715035.

65 Darren Waldron and Ros Murray, 'Troubling Transformations: Pedro Almodóvar's *La piel que habito / The Skin I Live In* (2011) and Its Reception', *Transnational Cinemas*, 5.1 (2014): 57–71 (62).
66 Waldron and Murray, 'Troubling Transformations', 57.
67 Quoted in Cristina Martínez-Carazo, 'Almodóvar in the USA/The USA in Almodóvar', in *(Re)viewing Creative, Critical and Commercial Practices in Contemporary Spanish Cinema*, ed. Duncan Wheeler and Fernando Canet (Bristol: Intellect, 2014), 263.
68 Pedro Lange-Churion, 'Pedro Almodóvar's *La piel que habito*: Of Late Style and Erotic Conservatism', *Bulletin of Hispanic Studies*, 93.3 (2016): 441–53 (448).
69 Waldron and Murray, 'Troubling Transformations', 61.
70 Francisco A. Zurian, '*La piel que habito*: A Story of Imposed Gender and the Struggle for Identity', in *A Companion to Pedro Almodóvar*, ed. Marvin D'Lugo and Kathleen M. Vernon (Chichester: Blackwell, 2013), 268.

Conclusion

Andrew Watts

Adaptation studies has long been focused on the source text, on how it translates into film, on what is lost and, potentially, gained in the process of adaptation. This book has not sought to argue that source texts do not matter in the adaptive process. Such an argument would be highly problematic in relation to works which explicitly market themselves as adaptations, seeking to exploit the popularity and renown of their source. But this book has sought to argue that to read adaptation with a binary focus on source text and subsequent adaptation alone is to ignore key facets of the adaptive process and to understand just part of that process. It has sought to speak to the historical turn in adaptation studies, driven by a core belief that adaptations are intriguing historical documents which sit at the confluence of multiple creative forces. They are shaped by the money behind them, by the cultural currency of their source text, by the creative personnel who make them and by the audiences for which they are destined. So too are they shaped by the politics of their target era, by the film movements which dominate in the era of their making, by the history which precedes them and by the historic comment they seek to offer. They are also moulded by the national space of their production and consumption. Adaptations, quite simply, are shaped by far more than just the source text, and this book has aimed to engage with and unpick the range and shape of these forces in order to underline the at times hidden histories of the adaptation of French sources.

Film versions of French literature offer a compelling framework through which to explore the complexities of the hidden histories of adaptation. French literature has always been, Chapter 1 argued, key to the development of film as a medium. At the outset of the silent era, filmmakers quickly recognized the potential for attracting paying audiences by recreating well-known works for the screen. In France, Georges Méliès drew extensively on popular fairy tales such as *Cinderella* and on the adventure novels of Jules Verne, which he re-imagined in his now-iconic *Le Voyage dans la lune* (1902). In the United States, early cinematographers showed similar enthusiasm for reinventing French sources and in films such as *The Count of Monte Cristo* (1913, dir. Porter) attempted to capitalize on the commercial success of long-running stage plays by adapting them for the nascent medium. However, if silent filmmakers viewed French literature as cheap and accessible material, money was only one of a variety of currencies that motivated them. For directors such as Alice Guy, adaptation represented a way of investing cinema with the kind of cultural prestige that it had not enjoyed in its earliest incarnation as a fairground entertainment. As production techniques improved, subsequent filmmakers sought to enrich the creative currency of cinema by developing it as an art form in its own right. Moving away from early film's reliance on the style and techniques of theatre, they explored the creative artistry of film. By the 1920s, key silent filmmakers used the practice of adaptation to reflect openly and self-reflexively on the technical capabilities of their medium. They contemplated the dual imperatives of art and money that had fuelled cinema in its early years. Marcel L'Herbier's version of *L'Argent* (1929) is a case in point. The plot revolves around the relentless movement of financial capital and emphasizes its complex cinematography through images of rotation and exchange. As Chapter 1 showed through its discussion of the multiple currencies that circulated during the silent era, French literature adaptations were integral both to establishing cinema as an art form and shaping the medium's complex sense of identity.

Chapter 2 focused on the people who drive adaptations, tracing the personal histories which shape the adaptive output between 1927 and 1939. All too often film adaptation is read in an intertextual context as viewers, critics and academics seek the source text in the subsequent adaptive work. But adaptations are made by people, for people. And we ignore the shaping influence of those people at our peril. The interpersonal networks via whom adaptations are produced are complex and numerous. Key to them is the source author, a figure whose text and media personality shape the adaptations made from them in telling ways. On both sides of the Atlantic in the inter-war years, studios returned time and again to the works and creative personalities of Hugo, Zola and Flaubert, as exemplified by versions of *Les Misérables* (1934, dir. Bernard) in France and *The Hunchback of Notre Dame* (1939, dir. Dieterle) in the United States. Moreover, this period witnessed a recurring interest in adapting popular but perhaps not quite canonical texts such as Dumas *père*'s *Les Trois Mousquetaires*, which Rowland V. Lee brought to the screen in 1935. But, as the interpersonal framework set out in the thought of Christiane Nord makes clear, legions of other people shape adaptive works as texts move between languages, media and nations. Chapter 2 thus reflected on the writers, actors, directors and often invisible technical staff. It contemplated the formative influence of stars in both Hollywood and other nations, assessing their varying impact in very different film systems, nations and gender frameworks. During this period, it was often the screen persona of leading men such as Douglas Fairbanks senior – rather than the source texts or their authors – which studios used to promote adaptations and imprint them on the memories of spectators. As this chapter argued, directors, too, mark their films with their own identities and personal visions of the material. In *La Bête humaine* (1938), for example, Jean Renoir acknowledges his artistic debt to Zola, not least by inserting an image of the novelist in the opening credits, and appropriating large sections of dialogue from the source text. At the same time, however, Renoir inscribes the film with his own creative signature, most notably by casting himself in a cameo role as the poacher Cabuche. He highlights his theft from his source author while crafting and making visible a complex and legible creative signature for himself in his images. Political figures, Chapter 2 argued, should also be incorporated in this interpersonal reading of film as censors, politicians and patrons shape films in visible and hidden ways. People are key to any understanding of the adaptive process.

Chapter 3 explored the impact of contemporary politics on adaptations. The German Occupation of France between 1940 and 1944 generated an intense and sometimes surprising enthusiasm for adapting French literature, particularly as filmmakers sought ways of avoiding censorship. During this four-year period, almost half of the films produced in France were based on plays or literary texts. This chapter showed how directors used adaptation to respond to the political circumstances of the time, whether this meant paying homage to the spirit of resistance in *Pontcarral, colonel d'empire* (1942, dir. Delannoy) or adopting a collaborationist stance in *La Main du diable* (1943, dir. Tourneur). However, if such films can be viewed as a reflection of the historical context in which they were produced, this discussion warned against attempting to place them into neat ideological categories. As the adaptive output of the Occupation period shows, the political content of these films is often difficult to determine with any certainty. Moreover, how we interpret the adaptations of this period is a matter of political perspective, which can change depending on who is watching a given film and in what context. This point was clearly not lost on the filmmakers of the time, who, in their attempts to avoid persecution at the hands of the Nazis, preferred to cultivate a sense of ambiguity in their films. Like the shifting camera work in Jacques Becker's *Goupi Mains Rouges*

(1942), the French literature adaptations of this period rarely settle fully on any one political position. More importantly, in their ideological ambivalence, many of these films can be seen as a barometer of the national schizophrenia that enveloped France under the Nazis. In a country riven by political enmities, filmmakers articulated the trauma of military defeat and occupation through the practice of adaptation and used French texts to vent their deep anxieties over what France had become under German rule. Ostensibly adaptations of earlier sources, many of the films made in this era also adapt and comment on the tense political context in which they were made.

Chapter 4 underlined the film movements within which adaptations are as potent and formative as politics. The Second World War was responsible in part for the Tradition of Quality movement in France. Following the Liberation in 1944, the French government initiated a drive towards re-establishing a robust national film industry that could compete with the commercial dominance of Hollywood. As Chapter 4 showed, these efforts resulted in the emergence of the Tradition of Quality in French filmmaking during the 1950s, a movement which scholars have typically associated with stale, uninspired filmmaking. This chapter confronted the critical prejudice towards this neglected period in French cinema, arguing that while the adaptations it produced were highly literary, they often reflected a careful attentiveness to techniques of cinematic representation. Moreover, it also argued that the influence of this movement tangibly shaped the adaptations made under its aegis. In his 1954 version of Stendhal's *Le Rouge et le Noir*, for example, Claude Autant-Lara aligns the film with its canonical source by superimposing the opening credits onto the pages of a book. His adaptation works to merge film and novel in intriguing ways, exploring the porous interstices between both, implying that the artistry of Stendhal's novel seeps over into its cinematic recreation. The movement which followed and reacted against the Tradition of Quality, the New Wave, was to prove no less potent an influence on the adaptations made during its ascendancy. In *Jules et Jim* (1962), based on the novel of the same title by Henri-Pierre Roché, François Truffaut adapts both his source novel and the social and artistic revolution which the New Wave sought to effect in film. In railing against the *cinéma de papa* through its own adaptive undertakings, the New Wave demonstrated that French literature adaptations do not simply recreate their source texts. Rather, they engage with earlier movements, moments and genres in film history and, in so doing, invite us to understand them as cultural mosaics. Otto Preminger's 1954 *Carmen Jones* works in a similar vein. It adapts and subverts the musical film genre within which it works, offering a cinematic experience which is as politically subversive in its comment on race in the United States as *Jules et Jim* is in relation to French society. The influence of movement on the adaptive process is tangibly underscored by the adaptation of the same text, Mérimée's *Carmen*, in the Italian Spaghetti Western movement. Adapted by Luigi Bazzoni as *Man, Pride, and Vengeance* (1967), *Carmen* becomes subtly other within the tropes of the Spaghetti Western, tropes which entrap and erase the novella's eponymous heroine even as they depend on her to sell the adaptation. This complex negotiation between source text and film movement or moment is echoed within Hrishikesh Mukherjee's *Anuradha* (1960), a film which clearly reworks Flaubert's *Madame Bovary* but does so in tandem with the key structures and philosophies characteristic of the Golden Age of Indian film within which it was made. Film movement and moment tangibly shape the adaptations they choose to remake as part of their output. We need, this book has argued, to read adaptations in the context of film history and its evolutions.

While this book has sought to offer a history of French literature on film, Chapter 5 turned to unpick the key term of its title: history. The case studies in this book constitute a cinematic history – that of French literature on film – but what happens when adaptations take history as their source? The chapter looked at history on multiple levels. It considered the way in which the *Emmanuelle* films, films sometimes authorized, more often not, adapted the changing social and artistic history of sex. They adapted the sexual revolution as much as, if not more so than, Emmanuelle Arsan's source novel. But they not only adapted history, they shaped it in cinematic terms. Just Jaeckin's 1974 soft-porn adaptation of Arsan's novel stands as a cinematic monument in the evolution of cinematic porn, a monument adapted and re-adapted like a talisman. The films analysed in this chapter considered what it means to adapt history. Heritage films dominated key moments in the case study years of this chapter as cinema screens were flooded with adaptations which claimed to take us back both to a source text and to an era long gone. But in his epic 1993 version of Zola's *Germinal*, Claude Berri both painstakingly recreates history as a monument and asks what history actually is. If Berri gently questions his film's heritage genre, the last two films discussed in this chapter – *Moulin Rouge!* (2001, dir. Luhrmann) and *Un long dimanche de fiançailles* (2004, dir. Jeunet) – deconstruct it more directly. Luhrmann's film underscores that history is as unstable and slippery a source as the multitude of source texts from which his film is exuberantly crafted. It is not something to which we can return but rather something which circles and re-circles dizzyingly in our present. For director Jean-Pierre Jeunet, in his adaptation of Sébastien Japrisot's novel *Un long dimanche de fiançailles*, history is a fictional work. Like adaptation, history is the product of multiple memories, voices and experiences and as such is both a created and creative construct.

Finally, this volume explored French literature adaptations produced outside of France between 1996 and 2016. Using the concept of adaptive diaspora, Chapter 6 considered the facility with which French texts have spread across national and cultural borders during this period. While such migratory movements have been a part of cinema's history since the silent era, the intense globalizing impulses of the late twentieth and early twenty-first centuries have made them especially visible and heightened our sensitivity to them. This final chapter in the book reflected on what happens to French works when they are adapted in cross-cultural contexts. It showed, first, how filmmakers have often reconfigured such material in ways that can highlight specific meanings and resonances in the source texts. In his 2001 version of *Planet of the Apes*, for example, Tim Burton baffled audiences and critics with an ending that depicted Earth still ruled by apes, but that actually renewed author Pierre Boulle's thesis that all civilizations must inevitably wither and die. The second component of the theory of adaptive diaspora explored how adaptations can blend material from different national literatures and cultural contexts, as evidenced by *Thirst* (2009, dir. Park), which combined Zola's Naturalist novel *Thérèse Raquin* with elements of vampire horror and situated them in a contemporary Korean setting. Third, this chapter reflected on the process of reinforcement and rethinking that can occur in cross-cultural adaptations such as *Phoenix* (2014, dir. Petzold), which transposes the setting of Hubert Monteilhet's novel *Le Retour des cendres* from Paris to Berlin. In so doing, director Christian Petzold not only foregrounds the theme of self-deception that runs through the source text but also remodels it into a wider reflection on Germany's national denial of Nazism and the Holocaust in the immediate aftermath of the Second World War. Lastly, this chapter argued that diasporic adaptations often expose a self-conscious awareness of their own status as cross-cultural artefacts. In particular, they can be seen to play on their connections to other cinematic works produced outside of France such as the *Twilight* saga, which directors Ormerod and Donnellan reference in their 2012 adaptation of Maupassant's *Bel Ami*. By casting Robert Pattinson as the predatory social climber Georges Duroy, the film invites spectators to compare the character to Pattinson's contemporaneous role as the vampire Edward Cullen in *Twilight*. In so doing, *Bel Ami* – like the other films discussed in this chapter – illustrates that the history of French literature on film is by no means an exclusively French concern but rather an ongoing exchange between different nations, cultures and cinematic traditions.

But the history of French literature on film does not close with the pages of this conclusion. Filmmakers continue to turn to French texts in search of material capable both of exciting their own imaginations and attracting spectators. Mindful of the commercial risks involved in bringing film projects to the screen, some directors continue to pursue the well-established strategy of adapting works that have already proved popular with readers, and which therefore have a strong chance of performing well at the box office. One of the most notable adaptations of recent times in this respect is Albert Dupontel's *Au revoir là-haut* (*See You Up There*) (2017). A reworking of the 2013 Goncourt Prize-winning novel of the same title by Pierre Lemaitre, the film revolves around the story of two French soldiers, Édouard Péricourt and Albert Maillard, and the devastating impact of the First World War on their lives. Following a short prologue in which Albert begins to explain how he came to be detained by the police in Morocco, the opening sequence of the film takes us into the trenches of an unnamed battlefield on 9 November 2018. Although the signing of the Armistice is only days away, the bloodthirsty French officer Pradelle orders his men over the top for a final assault on German lines. The attack leaves Albert fighting desperately for survival after he is buried in a deep shell-hole. In the act of saving his comrade, Édouard, meanwhile, is hit by a mortar blast that rips away his lower jaw and throat, leaving him horribly disfigured and unable to speak.

Like all of the case study adaptations in this book, *Au revoir là-haut* adapts more than just a source text. It adapts our memories of the First World War and contemporary condemnations of the horror and pointlessness of the war. The early sequences in the film emphasize the violence and physical horrors of the war. Following the initial battlefield scenes, we see Édouard in hospital and racked with pain as blood soaks through the bandages covering the lower half of his face and throat (see Figure C.1). In a close-up that can be interpreted as a metaphor for the human butchery of the conflict, Dupontel proceeds to show mince emerging from a meat grinder before a nurse administers it to the stricken Édouard via a feeding tube in his neck.

With a strong element of black comedy, the film nevertheless reaches beyond the brutal realities of the war to examine how France treated both

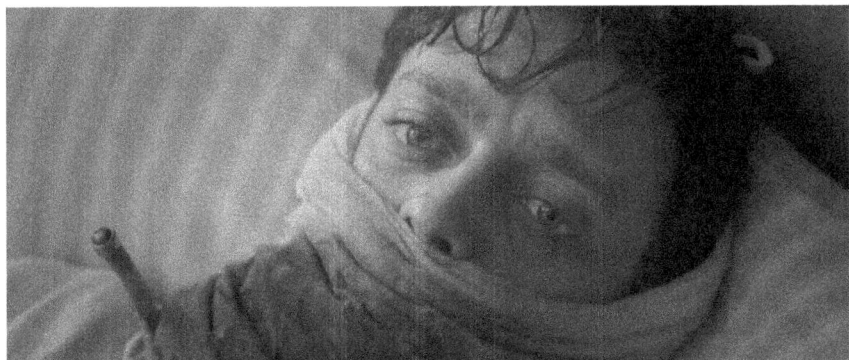

FIGURE C.1 Au revoir là-haut (See You Up There) *(2017, dir. Dupontel)*.

its dead and surviving combatants once the fighting was over. In particular, Dupontel reconfigures the novel's thesis that France cared little for the soldiers who returned home, or for those who had been killed on the battlefield. The film makes this point forcefully by juxtaposing two sequences set in Paris in 1920. In the first, Albert is shown stealing morphine from other wounded veterans in order to satisfy Édouard's addiction to the drug, even causing one old soldier to fall out of his wheelchair. The second sequence takes us inside a military cemetery, where the dead are being buried in the wrong graves because the Chinese gravediggers are unable to read the names on the coffins. Unconcerned by the error, the former officer Pradelle – who stands to profit financially from burying the dead in undersized coffins – reveals his complete indifference to their sacrifice by stepping across a line of tombstones as if jumping puddles in the trenches. Leaving a group of undertakers stunned, his proposed solution to the matter of the graves is simply to keep quiet about it. As these two sequences illustrate, Dupontel does not merely recreate the notion of the First World War as a bloodbath, but re-energizes the novel's position that France disrespected those who had fought on its behalf.

In addition to adapting modern history's contemporary judgement on the First World War, *Au revoir là-haut* references and adapts a wealth of preceding works. Its vision of its source era is profoundly intertextual. As Lemaitre explained in his postface to the source text, the novel drew inspiration from a number of other literary works. Declaring that he had 'borrowed here and there from several writers', Lemaitre went on to provide a comprehensive list of his influences, which included Louis Aragon, Ingmar Bergman, Gabriel García Márquez and Marcel Proust.[1] Not surprisingly, given the author's direct involvement in adapting his work for the screen, the film version of *Au revoir là-haut* evokes the intertextual presence of many of these literary figures. The battlefield sequence in the first part of the film is notable in this respect, not least because of the way in which it references Balzac's 1832 novella, *Le Colonel Chabert*. When Albert is blown backwards into a deep shell-hole and buried beneath piles of soil and debris, the moment recalls the plot of Balzac's text, in which the eponymous hero is thought to have been killed at the Battle of Eylau and thrown into a mass grave. A closer reading of this sequence shows, however, that Dupontel reformulates and rethinks this intertextual parallel using the techniques of his own medium. As Albert disappears beneath the avalanche of earth, the screen turns black, as if the light has been extinguished on his life. The director then reintroduces the character's voice-over, in which the soldier states that he believed himself dead. Finally, in a moment of visual horror, Albert realizes that he is staring at the body of a horse, its head partially illuminated by the light breaking through from the surface. In a manner reminiscent of Balzac's Chabert, who claws his way out of the burial pit using the severed arm of one of his dead comrades, Albert sucks the last pungent air from the horse's lungs, thus enabling him to survive until Édouard rescues him. Far from merely reproducing the intertexts featured in his source novel, Dupontel's version of *Au revoir là-haut* adapts and recasts them in its own cinematic terms.

If Dupontel adapts literature in its images, privileging its written heritage, Hélène Cattet and Bruno Forzani's *Laissez bronzer les cadavres* (*Let the Corpses Tan*) (2017) demonstrates that in specific modern adaptations cinema's early veneration of literature has shifted as cinema has become far more confident in its own film artistry. Based on the 1971 hard-boiled crime novel *Laissez bronzer les cadavres!* co-written by Jean-Patrick Manchette and film director Jean-Pierre Bastid, the film centres on a heist perpetrated by three gangsters, Rhino, Gros and Alex. Having robbed a security van containing 250 kilos of gold bullion, the men take refuge in a tumbledown hamlet in the south of France. Sharing the hideaway are the artist Luce and her former partner Max, who have previously used the remote hillside to stage erotic performances which appear in brief flashbacks during the film. The main narrative unfolds over the course of a day and night, during which the robbers return from the heist with three unexpected passengers, Max's estranged wife Mélanie, her son and a nanny. In pursuit are two police officers, whose arrival in the hamlet unleashes a violent shoot-out and a series of double-crosses in which each of the robbers attempts to escape with the gold.

In re-imagining Manchette and Bastid's text, *Laissez bronzer les cadavres* appears as a highly stylized work of cinema, confident in and of its own medium. As Christoph Huber observes, the film presents itself as 'an astonishingly cinematic experience [which] nevertheless feels operatic in its exuberant succession of extravagant and exquisite images'.[2] The action abounds in shots which call attention to the film's status as a cinematic artefact, from intense close-ups of eyes and wrinkled skin to low-angle shots of the protagonists silhouetted against the searingly blue Mediterranean sky. Moreover, Cattet and Forzani deploy a range of strikingly creative visual effects, such as a fantasy sequence in which the nanny is shot and her clothing ripped away piece by piece in a strobe-like hail of gunfire. The directors' depiction of the death of Gros, who is shot repeatedly as he attempts to flee with the bullion, is key to my line of argument here. The film sequence appropriates from the source text the inherently visual image of the gangster being caught in the headlights directed at him by the police officer Lambert. To that image, however, Cattet and Forzani add their own shots of Gros painted in the gold that he had coveted, followed by a series of close-ups of bullets as they penetrate his skin and bury themselves in his flesh, leaving a trail of blood behind them. Emphasizing the powerful visual contrast between the colours gold and red, the scene culminates in blood exploding over the criminal's face as the last bullet kills him. As opposed to presenting merely abstract visual effects, Cattet and Forzani use such distinctive images to adapt and imprint their own artistic vision on the source text. This film may remake a novel, but it is confident of the artistry in its own medium and does not seek validation from its literary source.

And *Laissez bronzer les cadavres* engages not with the history of literature but with the history of film, adapting material from a range of cinematic genres. Most obviously, it draws on the conventions of the Spaghetti Western, the movement explored in Chapter 4. At the level of plot, the confrontation between a gang of outlaws holding hostages and two officers of the law appears reminiscent of a Western-style shoot-out. Moreover, the sun-baked location in which the action takes place recalls the arid, dusty settings favoured by Sergio Leone in films such as *A Fistful of Dollars* (1964) and *The Good, the Bad, and the Ugly* (1966). Equally, Cattet and Forzani delight in mobilizing the artistic resources of more obscure genres, notably *giallo*. A genre that originated in Italy in the early 1960s, *giallo* films were for the most part crime thrillers that incorporated elements of horror and mystery. Given the variety of films that it encompassed, the genre remains difficult to define. However, *gialli* tended to feature melodramatic plots, aestheticized displays of graphic violence and eerie scores by composer Ennio Morricone. *Laissez bronzer les cadavres* is clearly inspired by many of these aspects. Reviewers were quick to notice the film's links with *giallo*. The 'Giallo-tinged visuals', wrote Ivan Radford, result 'in a montage of dazzling tropes and clichés ... Bullets, women painted in gold, people's insides on the outside – they all stack up with violent, garish, gleeful abandon.'[3] The film's score also includes several compositions by Morricone, notably the acapella children's chorus from Aldo Lado's 1972 *giallo Who Saw Her Die?*, which accompanies the decisive gun battle. Yet Cattet and Forzani's aim in incorporating such references is not to produce a pastiche or straightforward homage to *giallo*. Their recurring allusions to the genre function instead as artistic raw material from which the film generates a plethora of new meanings and resonances. The leather gloves and uniforms worn by the two police officers, for example, can be interpreted as a gesture towards one of the most familiar conventions of *giallo* films, which often feature murderers wearing black leather gloves. However, in the case of the female police officer played by Marilyn Jess (who appears in the credits under her birth name Dominique Troyes), the creaking leather uniform also appears as a nod to the actress's earlier career as a soft-porn actress and establishes a playful contrast with her role as a representative of law and order in this production (see Figure C.2). In their engagement with *giallo*, Cattet and Forzani do not imitate an old cinematic genre for the mere sake of doing so. They adapt and reshape it into a source of new artistic effects.

CONCLUSION

FIGURE C.2 Laissez bronzer les cadavres (Let the Corpses Tan) *(2017, dir. Cattet and Forzani)*.

But the contemporary landscape of film adaptation from French sources remains as diverse as the history this book has outlined. If *Laissez bronzer les cadavres* is self-reflexive about cinema's future, *Mademoiselle de Joncquières* (2018, dir. Mouret) looks back to cinema's past, inhabiting as it does the period costume drama genre. The film adapts the tale of the fictional Madame de La Pommeraye, one of the most well-known stories in Diderot's *Jacques le Fataliste* (1796). In Mouret's version, a serial womanizer, the Marquis des Arcis (Édouard Baer), succeeds in winning the affection of the widowed Madame de La Pommeraye (Cécile de France). However, when the Marquis's love for her begins to fade, La Pommeraye exacts revenge by tricking him into marrying the eponymous heroine, a former prostitute who masquerades as a devoutly religious virgin. While claiming to be only loosely inspired by Diderot's work, *Mademoiselle de Joncquières* exhibits key features of heritage cinema and its desire to take its viewer back to an authentic past. Most notably, the principal location for the film was the Château de Sourches, a neoclassical residence designed by the royal architect Gabriel de Lestrade and built between 1761 and 1786. In keeping with heritage conventions, the production also features authentic interiors and an array of lavish period costumes for which it won the prize for Best Costume Design at the 2019 César Awards. However, as we saw in Chapter 5, heritage films often reveal themselves as false antiques which create their own vision of the past. *Mademoiselle de Joncquières* proves no exception in this respect. As Elena Russo argues, Mouret applies his own artistic perspective to the eighteenth century by presenting it as a period of aristocratic idleness. 'All they do', observes Russo of the love affair between the Marquis and La Pommeraye, 'is walk in the park, stroll from room to room, read while standing up, read while lying down, and exchange

FIGURE C.3 Mademoiselle de Joncquières *(2018, dir. Mouret).*

amorous glances.'[4] While seeming to construct an authentic representation of its historical setting, *Mademoiselle de Joncquières* articulates its own vision of the eighteenth century, conscripting the prevalent vision of aristocratic excess and idleness so prevalent in period adaptations of the era to overwrite the more complex, diverse historical reality (see Figure C.3).

Mademoiselle de Joncquières is clearly a false antique not only in its partial vision of the eighteenth century. It merits this epithet for the past it offers us is shaped by the values of our present. Mouret's film stands out particularly for the way in which it reveals a much greater sensitivity to questions of sexual consent and male abuse of women than Diderot does in *Jacques le Fataliste*. The changes that the director makes to the source plot are significant in this respect. First, he inserts a scene – one that has no equivalent in the novel – in which the Marquis assures his new wife on their wedding night that he will not attempt to force a sexual relationship on her. Second, after the young woman has tried to commit suicide by throwing herself into the Seine, Mouret recreates the key episode from the novel in which the Marquis forgives her for her part in tricking him and cleanses her of her previous identity by addressing her as Madame la Marquise and Madame des Arcis. However, in contrast to Diderot's text, in which the eponymous heroine begs forgiveness on her knees, Mouret affords her the dignity of remaining standing. Only later in the scene does she collapse to the floor in an apparent state of exhaustion.[5] Mouret's adaptation can be seen to reflect a modern, politically correct attitude towards questions of gender equality and the rights of women in marriage and society. However, these departures from the source material take on a much more specific resonance when viewed within the context of the #MeToo movement and the allegations of sexual misconduct against film producer Harvey Weinstein that erupted in 2017. The release of *Mademoiselle de Joncquières* the following year quickly sparked a debate among reviewers over the extent to which the film engages with this contemporary context. Writing in *Le Journal du Dimanche*, Barbara Théate claimed that 'one cannot watch *Mademoiselle de Joncquières* without thinking of the #MeToo revolution, which today is redressing the balance for women'.[6] By contrast, other critics considered the film an anti-feminist work that ultimately sympathizes with its male protagonist. As Geneviève Sellier argued in her review for *Le Genre et l'écran*, Mouret offers a 'warning to women who would like to destabilize male dominance and give men some of their own medicine, a kind of anti-MeToo work'.[7] Attempting to determine which position the film adopts is less important, however, than the fact that it provoked such vibrant discussions in the first place. By inviting us to revisit issues of consent and the abuse of women, *Mademoiselle de Joncquières* does not simply echo the time in which it was made but serves as a driver of debate around such concerns.

Mademoiselle de Joncquières reflects the values of its present and markets itself in relation to adaptive predecessors which have done likewise to great acclaim. The film draws attention in particular to the similarities of plot and language that it shares with Laclos's *Les Liaisons dangereuses* and the 1988 adaptation of this novel directed by Stephen Frears. Several months before the premiere of *Mademoiselle de Joncquières* in September 2018, Indie Sales, the Paris-based company responsible for selling the international rights to the film, compared it to Laclos's work. 'The dialogues are subtle,' observed Indie Sales CEO Nicolas Eschbach, 'capturing perfectly the contradictory human emotions at play in the tale, in the vein of *Dangerous Liaisons*.'[8] Subsequent promotional materials for the film encouraged such comparisons, not least the posters which summarized its plot with five verbs: love, seduce, manipulate, scheme, take revenge. These attempts to link *Mademoiselle de Joncquières* to *Les Liaisons dangereuses* are understandable from the point of view of marketing the film outside of France, where spectators are likely to be more familiar with Laclos's novel – or the Frears adaptation of it – than with Diderot's work. *Mademoiselle de Joncquières* underlines that the history of adaptation of French sources continues to be complex, composite and compelling as it not only adapts a source and a vision of a historical era but also exploits the commercial successes of its genre.

It is entirely appropriate to close this book on the history of French literature on film on a note of commercial success. Novels, plays, poems and other literary pieces of literature written in French have generated millions for filmmakers around the world. They have also shaped the form and history of cinema as a genre. Our book has traced the thirst for such works from the dawn of cinema to the contemporary era, a thirst which shows no signs of abating. But it has not just charted trends and movements in the adaptation of French literature. It has also sought to underline the importance of the collective case studies in this book to adaptation studies as a whole. This volume has sought to feed into the historical turn in adaptation studies, unpicking the complex historical forces shaping adaptations above and beyond their source texts. Adaptations are the products of the money behind them, the legions of people who create and consume them. They are influenced by the politics of their moment. They are shaped by the history of their own medium: film. Together the case study films of this book offer a history of French literature on film, but key works among them turn to question what history is, how it influences them as adaptation, how and whether it can be adapted. That source texts matter to the creation of the adaptive outputs encompassed in this book is clear. But so too do the complex, intersecting range of other forces this book has highlighted, forces essential to an understanding of the art that is adaptation. Composites compellingly created from an overlapping range of historical forces, adaptations of French literature in film are much more than just their source texts.

Notes

1 Lemaitre, *Au revoir là-haut* (Paris: Albin Michel, 2013), 619.
2 Christoph Huber, 'Giving Credibility to the Universe: Hélène Cattet and Bruno Forzani on *Laissez bronzer les cadavres*', *Cinema Scope*, http://cinema-scope.com/cinema-scope-magazine/giving-credibility-to-the-universe-helene-cattet-bruno-forzani-on-laissez-bronzer-les-cadavres/.
3 Ivan Radford, '*Let the Corpses Tan (Laissez bronzer les cadavres)*', *Vodzilla*, 15 July 2018, http://vodzilla.co/reviews/vod-film-review-let-the-corpses-tan-laissez-bronzer-les-cadavres/.
4 Elena Russo, 'Mademoiselle de Joncquières or Diderot Updated and Corrected', *Fiction and Film for Scholars of France: A Cultural Bulletin* 9.5 (May 2019), https://h-france.net/fffh/reviews/mademoiselle-de-joncquieres-or-diderot-updated-and-corrected/.
5 For a detailed discussion of these changes, see Russo, '*Mademoiselle de Joncquières* or Diderot Updated and Corrected'.
6 Barbara Théate, 'Cécile de France et Édouard Baer badinent avec l'amour dans *Mademoiselle de Joncquières*', *Le Journal du Dimanche*, 12 September 2018, https://www.lejdd.fr/Culture/Cinema/cecile-de-france-et-edouard-baer-badinent-avec-lamour-dans-mademoiselle-de-joncquieres-3753179.

7 Geneviève Sellier, '*Mademoiselle de Joncquières*', *Le Genre et l'écran*, 14 September 2018, https://genre-ecran.net/?Mademoiselle-de-Joncquieres.

8 Melanie Goodfellow, 'Indie Sales Boards Emmanuel Mouret's Costume Drama *Mademoiselle de Joncquières*', *Screen Daily*, 16 January 2018, https://www.screendaily.com/news/indie-sales-boards-emmanuel-mourets-costume-drama-mademoiselle-de-joncquieres-exclusive/5125581.article.

Bibliography

Abel, Marco. 'Failing to Connect: Iterations of Desire in Oskar Roehler's Postromance Films'. *New German Critique* 37.1 (2010): 75–98.
Abel, Richard. *The Ciné Goes to Town: French Cinema 1896–1914*. Berkeley: University of California Press, 1998.
Abel, Richard. *French Cinema: The First Wave, 1915–1929*. Princeton, NJ: Princeton University Press, 1984.
Adams, Mark. '*Bel Ami*'. *Screen Daily*, 17 February 2012, https://www.screendaily.com/bel-ami/5038235.article. Accessed 4 April 2018.
Altman, Rick. 'Dickens, Griffith, and Film Theory Today'. In *Silent Film*, edited by Richard Abel, 145–62. London: Athlone Press, 1996.
Altman, Rick. *The American Film Musical*. Bloomington: Indiana University Press, 1987.
Andréoli, Max. 'Place de Balzac dans le cinéma français sous l'Occupation'. In *Balzac à l'écran*, edited by Anne-Marie Baron, *CinémAction* 173 (2019): 67–8.
Armes, Roy. 'Cinema of Paradox: French Film-making during the Occupation'. In *Collaboration in France: Politics and Culture during the Nazi Occupation, 1940–1944*, edited by Gerhard Hirschfeld and Patrick Marsh, 126–41. Oxford: Berg, 1989.
Armes, Roy. *French Cinema*. New York: Oxford University Press, 1985.
Arsan, Emmanuelle. *Emmanuelle*, translated by Lowell Bair. London: Harper Perennial, 2009.
Atack, Margaret, and Christopher Lloyd. *Framing Narratives of the Second World War and Occupation in France, 1939–2009*. Manchester: Manchester University Press, 2012.
Audiberti. '*Les Inconnus dans la maison*'. *Comœdia*, 23 May 1942, 5.
Baecque, Antoine de, and Serge Toubiana. *Truffaut: A Biography*. Berkeley: University of California Press, 2000.
Baguley, David. '*Riduttore, Traditore*? On Screening Zola'. *Excavatio* 21 (2006): 198–212.
Balio, Tino. *Hollywood in the New Millennium*. London: Palgrave, 2013.
Balzac, Honoré de. *La Comédie humaine*, edited by Pierre-Georges Castex et al., 12 vols. Paris: Gallimard, Bibliothèque de la Pléiade, 1976–81.
Baron, Anne-Marie, ed. '*Balzac à l'écran*'. *CinémAction* 173 (2019).
Baron, Anne-Marie. *Romans français du XIXe siècle à l'écran: problèmes de l'adaptation*. Clermont-Ferrand: Presses universitaires Blaise Pascal, 2008.
Bazin, André. *Jean Renoir*. New York: Da Capo Press, 1992.
Benoit, Pierre. *Atlantida*, translated by Mary C. Tongue and Mary Ross. New York: Ace, 1920.

Bertin-Maghit, Jean-Pierre. *Le Cinéma français sous l'Occupation: le monde du cinéma français de 1940 à 1946*. Paris: Perrin, 2002.
Bertin-Maghit, Jean-Pierre. 'L'éternel retour: un choix idéologique'. In *Cinéma et histoire: autour de Marc Ferro*, edited by François Garçon, 142–51. Courbevoie: CinémAction-Corlet, 1992.
Bihan, Max. '*Le Colonel Chabert*'. *Comœdia*, 11 December 1943, 5.
Billard, Pierre. *L'Âge Classique du cinéma français: du cinéma parlant à la Nouvelle Vague*. Paris: Flammarion, 1995.
Birch, Edmund. ' "Les Suites des suites": Alexandre Dumas' *Le Comte de Monte-Cristo* and the News'. *Dix-Neuf* 21 (2017): 223–30.
Birchard, Robert S. *Cecil B. DeMille's Hollywood*. Lexington: University Press of Kentucky, 2004.
Black, Claire. 'Saul Dibb on Shooting His New Film *Suite française*'. *Scotsman*, 10 March 2015, https://www.scotsman.com/arts-and-culture/film-and-tv/saul-dibb-on-shooting-his-new-film-suite-francaise-1-3715035. Accessed 5 April 2018.
Blake, Michael F. *The Films of Lon Chaney*. Lanham, MD: Vestal, 1998.
Bloom, Harold. *The Western Canon: The Books and School of the Ages*. San Diego: Harcourt Brace, 1994.
Bock, Hans-Michael. 'Erich Pommer'. In *The Oxford History of World Cinema*, edited by Geoffrey Nowell-Smith, 145. Oxford: Oxford University Press, 1996.
Bond, Lucy, and Jessica Rapson, eds. *The Transcultural Turn: Interrogating Memory Between and Beyond Borders*. Berlin: De Gruyter, 2014.
Boulanger, Pierre. *Le Cinéma colonial: de 'L'Atlantide' à 'Lawrence d'Arabie'*. Paris: Seghers, 1975.
Boulle, Pierre. *La Planète des singes*. Paris: Julliard, 1963.
Bouquet, José-Luis, and Marc Godin. *Henri-Georges Clouzot cinéaste*. Sèvres: La Sirène, 1993.
Bowser, Eileen. *The Transformation of Cinema: 1907–1915*. Vol. 2 of *History of the American Cinema*, edited by Charles Harpole. Berkeley: University of California Press, 1994.
Bradshaw, Peter. '*Atomised*'. *Guardian*, 14 July 2006, https://www.theguardian.com/film/2006/jul/14/comedy.worldcinema. Accessed 3 April 2018.
Bradshaw, Peter. '*Planet of the Apes*'. *Guardian*, 17 August 2001, https://www.theguardian.com/film/2001/aug/17/1. Accessed 2 April 2018.
Brockmann, Stephen. *A Critical History of German Film*. Rochester, NY: Camden House, 2010.
Brook, Tom. 'How the Global Box Office is Changing Hollywood'. 21 October 2014, http://www.bbc.com/culture/story/20130620-is-china-hollywoods-future. Accessed 9 April 2018.
Brooks, Peter. 'The Novel and the Guillotine; Or, Fathers and Sons in *Le Rouge et le Noir*'. *PMLA* 97.3 (1982): 348–62.
Brown, Mick. 'Carry On (and on) *Emmanuelle*'. *Sunday Times Magazine*, 21 November 1980, 21.
Bruhn, Jørgen, Anne Gjelsvik and Henriette Thune. 'Parallel Worlds of Possible Meetings in *Let the Right One In*'. *Word & Image* 27.1 (2011): 2–14.

Bunbury, Stephanie. 'In Search of Fresh Blood'. *Sydney Morning Herald*, 18 May 2012, https://www.smh.com.au/entertainment/movies/in-search-of-fresh-blood-20120517-1yrtp.html. Accessed 7 April 2018.

Burch, Noël, and Geneviève Sellier. *The Battle of the Sexes in French Cinema, 1930–1956*, translated by Peter Graham. Durham, NC: Duke University Press, 2014.

Certeau, Michel de. *The Practice of Everyday Life: Volume One*. Berkeley: University of California Press, 1984.

Chaffin-Quiray, Garrett. 'Emmanuelle Enterprises'. In *Alternative Europe: Eurotrash and Exploitation Cinema since 1945*, edited by Ernest Mathijs and Xavier Mendik, 134–45. London: Wallflower, 2004.

Chang, Justin. '*Bel Ami*'. *Variety*, 17 February 2012, https://variety.com/2012/film/markets-festivals/bel-ami-1117947114/. Accessed 4 April 2018.

Chung, Hye Seung, and David Scott Diffrient. *Movie Migrations: Transnational Genre Flows and South Korean Cinema*. New Brunswick, NJ: Rutgers University Press, 2015.

Cinéma de Vichy. Special Issue of *Les Cahiers de la Cinémathèque* 8 (Winter 1973).

Cohan, Steven, ed. *Hollywood Musicals: The Film Reader*. London: Routledge, 2002.

Collins, Andrew. 'The Epic Legacy of David Lean'. *Guardian*, 4 May 2008, https://www.theguardian.com/film/2008/may/04/features. Accessed 21 March 2019.

Colmeiro, José. 'Nationalising *Carmen*: Spanish Cinema and the Spectre of Francoism'. *Journal of Iberian and Latin American Research* 15.1 (2009): 1–26.

Cooke, Paul. *Contemporary German Cinema*. Manchester: Manchester University Press, 2012.

Coppola, Antoine, and Lee Ji-soon, 'L'adaptation transculturelle de *Thérèse Raquin* de Zola dans *Thirst*, film coréen'. *French Forum* 40.2–3 (2015): 141–55.

Corcy, Stéphanie. *La Vie culturelle sous l'Occupation*. Paris: Perrin, 2005.

Courtade, Francis. 'La Continental'. In *Tendres ennemis: cent ans de cinéma entre la France et l'Allemagne*, edited by Heike Hurst and Heiner Gassen, 216–30. Paris: L'Harmattan, 1991.

Courtade, Francis. *Les Malédictions du cinéma français: une histoire du cinéma français parlant, 1928–1978*. Paris: Alain Moreau, 1978.

Cousins, R. F. 'Adapting Zola for the Silent Cinema: The Example of Marcel L'Herbier'. *Literature/Film Quarterly* 12 (1984): 42–9.

Crisp, Colin. *French Cinema: A Critical Filmography*, 3 vols. Bloomington: Indiana University Press, 2015.

Crisp, Colin. *The Classic French Cinema, 1930–1960*. Bloomington: Indiana University Press, 1993.

D'Hugues, Philippe, and Michel Marmin. *Le Cinéma français: Le Muet*. Paris: Atlas, 1986.

Davies, Simon. *Laclos: 'Les Liaisons dangereuses'*. London: Grant & Cutler, 1987.

De Cesari, Chiara, and Ann Rigney, eds. *Transnational Memory: Circulation, Articulation, Scales*. Berlin: De Gruyter, 2014.

Delluc, Louis. 'Notes'. *Cinéa*, 10 June 1921, 9.

Deslauriers, Claire. 'Démodé et indémodable: Enjeux contemporains d'un style stendhalien'. *Dix-Neuf* 19.1 (2015): 22–32.
Diamant-Berger, Henri. *Il était une fois le cinéma*. Saint-Amand-Montrond: Éditions Jean-Claude Simoën, 1977.
Drazin, Charles. *The Faber Book of French Cinema*. London: Faber and Faber, 2011.
Duara, Ajit. 'A Touch of Realism', *The Hindu*, 3 September 2006, n.p.
Dubé, Pierre. 'Reflections on Chapter Titles in *Le Rouge et le Noir*'. *Dalhousie French Studies* 30 (1995): 45–54.
Dunne, Philip. *Take Two: A Life in Movies and Politics*. New York: Limelight, 1992.
Durovicova, Natasa, and Kathleen Newman, eds. *World Cinemas, Transnational Perspectives*. New York: Routledge, 2010.
Ebert, Roger. '*Diabolique*'. 22 March 1996, https://www.rogerebert.com/reviews/diabolique-1996. Accessed 7 April 2018.
Ehrlich, Evelyn. *Cinema of Paradox: French Filmmaking under the German Occupation*. New York: Columbia University Press, 1985.
Eibel, Alfred. 'Faut-il oublier Maurice Dekobra', http://www.lmda.net/din2/n_egar.php?Eg=MAT03298. Accessed 21 January 2019.
Eisner, Lotte. *Fritz Lang*. New York: Da Capo Press, 1986.
Eleftheriotis, Dimitris. *Popular Cinemas of Europe: Studies of Texts, Frameworks and Contexts*. London: Continuum, 2001.
Elliott, Kamilla. *Rethinking the Novel/Film Debate*. Cambridge: Cambridge University Press, 2003.
Epstein, Jean. *Écrits sur le cinema*, 2 vols. Paris: Seghers, 1974–5.
Erll, Astrid. 'Travelling Memory', *Parallax*, 17.4 (2011): 4–18.
Everson, William K. *American Silent Film*. New York: Da Capo Press, 1998.
Eyre, Jean. '*L'Auberge rouge*'. *Mon Ciné*, 4 October 1923, 19.
Eyre, Jean. 'Comment on tourne un orage la nuit'. *Mon Ciné*, 21 June 1923, 7.
Ezra, Elizabeth, ed. *European Cinema*. Oxford: Oxford University Press, 2004.
Ezra, Elizabeth. *Georges Méliès*. Manchester: Manchester University Press, 2000.
Ezra, Elizabeth, and Terry Rowden, eds. *Transnational Cinema: The Film Reader*. Abingdon: Routledge, 2006.
Faber, Claude. *Jules Verne: le roman de la terre*. Milan: Éditions Milan, 2005.
Fairbanks, Douglas. 'Kind of Crazy'. *Motion Picture Magazine*, November 1922, 43, 94.
Fauser, Annegret. 'Dixie Carmen: War, Race and Identity in Oscar Hammestein's *Carmen Jones* (1943)'. *Journal of the Society for American Music* 4.2 (2010): 127–74.
Fescourt, Henri. *La Foi et les montagnes ou la septième art au passé*. Paris: Photo-Cinéma/Paul Montel, 1959.
Feuillère, Edwige. *Les Feux de la mémoire*. Paris: Albin Michel, 1977.
Feyder, Jacques, and Françoise Rosay. *Le Cinéma, notre métier*. Geneva: Albert Skira, 1944.
Fisher, Jaimey. *Christian Petzold*. Urbana: University of Illinois Press, 2013.
Flaubert, Gustave. *Madame Bovary: Provincial Manners*, translated by Margaret Mauldon. Oxford: Oxford University Press, 2004.

Ford, Charles. *Jacques Feyder*. Paris: Seghers, 1973.
Fridlund, Bert. ' "First Class Pall-Bearer!": The Sartana/Sabata Cycle in Spaghetti Westerns'. *Film International* 6.3 (2008): 44–55.
Gaines, Jane M. 'Early Cinema's Heyday of Copying: The Too Many Copies of *L'Arroseur arrosé (The Waterer Watered)*'. *Cultural Studies* 20.2–3 (2006): 227–44.
Garcin, Hélène. '*Les Roquevillard*'. *Aujourd'Hui*, 30 August 1943, 2.
Garçon, François. 'Ce curieux âge d'or des cinéastes français'. *Politiques et pratiques culturelles dans la France de Vichy* (special issue of *Cahiers de l'Institut d'Histoire du Temps Présent*), 8 (June 1988): 193–206.
Garçon, François. *De Blum à Pétain: cinéma et société française (1936–1944)*. Paris: Du Cerf, 1984.
Garval, Michael D. *'A Dream of Stone': Fame, Vision and Monumentality in Nineteenth-Century French Literary Culture*. Newark: University of Delaware Press, 2004.
Gauteur, Claude, and Ginette Vincendeau. *Jean Gabin: anatomie d'un mythe*. Paris: Nouveau Monde, 2006.
Gellately, Robert, and Nathan Stoltzfus, *Social Outsiders in Nazi Germany*. Princeton, NJ: Princeton University Press, 2001.
Gerrard, Steven. *The Carry On Films*. London: Palgrave Macmillan, 2016.
Giddings, Robert, and Erica Sheen, eds. *The Classic Novel: From Page to Screen*. Manchester: Manchester University Press, 2000.
Gleizes, Delphine. 'Adapting *Les Misérables* for the Screen: Transatlantic Debates and Rivalries'. In *'Les Misérables' and Its Afterlives: Between Stage, Page and Screen*, edited by Kathryn M. Grossmann and Bradley Stephens, 129–42. London: Ashgate, 2015.
Gleizes, Delphine, ed. *L'Œuvre de Victor Hugo à l'écran: des rayons et des ombres*. Paris: L'Harmattan; Quebec: Presses de l'Université Laval, 2005.
Goffart, Juliette. '*Mademoiselle de Joncquières* d'Emmanuel Mouret: La Beauté et la Délicatesse'. *Critikat*, 11 September 2018, https://www.critikat.com/actualite-cine/critique/mademoiselle-de-joncquieres/. Accessed 28 July 2019.
Goodfellow, Melanie. 'Indie Sales Boards Emmanuel Mouret's Costume Drama *Mademoiselle de Joncquières*'. *Screen Daily*, 16 January 2018, https://www.screendaily.com/news/indie-sales-boards-emmanuel-mourets-costume-drama-mademoiselle-de-joncquieres-exclusive/5125581.article. Accessed 28 July 2019.
Gopal, Sangita, and Sujata Moorti. 'Bollywood in Drag: *Moulin Rouge!* and the Aesthetics of Global Cinema'. *Camera Obscura* 25.3 (2011): 29–67.
Grandy, Christine. *Heroes and Happy Endings: Class, Gender and Nation in Popular Film and Fiction in Interwar Britain*. Manchester: Manchester University Press, 2014.
Grant, Elliott M. *Zola's 'Germinal': A Critical and Historical Study*. Leicester: Leicester University Press, 1970.
Griffiths, Kate. *Émile Zola and the Artistry of Adaptation*. Oxford: Legenda, 2009.
Griffiths, Kate. 'Radio and the Space of Adaptation: Diana Griffiths' *Madame Bovary* (Radio 4, 2006)'. *Dix-Neuf* 18.2 (2014): 211–23.
Griffiths, Kate. *Zola and the Art of Television: Adaptation, Recreation, Translation*. Oxford: Legenda, 2019.

Grossman, Kathryn M. 'From Classic to Pop Icon: Popularizing Hugo'. *French Review* 74.3 (2001): 482–95.
Grossman, Kathryn M., and Bradley Stephens, eds. *'Les Misérables' and Its Afterlives: Between Stage, Page and Screen*. London: Ashgate, 2015.
Guilloux, Louis. 'Une heure chez le maître Anatole France: à propos de *Crainquebille*'. *Le Petit Journal*, 16 March 1923, 4.
Gunning, Tom. 'Cinema of Attractions: Early Film, Its Spectator and the Avant-Garde'. In *Early Cinema: Space Frame Narrative*, edited by Thomas Elsaesser and Adam Barker, 56–62. London: BFI, 1990.
Gunning, Tom. *The Films of Fritz Lang*. London: BFI, 2000.
Guy, Alice. *Mémoires: autobiographie de la première femme cinéaste*, edited by Catherine Laboubée. Paris: Autists Artists Associats, 2018.
'Gypsy Blood'. *Film Weekly*, 27 May 1932, 26.
Hanley, David. 'Serial Killers, Deals with the Devil, and the Madness of Crowds: The Horror Film in Nazi-Occupied France'. In *Recovering 1940s Horror Cinema: Traces of a Lost Decade*, edited by Mario DeGiglio-Bellemare, Charlie Ellbé and Kristopher Woofter, 181–202. Lanham, MD: Lexington, 2014.
Hassler-Forest, Dan, and Pascal Nicklas, eds. *The Politics of Adaptation: Media Convergence and Ideology*. London: Palgrave Macmillan, 2015.
Hayward, Susan. *French National Cinema*. London: Routledge, 1993.
Higashi, Sumiko. *Cecil B. DeMille and American Culture: The Silent Era*. Berkeley: University of California Press, 1994.
Higson, Andrew. 'Re-presenting the National Past: Nostalgia and Pastiche in the Heritage Film'. In *Film Genre Reader*, edited by Barry Keith Grant, 602–27. Austin: University of Texas Press, 2012.
Hill, Rodney. 'The New Wave Meets the Tradition of Quality: Jacques Demy's *The Umbrellas of Cherbourg*'. *Cinema Journal* 48.1 (2008): 27–50.
Hillairet, Prosper. 'Les Pieds dans le tapis: *L'Argent* de Marcel L'Herbier'. *Jeune Cinéma* 322–3 (Spring 2009): 102–5.
Holbane, Françoise. '*Les Inconnus dans la maison*'. *Paris-Midi*, 26 May 1942, 2.
Holloway, Richard. *Looking in the Distance*. Edinburgh: Canongate, 2004.
Houellebecq, Michel. *Atomised*, translated by Frank Wynne. London: Vintage, 2001.
Huber, Christoph. 'Giving Credibility to the Universe: Hélène Cattet and Bruno Forzani on *Laissez bronzer les cadavres*'. *Cinema Scope*, http://cinema-scope.com/cinema-scope-magazine/giving-credibility-to-the-universe-helene-cattet-bruno-forzani-on-laissez-bronzer-les-cadavres/. Accessed 27 July 2019.
Hudson, Elizabeth. '*Moulin Rouge!* and the Boundaries of Opera'. *Opera Quarterly* 27.2 (2011): 256–82.
Hunter, Russ. 'The Ecstasy of Gold: Love, Greed and Homosociality in the *Dollars* Trilogy'. *Studies in European Cinema* 9.1 (2012): 69–78.
Jackson, Julian. *France: The Dark Years, 1940–1944*. Oxford: Oxford University Press, 2001.
Jeanne, René, and Charles Ford. *Abel Gance*. Paris: Seghers, 1963.
Jefferey, Keith. 'Ireland and World War One', 3 October 2011, http://www.bbc.co.uk/history/british/britain_wwone/ireland_wwone_01.shtml. Accessed 6 May 2019.

Johnson, David. 'Adaptation and Fidelity'. In *The Oxford Handbook of Adaptation Studies*, edited by Thomas Leitch, 87–100. New York: Oxford University Press, 2017.

Kaplan, E. Ann *Women and Film. Both Sides of the Camera*. New York: Methuen, 1983.

Kauf. '*Unholy Love*', *Variety*, 30 August 1932, 21.

Kaufman, Anthony. 'The Lonely Subtitle: Here's Why US Audiences Are Abandoning Foreign-Language Films'. 6 May 2014, https://www.indiewire.com/2014/05/the-lonely-subtitle-heres-why-u-s-audiences-are-abandoning-foreign-language-films-27051/. Accessed 3 April 2018.

Kehler, Grace. 'Still for Sale: Love Songs and Prostitutes from *La Traviata* to *Moulin Rouge!*' *Mosaic: A Journal for the Interdisciplinary Study of Literature* 38.2 (2005): 145–63.

Kim, Kyu Hyun, 'Park Chan-wook's *Thirst*: Body, Guilt and Exsanguination'. In *Korean Horror Cinema*, edited by Alison Peirse and Daniel Martin, 199–215. Edinburgh: Edinburgh University Press, 2013.

King, Norman. *Abel Gance: A Politics of Spectacle*. London: BFI, 1984.

Kleinhans, Chuck. 'The Change from Film to Video Pornography: Implications for Analysis'. In *Pornography: Film and Culture*, edited by Peter Lehman, 154–66. New Brunswick, NJ: Rutgers University Press, 2006.

Koszarski, Richard. *An Evening's Entertainment: The Age of the Silent Feature Picture, 1915–1928*. Vol. 3 of *History of the American Cinema*, edited by Charles Harpole. Berkeley: University of California Press, 1994.

Kramer, Stephen Philip, and James Michael Welsh. *Abel Gance*. Boston: Twayne, 1978.

Kranz, David L., and Nancy C. Mellerski, eds. *In/Fidelity: Essays in Film Adaptation*. Newcastle: Cambridge Scholars, 2008.

L'Herbier, Marcel. *La Tête qui tourne*. Paris: Belfond, 1979.

Laclos, Choderlos de. *Les Liaisons dangereuses*, translated by Douglas Parmée. Oxford: Oxford University Press, 1995.

Lange-Churion, Pedro. 'Pedro Almodóvar's *La piel que habito*: Of Late Style and Erotic Conservatism'. *Bulletin of Hispanic Studies* 93.3 (2016): 441–53.

Lanzoni, Rémi Fournier. *French Cinema: From Its Beginnings to the* Present. New York: Bloomsbury, 2015.

Lapierre, Marcel. *Les Cent Visages du cinéma*. Paris: Grasset, 1948.

Larson, Katherine. 'Silly Love Songs: The Impact of Puccini's *La Bohème* on the Intertextual Strategies of *Moulin Rouge!*' *Journal of Popular Culture* 42.6 (2009): 1040–52.

Lefebvre, Thierry. '*A Trip to the Moon*: A Composite Film'. In *Fantastic Voyages of the Cinematic Imagination: Georges Méliès's 'Trip to the Moon',* edited by Matthew Solomon, 49–63. Albany: State University of New York Press, 2011.

Lefevere, André, ed. *Translation, History, Culture: A Sourcebook*. London: Routledge, 1992.

Lefevere, André. *Translation, Rewriting and the Manipulation of Literary Fame*. London: Routledge 2016.

Lehman, Peter. 'Revelations about Pornography'. In *Pornography: Film and Culture*, edited by Peter Lehman, 87–98. New Brunswick, NJ: Rutgers University Press, 2006.

Lejeune, Caroline. 'I Knew Donat When'. *Picturegoer Weekly*, 28 September 1935, 16.
Lemaitre, Pierre. *Au revoir là-haut*. Paris: Albin Michel, 2013.
Leplat, Thibault. 'Quel rapport entre un match de foot et *Hamlet*'. *Le Nouvel Observateur*, 18 March 2019. https://bibliobs.nouvelobs.com/screenshot/20190318.OBS1980/quel-rapport-entre-un-match-de-foot-et-hamlet.html. Accessed 20 March 2019.
Leprohon, Pierre. *Cinquante ans de cinéma français (1895–1945)*. Paris: Cerf, 1954.
Leteux, Christine. *Maurice Tourneur: réalisateur sans frontières*. Hellenvilliers: La Tour verte, 2015.
Lloyd, Christopher. *Collaboration and Resistance in Occupied France: Representing Treason and Sacrifice*. London: Palgrave Macmillan, 2003.
Lloyd, Christopher. *Henri-Georges Clouzot*. Manchester: Manchester University Press, 2007.
Lodge, Guy. '*Suite française*'. *Variety*, 10 March 2015, https://variety.com/2015/film/global/film-review-suite-francaise-1201447199/. Accessed 25 April 2018.
Lowe, Victoria. '"Something That Is US": Robert Donat, Screen Performance, and Stardom in the 1930s'. *Journal of Film and Video* 63.3 (2011): 13–29.
MacArthur, Elizabeth J. 'Trading Genres: Epistolarity and Theatricality in *Britannicus* and *Les Liaisons dangereuses*'. *Yale French Studies* 76 (1989): 243–64.
MacCabe, Colin, Kathleen Murray and Rick Warner, eds. *True to the Spirit: Film Adaptation and the Question of Fidelity*. Oxford: Oxford University Press, 2011.
Macnab, Geoffrey. 'A Berlin Thriller with Hints of Hitchcock and Plenty of Plot Twists'. *Independent*, 7 May 2015, https://www.independent.co.uk/arts-entertainment/films/reviews/phoenix-film-review-a-berlin-thriller-with-hints-of-hitchcock-and-plenty-of-plot-twists-10233527.html. Accessed 4 April 2018.
Macnab, Geoffrey. '*Suite française*'. *Independent*, 12 March 2015, https://www.independent.co.uk/arts-entertainment/films/reviews/suite-fran-aise-film-review-a-romantic-but-discordant-dispatch-on-love-and-war-10104994.html. Accessed 9 April 2018.
Marcus, Millicent. *Filmmaking by the Book: Italian Cinema and Literary Adaptation*. Baltimore: Johns Hopkins University Press, 1993.
Marel, Henri. 'Etienne Lantier et les chefs syndicalistes'. *Cahiers naturalistes* 50 (1976): 26–39.
Marsans-Sakly, Silvia. 'Geographies of Vengeance in Alexandre Dumas' *The Count of Monte Cristo*'. *Journal of North African Studies* 24.5 (2018): 738–57.
Martin-Jones, David. 'Transnational Allegory/Transnational History: *Se sei vivo spara/Django Kill ... If You Live, Shoot!*' *Transnational Cinemas* 2 (2012): 179–95.
Martínez-Carazo, Cristina. 'Almodóvar in the USA/The USA in Almodóvar'. In *(Re)viewing Creative, Critical and Commercial Practices in Contemporary Spanish Cinema*, edited by Duncan Wheeler and Fernando Canet, 259–70. Bristol: Intellect, 2014.
Mastorou, Elli. *Les Adaptations d'Émile Zola au cinéma: étude transnationale*. Saarbrücken: Éditions universitaires européennes, 2016.

Mazdon, Lucy. *Encore Hollywood: Remaking French Cinema*. London: BFI, 2000.
McCann, John. *Michel Houellebecq: Author of our Times*. Bern: Peter Lang, 2010.
McClary, Susan. *Georges Bizet: Carmen*. Cambridge: Cambridge University Press, 1992.
McFarlane, Brian. *Novel to Film: An Introduction to the Theory of Adaptation*. Oxford: Clarendon Press, 1996.
McGilligan, Patrick. *Cagney: The Actor as Auteur*. South Brunswick, NJ: A. S. Barnes, 1975.
McMahan, Alison. *Alice Guy Blaché: Lost Visionary of the Cinema*. New York: Continuum, 2002.
Mendik, Xavier. 'Black Sex, Bad Sex: Monstrous Ethnicity in the Black Emanuelle Films'. In *Alternative Europe: Eurotrash and Exploitation Cinema since 1945*, edited by Ernest Mathijs and Xavier Mendik, 146–59. London: Wallflower, 2004.
Moine, Raphaëlle. *Remakes: les films français à Hollywood*. Paris: CNRS, 2007.
Monteilhet, Hubert. *Le Retour des cendres*. Paris: Fallois, 1991.
Monteilhet, Véronique. 'Les adaptations balzaciennes sous l'Occupation'. *L'Année balzacienne* 3.1 (2002): 327–47.
Morrey, Douglas. *Michel Houellebecq: Humanity and Its Aftermath*. Liverpool: Liverpool University Press, 2013.
Motion Picture Association of America. 'Theatrical Market Statistics (2016)'. https://archive.org/details/MPAATheatricalMarketStatistics2016/page/n5. Accessed 5 April 2017.
Murphy, Mekado. 'Faith and Fangs: An Interview with Park Chan-wook'. 30 July 2009, https://artsbeat.blogs.nytimes.com/2009/07/30/faith-and-fangs-an-interview-with-park-chan-wook/. Accessed 25 March 2017.
Murray, Alison. 'Film as National Icon: Claude Berri's *Germinal*'. *French Review* 76.5 (2003): 906–16.
Murray, Simone. *The Adaptation Industry: The Cultural Economy of Contemporary Literary Adaptation*. New York: Routledge, 2012.
Naficy, Hamid. *An Accented Cinema: Exilic and Diasporic Filmmaking*. Princeton, NJ: Princeton University Press, 2011.
Nicholls, Bill, ed. *Movies and Methods. Volume One. An Anthology*. Berkeley: University of California Press, 1976.
Nord, Christiane. 'Function Plus Loyalty: Ethics in Professional Translation'. *Génesis. Revista Científica do ISAG* 6 (2006–7): 7–17.
Nord, Christiane. *Translating as a Purposeful Activity: Functionalist Approaches Explained*. Manchester: St Jerome, 1997.
Nowell-Smith, Geoffrey, and Steven Ricci, eds. *Hollywood and Europe: Economics, Culture, National Identity, 1945–1995*. London: BFI, 1998.
'On the Tender Tale of Cinderella Penguin and When the Day Breaks'. https://www.youtube.com/watch?v=KAIwUmd3XAU. Accessed 29 July 2019.
Paquet, Darcy. 'An Interview with E. J-yong'. 10 October 2003, https://koreanfilm.org/ejyong.html.
Paquet, Darcy. *New Korean Cinema: Breaking the Waves*. London: Wallflower, 2009.
Paqui, Guy. *Jean Delannoy: ses années lumière, 1938–1992*. Toulon: Les Presses du Midi, 2010.

Park-Finch, Heebon. 'From *Madame Bovary* to *Ryan's Daughter*: Literary, Cultural, and Historical Palimpsests'. *Adaptation* 10.1 (2017): 51–72.

Petrey, Sandy. *Realism and Revolution: Balzac, Stendhal, Zola and the Performances of History*. Ithaca, NY: Cornell University Press, 1988.

Pizzello, Chris. 'Bringing the Dark Side of Character to Light in *Diabolique*'. *American Cinematographer* 77.4 (April 1996): 36–44.

Place, Janey, and Lowell Peterson. 'Some Visual Motifs of *Film Noir*'. In *Film Noir Reader*, edited by Alain Silver and James Ursini, 65–76. New York: Limelight Editions, 1996.

Powrie, Phil. '1915: The Year of the Two *Carmens* (DeMille, Walsh)'. In *Carmen on Film: A Cultural History*, edited by Phil Powrie, Bruce Babington, Anne Davies and Chris Perriam, 41–54. Bloomington: Indiana University Press, 2007.

Prédal, René. *La Société française (1914–1945) à travers le cinéma*. Paris: Armand Colin, 1972.

Radford, Ivan. '*Let the Corpses Tan* (*Laissez bronzer les cadavres*)'. *Vodzilla*, 15 July 2018, http://vodzilla.co/reviews/vod-film-review-let-the-corpses-tan-laissez-bronzer-les-cadavres/.

Ragache, Gilles, and Jean-Robert Ragache. *La Vie quotidienne des écrivains et des artistes sous l'Occupation 1940–1944*. Paris: Hachette, 1988.

Raghavendra, M. K. *Seduced by the Familiar: Narration and Meaning in Indian Popular Cinema*. Oxford: Oxford University Press, 2008.

Raw, Laurence. 'Aligning Adaptation Studies with Translation Studies'. In *The Oxford Handbook of Adaptation Studies*, edited by Thomas Leitch, 494–508. New York: Oxford University Press, 2017.

Reader, Keith. 'Raymond Bernard's *Les Misérables* (1933)'. In *Studies in French Cinema: UK Perspectives, 1985–2010*, edited by Will Higbee and Sarah Leahy, 309–20. Bristol: Intellect, 2011.

Reader, Keith. *Robert Bresson*. Manchester: Manchester University Press, 2000.

Rebatet, Lucien. *Quatre ans de cinéma (1940–1944)*, edited by Philippe d'Hugues, Philippe Billé, Pascal Manuel Heu and Marc Laudelout. Pardès: Grez-sur-Loing, 2009.

Régent, Roger. *Cinéma de France de 'La Fille du Puisatier' aux 'Enfants du Paradis.'* Paris: Bellefaye, 1948.

Reid, Donald. 'Claude Berri's *Germinal*'. *Radical History Review* 66 (1996): 146–62.

René-Jeanne, 'La Semaine cinématographique'. *Le Petit Journal*, 21 October 1921, 4.

Renoir, Jean. *Renoir on Renoir: Interviews, Essays, Remarks*. Cambridge: Cambridge University Press, 1990.

Rentschler, Eric, ed. *German Film and Literature. Adaptations and Transformations*. London: Methuen, 1986.

Reyes, Xavier Aldana. 'Skin Deep? Surgical Horror and the Impossibility of Becoming Woman in Almodóvar's *The Skin I Live In*'. *Bulletin of Hispanic Studies* 90.7 (2013): 819–34.

Riding, Alan. *And the Show Went On: Cultural Life in Nazi-Occupied Paris*. London: Duckworth Overlook, 2011.

Roché, Henri-Pierre. *Jules et Jim*, translated by Patrick Evans. London: Penguin, 2011.

Rubin, Martin. *Showstoppers: Busby Berkeley and the Tradition of Spectacle*. New York: Columbia University Press, 1993.
Russo, Elena. 'Mademoiselle de Joncquières or Diderot Updated and Corrected'. *Fiction and Film for Scholars of France: A Cultural Bulletin* 9.5 (May 2019), https://h-france.net/fffh/reviews/mademoiselle-de-joncquieres-or-diderot-updated-and-corrected/.
Sadoul, Georges. *L'Art muet, 1919–1929*. Vol. 5.1 of *Histoire Générale du Cinéma* (*L'Après-guerre en Europe*). Paris: Denoël, 1975.
Sadoul, Georges. *Le Cinéma français (1890–1962)*. Paris: Flammarion, 1962.
Sadoul, Georges. *Les Pionniers du cinéma (de Méliès à Pathé), 1897–1909*. Vol. 2 of *Histoire Générale du Cinéma*. Paris: Denoël, 1947.
Sanders, Julie. *Adaptation and Appropriation*. London: Routledge, 2006.
Savas, Minae Yamamoto. 'The Art of Japanese Noh Theatre in Akira Kurosawa's *Throne of Blood*'. *Bridgewater Review* 30.2 (2011): 19–23.
Schatz, Thomas. *Hollywood Genres: Formulas, Filmmaking and the Studio System*. New York: Random House, 1981.
Schofield, Hugo. 'The French Spy Who Wrote *The Planet of the Apes*'. 4 August 2014, https://www.bbc.co.uk/news/magazine-28610124. Accessed 3 April 2018.
Scott, Maria. 'Acts of Suppression: Adapting *Le Rouge et le Noir*'. *Literature/Film Quarterly* 3.35 (2007): 237–43.
Sellier, Geneviève. '*Mademoiselle de Joncquières*'. *Le Genre et l'écran*, 14 September 2018, https://genre-ecran.net/?Mademoiselle-de-Joncquieres.
Semenza, Greg M. Colón, and Bob Hasenfratz. *The History of British Literature on Film, 1895–2015*. New York: Bloomsbury, 2015.
Sémolué, Jean. *Bresson ou l'acte pur des metamorphoses*. Saint-Amand-Montrond: Flammarion, 1993.
Sexton, David. '*Suite française*'. *Evening Standard*, 13 March 2015, https://www.standard.co.uk/go/london/film/suite-francaise-film-review-michelle-williams-touching-in-poor-adaptation-of-ir-ne-n-mirovsky-s-10105862.html. Accessed 7 April 2018.
Sheen, Erica. 'Anti-Anti-Fidelity: Truffaut, Roché, Shakespeare'. *Adaptation* 6.3 (December 2013): 243–59.
Shin, Jeeyoung. 'Globalisation and New Korean Cinema'. In *New Korean Cinema*, edited by Chi-Yun Shin and Julian Stringer, 51–62. Edinburgh: Edinburgh University Press, 2005.
Siclier, Jacques. *La France de Pétain et son cinéma*. Paris: Henri Veyrier, 1981.
Simenon, Georges. *Les Inconnus dans la maison*. Paris: Gallimard, 1941.
Simon, Joan, ed. *Alice Guy Blaché: Cinema Pioneer*. New Haven: Yale University Press, 2010.
Sims, Gregory. 'Returning to the Fold: Questions of Ideology in Jacques Becker's *Goupi Mains Rouges* (1942)'. *French Cultural Studies* 13 (2002): 5–31.
Slide, Anthony. '*Banned in the USA*' *British Films in the United States and Their Censorship 1933–1960*. New York: I.B. Tauris, 1998.
Soloman, Matthew, ed. *Fantastic Voyages of the Cinematic Imagination: Georges Méliès's 'Trip to the Moon'*. Albany: State University of New York Press, 2011.
Stam, Robert. 'Beyond Fidelity: The Dialogics of Adaptation'. In *Film Adaptation*, edited by James Naremore, 54–76. London: Athlone Press, 2000.

Stam, Robert. 'Revisionist Adaptation: Transtextuality, Cross-Cultural Dialogism, and Performative Infidelities'. In *The Oxford Handbook of Adaptation Studies*, edited by Thomas Leitch, 239–50. New York: Oxford University Press, 2017.
Stam, Robert. 'The Theory and Practice of Adaptation'. In *Literature and Film: A Guide to the Theory and Practice of Film Adaptation*, edited by Robert Stam and Alessandra Raengo, 1–52. Oxford: Blackwell, 2005.
Steeman, Stanislas-André. *L'Assassin habite au 21*. Paris: Poche, 1939.
Stephens, Bradley. 'Animating Animality through Dumas, D'Artagnan and Dogtanian'. *Dix-Neuf* 18 (2014): 193–210.
Struve-Debeaux, Anne. *Pierre Benoit: maître du roman d'aventures*. Paris: Hermann, 2015.
Sweeney, Carole. *Michel Houellebecq and the Literature of Despair*. London: Bloomsbury, 2013.
Taves, Brian. *Hollywood Presents Jules Verne: The Father of Science Fiction on Screen*. Lexington: University Press of Kentucky, 2015.
Temple, Michael, and Michael Witt, eds. *The French Cinema Book*. London: BFI, 2004.
Théate, Barbara. 'Cécile de France et Édouard Baer badinent avec l'amour dans *Mademoiselle de Joncquières*'. *Le Journal du Dimanche*, 12 September 2018, https://www.lejdd.fr/Culture/Cinema/cecile-de-france-et-edouard-baer-badinent-avec-lamour-dans-mademoiselle-de-joncquieres-3753179. Accessed 28 July 2019.
Thompson, David. 'Three Films with Gérard Philipe'. *Sight & Sound* 26.4 (April 2016): 100–1.
Tobing-Ronay, Fatimah. *The Third Eye: Race, Cinema and Ethnographic Spectacle*. Durham, NC: Duke University Press, 1996.
Travers, James. '*Le Colonel Chabert* (1943)'. *Films de France*, 2007, http://www.filmsdefrance.com/review/le-colonel-chabert-1943.html. Accessed 5 October 2016.
Truffaut, François. 'André Bazin, the Occupation, and I'. In *French Cinema of the Occupation and Resistance: The Birth of a Critical Esthetic*, edited by André Bazin; introduction by François Truffaut; translated by Stanley Hochman, 1–21. New York: Frederick Ungar, 1984.
Unwin, Timothy. *Jules Verne: Journeys in Writing*. Liverpool: Liverpool University Press, 2005.
Vance, Jeffrey. *Douglas Fairbanks*. Berkeley: University of California Press, 2008.
Véry, Pierre. *Œuvres complètes*, edited by Jacques Baudou. 3 vols. Paris: Éditions du Masque-Hachette Livre, 1997.
Vincendeau, Ginette. 'Show Me the Money'. *Sight and Sound* 19 (January 2009): 92.
Virdi, Jyotika. *The Cinematic ImagiNation: Indian Popular Films as Social History*. New Brunswick, NJ: Rutgers University Press, 2003.
Waldman, Harry. *Maurice Tourneur: The Life and Films*. Jefferson, NC: McFarland, 2001.
Waldron, Darren and Ros Murray. 'Troubling Transformations: Pedro Almodóvar's *La piel que habito/The Skin I Live In* (2011) and Its Reception'. *Transnational Cinemas* 5.1 (2014): 57–71.

Wallace, Leonard, ed. 'Grand Opera Comes to the Talkies'. *The Film Weekly*, 7 November 1931, https://search-proquest-com.abc.cardiff.ac.uk/docview/1705133197?rfr_id=info%3Axri%2Fsid%3Aprimo. Accessed 21 January 2019.

Watts, Andrew. 'Diamond Thieves and Gold Diggers: Balzac, Silent Cinema and the Spoils of Adaptation'. In *Adapting Nineteenth-Century France: Literature in Film, Theatre, Television, Radio and Print*, edited by Kate Griffiths and Andrew Watts, 47–79. Cardiff: University of Wales Press, 2013.

Watts, Andrew. '"Rien ne crie plus fort que le silence": *L'Auberge rouge* de Jean Epstein'. In *Balzac à l'écran*, edited by Anne-Marie Baron, *CinémAction* 173 (2019): 42–51.

Weitzel, Edward. 'Twenty Thousand Leagues under the Sea'. *The Moving Picture World*, 13 January 1917, 240.

Weitzman, Elizabeth. 'Robert Pattinson Falls Short as French Social Climber in *Bel Ami*'. *New York Daily News*, 7 June 2012, https://www.nydailynews.com/entertainment/tv-movies/movie-review-robert-pattinson-falls-short-french-social-climber-bel-ami-article-1.1091551. Accessed 7 April 2018.

Whelehan, Imelda. 'Adaptations: The Contemporary Dilemmas'. In *Adaptations: From Text to Screen, Screen to Text*, edited by Deborah Cartmell and Imelda Whelehan, 3–19. London: Routledge, 1999.

Whitney, Grace. *Lotte Reiniger: Pioneer of Film Animation*. Jefferson, NC: McFarland, 2017.

Wild, Florianne. 'The Case of the Undead Emperor: Familial and National Identity in Jacques Becker's *Goupi Mains Rouges*'. In *France in Focus: Film and National Identity*, edited by Elizabeth Ezra and Sue Harris, 157–67. Oxford: Berg, 2000.

Williams, Tony. '*Goupi Mains Rouges*'. *Senses of Cinema*, November 2014, http://sensesofcinema.com/2014/cteq/goupi-mains-rouges/. Accessed 23 November 2016.

Woolf, Matt. 'One Cool Jude'. *Observer*, 14 December 2003, 5.

Zakarian, Richard. *Zola's 'Germinal': A Critical Study of its Primary Sources*. Geneva: Droz, 1972.

Zola, Émile. *Germinal*, translated by Havelock Ellis. London: Dent, 1885.

Zola, Émile. *Thérèse Raquin*. Paris: Gallimard, [1868] 1970.

Zurian, Francisco A. '*La piel que habito*: A Story of Imposed Gender and the Struggle for Identity'. In *A Companion to Pedro Almodóvar*, edited by Marvin D'Lugo and Kathleen M. Vernon, 262–78. Chichester: Wiley-Blackwell, 2013.

Index

Abel, Alfred 54
Abel, Marco 247
Abel, Richard 21, 46–50, 56, 59 n.18, 59 n.20, 61 n.53
Adams, Mark 252
Académie française 136
adaptive canon 67–78
adaptive currencies 19–62
adaptive diaspora 225–65
Adjani, Isabelle 233–4, 235–6
L'Affaire Crainquebille (*The Crainquebille Affair*) (novella) 45
African American cast 161
African American vernacular 161
Agnes and His Brothers (2004) 247
Albertini, Alderberto 197
Alcohol and Its Victims (1902) 6
Alcover, Pierre 54
Algeria 43, 112, 115
Allégret, Marc 111
'Allo! 'Allo! 255
Almirante, Mario 100 n.38
Almodóvar, Pedro 226, 257–60
Altman, Rick 3–4, 160
Amazon Prime 228
American Psycho (novel) 247
Amphitryon (1935) 100 n.40
Anaya, Elena 257
animation 15, 189, 190
animatograph 22
Angst (2003) 247
Anti-Semitism 111, 120
Anuradha (1960) 13, 169–74, 271
Aragon, Louis 274
L'Arche de Noé (*Noah's Ark*) (novel) 110–11
L'Argent (*Money*) (novel) 120
L'Argent (*Money*) (1929) 11, 21, 54–7, 268

Argentina 7
Armes, Roy 109
Armont, Paul 9
Arsan, Emmanuelle 9, 191, 195, 271
'art films' 29
L'Assassin habite au 21 (*The Murderer Lives at Number 21*) (1942) 107, 110, 133–5
L'Assassinat du Duc de Guise (*The Assassination of the Duke of Guise*) (1908) 28–30
L'Assassinat du Père Noël (*The Killing of Santa Claus*) (novel) 138
L'Assassinat du Père Noël (*The Killing of Santa Claus*) (1941) 69, 107, 109, 136–41
L'Assommoir (novel) 3, 6
L'Assommoir (*The Drinking Den*) (1909) 30
'Astronomic Club' 25
L'Atlantide (*Atlantida*) (novel) 42
L'Atlantide (*Atlantida*) (1921) 42–5
L'Atlantide (*Atlantida*) (1934) 93
Atomised (2006) 227, 247–50
L'Auberge rouge (*The Red Inn*) (1923) 49–51, 58
Aubert-Palace 56
Au bonheur des dames (*The Ladies' Paradise*) (1943) 109
Au cœur de l'orage (*In the Eye of the Storm*) (1944-45) 111
Auschwitz 254
Austen, Jane 98 n.4
Australia 239
Auteur 81–90, 96
Aurenche, Jean 149, 150, 153
Au revoir là-haut (*See You Up There*) (novel) 273

Au revoir là-haut (See You Up There) (2017) 273–5
Autant-Lara, Claude 1, 2, 13, 150, 151, 153–5
Autour de la lune (*Around the Moon*) (novel) 25

Babelsberg Studios 230
Bach, Johann Sebastian 238–9
Bacon, Lloyd 131
Baer, Edouard 277
Bakhtin, Mikhail 227, 251
Baledón, Rafael 17 n.10
Balio, Tino 21, 39–40
Balzac, Honoré de 68, 79, 94, 105, 106, 109, 110, 112, 120, 136, 137, 138, 274
Banderas, Antonio 257, 260
Bangkok 191, 195
Bara, Theda 100 n.42
Basic Instinct (1992) 236
Baron, Anne-Marie 137
Baroncelli, Jacques de 47, 110, 111
Bary, Léon 102 n.63
Bastid, Jean-Pierre 275
Bataille, Henri 79
Bates, Kathy 236
Baur, Harry 68, 69, 138
Bazin, André 106, 165
Bazzoni, Luigi 13, 165–9, 171, 182, 271
BBC, the 7, 180
Becker, Jacques 13, 110, 125–8, 141
Belafonte, Harry 163
Bel Ami (novel) 226
Bel Ami (2012) 251–61, 272
Benacquista, Tonino 231
Ben-Hur (1959) 35
Benoit, Pierre 42, 45, 93, 136, 138, 145 n.60
Bergman, Ingmar 274
Berkeley, Busby 131–2
Berlin Wall 244, 247
Bernon, Bleuette 23
Berr, Georges 79
Berri, Claude 190, 202–8, 218, 221 n.30
Berthomieu, André 123
Bertin-Maghit, Jean-Pierre 106
Bertolucci, Bernardo 193
Bertram, Hans 69
Besson, Luc 230
La Bestia humana (1957) 17 n.7
La Bête humaine (*Judas Was a Woman*) (1938) 11, 65, 66, 71, 90, 269
Bhowmick, Sachin 169–71
Bibidh, Marayat 195
Bihan, Max 136
Bildungsroman 191
Billard, Pierre 114, 120
Birabeau, André 79
Birch, Edmund 74
A Bit of a Fillum (2009) 180
Bizet, Georges 33–4, 79, 80, 94, 161, 163, 164, 167
Black Cobra Woman (*Eva Nera*) (1976) 195
Black Emanuelle 190, 195, 197
The Black Tulip (1937) 99 n.23
Blake, Michael F. 58 n.2, 61 n.60
Blanchar, Pierre 114
Blum–Byrnes agreement 149
Bloom, Harold 67, 70, 74
Blu-Ray 228
La Bohème (opera) 9, 18 n.13, 208–10
Bock, Hans-Michael 52
Boileau-Narcejac 233, 237, 258
Bollywood 210–12, 251
Bolt, Robert 175, 176, 178
Bond, Lucy 228
Bordeaux, Henry 123–5
Bosco the Musketeer (1933) 99 n.23
Bost, Pierre 149, 150, 153
Boston Symphony Hall 33
Botticelli, Sandro 158
Boublil, Alain 225
Boudu sauvé des eaux (*Boudu saved from drowning*) (1932) 102 n.69
Bouilhet, Louis 178
Boulle, Pierre 226, 231–3, 260, 272
Bourdieu, Pierre 20
Bousquet, Jacques 79
Bowie, David 213
Bowie, Malcolm 179

Bowser, Eileen 32
Bradshaw, Peter 232, 249
Bresslaw, Bernard 197
Brief Encounter (1945) 256, 257
Bright Road (1953) 163
Brissot, Jacques Pierre 117
Britain 22, 64–6, 76, 96, 134, 135, 198, 199, 225, 254
British Board of Film Censors (BBFC) 96, 104 n.85
Brockmann, Stephen 51, 53
Brook, Tom 231
Brooks, Peter 183 n.13
Brothers Grimm 202
Brown, Mick 220 n.11
Bruhn, Jørgen 227
Bryce, Alex 99 n.23
Bunbury, Stephanie 253
Burch, Noël 114–15
Burke, Tom 80, 81
Burton, Richard 198
Burton, Tim 16, 231–3, 260, 272
Busnach, William 3
Butterworth, Peter 197

Cagney, James 81
Cahuet, Albéric 112
Cain, James M. 245
Calmettes, André 28, 30
Cameron, James 238
Camille (1936) 65–6, 85–7, 210
Campogalliani, Carlo 99 n.23
Canon, the 99 n.28, 148–51, 155, 164, 200, 201
Capellani, Albert 30
Capus, Alfred 79
Card Game (1895) 22
Carleton, Lloyd B. 36
Carmen (1915) 32–6
Carmen Jones (1954) 159–64, 182, 185 n.36, 186 n.38, 270
Carmen, the Girl from Triana (*Carmen, la de Triana*) (1938) 12, 67, 95, 103 n.83
Carné, Marcel 69
Carnival of Souls (1962) 245
Carry On Camping (1969) 197, 249
Carry On Cleo (1964) 198

Carry On Don't Lose Your Head (1967) 198
Carry On Emmanuelle (1978) 14, 90, 198–200
Carry On Screaming (1966) 198
Carry On Spying (1964) 198
Carry On Up the Khyber (1969) 197
Cartmell, Deborah 58 n.3
Cattet, Hélène 275, 276
Caulwelaert, Didier Van 230
Cayatte, André 108, 109
Cécile est morte! (*Cécile Is Dead!*) (1944) 111
Céline 123
Celle qui n'était plus (*She Who Was No More*) (novel) 233, 236
Cendrillon (*Cinderella*) (1899) 23–5
censorship 69, 96, 105, 111, 112, 116, 126, 128, 141, 237, 269
Centre National de la Cinématographie (CNC) 149
'A Certain Tendency of the French Cinema', Truffaut 153
Certeau, Michel de 72
Cervantes, Miguel de 68
Chaffin-Quiray, Garrett 191, 192
Chang, Justin 252
Chaplin, Charlie 39
Charlotte Gray (2001) 255
La Chartreuse de Parme (*The Charterhouse of Parma*) (novel) 151
La Chartreuse de Parme (*The Charterhouse of Parma*) (1948) 151
Chechik, Jeremiah 227, 233–7
Cheeky Devil, The (1932) 93–4
La Chienne (*The Bitch*) (novel) 102 n.69
La Chienne (*The Bitch*) (1931) 66, 90
China 63, 225, 228
The Children of Captain Grant (1936) 97 n.1
Chocolat 211–12
Choderlos de Laclos, Pierre 263 n.32, 279
Chosun Dynasty (1392–1897) 239
Chowdhary, Nirmal 169
Christensen, Benjamin 8

INDEX

Christian-Jaque 69, 109, 136, 138–41
Chung, Hye Seung 239–40
cinema of attractions 59 n.4
Cinémathèque Royale 30
Cinéromans film company 54
Cité Elgé 26
Clair, René 108
Class system, the 198, 199
The Clay Cart (*Mrichhakatika*) (play) 211
Clément, René 183 n.4
Cleopatra (1963) 198
Close, Glenn 230
Clouzot, Henri-Georges 107, 110, 119–22, 129–35, 229, 233–6
Cohan, Steven 159
Cohen, Jacques 110
Collaboration 116–19, 123, 139, 141
Collet-Serra, Jaume 230
Collins, Andrew 176
Colman, Ronald 76
Le Colonel Chabert (Colonel Chabert) (novella) 274
Le Colonel Chabert (Colonel Chabert) (1943) 107, 136, 137, 141
Colmeiro, José 95
La Comédie-Française 28
Comité de l'Organisation de l'Industrie Cinématographique (COIC) 149
Communism 206
Le Comte de Montecristo (*The Count of Monte Cristo*) (1929) 99 n.23
Condon, Bill 18 n.19
Connor, Kenneth 197
Continental (film company) 69, 109–11, 116, 119, 129, 131, 132, 134, 135, 138, 139
Coppola, Francis Ford 218
Copyright 20, 25, 32, 220 n.11, 235
Le Corbeau (*The Raven*) (1943) 110
Corrado, Gino 102 n.63
Les Corrupteurs (The Corrupters) (1941) 120–1
Count of Monte Cristo, The (1913) 21, 268
Count of Monte Cristo, The (1934) 75, 76, 78
Courtade, François 114
Le Cousin Pons (1924) 48

Crainquebille (*Bill / Old Bill of Paris*) (1922) 45–48
Crewe Jones, Florence 88
Crisp, Colin 111, 121, 135
Crossroads, The (1942) 123
Crosland, Alan 19
Crowe, Russell 225
Crowther, Bosley 117
Cruz, Penelope 103 n.83
Cubitt, Sean 228
Cukor, George 65, 85, 210
Currency of adaptation 19–62

Dale, Jim 197
d'Amato, Joe 14, 190, 195–7
D'Arrast, D'Abbadie 100 n.38
La Dame aux camélias (*The Lady with the Camellias*) (novel and play) 30, 65, 85, 210
La Dame aux camélias (*The Lady with the Camellias*) (1912) 30
Damiano, Gerard 193
Dandridge, Dorothy 163
Dangerous Liaisons (1988) 239
Dante 68
Danton, Georges 154
Dark Castle Entertainment 230
Dauphin, Claude 111
Davies, Simon 240
Déat, Marcel 116
De Brulier, Nigel 81, 85
Decoin, Henri 107, 119–21
Decourcelle, Pierre 30
Deep Throat (1972) 193
Dekobra, Maurice 79
Delair, Suzy 133
Delannoy, Jean 13, 107, 112–15, 269
De la Terre à la lune (*From the Earth to the Moon*) (novel) 25
Delluc, Louis 43
DeMille, Cecil B. 32–6
De Niro, Robert 231
D'entre les morts (*Among the Dead*) (novel) 258
Depardieu, Gérard 206
Le Dernier des six (*The Last of the Six*) (1941) 107, 110, 129–33, 135
Deslauriers, Claire 150

Devaivre, Jean 117
Devant, David 22
Diabolique (1996) 227, 229, 233–7
Les Diaboliques (1955) 229, 233–6
Le Diable au corps (*Devil in the Flesh*) (1947) 151
Diamant-Berger, Henri 40
Diaspora 226, 227
Dibb, Saul 254–7
DiCaprio, Leonardo 230
Dickens, Charles 98 n.4
Diderot, Denis 277–9
Dieterle, William 11, 65
Diffrient David Scott 239, 240
Dolley, Georges 79
'domestication' 229
dominant poetics 147–88
Donat, Robert 66, 75–7, 81
Donnellan, Declan 16, 226, 251, 252, 272
Drazin, Charles 153
Dréville, Jean 123–5, 131
Dreyfus Affair, The 24, 111
Drunkard's Reformation, The (1909) 3, 4
Dubé, Pierre 184 n.20
Ducaux, Annie 114
La Duchesse de Langeais (*The Duchess of Langeais*) (1941) 110, 111
Dumas, Alexandre *père* 85, 99 n.22, 230, 269
Dumas, Alexandre, *fils* 30, 210, 211
Dumasy, Lise 74
Dunne, Philip 75
Dunquin 180
Dupontel, Albert 273–5
Duvivier, Julien 108
DVD 7, 34, 69, 228, 232
Dwan, Allan 11, 65, 82, 83, 85
Dyke, W. S. Van 107

Easton Ellis, Brett 247
Ebert, Roger 235
Edison 100 n.42
Ehrlich, Evelyn 109, 131, 132, 141
Eibel, Alfred 79
Eichinger, Bernd 248

Eisner, Lotte 102 n.70
E. J-yong 227, 238
El Boassa (1944) 98 n.4
Eleftheriotis, Dimitris 166
Elliott, Kamilla 3
Elsner, Gisela 247
Emmanuelle (novel) 9, 191, 194–98
L'Enfant de la barricade (*The Child of the Barricade*) (1907) 28
Les Enfants du Capitaine Grant (*In Search of the Castaways*) (1914) 36
English Patient, The (1996) 255, 256
Epic Cinema 147
epigraph 150, 153–5
Erll, Astrid 228
Eschbach, Nicolas 279
Esmeralda (1905) 20, 26–7
EuroCorp 230
Evening Standard 254
Everson, William K. 32
Eyre, Jean 49
Ezra, Elizabeth 228

Faber, Claude 8
Fabulous World of Jules Verne, The (*Vynález zkázy*) (1958) 9
Fairbanks Junior, Douglas 83, 96
Fairbanks Senior, Douglas 39, 40–2, 66, 76, 79, 81–6, 101 n.50, 269
fairy tales 10, 15, 23, 138, 190, 202, 268
Falk, Henri 79
Family, The (2013) 230–1
Fanny (1932) 78
Far from the Madding Crowd (novel) 179
Fares, Abbas 98 n.5
Farrar, Geraldine 33–5
Fauser, Annegret 185 n.36
La Fausse Maîtresse (*The False Mistress*) (novel) 109
La Fée aux choux (*The Cabbage Fairy*) (1896) 26
Félicie Nanteuil (1943) 111
Feuillère, Edwige 110
Ferragus (1924) 48
Fescourt, Henri 29
Feyder, Jacques 29, 42–8

Fiennes, Ralph 255
Film d'Art 28–30
First World War 6, 15, 31–2, 42, 51, 58, 96, 175, 177, 180, 190, 215, 217, 219, 273, 274
Firth, Colin 256
Fisher, Jaimey 244
A Fistful of Dollars (1964) 165, 276
Flaubert, Gustave 73, 169–80, 251, 268, 271
Footit, Georges 212
Ford, Charles 45
  Formative function of film genre 147–88
  Forst, Willi 100 n.40
  42nd Street (1933) 131
Forzani, Bruno 275–6
Foster, Jodie 215
The Four Musketeers (*I Quattro moschettieri*) (1936) 99 n.23
Fouchardière, Georges de la 102 n.69
Fournier Lanzoni, Rémi 9, 70, 78
Fragonard, Jean Honoré 92–3
France, Anatole 45, 48, 111
France, Cécile de 277
Franco 95, 103 n.83
Franju, Georges 257
French Revolution, The 71, 117
Frears, Stephen 239, 279
Fred Astaire–Ginger Rogers series 159
French New Wave movement 13, 147, 151–2, 155–9, 182, 191
French Occupation cinema 12, 69, 105–45, 254, 269–70
Fresnay, Pierre 116, 121, 129
Freund, Karl 66, 88–9
Fridlund, Bert 168, 186 n.40

Gabin, Jean 11, 66, 70–1, 108
Gaines, Jane M. 20
Galatea 89
Galdós, Benito Pérez 259
  Gandéra, Félix 9
  Garbo, Greta 11, 66, 81, 85–8
Garcin, Hélène 124
Garçon, François 106
Garland, Judy 214
Gasnier, Louis J. 78

Gastineau, Octave 3
Gaumont, 26–7, 109
Gautier, Théophile 74
Gemser, Laura 195
gender 64, 66, 81, 85, 259, 269, 278
Genette, Gérard 251
Gentleman (1995) 247
Georges (novel) 99 n.28
Germany 7, 12, 19, 51, 54, 64, 65, 67, 79, 88, 93–5, 117, 134, 180, 220 n.11, 225, 228, 245–7, 250, 260, 261, 272
Germinal (1993) 5, 14, 190, 202–8, 218, 221 n.30, 271
Gerrard, Steven 197–8, 199
Gervaise (1956) 183 n.4
Gestapo 70
Giallo 276
Giant, The (*Kyojin-den*) (1938) 67
Giraud, Henri 115
The Girl of your Dreams (*La niña de tus ojos*) (1999) 103 n.83
Gjelsvik, Anne 227
Gleizes, Delphine 26
Glenister, Philip 252
Glory, Marie 54
Godfather, The (1972) 218
Goebbels, Joseph 12, 67, 69, 94–5, 97, 109
The Gold Diggers of 1933 (1933) 131
Good, the Bad, and the Ugly, The (1966) 276
Golden Age of Indian Cinema 173, 182
The Golden Anchor (1932) 100 n.38
Gopal, Sangita 210–12
Gorostiza, Celestino 17 n.10
Gothic, the 27, 138, 243–4
Goupi Mains Rouges (*It Happened at the Inn*) (1943) 13, 110, 125–9, 141, 269–70
Grable, Betty 159
La Grande Bretèche (1909) 30
Grand opera 33, 80–1
Grandy, Christine 102 n.68, 104 n.85
Great Depression 63
Great Escape, The (1963) 255, 256

Greece 165
Greven, Alfred 109
Griffith, D. W. 3, 40, 48
Griffiths, Kate 37, 61 n.51, 98 n.19, 103 n.72
Grossman, Kathryn M. 68, 98 n.4
Grund, Helen 156
The Guardian 232, 249
Gunning, Tom 91, 102 n.70
Guy, Alice 20–1, 26, 58, 268
Gypsy Blood (1932) 79–81, 100 n.42, 168

Hammerstein, Oscar 162, 185 n.36, 186 n.38
Hammett, Dashiell 132
Hanley, David 143 n.30
hard-core porn 193, 194
Hardwicke, Catherine 18 n.19
Hardy, Thomas 179
Harman, Hugh 99 n.23
Hasenfratz, Bob 2–4
Hassler-Forest, Dan 106
Hathaway, Anne 225
Hawtrey, Charles 197
Hays Code 72
Hayward, Susan 21, 44, 106, 107, 115, 139, 149
Helm, Brigitte 54
Hénaff, René Le 107, 136–8, 141
heritage films 5, 189–90, 202–4, 208, 212–16, 218, 271, 277
heroes 81, 97, 177, 232
heroines 86, 94, 97, 102 n.68, 237
Hessel, Franz 156
Heston, Charlton 232
Hibbard, Lucien 8
Higashi, Sumiko 33
Higson, Andrew 203, 212–13
Hill, Rodney 149
Hindu films 172
Hispano-Film-Produktion 95
Histoire comique (novella) 111
L'Histoire d'Adèle H. (The Story of Adèle H.) (1975) 235–6
Histoires ou contes du temps passé (Histories or Tales of Past Time) (fairy tales) 200

Hitchcock, Alfred 227, 258–9
Holbane, Françoise 122
Holloway, Richard 247
Hollywood 27, 40, 42, 49, 51, 54, 66, 76, 82, 86, 88, 90, 91, 93, 95, 108, 121, 134, 193, 228–30, 269
Hollywood Anti Nazi League 185 n.36
Hollywood cinema 131, 135, 194, 226, 228–33, 235–7, 230, 258, 260
Hollywood musical tradition 131, 135
Holocaust, The 272
Holt, Nora 162
Hong Kong cinema 238
Hooper, Tom 225
Horne, Marilyn 163
Hors de moi (*Enraged*) (novel) 230
Hoss, Nina 245
Houellebecq, Michel 226–7, 247–50
Howard, Trevor 256
Huber, Christoph 275
Hudson, Elizabeth 210
Hugo, Victor 11, 26, 58, 65, 67, 98 n.4, 225, 235
Human Desire (1954) 66, 90
Hunchback of Notre Dame, The (1939) 11, 65, 268
Hunter, Russ 168, 186 n.42
Hutcheon, Linda 229
Hutcherson, LeVern 163

L'Ile mystérieuse (*The Mysterious Island*) (novel) 38
Impressionism 92
Les Inconnus dans la maison (*Strangers in the House*) (novel) 109, 122
Les Inconnus dans la maison (*Strangers in the House*) (1942) 107, 110, 119–23, 141
Independent, The 246, 256
India 13, 39, 147, 148, 169, 172–4, 182, 211, 251, 271
'indigenization' 229, 251
In Search of the Castaways (1914) 36
In Secret (2013) 230
interpersonal transactions 61–104
Ireland 175, 180–1
Irish Republican Army (IRA) 181

Irish Republican Brotherhood (IRB) 178, 180
Iron Mask, The (1929) 11, 65, 66, 82–5
Iron Mask, The (1939) 85
Israel 165, 226
Italian Spaghetti Western 13, 148, 165–9, 271
Italy 7, 14, 24, 124, 148, 165, 190, 220 n.11, 276
Itami, Mansaku 67

Jackman, Hugh 225
Jackson, Julian 122
Jacques, Hattie 197
Jacques le Fataliste et son maître (Jacques the Fatalist and his Master) (novel) 277–8
Jaeckin, Just 10, 14, 190–9, 271
James, Sid 197
Japan 63, 67, 227, 241, 242
Japrisot, Sébastien 190, 215, 219
Jasset, Victorin 36
Jazz Singer, The 19
Jeffery, Keith 181
Jerichow (2008) 245
Jess, Marilyn 276
Jeunet, Jean-Pierre 15, 190, 214–19, 271
  Jeux interdits (Forbidden Games) (1952) 183 n.4
John, Elton 213
Johnson, Celia 256
Johnson, David, 3
Jonquet, Thierry 226, 257, 259
Jules et Jim (Jules and Jim) (novel) 9, 270
Jules et Jim (Jules and Jim) (1962) 9, 13, 155–6, 159, 182, 191–2, 270
Jurassic Park (1993) 237

Kael, Pauline 175
Kane, Robert 78
Kaplan, E. Ann 86–7
Kehler, Grace 208
Khleifi, Michel 226
Kiki (1932) 93
Kim Young-sam 237
King Jeongjo (r. 1776–1800) 239

Kistemaekers, Henri 79
Kleinhans, Chuck 194, 219 n.8
Knoblock, Edward 84
Korda, Alexander 78, 100 n.38
Korean New Wave 237
Kranz, David. L 3
Kristel, Sylvia 198
Kristeva, Julia 251
Kuhn, Annette 96
Kurosawa, Akira 241

Lacombe, Henri 107, 129–33, 135
The Ladies Paradise (Zum Paradies des Damen) (1922) 17 n.8
Lado, Aldo 276
Laissez bronzer les cadavres! (Let the Corpses Tan!) (novel) 275
Laissez bronzer les cadavres (Let the Corpses Tan) (2017) 275–7
Lafitte, Paul 28
Lamac, Carl 93
Lamartine, Alphonse de 172
Lamprecht, Gerhard 100 n.40
Landi, Elissa 77
Lange-Churion, Pedro 258
Lang, Fritz 51, 66, 90, 102 n.70
Langton, Simon 17 n.11
Larson, Katherine 209, 222 n.48
Lasky, Jesse 32–3, 35
Last Tango in Paris (1972) 193
Laughton, Charles 27
Lavedan, Henri 29
'La Vénus d'Ille' ('The Venus of Ille') (short story) 158
Lawrence, Gertrude 102 n.68
20,000 Leagues under the Sea (1916) 36–8
LD Entertainment 230
Lean, David 13, 147, 175–82, 256–7
Le Bargy, Charles 28
Le Chanois, Jean-Paul 111, 116–17
Lee, Rowland V. 11, 65, 75, 85, 99 n.23, 269
Lefebvre, Thierry 25
Lehman, Peter 194
Lefevere, André 5, 12, 63–5, 67, 97, 147–8, 183 n.1
Lejeune, Caroline 76

Le Journal du Dimanche 279
Lemaitre, Pierre 273
Leni, Paul 52
Leone, Sergio 165, 186 n.40, 276
Leone, Vincenzo 186 n.40
Leplat, Thibaud 164
Le Roy, Mervyn 131
Lestrade, Gabriel de 277
les femmes tondues 181
Les Halles 47, 206, 215
L'Herbier, Marcel 11, 21, 54–8, 268
Les Liaisons dangereuses (*Dangerous Liaisons*) (novel) 227, 238–41, 246, 279
Lewis, Cecil 80–1
Lewis, Jon 193
Lodge, Guy 254, 256
London Philharmonic Orchestra 34
Lorre, Peter 11, 66, 81, 88, 102 n.70
Louis XIV 64, 230
Lowe, Victoria 76
Loy, Myrna 132
loyalty 64
Lourdes (novel) 7
Luhrmann, Baz 9, 15, 190, 208–14, 215, 218, 271
Lumière brothers 6, 19, 22
Lyric Theatre Broadway 84

M (1931) 88
Macnab, Geoffrey 246, 256
Madame Bovary (novel) 13, 72–3, 169, 175, 182, 251, 271
Madame Bovary (1937) 100 n.40
Madeleine Férat (novel) 7
Mademoiselle de Joncquières (2018) 277–9
Mad Love (1935) 66, 88–9
Madonna 213
Magic Lantern Tradition 6
La Main du diable (*Carnival of Sinners*) (1943) 13, 107, 111, 116–19, 141, 143 n.30
La Main enchantée (*The Enchanted Hand*) (novella) 111, 116
Les Mains d'Orlac (*The Hands of Orlac*) (novel) 66, 88
Maisch, Herbert 67, 95

Malavita (2004) (novel) 231
Man With No Name (*Mensch ohne namen*) (1932) 100 n.40
Manchette, Jean-Patrick 275
Manet, Édouard 239
Mangeshkar, Lata 172
Man in the Iron Mask, The (1998) 230
Man, Pride, and Vengeance (*L'uomo, l'orgoglio, la vendetta*) (1967) 13, 165–9, 182, 271
Manon Lescaut (1926) 51
Maquet, Auguste 75
Marcus, Millicent 172
Mari, Febo 7
Mark of Zorro, The (1920) 40
Márquez, Gabriel García 274
Martin-Jones, David 186 n.41, 187 n.43
Marsans-Sakly, Silvia 99 n.28
Ma sœur et moi (*My Sister and I*) (play) 79
Masterpiece Theater 7
Masterplan 198
Mathot, Léon 31, 49
Marius (1931) 78, 100 n.38
Maya Memsaab (1993) 251
Maupassant, Guy de 16, 92, 226, 251, 272
Mazdon, Lucy 236
May 1968 207, 249
Mayer, Gerald 163
McClary, Susan 100 n.42
McClintock, Anne 195
McGilligan, Patrick 81–2
McMahan, Alison 28
McQueen, Steve 255
Meet Me in St Louis (1944) 214
Mehta, Ketan 251
Méliès, Georges 6, 10, 21–6, 57, 268
Mendik, Xavier 195
Mercury, Freddie 213
Mérimée, Prosper 30, 32, 79, 80, 94–5, 103 n.83, 158, 164–8
#MeToo revolution 278, 279
Mexico 7
MGM/Metro-Goldwyn-Mayer 132, 159

Michael Strogoff (novel) 36
Mills, John 175
Mimi (1935) 9, 65, 96, 208
Minelli, Vincent 214
Minghella, Anthony 255
Minogue, Kylie 213
Miou Miou 206
The Miracle (*Miraklet*) (1913) 7
Le Miroir à deux faces (*The Mirror Has Two Faces*) (1958) 229
Les Misérables (novel) 67, 225
Les Misérables (1911) 30
Les Misérables (1934) 11, 65, 67, 69, 268
Les Misérables (1935) 67
Moine, Raphaëlle 234, 235
Molière 52, 79
Monroe, Marilyn 213
monstrosity 196
Montaigne, Michel de 68
Monteilhet, Hubert 227, 245, 246, 250, 261
Monteilhet, Véronique 137
Moorti, Sujata 210–12
Morgan Creek 235
Morrey, Douglas 248
Morricone, Ennio 276
Motion Picture Association of America 230
Motion Picture Code 72
Motion Picture Magazine 41
Motion Picture World 31
Motte, Marguerite de la 101 n.63
Moulin Rouge! (2001) 9, 15, 190, 208–14, 218, 271
Mouloudji, Marcel 120
Mouret, Emmanuel 277–9
Mukherjee, Hrishikesh 13, 14, 169–75, 182, 271
Murger, Henri 9, 18 n.13, 96, 102 n.68, 208, 211
Murphy, Mekado 263 n.36
Murray, Alison 221 n.30
Murray, Ros 257
Murray, Simone 4
Mygale (*Tarantula*) (novel) 226, 257, 260

My Sister and I (*Meine Schwester und ich*) (1929) 79

Naderi, Amir 226
Naficy, Hamid 226
Naidu, Leela 172
Namara, Marguerite 80
Nana (novel) 102 n.69
Nana (1926) 102 n.69
Nana (1944) 17 n.10
Nana (1985) 17 n.10
Nandagaon 169
Napoleonic Empire 112
Natanson, Jacques 79
National Board of Review of Motion Pictures 75
National Urban League 185 n.36
naturalism 6, 7, 70, 203, 213
Naturalist theory 242–4, 261, 272
Nazi Germany 93, 95, 117
Nazism 103 n.75
Negri, Pole 100 n.42
La Neige sur les pas (*The Snow on the Footsteps*) (1941), 123
Némirovsky, Irène 254–5
Nero-AG 93
Nero, Franco 165
Nerval, Gérard de 111, 116, 118
Netflix 228
Neupert, Richard 183 n.4
New Korean Cinema 237–8
New Symphony Orchestra 80
New York Daily News 252
New York Dramatic Mirror 33
New York Times 117
The Song of the Nibelungs (*Die Nibelungen*) (1924) 51
Niblo, Fred 85
Nichols, Bill 148–9
Nicklas, Pascal 106
Nights in Andalusia (*Andalusische Nächte*) (1938) 67, 95
Noa, Manfred 79
No Place to Go (2000) 247
Nord, Christiane 11, 63–5, 97, 269
North Africa 44, 45
North Carolina 161

INDEX

Novak, Kim 258
Notre-Dame de Paris (novel) 20, 26–7
Nowell-Smith, Geoffrey 229
La Nuit du carrefour (*Night at the Crossroads*) (novel) 102 n.69

Offenbach, Jacques 25–6
Olympia (painting) 239
Ondaatje, Michael 255
Ondra, Anny 93
O'Neill, James 21, 32
Opera 33–5, 79–81, 96, 102 n.68, 163–4, 208–10
Orientalism 99 n.28, 211
Ormerod, Nick 16, 226, 251–2, 272

Pabst, G. W. 93
Pagnol, Marcel 11, 65, 78
Palette, Eugene 102 n.63
Pan-American Exhibition 25
Paquet, Darcy 237, 244
Paramount 78, 103 n.74
Paraz, Albert 110
Paris Stock Exchange 54, 55
Park Chan-wook 7, 226, 242–4, 261, 272
Park-Finch, Heebon 178–9
Les Particules élémentaires (*The Elementary Particles*) (novel) 226, 227, 247–50
Pathé 30, 60 n.38, 100 n.42, 109, 112
Partie d'écarté (*Card Game*) (1895) 22
Passek, Jean-Loup 98 n.14
Pattinson, Robert 251–4, 272
Paton, Stuart 36–9, 58
patronage 64–5
Paul, Robert William 22
Le Père Goriot (*Old Goriot*) (novel) 47
Le Père Goriot (*Old Goriot*) (1921) 47
Perlman, Janet 15, 190, 200–2, 218–19
Perrault, Charles 15, 23, 190, 200–2, 218–19
Pétain, Marshal 106, 115, 119, 122–7, 129
Peterson, Lowell 151
La Petite Marchande d'allumettes (*The Little Match Girl*) (1928) 102 n.69

Petrey, Sandy 153, 154
Petzold, Christian 227, 245–6, 250, 261, 272
Peyrie, Clément 233
Pfeiffer, Michelle 231
Philipe, Gérard 1, 151–2
Phoenix (2014) 227, 244–50, 261, 272
'photosphere' 36
Picard, André 93
Pick, Lupu 17 n.7
Pickford, Mary 39, 40, 82
Picpus (1942) 111, 116
Picture-Play 82
Place, Janey 151
plagiarism and financial profiteering 20
La Planète des singes (novel) 226, 231, 233
Planet of the Apes (1968) 232
Planet of the Apes (2001) 16, 226, 227, 229, 231–3, 260, 272
Playboy 194
Plaza de Toros, Seville 35
poetic realism 70
Poff, Lon 101 n.63
politics of adaptation 105–45
Pommer, Erich 52
Popular Plays and Players 36
pornography 190, 193
Pontcarral, colonel d'empire (*Pontcarral, Colonel of the Empire*) (1942) 13, 107, 112–16, 269
Porter, Edwin S. 21, 32, 268
Portugal 165
Postman Always Rings Twice, The (1934) (novel) 245
Postman Always Rings Twice, The (1946) 245
Pottier, Richard 111
Pouctal, Henri 30, 31, 47
Powell, William 132
Powrie, Phil 34, 60 n.27
Preminger, Otto 13, 159–65, 168, 182, 185 n.36, 186 n.38, 270
Private Life of Henry VIII, The (1933) 76
Propaganda Abteilung 111
Proust, Marcel 274

Puccini, Giacomo 9, 18 n.13, 65, 96, 102 n.68, 208, 211
Putti, Lya de 53–4

Quatre-vingt-treize (*Ninety-Three*) (1914) 30

Radford, Ivan 276
Raghavendra, M. K. 172
Rapson, Jessica 228
Ravel, Gaston 48
Ray, Albert 72–4
Reader, Keith 67, 69
Rear Window (1954) 258
Rebatet, Lucien 123, 136
Redmond, John 181
Reid, Donald 203, 206–7
Régent, Roger 125
Regiani, Maximilien 206
Reiniger, Lotte 94, 103 n.75
Relativity Media 230
Rembrandt lighting 35
Renard, Maurice 66, 88
Renaud 206–7
Renoir, Jean 11, 66, 69–72, 89–90, 102 n.69, 108, 110
Republicans 180–1
Resines, Antonio 103 n.83
Resistance 107, 111–16
Le Retour des cendres (*Return from the Ashes*) (novel) 227, 245, 246, 261, 272
Return of Monte Cristo, The (1946) 75
Reuze, André 9
Rey, Florián 95, 112
Ricci, Christina 252
Richelieu, Cardinal 41, 42, 85
Rizk, Amina 98 n.5
RKO Radio Pictures 159–60
Roberti, Roberto 7
Robison, Arthur 51–4
Roché, Henri-Pierre 155–9
Roehler, Oskar 226, 247–50
Roh Tae-woo 237
Les Roquevillard (novel) 123
Les Roquevillard (1943) 123–5
Le Rouge et le Noir (*The Red and the Black*) (novel) 1, 13, 150, 154, 270

Le Rouge et le Noir (*The Red and the Black*) (1954) 1, 13, 150–5, 182, 270
Rowden, Terry 228
Russia 63
Russo, Elena 277
Ryan's Daughter (1970) 13, 175–82
'*Ryan's Daughter* Revisited' 180

Sadoul, Georges 23, 24, 27, 43, 48
Sanders, Julie 4, 80, 202
Sandford, Stanley J. 102 n.63
Sapène, Jean 57
Sardou, Victorien 79
Sargeant, Malcolm 80
Saving Private Ryan (1998) 217
Scarlet Street (1945) 66, 90, 91
Scènes de la vie de bohème (*Scenes of Bohemian Life*) (novel) 102 n.68, 208
Schaffner, Franklin J. 231–2, 233
Schaeffer, Armand 99 n.23
Schatz, Thomas 160
Schindler's List (1993) 217
Schneider, Pierre 193
Schönberg, Claude-Michel 225
Schwarzenegger, Arnold 232
Scott, Maria 184 n.17
Scott Thomas, Kristin 253–6
Screen Daily 252
Second World War 79, 105, 136, 149, 161, 181, 217, 246, 250, 254–6, 261, 270, 272
'segyehwa' 237
Selig 20
Sellier, Geneviève 114–15
Semenza, Greg 2–4
Sepoy Rebellion of 1857 39
serials/*roman feuilleton* 74
Sexton, David 254–5
Shakespeare, William 68, 92
Sheen, Erica 155
Shin, Jeeyoung 238
Shiri (*Kang Je-gyu*) (1999) 238
Shortt, Edward 96
Siclier, Jacques 125–6
Siegmann, George 102 n.63
Silbermann, Marc 94–5

silent film 19–62
Simenon, Georges 102 n.69, 105, 109, 111, 116, 119–22
Simon, Simone 108
Sims, Gregory 126
Sims, Joan 197
Siodmak, Robert 94
Sjöström, Victor 7
Skin I Live In, The (*La piel que habito*) (2011) 226–7, 257–61
Slade, David 18 n.19
Small, Edward 76
Sociological approach to adaptation 4
soft-core porn 193
Solomon, Matthew 25, 59 n.7
Son of Monte Cristo, The (1940) 75
Song At Midnight (1937) 97 n.1
Sorel, René 79
La Sortie de l'usine Lumière à Lyon (*Workers Leaving the Lumière Factory in Lyon*) (1895) 26
Sound of Music, The (1965) 213
South Korean cinema 237–8
Soviet Russia 63
Spaak, Charles 138
Spain 12, 64, 67, 95, 103 n.83, 164–6, 225, 257–8
Spielberg, Steven 217–18, 237
Stam, Robert 251
stars 7, 11, 20, 32, 39, 42, 63, 66, 70, 76, 79–83, 88, 89, 93
star system 39–40, 53
Star Film Company 23
Steeman, Stanislas-André 107, 109, 129–31, 133–5
Stein, Paul L. 208
Stendhal 1, 8, 13, 150–1, 153–5, 270
Stephens, Bradley 98 n.4, 99 n.22
Stevens, Charles 102 n.63
Stewart, Kristen 252
Sting 213
Stone, Sharon 234, 236
Stratton, Charlie 30
studios 20, 26, 31, 39, 40, 42, 48, 51, 65, 66, 76, 78, 95, 103 n.74, 230, 268, 269
Sturges, John 255
Suite française (2015) 227, 251–7

superproduction 42–5, 48, 58
'Sur une barricade' ('On a barricade') 28
Sweeney, Carole 249
'The Swing' (painting) 92
La Symphonie pastorale (*Pastoral Symphony*) (1947) 183 n.4
Symphony of Life (*Symphonie eines lebens*) (1942) 69

tableaux vivants 192–3
Taine, Hippolyte 7, 242
Tartuffe (play) 52
Tartuffe (*Herr Tartüff*) (1925) 52
Tati, Jacques 218
Taves, Brian 36, 38, 39
Taylor, Elizabeth 198
Taylor, Robert 87
Ten Commandments, The (1956) 35
Tender Tale of Cinderella Penguin, The (1981) 15, 190, 200–2, 218
Théate, Barbara 279
theatre
  Broadway 84, 160
  of horrors 89
  Théâtre filmé 32
Théâtre Robert-Houdin 22–4
Thelma and Louise (1991) 237
Thérèse Raquin (novel) 7, 16, 226, 230, 242–3, 261, 272
Thin Man, The (novel) 132
Thin Man, The (1934) 107, 133–4
Third Man, The (1949) 218
Third Republic, The 119, 205
Thirst (2009) 7, 16, 226, 242–4, 253
Thompson, David 151
Three Musketeers, The (1921) 40–2, 85
Three Musketeers, The (1935) 11, 65, 85, 99 n.23
Throne of Blood (1957) 241
Thune, Henriette 227
Thurman, Uma 251
Tie Me Up! Tie Me Down! (1989) 259
Tinayre, Daniel 17 n.7
Titanic (1997) 230, 238
Tobing-Ronay, Fatimah 197
Tobis-Klangfilm 103

Topaze (1933) 78, 100 n.38
Toulouse Lautrec, Henri de 212
Tourneur, Maurice 269
Tournier, Maurice 8
Tradition of Quality 2, 13, 147–53, 155, 182, 183 n.4, 184 n.16, 270
  Travail (*Work*) (1920) 30, 47
La Traviata (opera) 65, 210
Translation theory *see* Nord, Christiane; Lefevere, André
Travers, James 136, 140
Triangle Pictures 40
Les Trois Mousquetaires (novel) 40, 269
Les Trois Mousquetaires (*The Three Musketeers*) (1921) 40–1
Les Trois Mousquetaires (*The Three Musketeers*) (1932) 99 n.23
Les Trois Mousquetaires (*The Three Musketeers*) (1933) 99 n.23
Les Trois Mousquetaires (*The Three Musketeers*) (1935) 99 n.23
Trueba, Fernando 103 n.83
Truffaut, François 106, 148–50, 152–3, 155–9, 182, 191, 235, 270
Turkey 225
Twentieth-Century Fox 232
Twilight (2008-12) 227, 252–4, 272
Twilight, Breaking Dawn–Part 2 (2012) 252

Ucicky, Gustav 94
UFA 93–4, 103 n.83, 109, 51–2, 54, 95
Ulmen, Christian 248
Unholy Love (1932) 11, 65, 72, 73
United Artists 101 n.50
United Kingdom 148, 225
United States 7, 11, 19–21, 24, 26, 31–2, 36, 37, 39–40, 42, 48, 58, 64, 65, 67, 75–7, 100 n.38, 148, 161, 165, 180, 193, 194, 219 n.8, 220 n.13, 230–1, 234, 258, 260, 268, 270
Universal 37, 230
Un long dimanche de fiançailles (*A Very Long Engagement*) (2004) 15, 214–19, 271

'Une partie de campagne' ('A Day in the Country') (story) 92
Une partie de cartes (*Playing Cards*) (1896) 22
  Unknown (2011) 230
Untold Scandal (2003) 227, 238–42
Unwin, Timothy 9

vampirism 242–3, 252, 253, 263 n.37
Vance, Jeffrey 41–2, 82
Vanel, Charles 123, 236
Variety 252, 254, 256
Vautrin (1943) 120
Vaynshtok, Vladimir 97 n.1
Verdi, Giuseppe 85, 210–11
Verhoeven, Paul 236
Verne, Jules 6, 8–10, 25–6, 32, 36–9, 97 n.1, 268
Verneuil, Louis 9, 79, 94
Vertigo (1958) 258–9
Véry, Pierre 105, 109, 110, 125–8, 138
Vichy regime 115, 118, 125
Le Vicomte de Bragelonne ou dix ans plus tard (*The Viscount of Bragelonne or Ten Years Later*) (novel) 230
video 149, 194, 220 n.12
Vienna Academy of Art 116
Vincendeau, Ginette 55
Vingt mille lieues sous les mers (*20,000 Leagues under the Sea*) (novel) 36–9
Virdi, Jyotika 173–4
Vitagraph 20
Le Voyage dans la lune (*A Trip to the Moon*) (1902) 24–6, 59 n.7, 268
Vorins, Henry 27

Wahlberg, Mark 232
Waldron, Darren 257, 259
Wallace, Leonard 80
Wallace, Randall 230
Watts, Andrew 61 n.51
Wayne, John 232
Weibang, Ma-Xu 97 n.1
Weitzel, Edward 37–8
Weitzman, Elizabeth 252
Wendhausen, Fritz 100 n.38

Western cultural hegemony 238
Whale, James 85
Whelehan, Imelda 58 n.3
Who Saw Her Die? (1972) 276
Wild, Florianne 106, 142 n.3
Williams, Kenneth 197
Williams, Tony 128
Williamson, George and Ernest 36
Windsor, Barbara 197
Winslet, Kate 230
Woods, Lotta 41
Wyckoff, Alvin 35

Yamamoto Savas, Minae 241
Les Yeux sans visage (*Eyes Without a Face*) (1960) 257

Yella (2007) 245
YouTube 228
Yugoslavia 165

Zakarian, Richard 205
Zecca, Ferdinand 6
Zeman, Karel 9
Zola, Émile 3, 6–8, 11, 16, 19, 30, 47, 54, 55, 65, 67, 70–2, 90, 102 n.69, 106, 109, 120, 190, 202–7, 221 n.30, 222 n.38, 226, 230, 242–4, 261, 268, 269, 271, 272
Zurian, Francisco 259

www.ingramcontent.com/pod-product-compliance
Lightning Source LLC
Chambersburg PA
CBHW072122290426
44111CB00012B/1746